NEGIMA! 10

Ken Akamatsu

TRANSLATED BY
Toshifumi Yoshida

ADAPTED BY
T. Ledoux

LETTERING AND RETOUCH BY
Steve Palmer

DEL REY

BALLANTINE BOOKS · NEW YORK

Negima! volume 10 is a work of fiction. Names, characters, places, and incidents are the products of the author's imagination or are used fictitiously. Any resemblance to actual events, locales, or persons, living or dead, is entirely coincidental.

A Del Rey Trade Paperback Original

Published in the United States by Del Rey Books, an imprint of The Random House Publishing Group, a division of Random House, Inc., New York.

Publication rights arranged through Kodansha Ltd.

First published in Japan in 2005 by Kodansha Ltd., Tokyo

ISBN 0-345-48441-X

Printed in the United States of America

www.delreymanga.com

9 8 7 6

Translator —Toshifumi Yoshida
Adaptor—T. Ledoux
Lettering and Retouch—Steve Palmer
Cover Design—David Stevenson

A Word from the Author

Day One of "MahoraFest" has begun!

The Mahora Festival isn't something put on by just the junior high kids, after all; the high school and university students are involved, too—it's a campus-wide event.

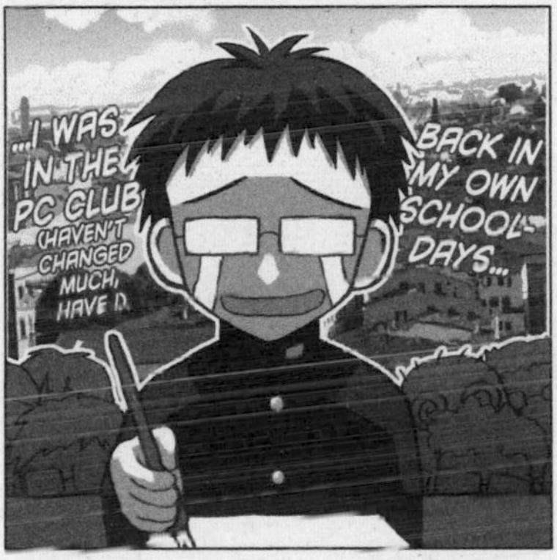
BACK IN MY OWN SCHOOL DAYS...
...I WAS IN THE PC CLUB
(HAVEN'T CHANGED MUCH, HAVE I)

Whatever can this miraculous invention that supposedly will save Negi from his insanely overbooked schedule be...?!

Speaking of school cultural festivals, when I myself was in high school (all boys), I helped out with a booth that did "Computer Matchmaking Compatibility" charts. How sad is that...? (Heh.) This was in the days before even the PC88SR, mind you.

Ken Akamatsu
www.ailove.net

Honorifics

Throughout the Del Rey Manga books, you will find Japanese honorifics left intact in the translations. For those not familiar with how the Japanese use honorifics and, more important, how they differ from American honorifics, we present this brief overview.

Politeness has always been a critical facet of Japanese culture. Ever since the feudal era, when Japan was a highly stratified society, use of honorifics—which can be defined as polite speech that indicates relationship or status—has played an essential role in the Japanese language. When addressing someone in Japanese, an honorific usually takes the form of a suffix attached to one's name (example: "Asuna-san"), or as a title at the end of one's name or in place of the name itself (example: "Negi-sensei," or simply "Sensei!").

Honorifics can be expressions of respect or endearment. In the context of manga and anime, honorifics give insight into the nature of the relationship between characters. Many translations into English leave out these important honorifics, and therefore distort the "feel" of the original Japanese. Because Japanese honorifics contain nuances that English honorifics lack, it is our policy at Del Rey not to translate them. Here, instead, is a guide to some of the honorifics you may encounter in Del Rey Manga.

-*san:* This is the most common honorific, and is equivalent to Mr., Miss, Ms., or Mrs. It is the all-purpose honorific and can be used in any situation where politeness is required.

-*sama:* This is one level higher than "-san." It is used to confer great respect.

-*dono:* This comes from the word "tono," which means "lord." It is an even higher level than "-sama," and confers utmost respect.

-kun: This suffix is used at the end of boys' names to express familiarity or endearment. It is also sometimes used by men among friends, or when addressing someone younger or of lower station.

-chan: This is used to express endearment, mostly toward girls. It is also used for little boys, pets, and even among lovers. It gives a sense of childish cuteness.

Bozu: This is an informal way to refer to a boy, similar to the English term "kid" or "squirt."

Senpai/sempai: This title suggests that the addressee is one's senior in a group or organization. It is most often used in a school setting, where underclassmen refer to their upperclassmen as "senpai." It can also be used in the workplace, such as when a newer employee addresses an employee who has seniority in the company.

Kohai: This is the opposite of "sempai," and is used toward underclassmen in school or newcomers in the workplace. It connotes that the addressee is of lower station.

Sensei: Literally meaning "one who has come before," this title is used for teachers, doctors, or masters of any profession or art.

Anesan: Anesan (or nesan) is a generic term for a girl, usually older, that means sister.

Ojôsama: Ojôsama is a way of referring to the daughter or sister of someone with high political or social status.

-[blank]: Usually forgotten in these lists, but perhaps the most significant difference between Japanese and English. The lack of honorific means that the speaker has permission to address the person in a very intimate way. Usually, only family, spouses, or very close friends have this kind of permission. Known as *yobisute,* it can be gratifying when someone who has earned the intimacy starts to call one by one's name without an honorific. But when that intimacy hasn't been earned, it can also be very insulting.

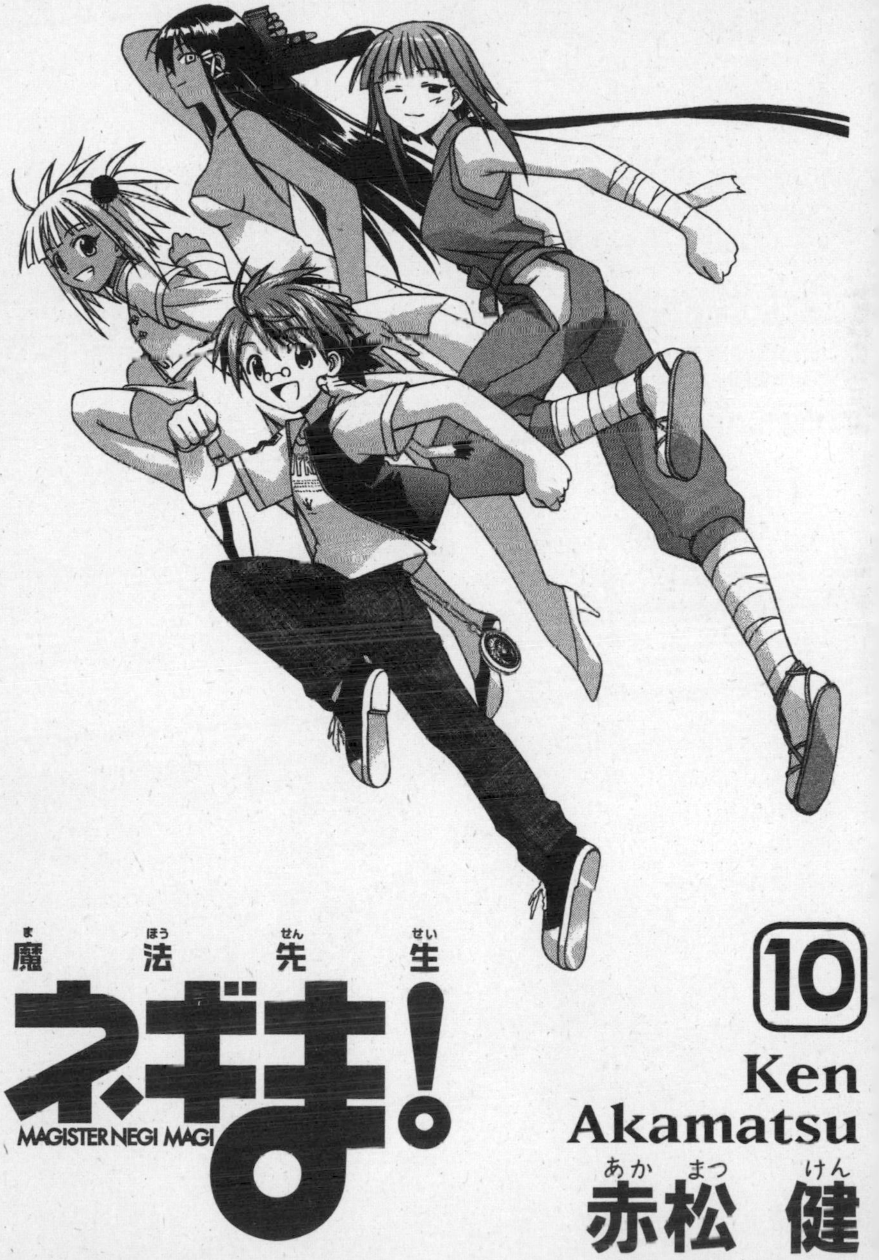

魔法先生ネギま!

MAGISTER NEGI MAGI

10

Ken Akamatsu

赤松健

Contents

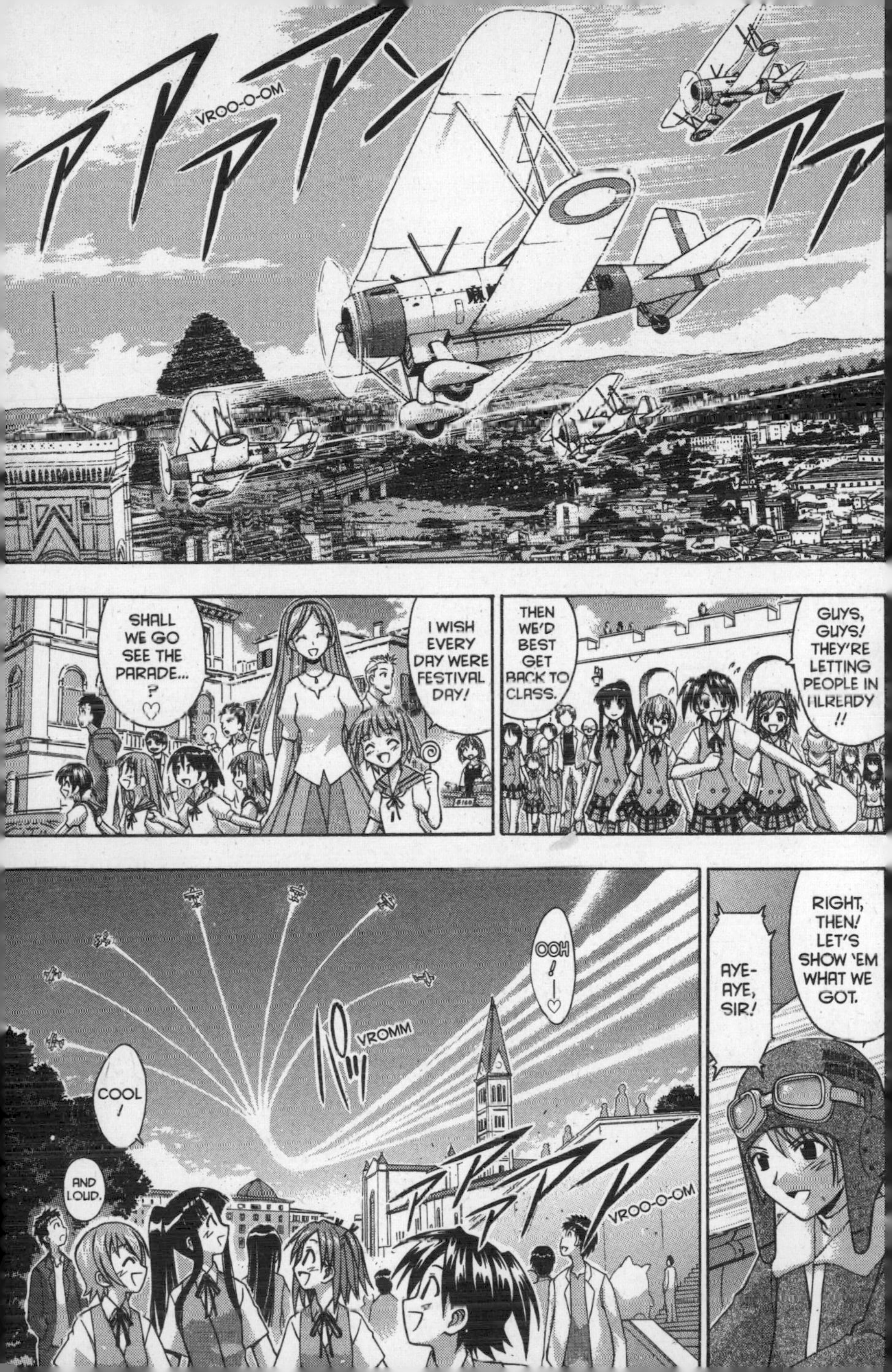
VROO-O-OM
GUYS, GUYS! THEY'RE LETTING PEOPLE IN ALREADY!!
THEN WE'D BEST GET BACK TO CLASS.
I WISH EVERY DAY WERE FESTIVAL DAY!
SHALL WE GO SEE THE PARADE...? ♡
RIGHT, THEN! LET'S SHOW 'EM WHAT WE GOT.
AYE-AYE, SIR!
OOH! —♡
VROMM
COOL!
AND LOUD.
VROO-O-OM

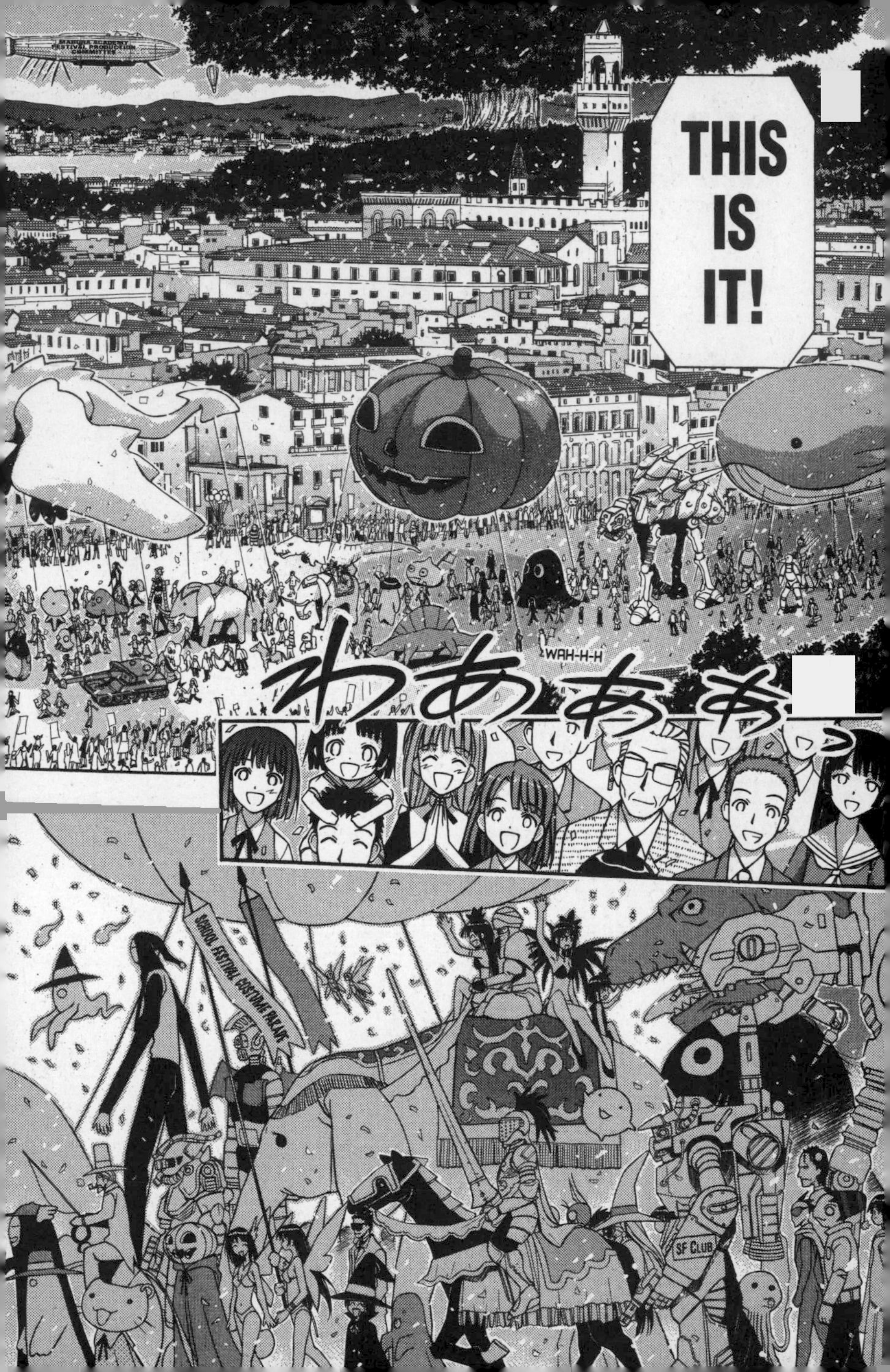
MAHORA ACADEMY FESTIVAL PRODUCTION COMMITTEE
THIS IS IT!
WAH-H-H
わあああっ
SCHOOL FESTIVAL COSTUME PARADE
SF CLUB

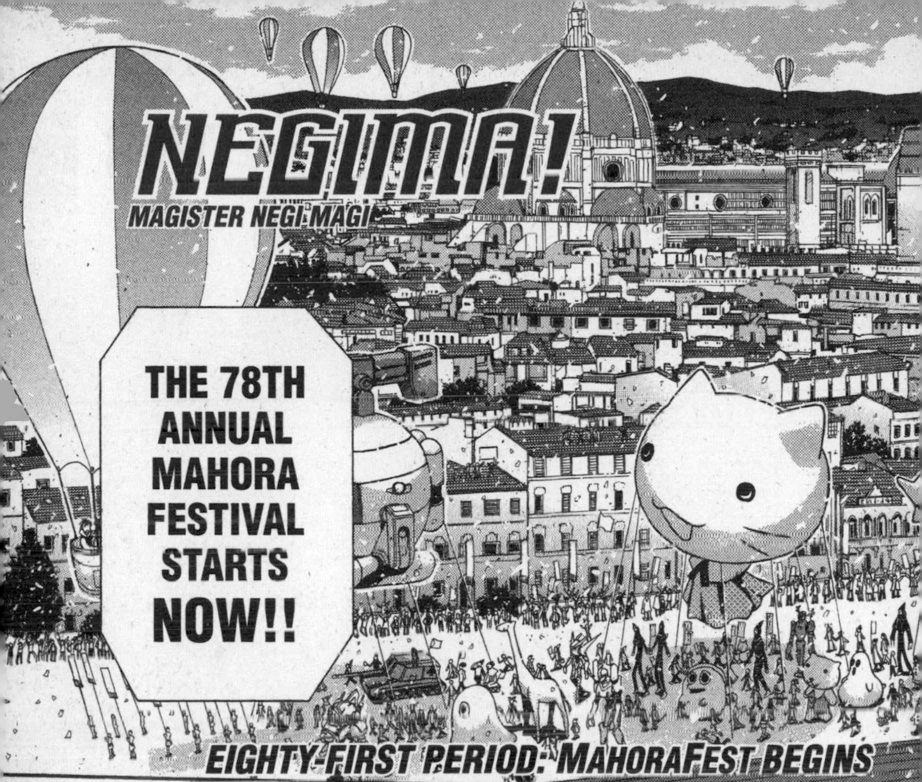
NEGIMA!
MAGISTER NEGI MAGI
THE 78TH ANNUAL MAHORA FESTIVAL STARTS NOW!!
EIGHTY-FIRST PERIOD: MahoraFest BEGINS

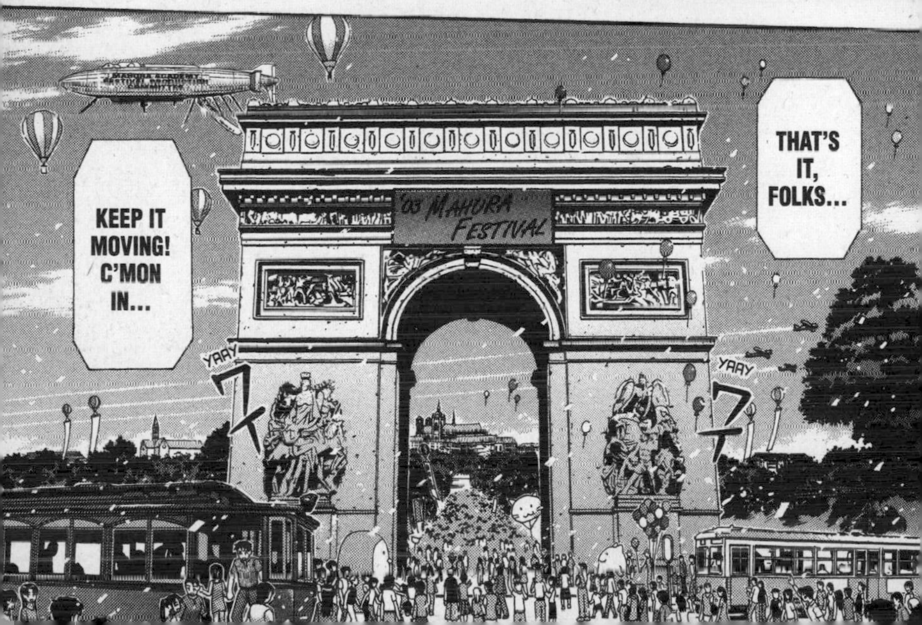
THAT'S IT, FOLKS...
'03 MAHORA FESTIVAL
YAAY
YAAY
KEEP IT MOVING! C'MON IN...

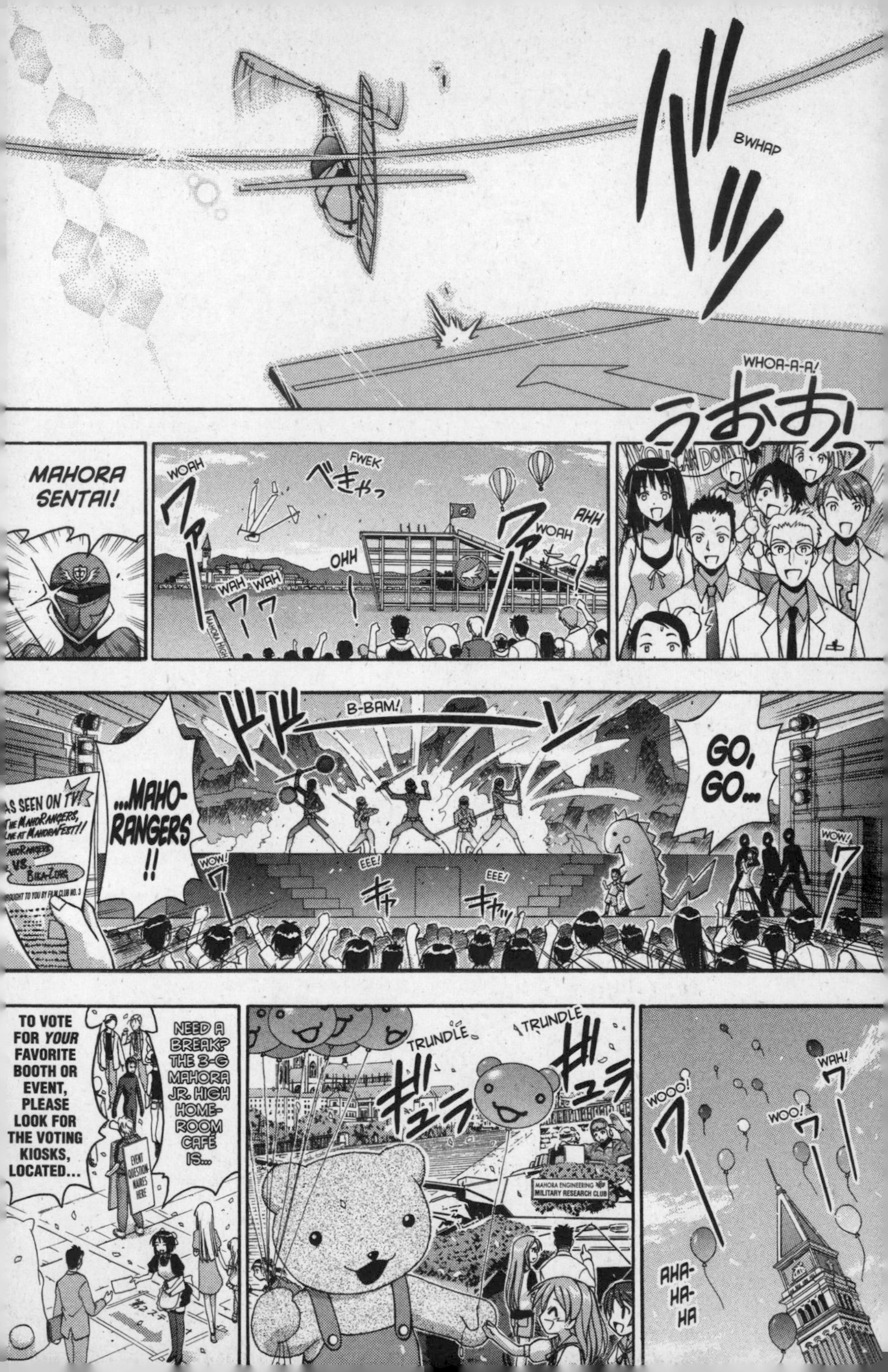
ブヅ
BWHAP
WHOA-A-A!
うおおっ
FWEK
べきゃっ
AHH
WOAH
ワァー
OHH
WAH WAH
ワワ
WOAH
ワァー
MAHORA HIGH
MAHORA SENTAI!
GO, GO...
B-BAM!
ドドーン
...MAHO-RANGERS!!
WOW!
ワ
EEE!
キャッ
EEE!
キャ
WOW!
ワ
AS SEEN ON TV!
MAHORANGERS
VS.
BIKA-ZORG
WAH!
ワー
WOO!
ワー
WOOO!
ワー
AHA-HA-HA
TRUNDLE
ギュラ
TRUNDLE
ギュラ
MAHORA ENGINEERING
MILITARY RESEARCH CLUB
NEED A BREAK? THE 3-G MAHORA JR. HIGH HOME-ROOM CAFÉ IS...
TO VOTE FOR YOUR FAVORITE BOOTH OR EVENT, PLEASE LOOK FOR THE VOTING KIOSKS, LOCATED...
EVENT QUESTION-NAIRES HERE

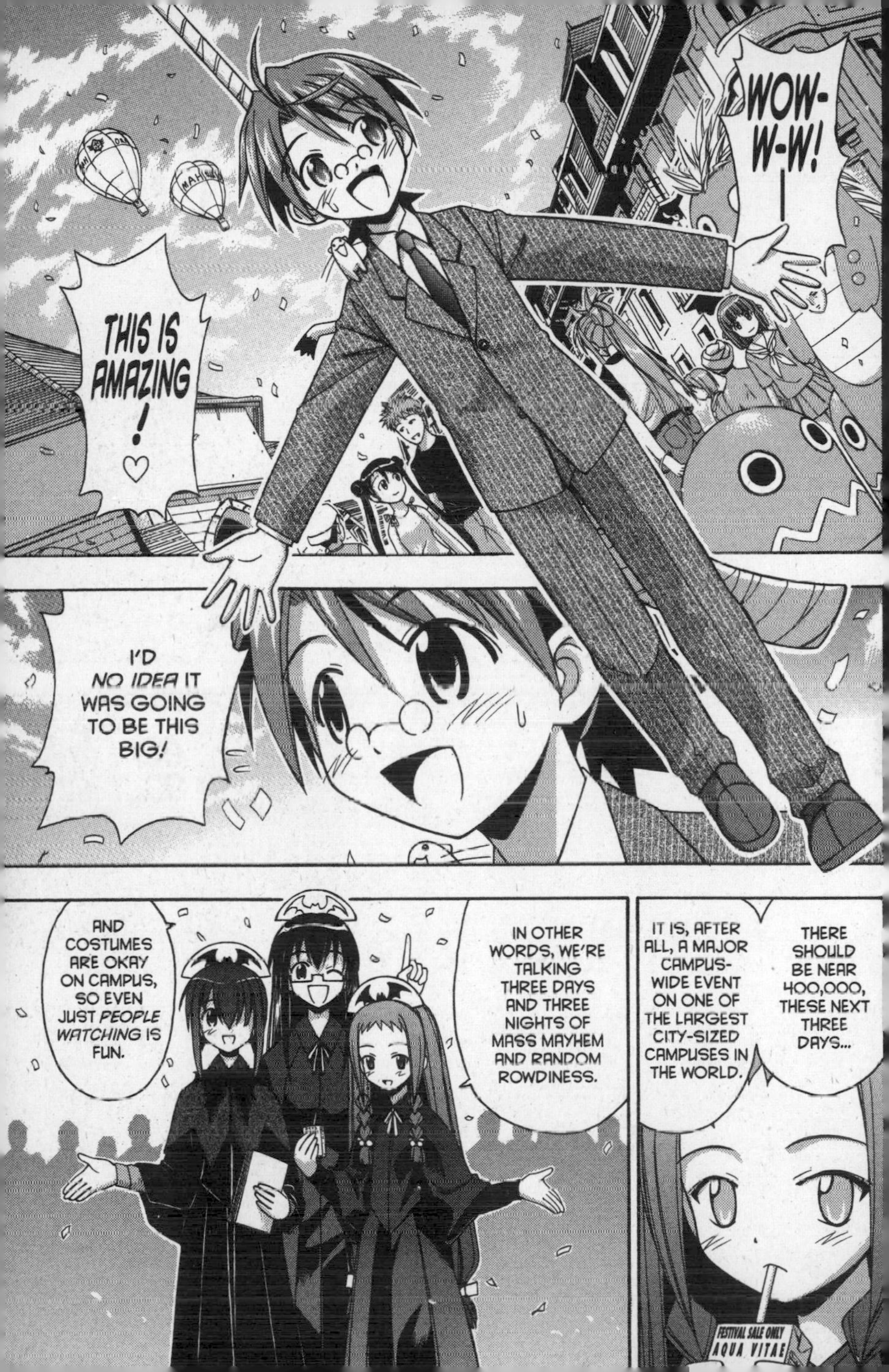
WOW-W-W!
THIS IS AMAZING! ♡
I'D NO IDEA IT WAS GOING TO BE THIS BIG!
THERE SHOULD BE NEAR 400,000, THESE NEXT THREE DAYS...
IT IS, AFTER ALL, A MAJOR CAMPUS-WIDE EVENT ON ONE OF THE LARGEST CITY-SIZED CAMPUSES IN THE WORLD.
FESTIVAL SALE ONLY AQUA VITAE
IN OTHER WORDS, WE'RE TALKING THREE DAYS AND THREE NIGHTS OF MASS MAYHEM AND RANDOM ROWDINESS.
AND COSTUMES ARE OKAY ON CAMPUS, SO EVEN JUST PEOPLE WATCHING IS FUN.

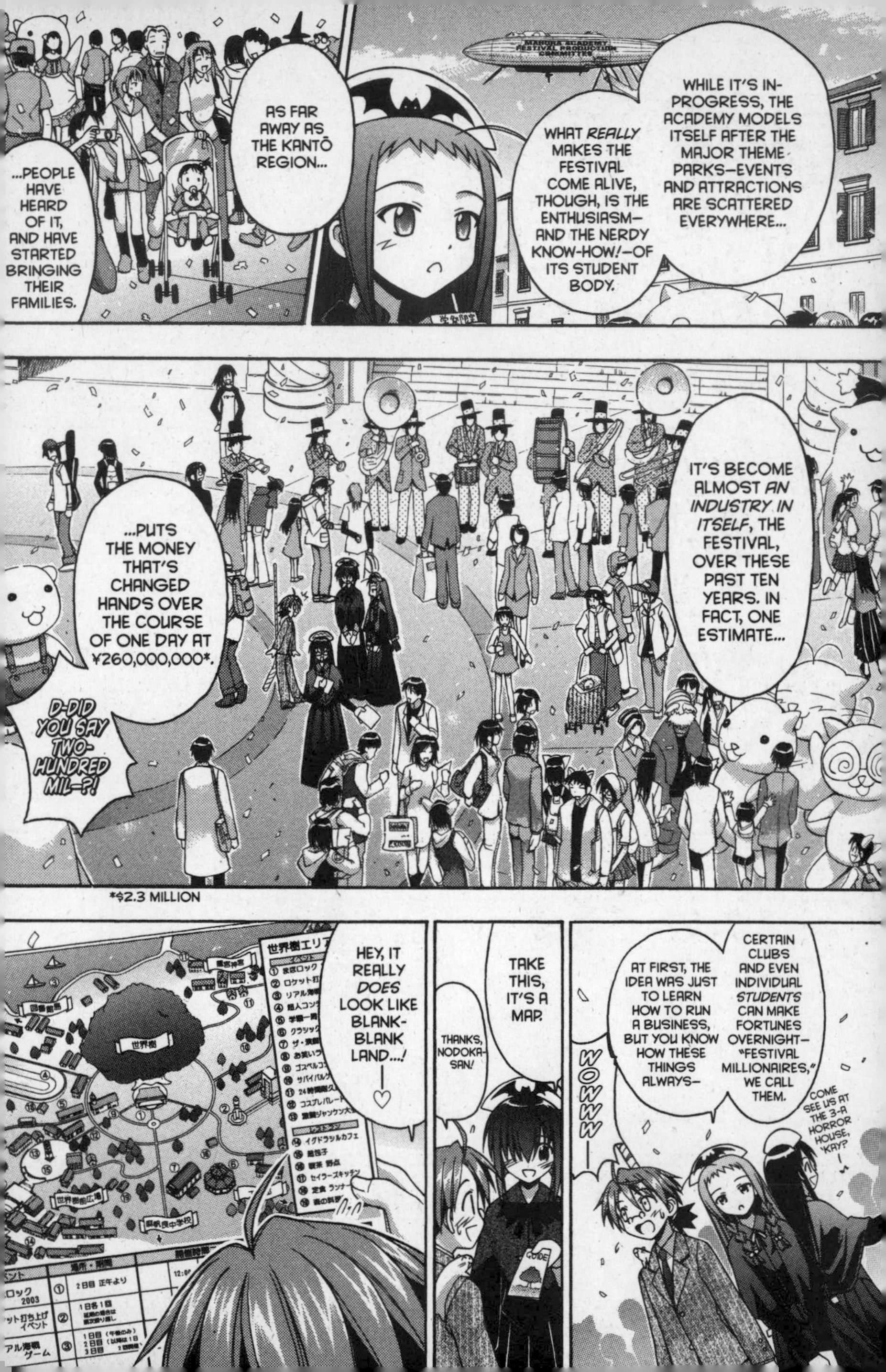
MAHORA ACADEMY FESTIVAL PRODUCTION COMMITTEE
WHILE IT'S IN-PROGRESS, THE ACADEMY MODELS ITSELF AFTER THE MAJOR THEME PARKS—EVENTS AND ATTRACTIONS ARE SCATTERED EVERYWHERE...
WHAT *REALLY* MAKES THE FESTIVAL COME ALIVE, THOUGH, IS THE ENTHUSIASM—AND THE NERDY KNOW-HOW!—OF ITS STUDENT BODY.
AS FAR AWAY AS THE KANTŌ REGION...
...PEOPLE HAVE HEARD OF IT, AND HAVE STARTED BRINGING THEIR FAMILIES.
IT'S BECOME ALMOST *AN INDUSTRY IN ITSELF*, THE FESTIVAL, OVER THESE PAST TEN YEARS. IN FACT, ONE ESTIMATE...
...PUTS THE MONEY THAT'S CHANGED HANDS OVER THE COURSE OF ONE DAY AT ¥260,000,000*.
D-DID YOU SAY TWO-HUNDRED MIL—?!
AT FIRST, THE IDEA WAS JUST TO LEARN HOW TO RUN A BUSINESS, BUT YOU KNOW HOW THESE THINGS ALWAYS—
CERTAIN CLUBS AND EVEN INDIVIDUAL *STUDENTS* CAN MAKE FORTUNES OVERNIGHT—"FESTIVAL MILLIONAIRES," WE CALL THEM.
COME SEE US AT THE 3-A HORROR HOUSE, 'KAY?
TAKE THIS, IT'S A MAP.
THANKS, NODOKA-SAN!
WOWWW—
HEY, IT REALLY *DOES* LOOK LIKE BLANK-BLANK LAND...!
GUIDE

*$2.3 MILLION

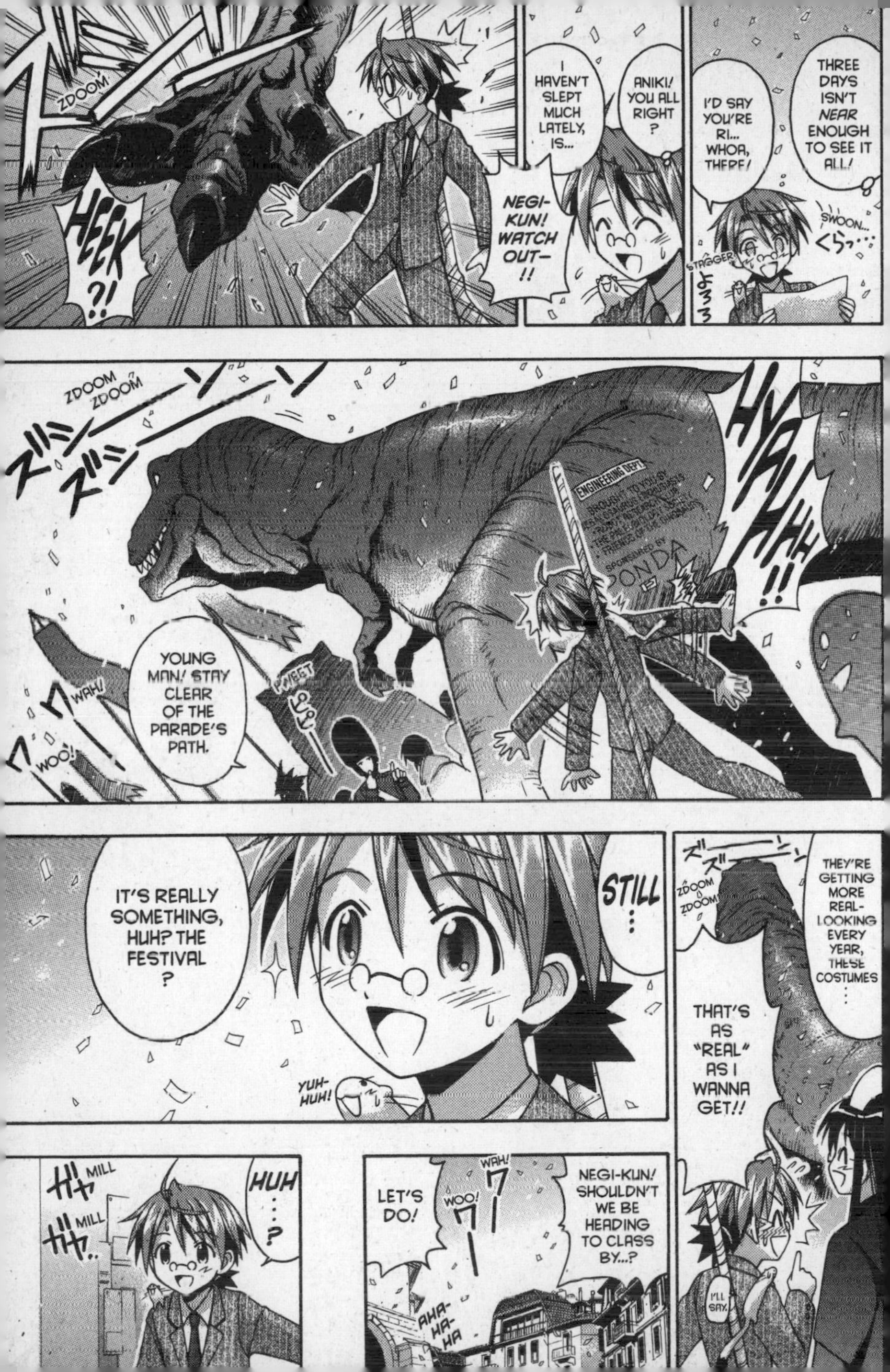
THREE DAYS ISN'T NEAR ENOUGH TO SEE IT ALL!
SWOON... くらっ…
I'D SAY YOU'RE RI... WHOA, THERE!
STAGGER
ANIKI! YOU ALL RIGHT?
I HAVEN'T SLEPT MUCH LATELY, IS...
NEGI-KUN! WATCH OUT—!!
ZDOOM
HEEK?!
HYAAAHH!!
ZDOOM ZDOOM
ENGINEERING DEPT.
YOUNG MAN! STAY CLEAR OF THE PARADE'S PATH.
PWEET ピッ
WAH!
WOO!
THEY'RE GETTING MORE REAL-LOOKING EVERY YEAR, THESE COSTUMES...
ZDOOM ZDOOM
THAT'S AS "REAL" AS I WANNA GET!!
I'LL SAY.
STILL...
IT'S REALLY SOMETHING, HUH? THE FESTIVAL?
YUH-HUH!
NEGI-KUN! SHOULDN'T WE BE HEADING TO CLASS BY...?
WAH!
WOO!
LET'S DO!
AHAHAHA
HUH...?
MILL
MILL

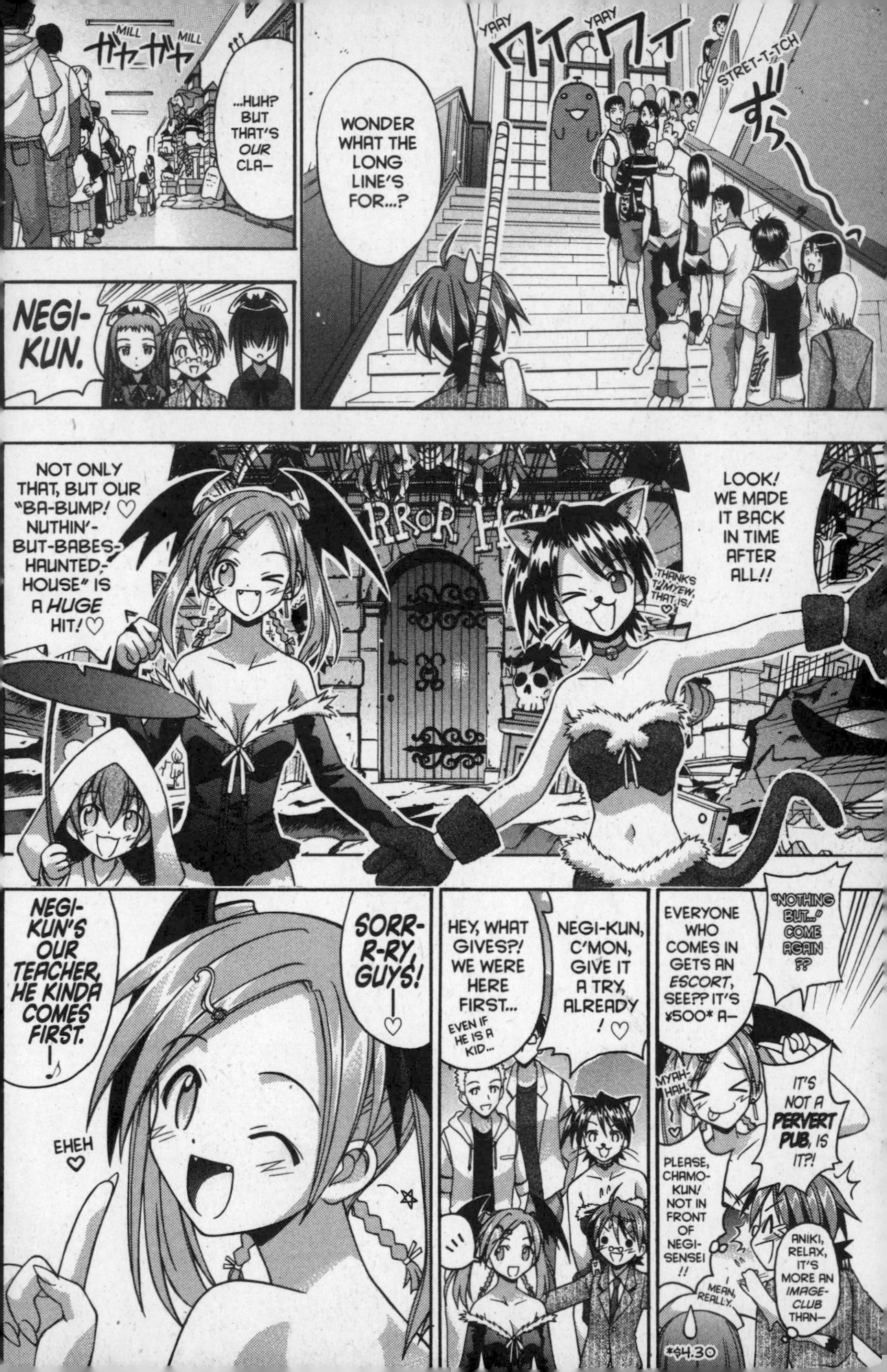
YAAY YAAY
ワイワイ
STRET-T-TCH
ずら〜
WONDER WHAT THE LONG LINE'S FOR...?
MILL MILL
ガヤガヤ
...HUH? BUT THAT'S *OUR* CLA–
NEGI-KUN.
LOOK! WE MADE IT BACK IN TIME AFTER ALL!!
THANKS T'MYEW, THAT IS! ♡
NOT ONLY THAT, BUT OUR "BA-BUMP! ♡ NUTHIN'-BUT-BABES-HAUNTED-HOUSE" IS A *HUGE* HIT! ♡
"NOTHING BUT..." COME AGAIN??
EVERYONE WHO COMES IN GETS AN *ESCORT*, SEE?? IT'S ¥500* A–
IT'S NOT A **PERVERT PUB**, IS IT?!
MYAH-HAH. ♡
ANIKI, RELAX, IT'S MORE AN *IMAGE-CLUB* THAN–
PLEASE, CHAMO-KUN! NOT IN FRONT OF NEGI-SENSEI!!
I MEAN, REALLY.
*$4.30
NEGI-KUN, C'MON, GIVE IT A TRY, ALREADY! ♡
HEY, WHAT GIVES?! WE WERE HERE FIRST...
EVEN IF HE IS A KID...
SORRR-R-RY, GUYS! ♡
NEGI-KUN'S OUR TEACHER, HE KINDA COMES FIRST. ♪
EHEH ♡

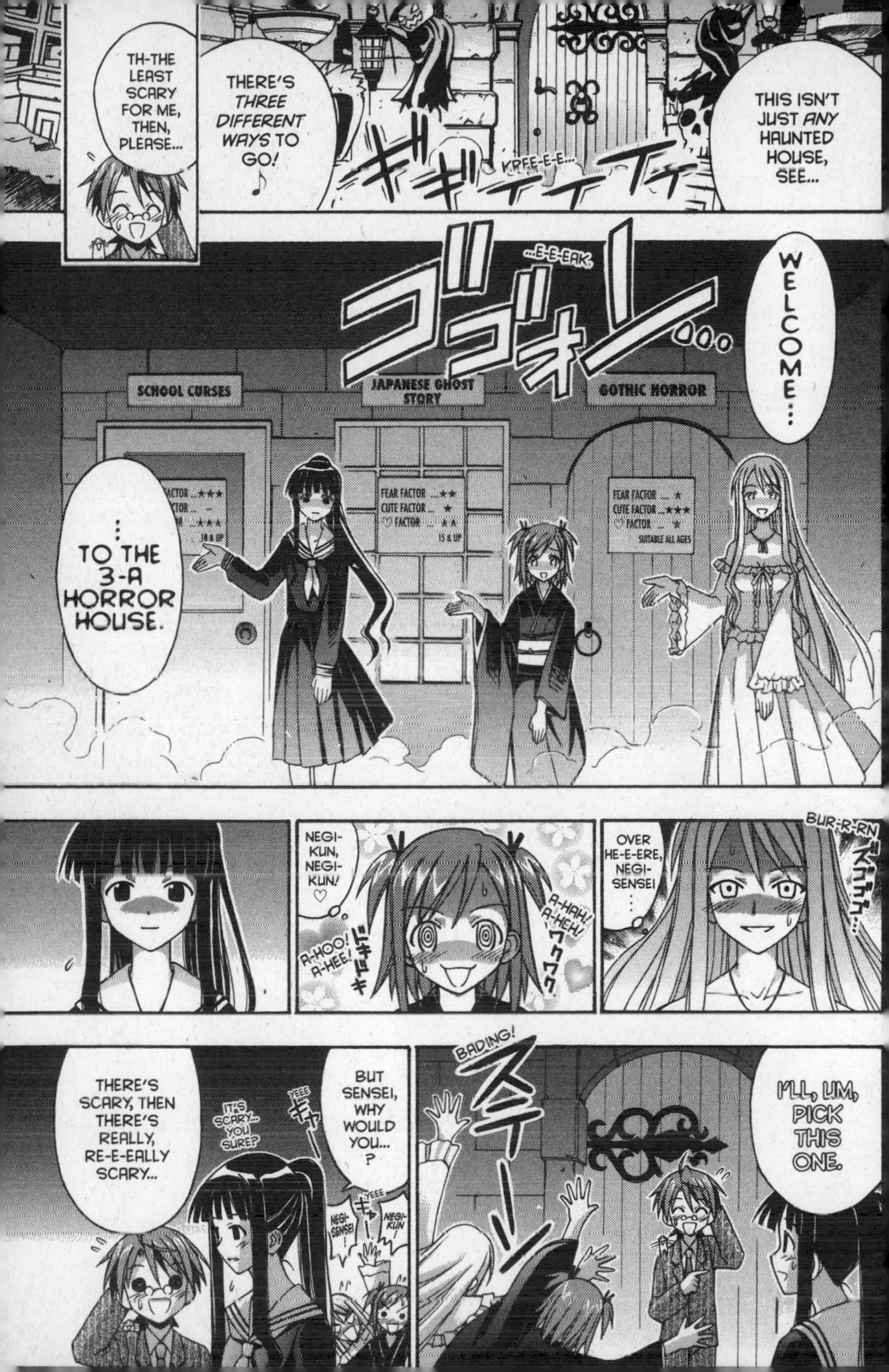

THIS ISN'T JUST ANY HAUNTED HOUSE, SEE...
KREE-E-E...
THERE'S THREE DIFFERENT WAYS TO GO! ♪
TH-THE LEAST SCARY FOR ME, THEN, PLEASE...
WELCOME...
...E-E-EAK.
GOTHIC HORROR
FEAR FACTOR ... ★
CUTE FACTOR ...★★★
♡ FACTOR ... ★
SUITABLE ALL AGES
JAPANESE GHOST STORY
FEAR FACTOR ...★★
CUTE FACTOR ... ★
♡ FACTOR ... ★★
15 & UP
SCHOOL CURSES
18 & UP
...TO THE 3-A HORROR HOUSE.
BUR-R-RN
OVER HE-E-ERE, NEGI-SENSEI ...
A-HAH! A-HEH!
NEGI-KUN, NEGI-KUN! ♡
A-HOO! A-HEE!
I'LL, UM, PICK THIS ONE.
BADING!
BUT SENSEI, WHY WOULD YOU...?
YEEE
IT'S SCARY... YOU SURE?
THERE'S SCARY, THEN THERE'S REALLY, RE-E-EALLY SCARY...
YEEE
NEGI-KUN!
NEGI-SENSEI!

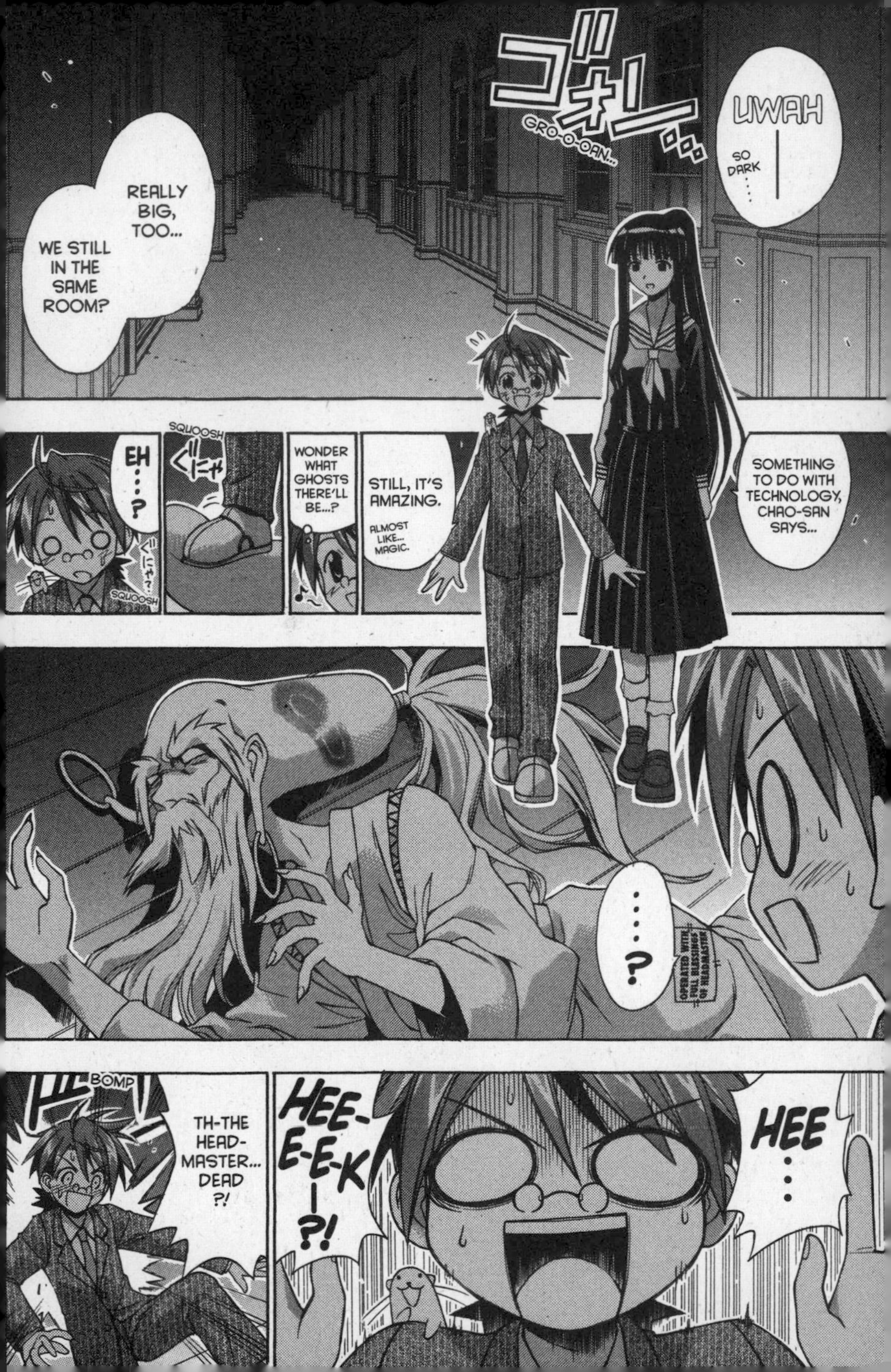
ゴオーン
GRO-O-OAN...
UWAH—
SO DARK...
REALLY BIG, TOO...
WE STILL IN THE SAME ROOM?
SOMETHING TO DO WITH TECHNOLOGY, CHAO-SAN SAYS...
STILL, IT'S AMAZING.
ALMOST LIKE... MAGIC.
WONDER WHAT GHOSTS THERE'LL BE...?
SQUOOSH
ぐにゃ
EH...?
ぐにゃ?
SQUOOSH
...?
OPERATED WITH FULL BLESSINGS OF HEADMASTER
HEE...
HEE-E-E-K-I-?!
BOMP
TH-THE HEAD-MASTER... DEAD?!

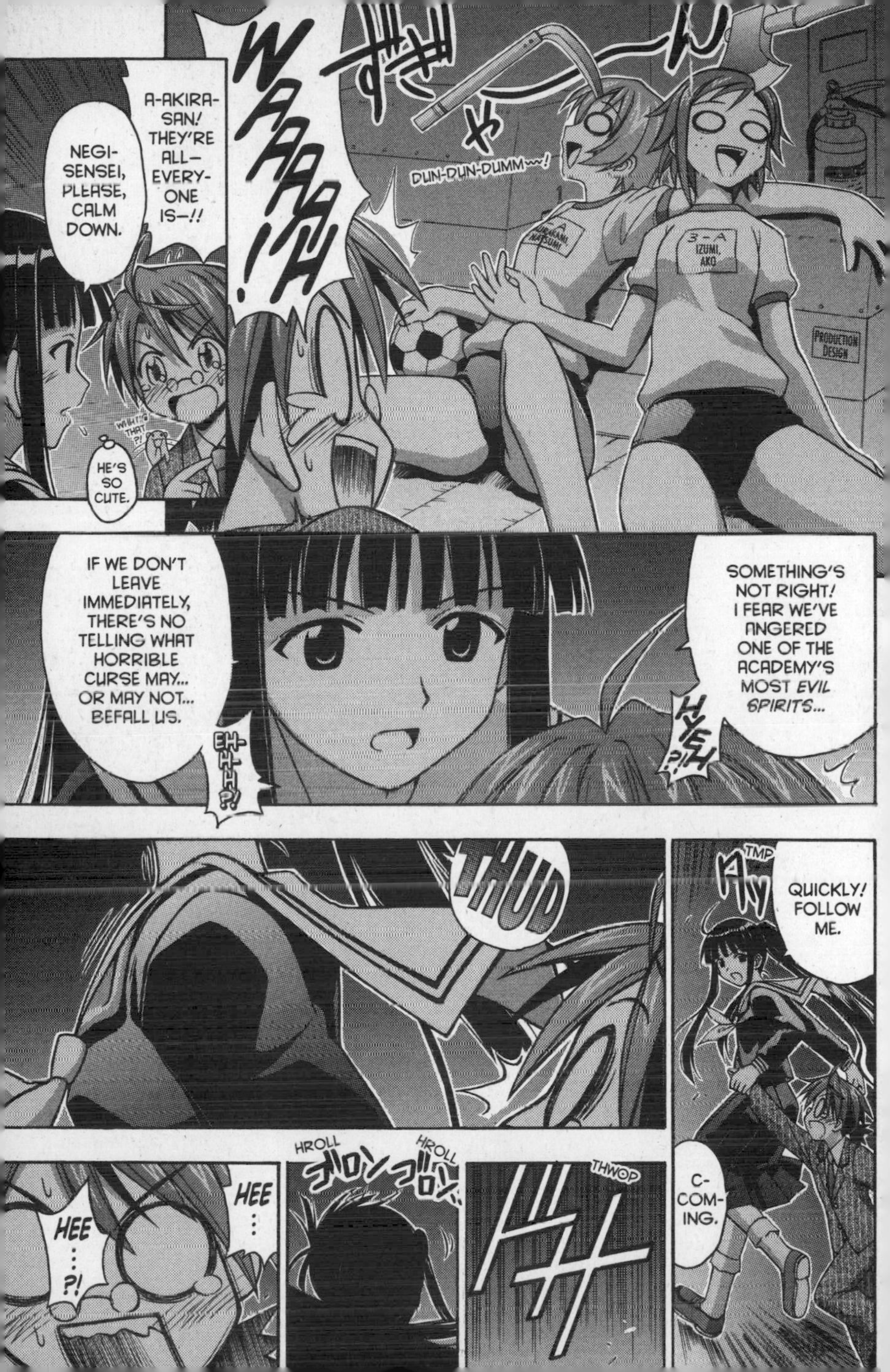
DUN-DUN-DUMM~~!
3-A
IZUMI, AKO
PRODUCTION DESIGN
WAAAAAH!
A-AKIRA-SAN! THEY'RE ALL— EVERYONE IS—!!
NEGI-SENSEI, PLEASE, CALM DOWN.
WHAT'S THAT?!
HE'S SO CUTE.
SOMETHING'S NOT RIGHT! I FEAR WE'VE ANGERED ONE OF THE ACADEMY'S MOST *EVIL SPIRITS*...
HYEH?!
IF WE DON'T LEAVE IMMEDIATELY, THERE'S NO TELLING WHAT HORRIBLE CURSE MAY... OR MAY NOT... BEFALL US.
EH-H-H?!
TMP
QUICKLY! FOLLOW ME.
C-COMING.
THUD
THWOP
HROLL
HROLL
HEE
HEE...?!

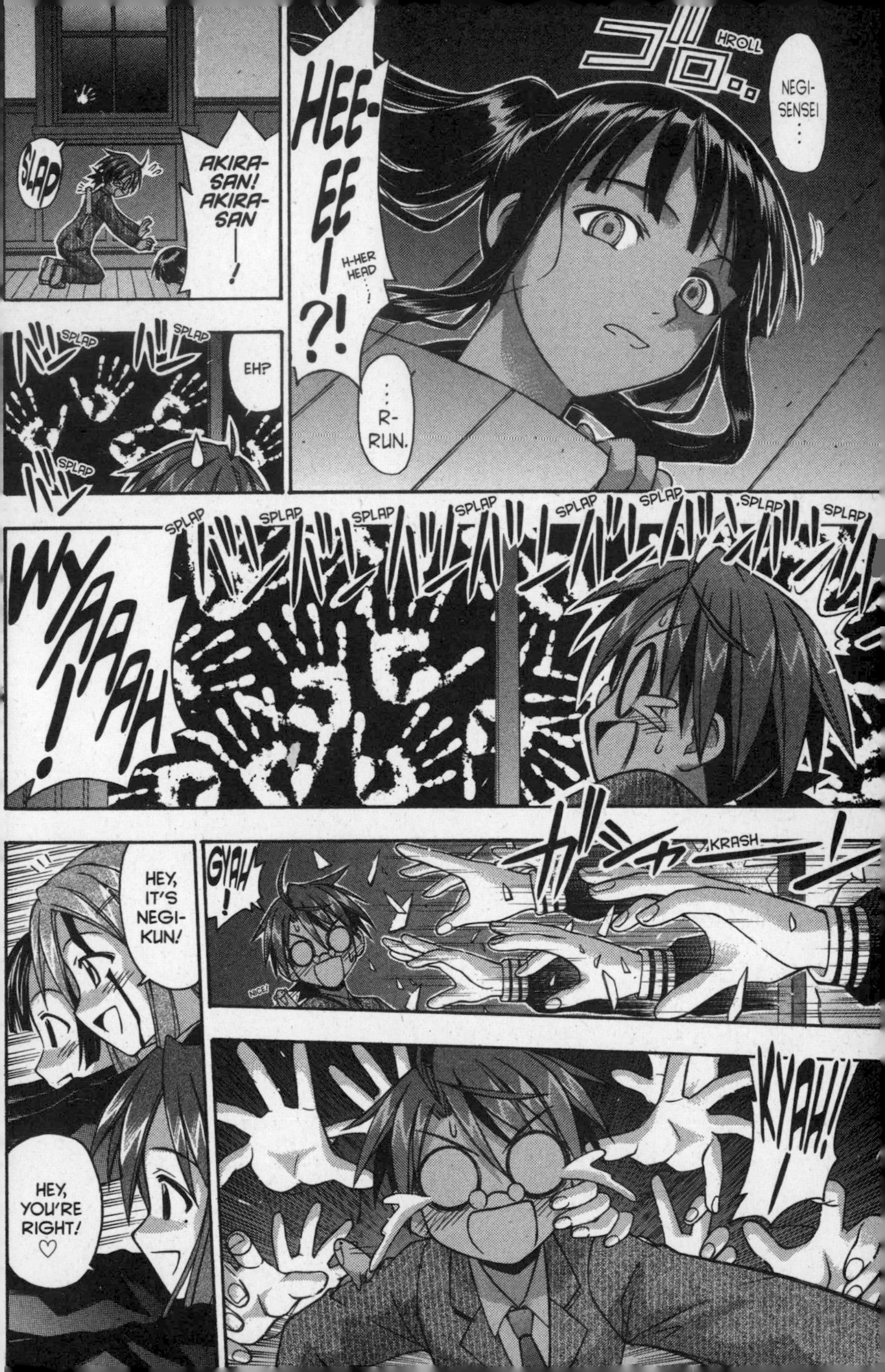
HROLL
NEGI-SENSEI...
HEE-EE-I?!
H-HER HEAD...!
...R-RUN.
SLAP
AKIRA-SAN! AKIRA-SAN—!
SPLAP
SPLAP
EH?
SPLAP
SPLAP
SPLAP
SPLAP
SPLAP
SPLAP
SPLAP
SPLAP
SPLAP
WYAAAAH!
KRASH
GYAH!
NICE!
HEY, IT'S NEGI-KUN!
KYAH!!
HEY, YOU'RE RIGHT! ♡

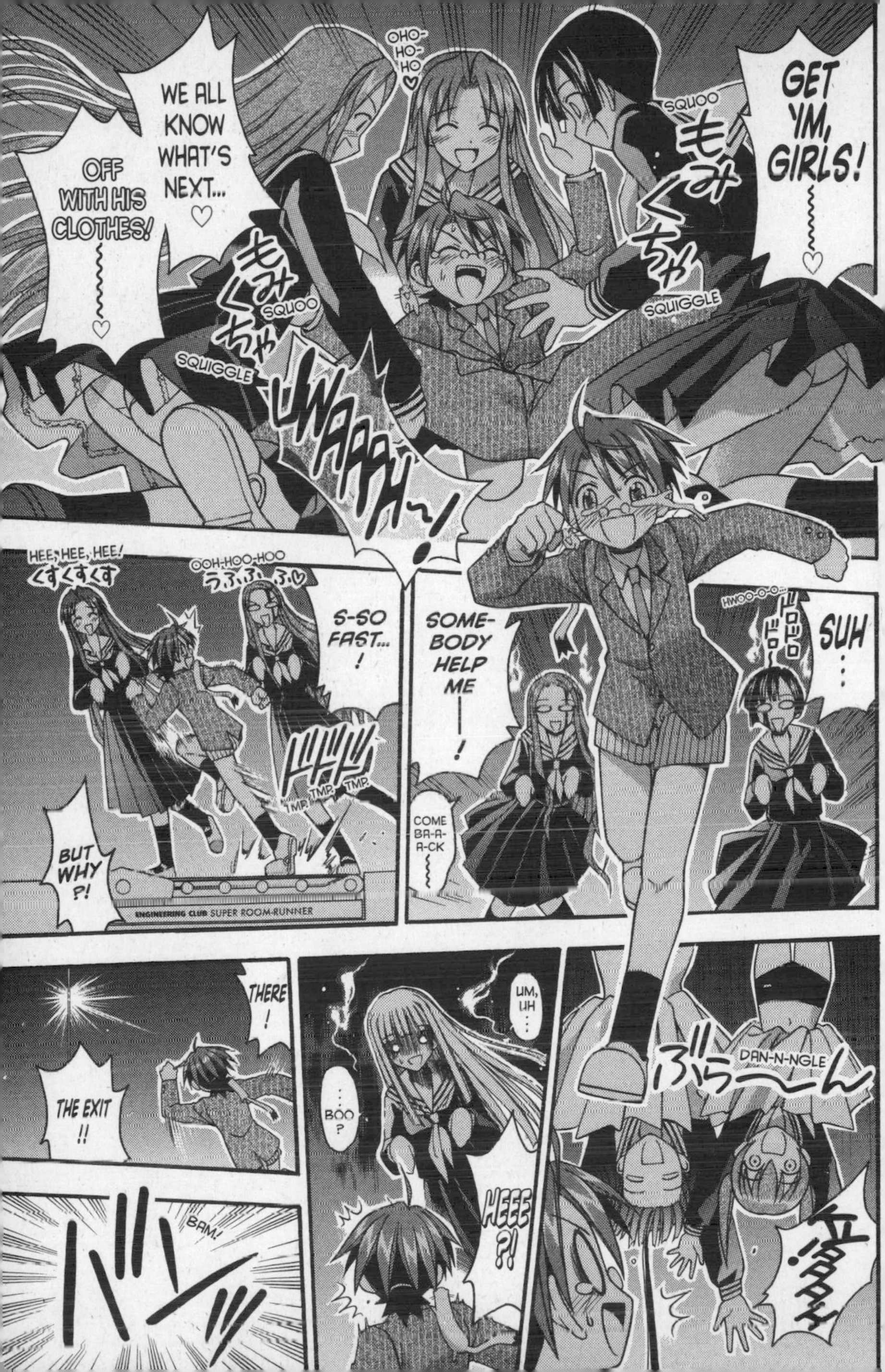

GET 'IM, GIRLS! ~~~♡
SQUOO
もみくちゃ
SQUIGGLE
OHO-HO-HO♡
WE ALL KNOW WHAT'S NEXT...♡
OFF WITH HIS CLOTHES! ~~~♡
もみくちゃ
SQUOO
SQUIGGLE
WAAAAH~!
HWOO-O-O...
ドロドロ~ドロ~
SUH...
SOMEBODY HELP ME—!
COME BA-A-A-CK ~~~
S-SO FAST...!
OOH-HOO-HOO
うふふふ♡
HEE, HEE, HEE!
くすくすくす
ドドドド
TMP. TMP. TMP.
BUT WHY?!
ENGINEERING CLUB SUPER ROOM-RUNNER
ぶら〜ん
DAN-N-NGLE
UM, UH...
...BOO?
HEEE?!
THERE!
THE EXIT!!
BAM!
バン!!

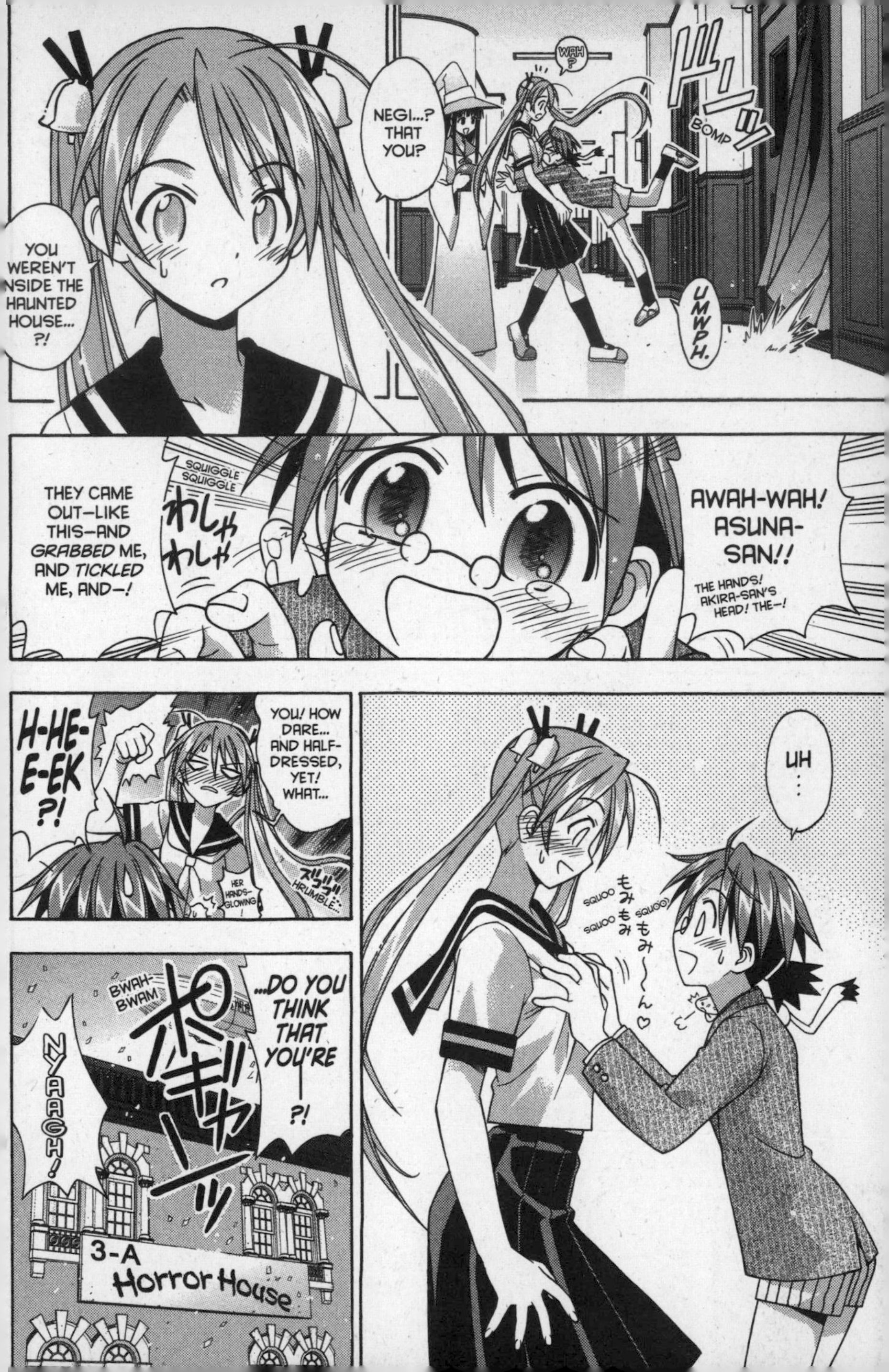
WAH?
BOMP
UMWPH.
NEGI...? THAT YOU?
YOU WEREN'T INSIDE THE HAUNTED HOUSE...?!
AWAH-WAH! ASUNA-SAN!!
THE HANDS! AKIRA-SAN'S HEAD! THE—!
SQUIGGLE SQUIGGLE
わしゃわしゃ
THEY CAME OUT—LIKE THIS—AND GRABBED ME, AND TICKLED ME, AND—!
UH...
もみもみもみ～ん♡
SQUOO SQUOO SQUOO
YOU! HOW DARE... AND HALF-DRESSED, YET! WHAT...
H-HE-E-EK?!
HER HANDS-GLOWING!
ズゴゴゴ HRUMBLE...
...DO YOU THINK THAT YOU'RE—?!
BWAH-BWAM
ポギャーッ
NYAAAGH!
3-A Horror House

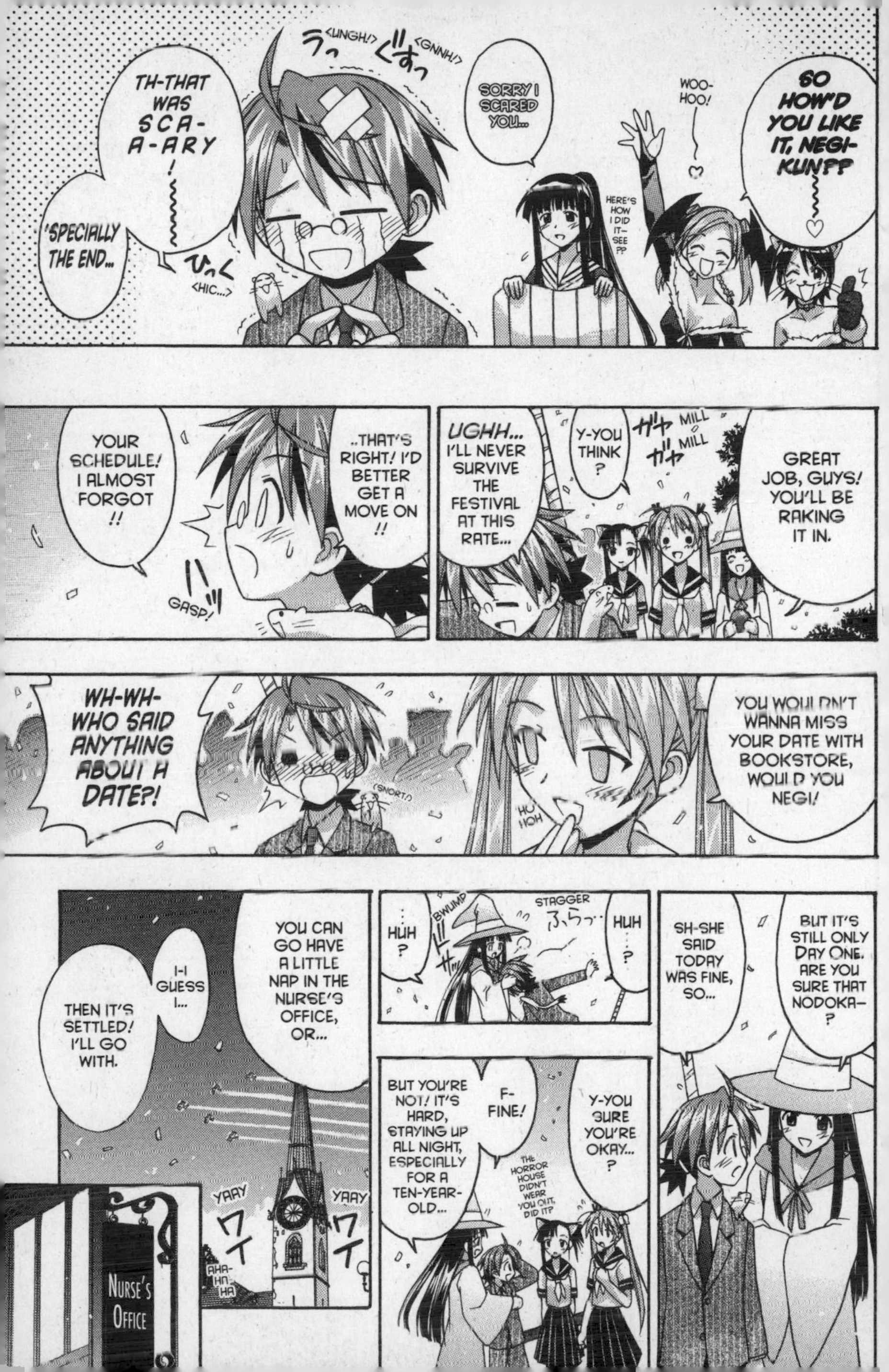
SO HOW'D YOU LIKE IT, NEGI-KUN??
WOO-HOO!
HERE'S HOW I DID IT—SEE??
SORRY I SCARED YOU...
ぐずっ <GNNH!>
うっ <UNGH!>
TH-THAT WAS SCA-A-ARY!
'SPECIALLY THE END...
ひっく <HIC...>
GREAT JOB, GUYS! YOU'LL BE RAKING IT IN.
ガヤ ガヤ MILL MILL
Y-YOU THINK?
UGHH... I'LL NEVER SURVIVE THE FESTIVAL AT THIS RATE...
..THAT'S RIGHT! I'D BETTER GET A MOVE ON!!
YOUR SCHEDULE! I ALMOST FORGOT!!
ハッ GASP!
YOU WOULDN'T WANNA MISS YOUR DATE WITH BOOKSTORE, WOULD YOU NEGI!
HO HOH
(SNORT.)
WH-WH-WHO SAID ANYTHING ABOUT A DATE?!
BUT IT'S STILL ONLY DAY ONE. ARE YOU SURE THAT NODOKA—?
SH-SHE SAID TODAY WAS FINE, SO...
HUH...?
ふらっ STAGGER
...HUH?
BWUMP
Y-YOU SURE YOU'RE OKAY...?
THE HORROR HOUSE DIDN'T WEAR YOU OUT, DID IT?
F-FINE!
BUT YOU'RE NOT! IT'S HARD, STAYING UP ALL NIGHT, ESPECIALLY FOR A TEN-YEAR-OLD...
YOU CAN GO HAVE A LITTLE NAP IN THE NURSE'S OFFICE, OR...
I-I GUESS I...
THEN IT'S SETTLED! I'LL GO WITH.
ワイ YAAY
ワイ YAAY
AHA-HA-HA
NURSE'S OFFICE

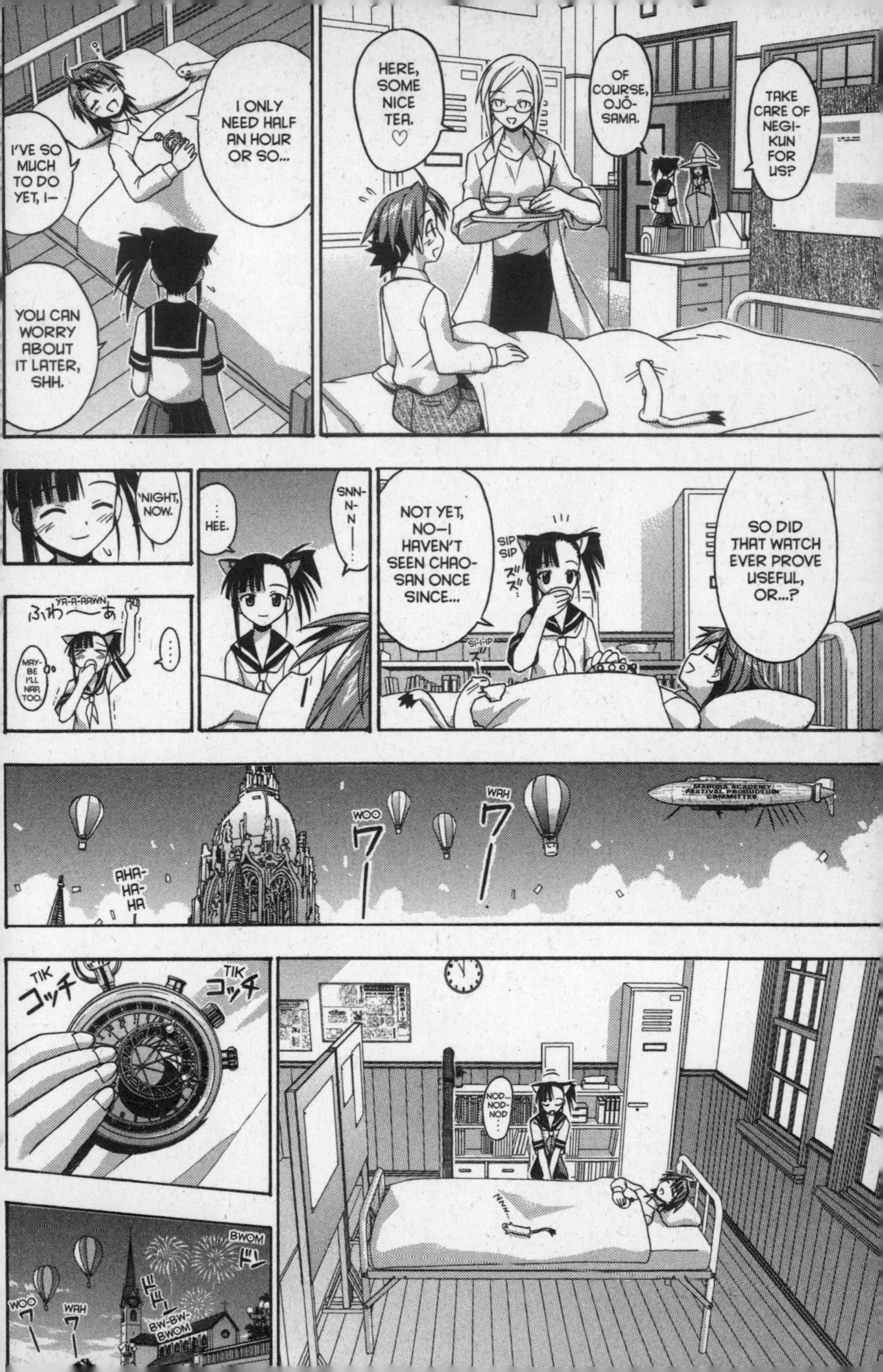
TAKE CARE OF NEGI-KUN FOR US?
OF COURSE, OJŌ-SAMA.
HERE, SOME NICE TEA. ♡
I ONLY NEED HALF AN HOUR OR SO...
I'VE SO MUCH TO DO YET, I—
YOU CAN WORRY ABOUT IT LATER, SHH.
SO DID THAT WATCH EVER PROVE USEFUL, OR...?
SIP SIP
NOT YET, NO—I HAVEN'T SEEN CHAO-SAN ONCE SINCE...
SI-I-IP
SNN-N-N—...
...HEE.
'NIGHT, NOW.
...
YA-A-AAWN
ふわ〜〜あ
MAY-BE I'LL NAP, TOO.
WAH
WOO
AHA-HA-HA
NOD... NOD... NOD...
NNH...
TIK
コッチ
TIK
コッチ
BWOM
BW-BW-BWOM
WAH
WOO

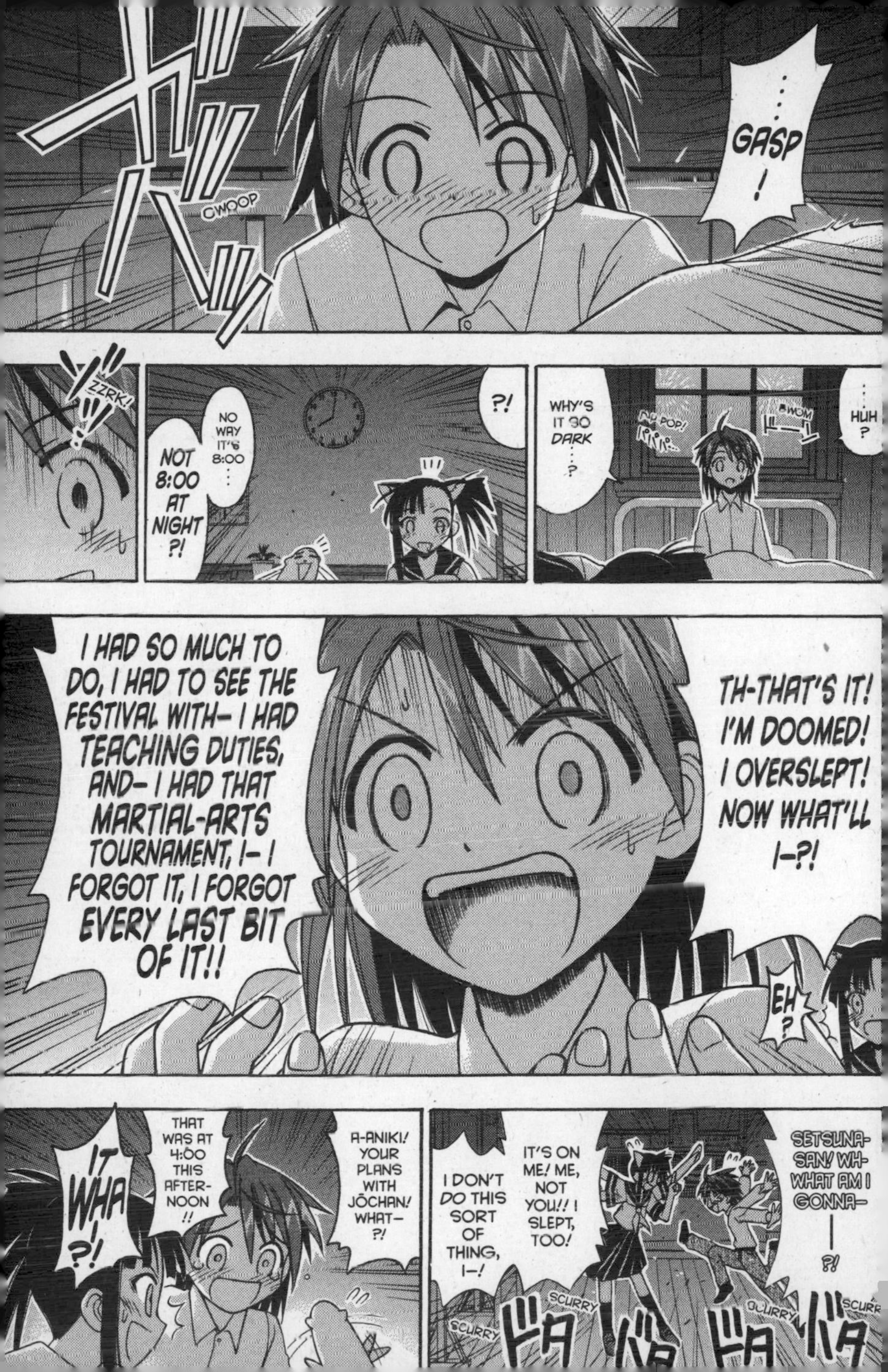
...GASP!
CWOOP
...HUH?
WOM
POP!
WHY'S IT SO DARK...?
?!
NO WAY IT'S 8:00...
NOT 8:00 AT NIGHT?!
ZZRK!
TH-THAT'S IT! I'M DOOMED! I OVERSLEPT! NOW WHAT'LL I-?!
I HAD SO MUCH TO DO, I HAD TO SEE THE FESTIVAL WITH- I HAD TEACHING DUTIES, AND- I HAD THAT MARTIAL-ARTS TOURNAMENT, I- I FORGOT IT, I FORGOT EVERY LAST BIT OF IT!!
EH?
SETSUNA-SAN! WH-WHAT AM I GONNA—?!
IT'S ON ME! ME, NOT YOU!! I SLEPT, TOO!
I DON'T DO THIS SORT OF THING, I—!
SCURRY
SCURRY
SCURRY
A-ANIKI! YOUR PLANS WITH JŌCHAN! WHAT—?!
THAT WAS AT 4:00 THIS AFTERNOON!!
IT WHA—?!

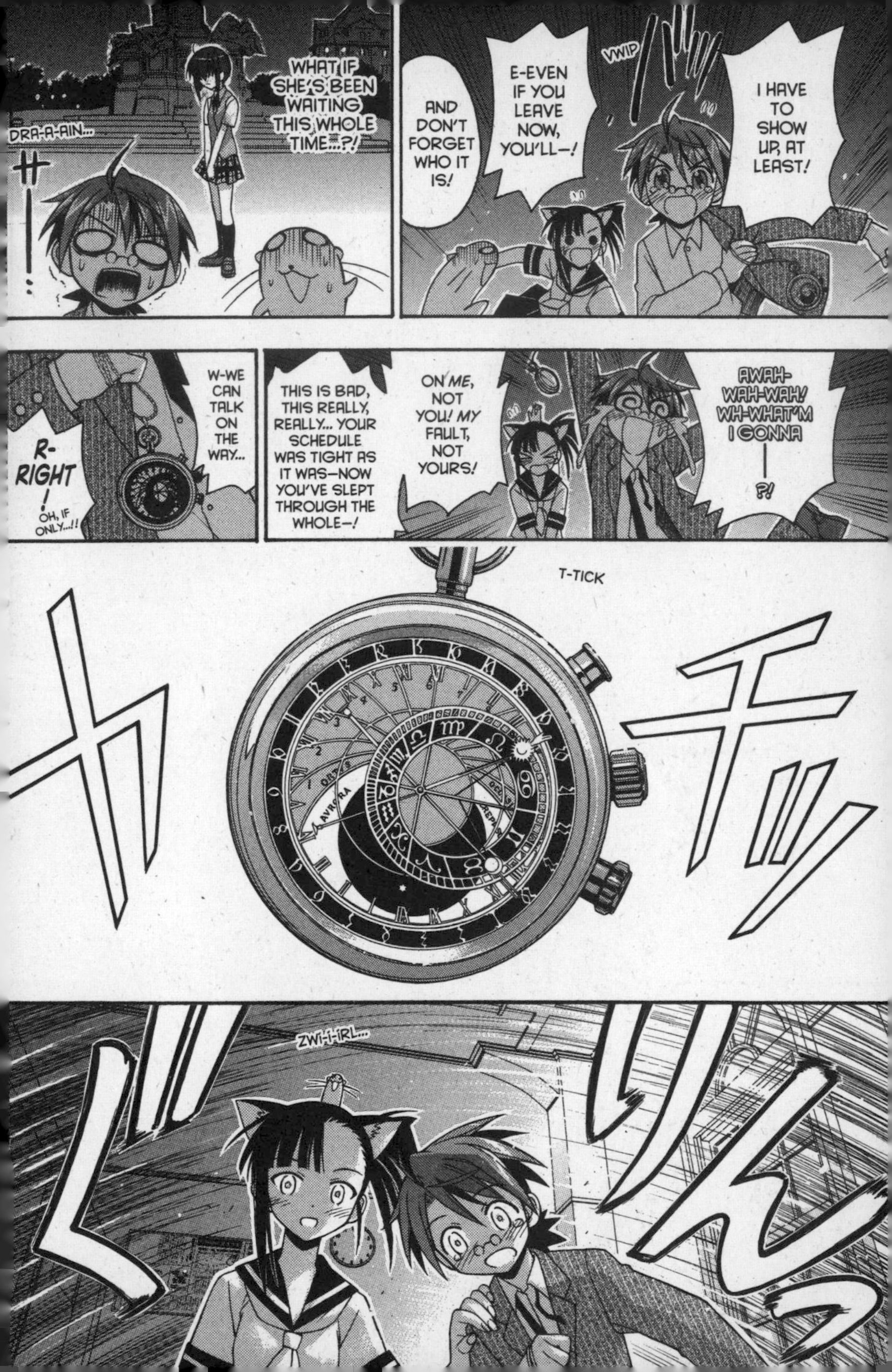
I HAVE TO SHOW UP, AT LEAST!
VWIP
E-EVEN IF YOU LEAVE NOW, YOU'LL—!
AND DON'T FORGET WHO IT IS!
WHAT IF SHE'S BEEN WAITING THIS WHOLE TIME...?!
DRA-A-AIN...
H—!...
AWAH-WAH-WAH! WH-WHAT'M I GONNA —?!
ON ME, NOT YOU! MY FAULT, NOT YOURS!
THIS IS BAD, THIS REALLY, REALLY... YOUR SCHEDULE WAS TIGHT AS IT WAS—NOW YOU'VE SLEPT THROUGH THE WHOLE—!
W-WE CAN TALK ON THE WAY...
R-RIGHT!
OH, IF ONLY...!!
T-TICK
AVRORA
ZWI-I-IRL...

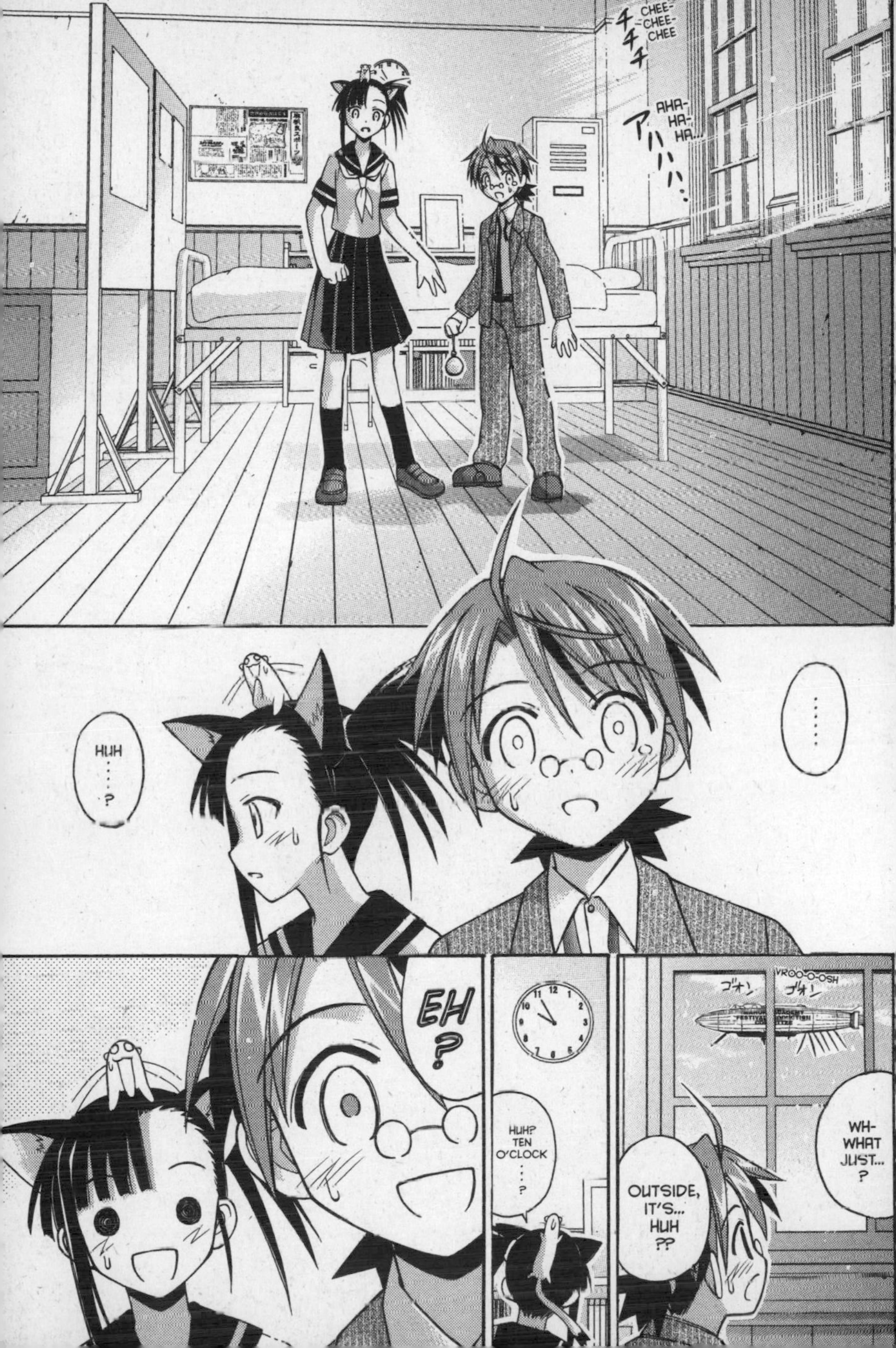
チチチ
CHEE-CHEE-CHEE
アハハハ...
AHA-HA-HA...
......
HUH ......?
ゴォン ゴォン
VROO-O-OSH
WH-WHAT JUST...?
OUTSIDE, IT'S... HUH ??
HUH? TEN O'CLOCK ....?
EH ?

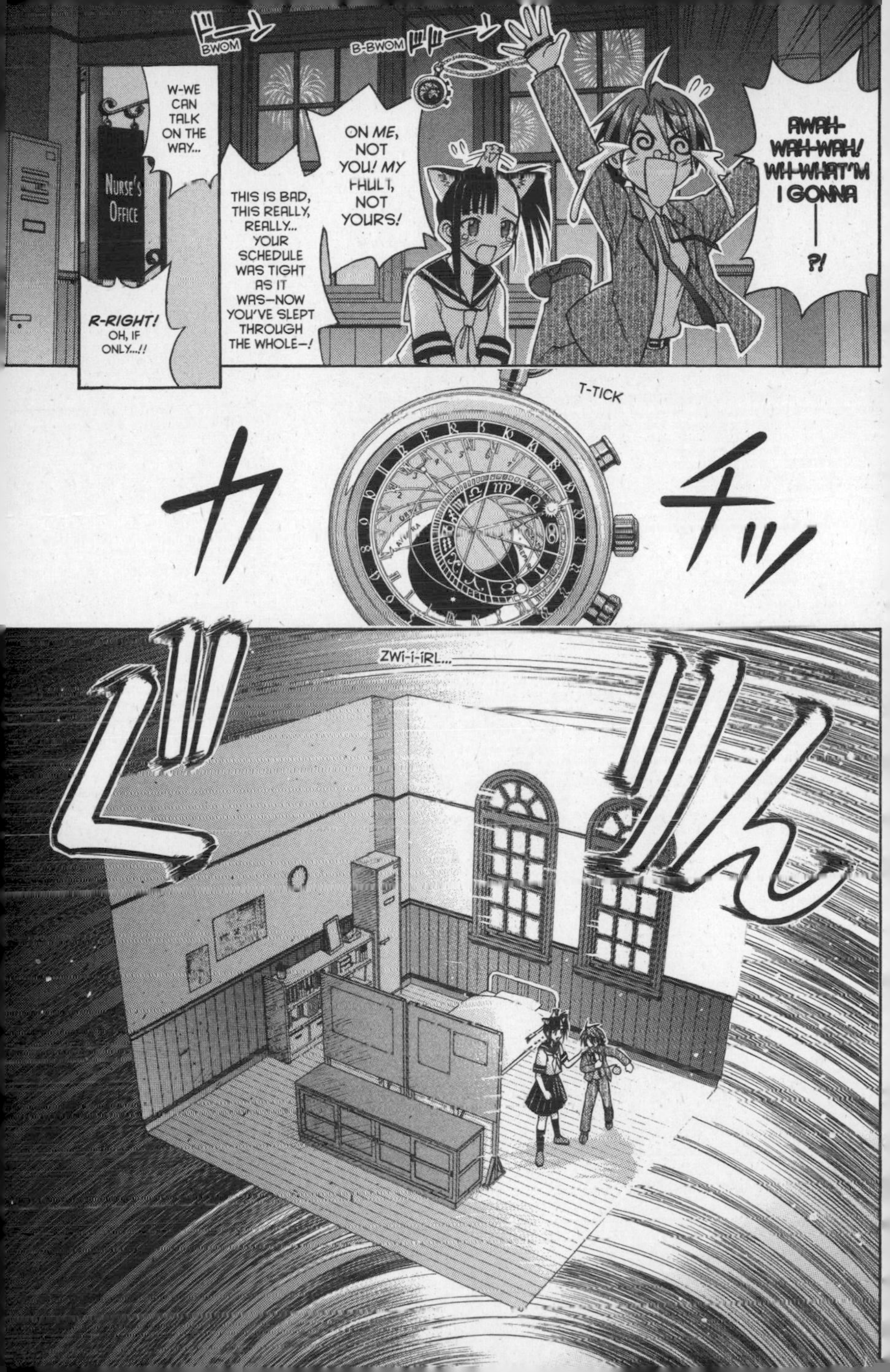
AWAH-WAH-WAH! WH-WHAT'M I GONNA—?!
B-BWOM
ON ME, NOT YOU! MY FAULT, NOT YOURS!
BWOM
W-WE CAN TALK ON THE WAY...
THIS IS BAD, THIS REALLY, REALLY... YOUR SCHEDULE WAS TIGHT AS IT WAS—NOW YOU'VE SLEPT THROUGH THE WHOLE—!
NURSE'S OFFICE
R-RIGHT! OH, IF ONLY...!!
T-TICK
カチッ
ZWI-I-IRL...

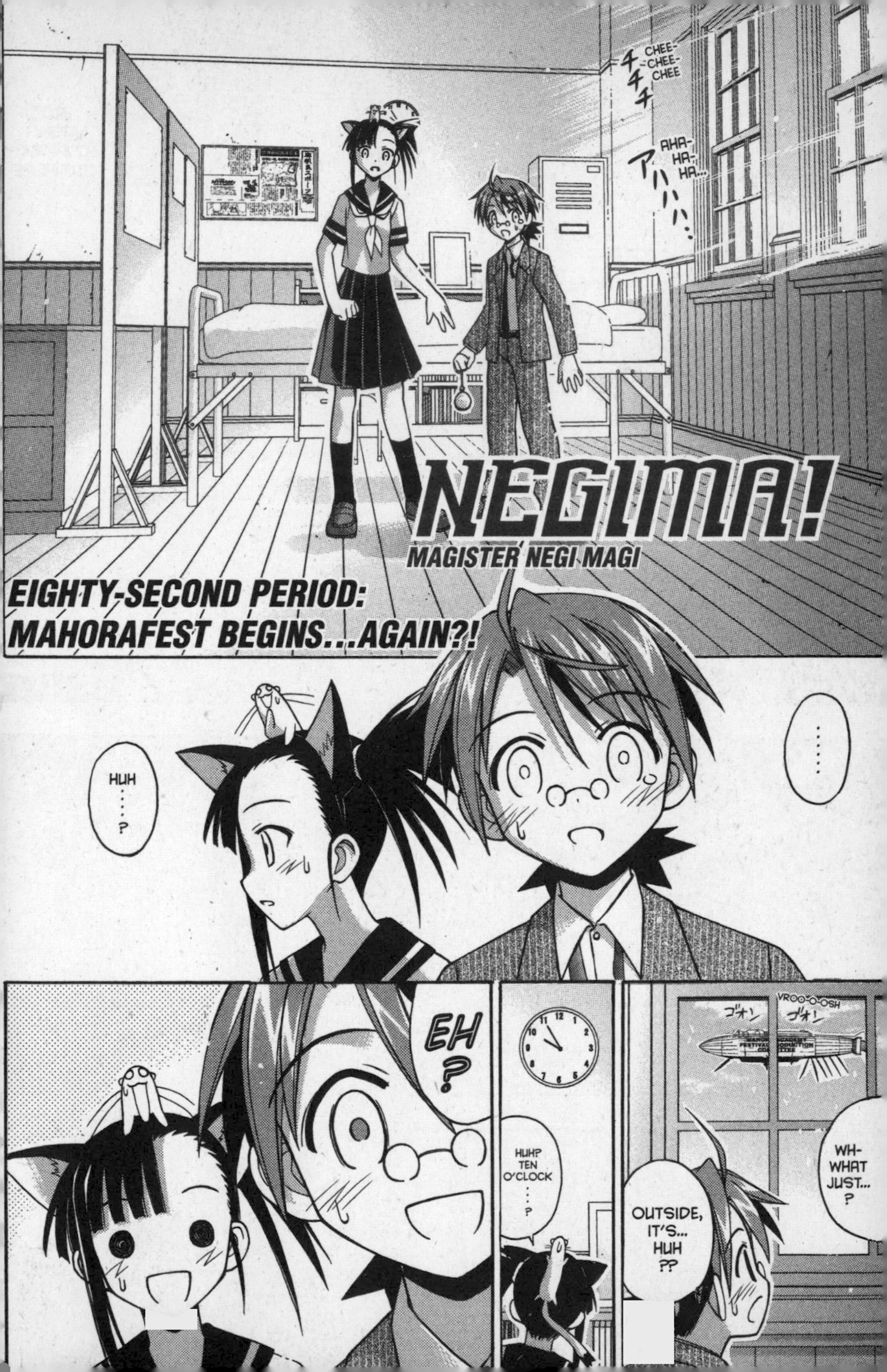
CHEE-CHEE-CHEE
チチチ
AHA-HA-HA...
アハハハ...
NEGIMA!
MAGISTER NEGI MAGI
EIGHTY-SECOND PERIOD: MAHORAFEST BEGINS...AGAIN?!
......
HUH ...?
VROO-O-OSH
ゴオン ゴオン
WH- WHAT JUST...?
OUTSIDE, IT'S... HUH ??
HUH? TEN O'CLOCK ...?
EH ?

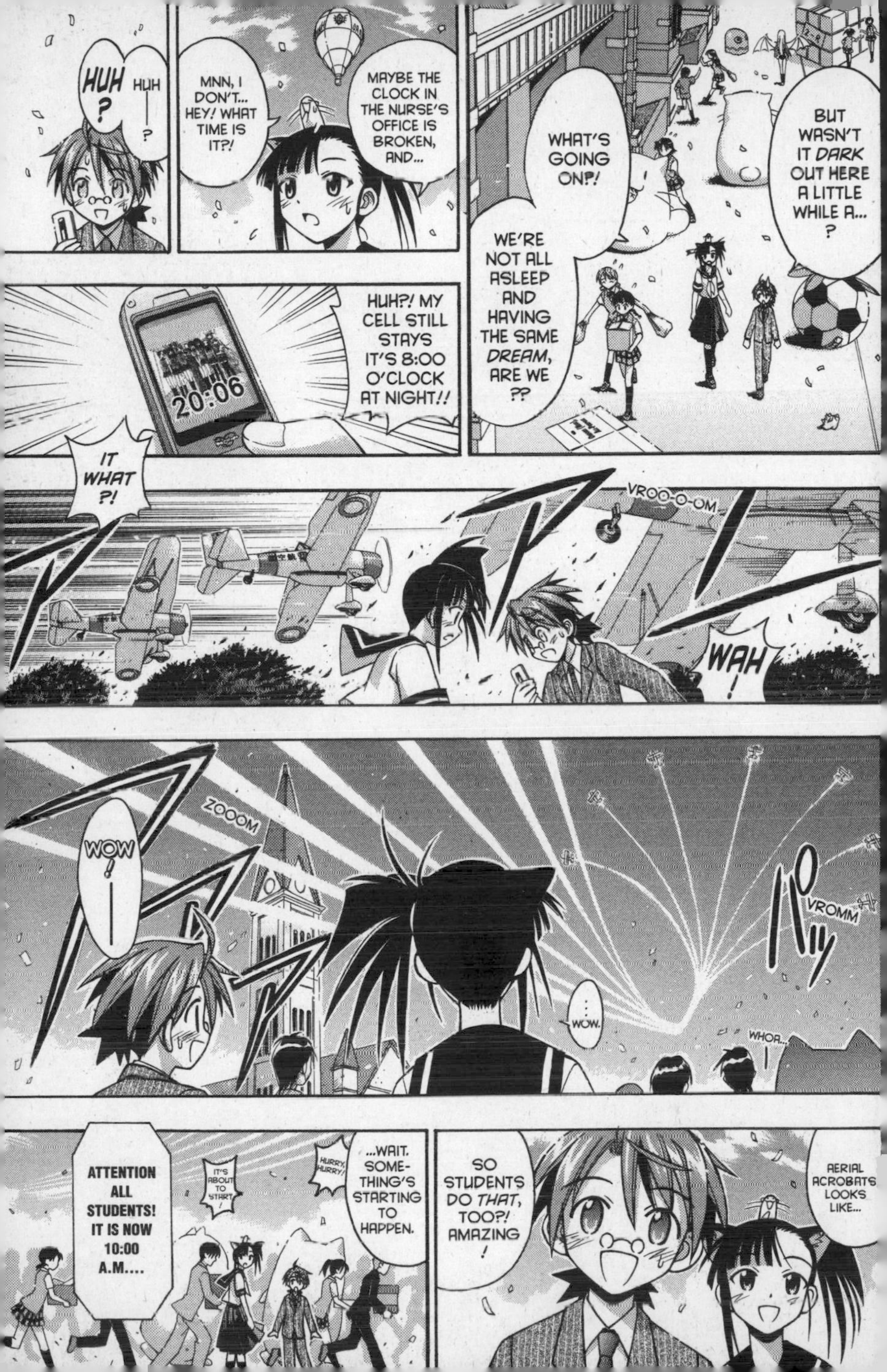

BUT WASN'T IT *DARK* OUT HERE A LITTLE WHILE A...?
WHAT'S GOING ON?!
WE'RE NOT ALL ASLEEP AND HAVING THE SAME *DREAM*, ARE WE??
MAYBE THE CLOCK IN THE NURSE'S OFFICE IS BROKEN, AND...
MNN, I DON'T... HEY! WHAT TIME IS IT?!
HUH?
HUH—?
HUH?! MY CELL STILL STAYS IT'S 8:00 O'CLOCK AT NIGHT!!
20:06
IT WHAT?!
VROO-O-OM
WAH!
ZOOOM
WOW!—
VROMM
WHOA...!
...WOW.
AERIAL ACROBATS LOOKS LIKE...
SO STUDENTS DO *THAT*, TOO?! AMAZING!
...WAIT. SOMETHING'S STARTING TO HAPPEN.
HURRY, HURRY!
IT'S ABOUT TO START!
ATTENTION ALL STUDENTS! IT IS NOW 10:00 A.M....

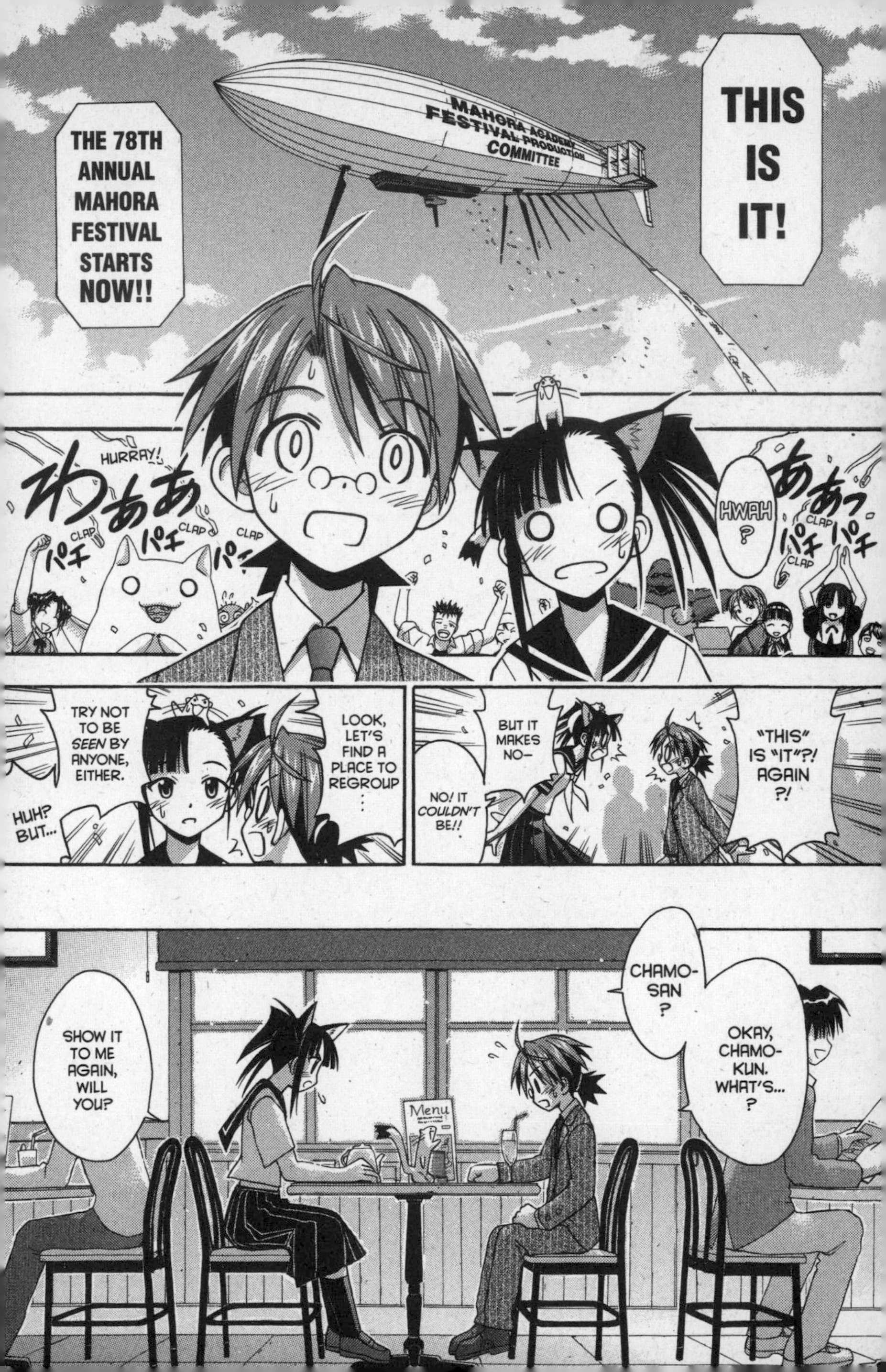
THIS IS IT!
MAHORA ACADEMY FESTIVAL PRODUCTION COMMITTEE
THE 78TH ANNUAL MAHORA FESTIVAL STARTS NOW!!
ああっ
CLAP パチ CLAP パチ
HWAH?
わあああ
HURRAY!
CLAP パチ CLAP パチ CLAP パ
"THIS" IS "IT"?! AGAIN?!
BUT IT MAKES NO—
NO! IT *COULDN'T* BE!!
LOOK, LET'S FIND A PLACE TO REGROUP...
TRY NOT TO BE *SEEN* BY ANYONE, EITHER.
HUH? BUT...
CHAMO-SAN?
OKAY, CHAMO-KUN. WHAT'S...?
Menu
SHOW IT TO ME AGAIN, WILL YOU?

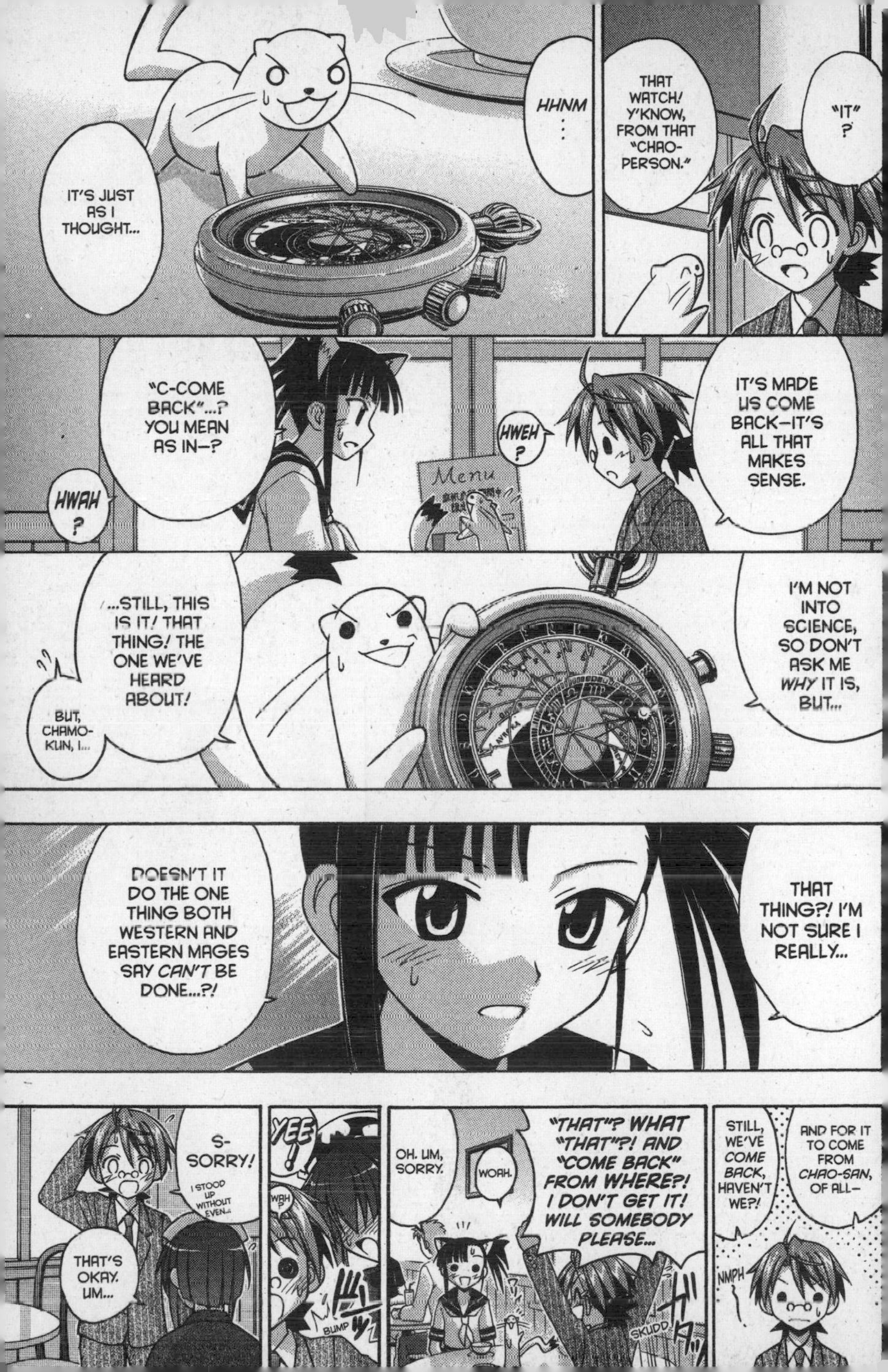
"IT"?
THAT WATCH! Y'KNOW, FROM THAT "CHAO-PERSON."
HHNM ...
IT'S JUST AS I THOUGHT...
IT'S MADE US COME BACK—IT'S ALL THAT MAKES SENSE.
HWEH?
"C-COME BACK"...? YOU MEAN AS IN—?
HWAH?
I'M NOT INTO SCIENCE, SO DON'T ASK ME WHY IT IS, BUT...
...STILL, THIS IS IT! THAT THING! THE ONE WE'VE HEARD ABOUT!
BUT, CHAMO-KUN, I...
THAT THING?! I'M NOT SURE I REALLY...
DOESN'T IT DO THE ONE THING BOTH WESTERN AND EASTERN MAGES SAY CAN'T BE DONE...?!
AND FOR IT TO COME FROM CHAO-SAN, OF ALL—
STILL, WE'VE COME BACK, HAVEN'T WE?!
NMPH
"THAT"? WHAT "THAT"?! AND "COME BACK" FROM WHERE?! I DON'T GET IT! WILL SOMEBODY PLEASE...
WOAH.
OH. UM, SORRY.
SKUDD
YEE
WAH?
BUMP
S-SORRY!
I STOOD UP WITHOUT EVEN...
THAT'S OKAY. UM...

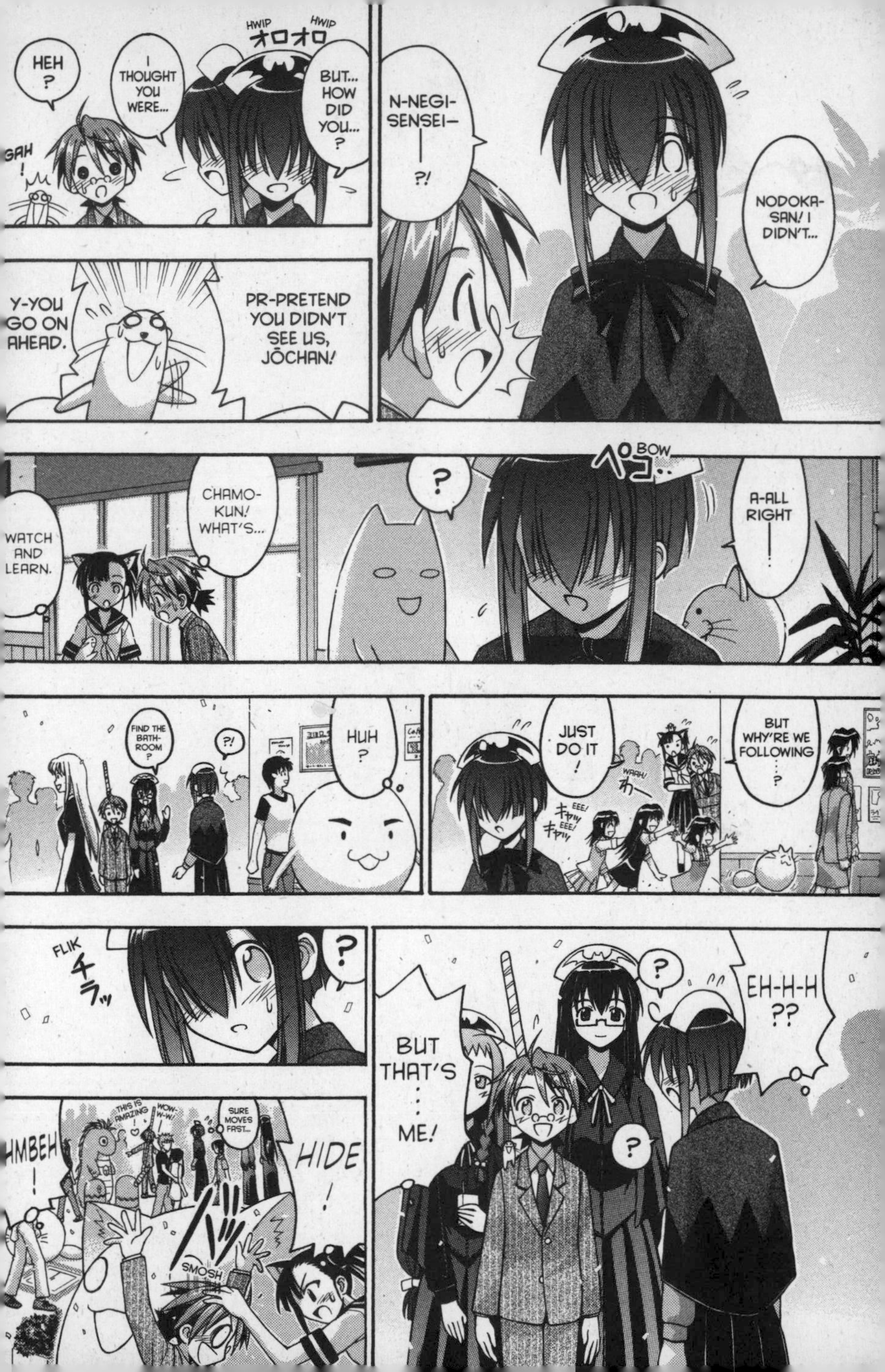
NODOKA-SAN! I DIDN'T...
N-NEGI-SENSEI— —?!
BUT... HOW DID YOU...?
HWIP HWIP
オロオロ
I THOUGHT YOU WERE...
HEH?
GAH!
PR-PRETEND YOU DIDN'T SEE US, JŌCHAN!
Y-YOU GO ON AHEAD.
A-ALL RIGHT—!
BOW
ペコ..
?
CHAMO-KUN! WHAT'S...
WATCH AND LEARN.
BUT WHY'RE WE FOLLOWING...?
JUST DO IT!
WAAH!
わー
EEE! EEE!
キャッ キャッ
HUH?
?!
FIND THE BATH-ROOM?
EH-H-H??
?
BUT THAT'S... ME!
?
?
FLIK
チラッ
HIDE!
SURE MOVES FAST...
WOW-W-W!
THIS IS AMAZING!
SMOSH
HMBEH!

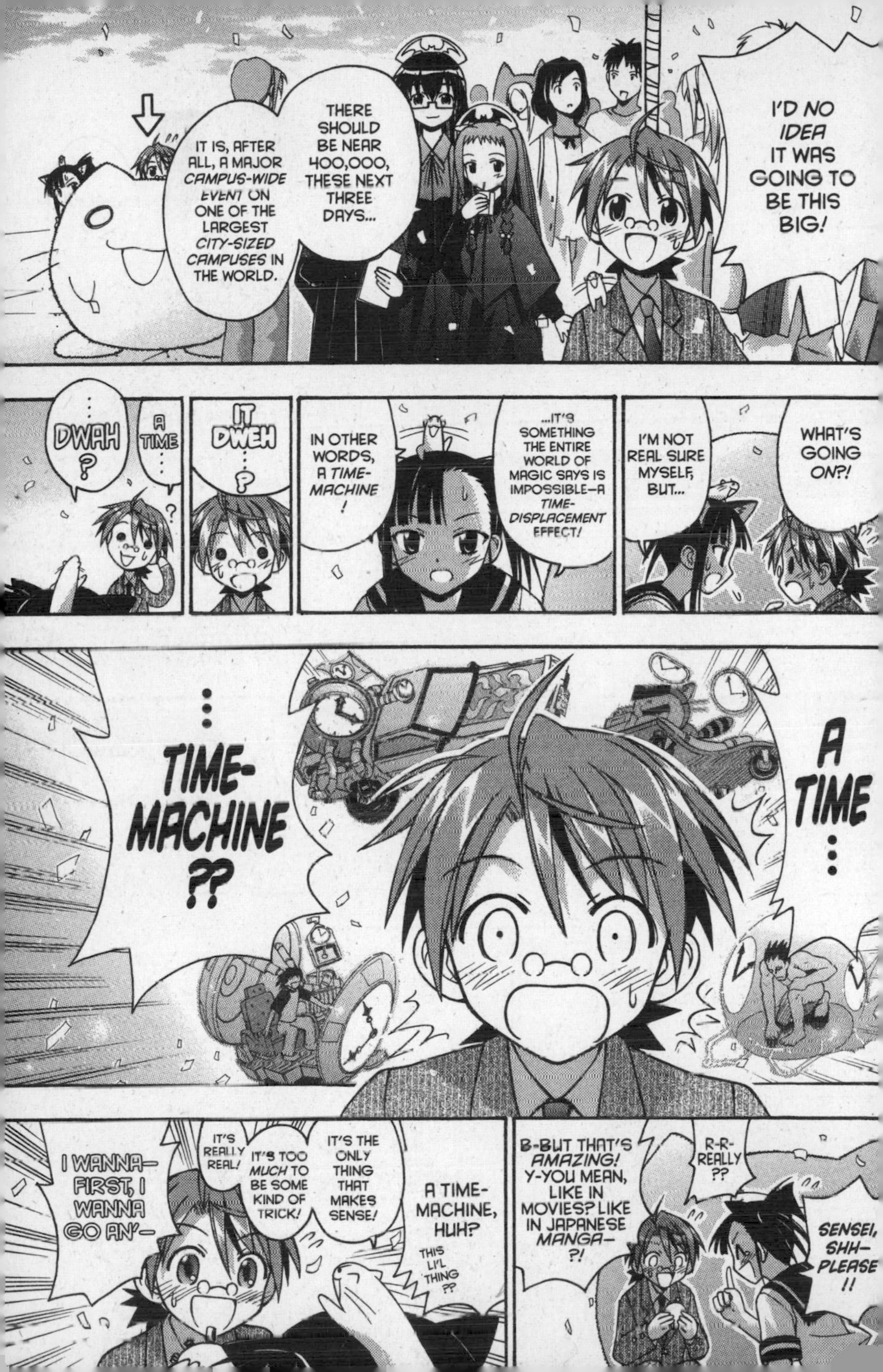

I'D NO IDEA IT WAS GOING TO BE THIS BIG!
THERE SHOULD BE NEAR 400,000, THESE NEXT THREE DAYS...
IT IS, AFTER ALL, A MAJOR CAMPUS-WIDE EVENT ON ONE OF THE LARGEST CITY-SIZED CAMPUSES IN THE WORLD.
WHAT'S GOING ON?!
I'M NOT REAL SURE MYSELF, BUT...
...IT'S SOMETHING THE ENTIRE WORLD OF MAGIC SAYS IS IMPOSSIBLE—A TIME-DISPLACEMENT EFFECT!
IN OTHER WORDS, A TIME-MACHINE!
IT DWEH...?
A TIME...
...DWAH?
A TIME...
...TIME-MACHINE??
R-R-REALLY??
B-BUT THAT'S AMAZING! Y-YOU MEAN, LIKE IN MOVIES? LIKE IN JAPANESE MANGA—?!
SENSEI, SHH PLEASE!!
A TIME-MACHINE, HUH?
THIS LI'L THING??
IT'S THE ONLY THING THAT MAKES SENSE!
IT'S TOO MUCH TO BE SOME KIND OF TRICK!
IT'S REALLY REAL!
I WANNA— FIRST, I WANNA GO AN'—

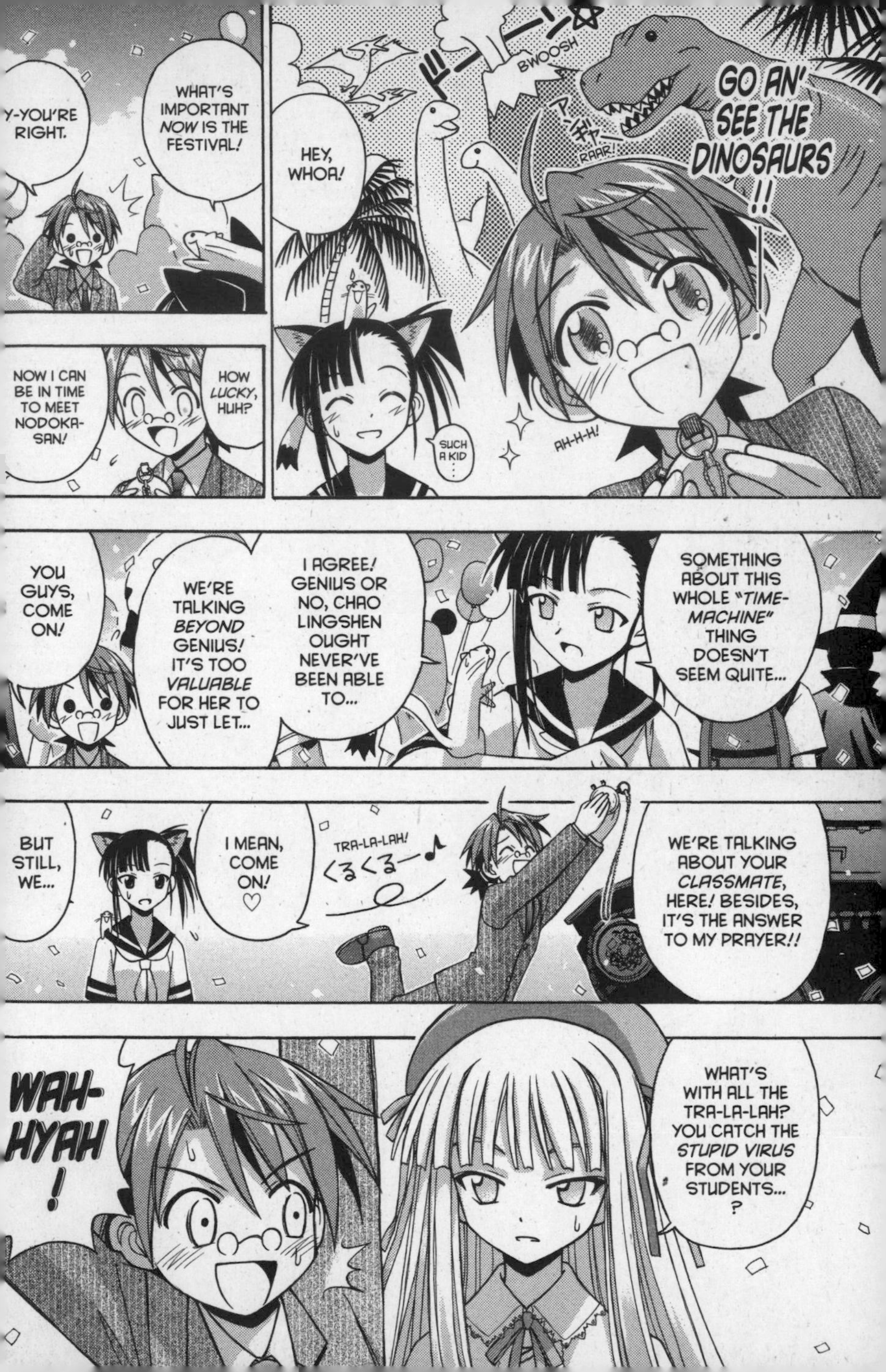
GO AN' SEE THE DINOSAURS!!
BWOOSH
ドーーン
アギャー
RAAR!
HEY, WHOA!
AH-H-H!
SUCH A KID...
WHAT'S IMPORTANT NOW IS THE FESTIVAL!
Y-YOU'RE RIGHT.
HOW LUCKY, HUH?
NOW I CAN BE IN TIME TO MEET NODOKA-SAN!
SOMETHING ABOUT THIS WHOLE "TIME-MACHINE" THING DOESN'T SEEM QUITE...
I AGREE! GENIUS OR NO, CHAO LINGSHEN OUGHT NEVER'VE BEEN ABLE TO...
WE'RE TALKING BEYOND GENIUS! IT'S TOO VALUABLE FOR HER TO JUST LET...
YOU GUYS, COME ON!
WE'RE TALKING ABOUT YOUR CLASSMATE, HERE! BESIDES, IT'S THE ANSWER TO MY PRAYER!!
TRA-LA-LAH!
くるくるー
I MEAN, COME ON! ♡
BUT STILL, WE...
WHAT'S WITH ALL THE TRA-LA-LAH? YOU CATCH THE STUPID VIRUS FROM YOUR STUDENTS...?
WAH-HYAH!

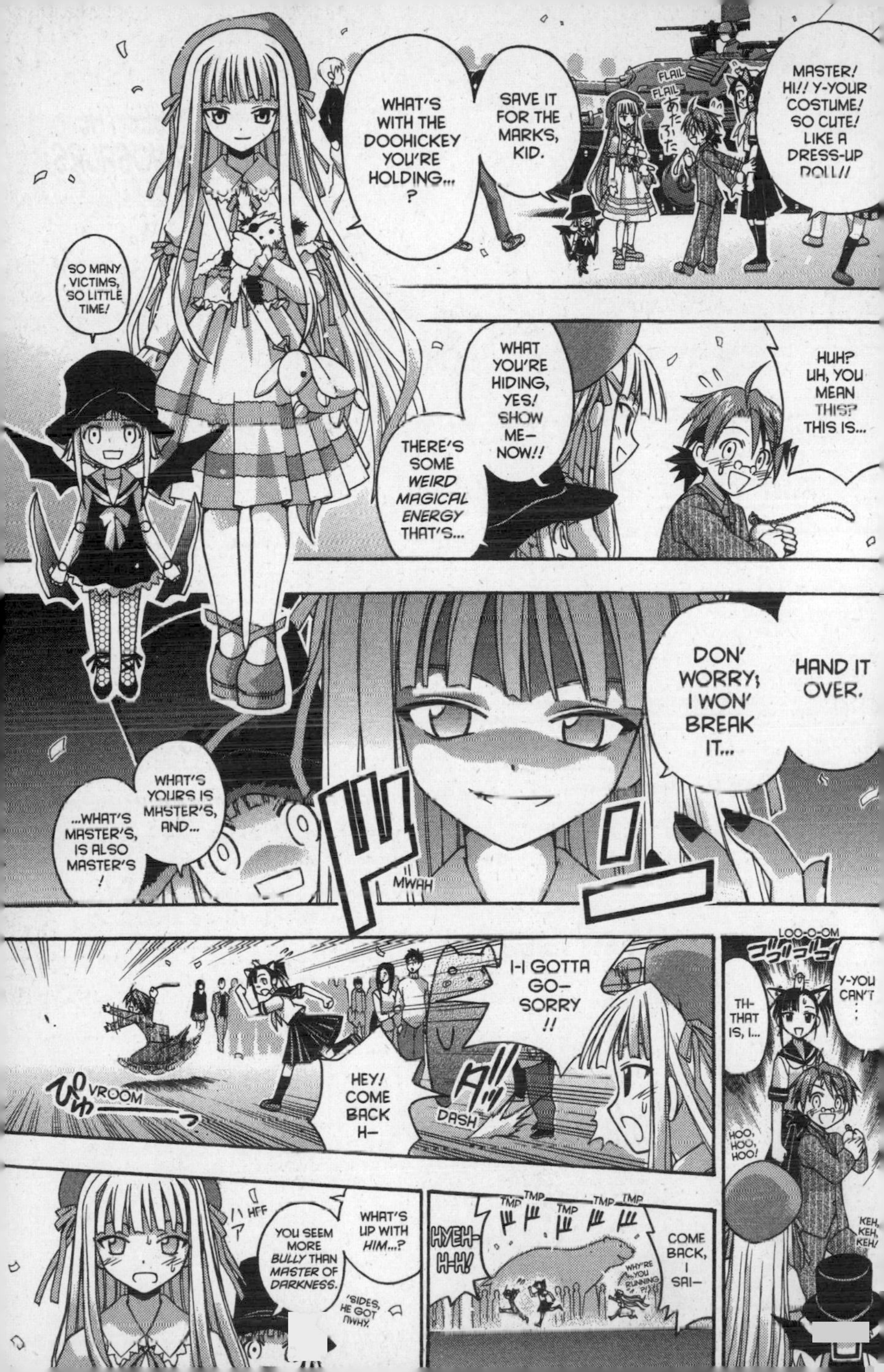
MASTER! HI!! Y-YOUR COSTUME! SO CUTE! LIKE A DRESS-UP DOLL!!
FLAIL
FLAIL
あたふた
SAVE IT FOR THE MARKS, KID.
WHAT'S WITH THE DOOHICKEY YOU'RE HOLDING...?
HUH? UH, YOU MEAN THIS? THIS IS...
WHAT YOU'RE HIDING, YES! SHOW ME— NOW!!
THERE'S SOME WEIRD MAGICAL ENERGY THAT'S...
SO MANY VICTIMS, SO LITTLE TIME!
HAND IT OVER.
DON' WORRY; I WON' BREAK IT...
MWAH
WHAT'S YOURS IS MASTER'S, AND...
...WHAT'S MASTER'S, IS ALSO MASTER'S!
LOO-O-OM
Y-YOU CAN'T...
TH-THAT IS, I...
HOO, HOO, HOO!
I-I GOTTA GO- SORRY!!
DASH
HEY! COME BACK H—
VROOM
KEH, KEH, KEH!
COME BACK, I SAI—
TMP TMP TMP TMP TMP
WHY'RE YOU RUNNING?!
HYEH-H-H!
WHAT'S UP WITH HIM...?
YOU SEEM MORE BULLY THAN MASTER OF DARKNESS.
'SIDES, HE GOT AWAY.
HFF

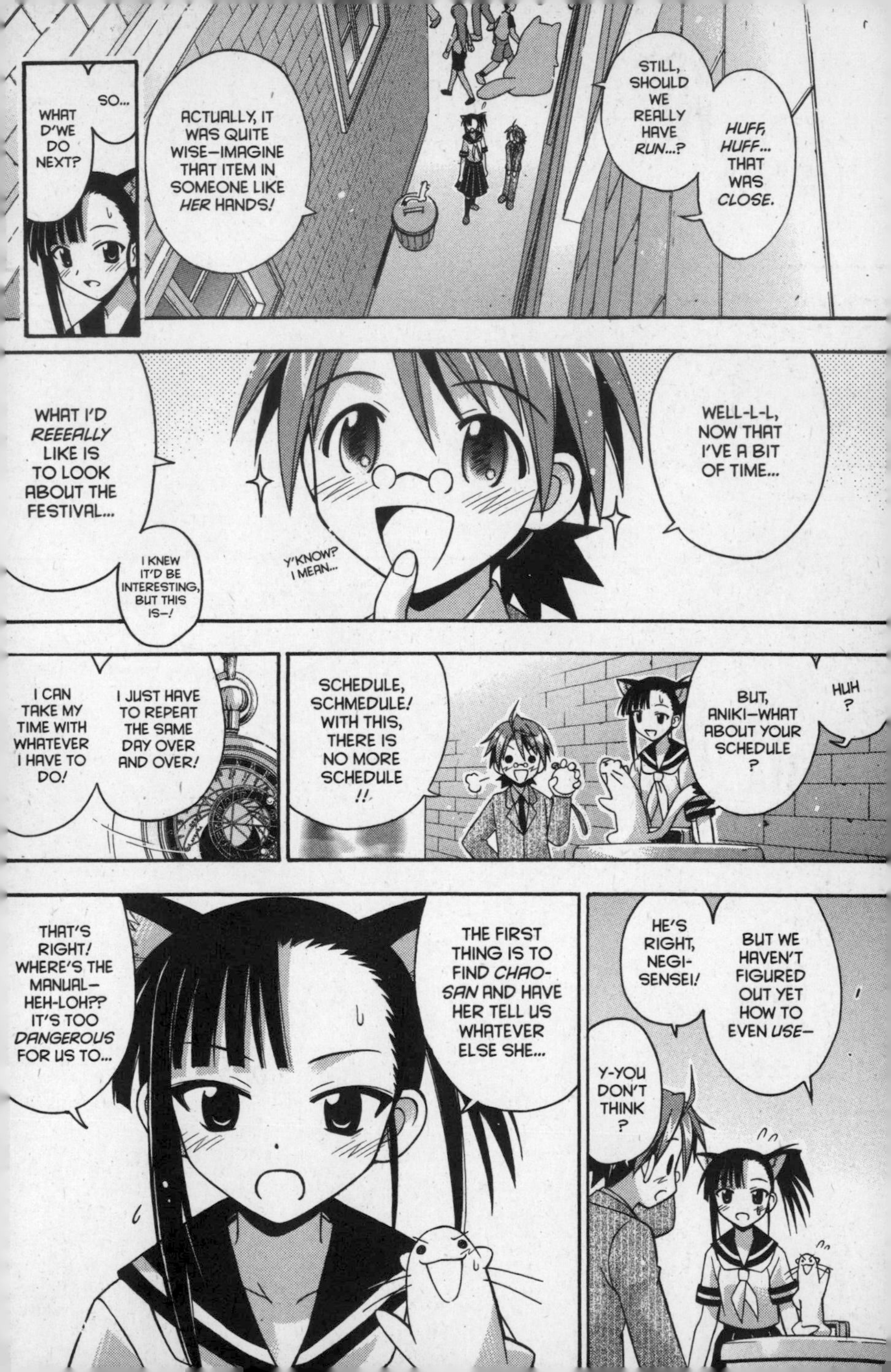
HUFF, HUFF... THAT WAS CLOSE.
STILL, SHOULD WE REALLY HAVE RUN...?
ACTUALLY, IT WAS QUITE WISE—IMAGINE THAT ITEM IN SOMEONE LIKE HER HANDS!
SO... WHAT D'WE DO NEXT?
WELL-L-L, NOW THAT I'VE A BIT OF TIME...
Y'KNOW? I MEAN...
WHAT I'D REEEALLY LIKE IS TO LOOK ABOUT THE FESTIVAL...
I KNEW IT'D BE INTERESTING, BUT THIS IS—!
HUH?
BUT, ANIKI—WHAT ABOUT YOUR SCHEDULE?
SCHEDULE, SCHMEDULE! WITH THIS, THERE IS NO MORE SCHEDULE!!
I JUST HAVE TO REPEAT THE SAME DAY OVER AND OVER!
I CAN TAKE MY TIME WITH WHATEVER I HAVE TO DO!
BUT WE HAVEN'T FIGURED OUT YET HOW TO EVEN USE—
HE'S RIGHT, NEGI-SENSEI!
Y-YOU DON'T THINK?
THE FIRST THING IS TO FIND CHAO-SAN AND HAVE HER TELL US WHATEVER ELSE SHE...
THAT'S RIGHT! WHERE'S THE MANUAL—HEH-LOH?? IT'S TOO DANGEROUS FOR US TO...

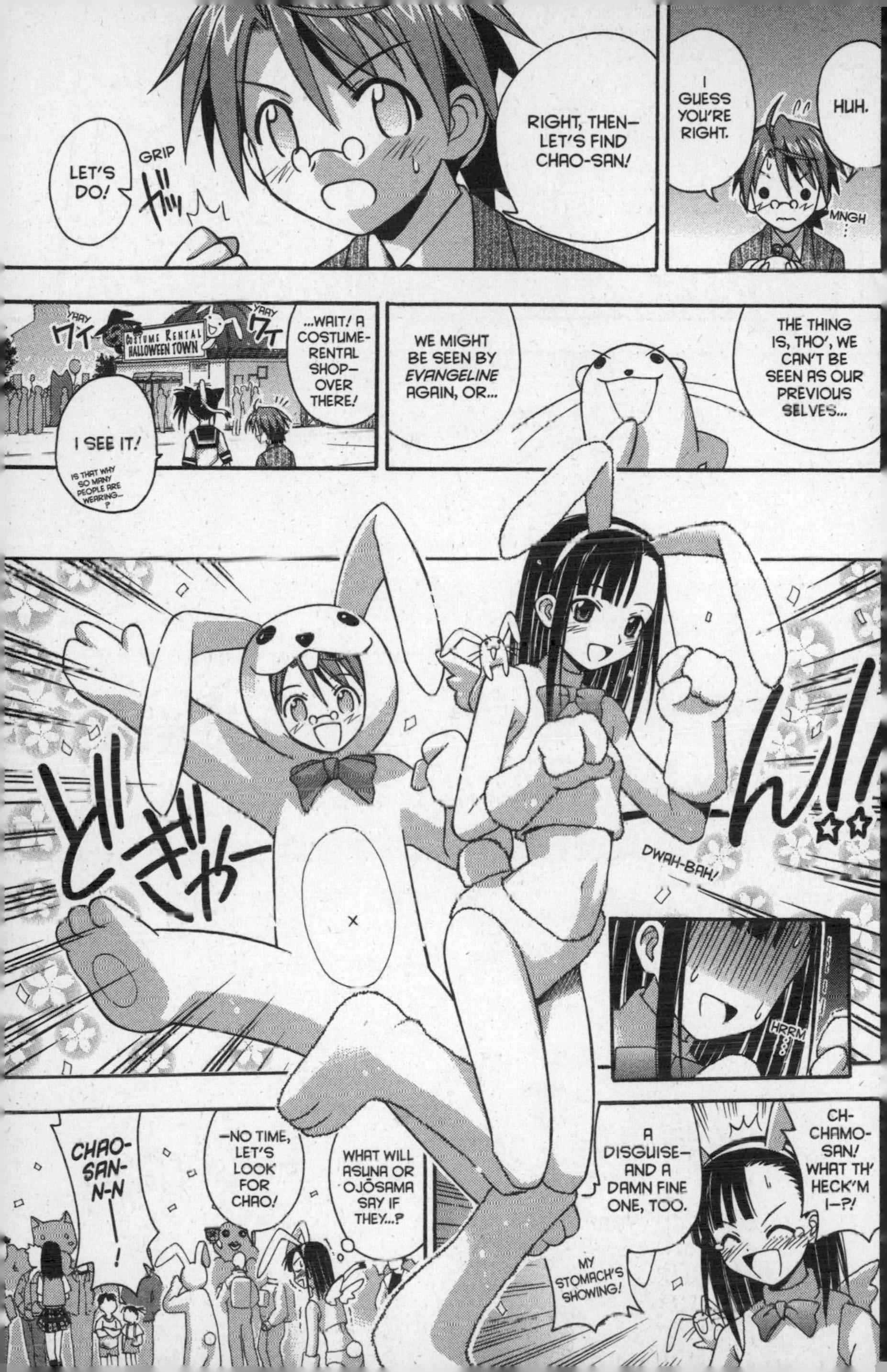
HUH.
I GUESS YOU'RE RIGHT.
MNGH...
RIGHT, THEN— LET'S FIND CHAO-SAN!
GRIP
LET'S DO!
THE THING IS, THO', WE CAN'T BE SEEN AS OUR PREVIOUS SELVES...
WE MIGHT BE SEEN BY *EVANGELINE* AGAIN, OR...
...WAIT! A COSTUME-RENTAL SHOP— OVER THERE!
YAAY
COSTUME RENTAL
HALLOWEEN TOWN
YAAY
I SEE IT!
IS THAT WHY SO MANY PEOPLE ARE WEARING...?
DWAH-BAH!
HRRM...
CH-CHAMO-SAN! WHAT TH' HECK'M I—?!
A DISGUISE— AND A DAMN FINE ONE, TOO.
MY STOMACH'S SHOWING!
WHAT WILL ASUNA OR OJŌSAMA SAY IF THEY...?
—NO TIME, LET'S LOOK FOR CHAO!
CHAO-SAN-N-N—!

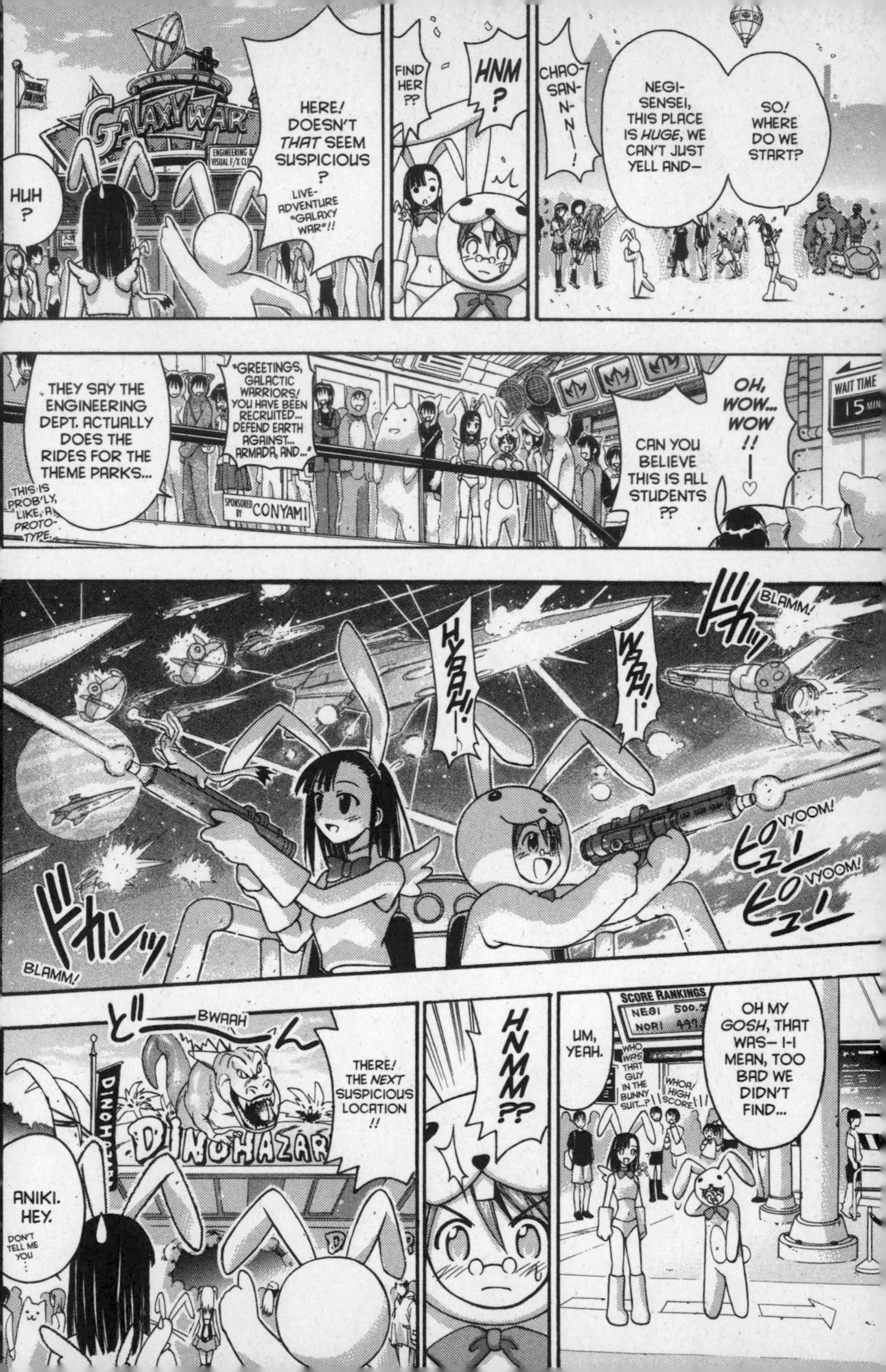
SO! WHERE DO WE START?
NEGI-SENSEI, THIS PLACE IS HUGE, WE CAN'T JUST YELL AND—
CHAO-SAN-N-N—!
HNM?
FIND HER??
HERE! DOESN'T THAT SEEM SUSPICIOUS?
LIVE-ADVENTURE "GALAXY WAR"!!
GALAXY WAR
ENGINEERING & VISUAL F/X CLU
HUH?
WAIT TIME 15 MIN
OH, WOW... WOW!! ♡
CAN YOU BELIEVE THIS IS ALL STUDENTS??
"GREETINGS, GALACTIC WARRIORS! YOU HAVE BEEN RECRUITED... DEFEND EARTH AGAINST... ARMADA, AND..."
SPONSORED BY CONYAMI
THEY SAY THE ENGINEERING DEPT. ACTUALLY DOES THE RIDES FOR THE THEME PARKS...
THIS IS PROB'LY, LIKE, A PROTO-TYPE.
BLAMM!
WAAH!
HYAAH!
VYOOM!
VYOOM!
BLAMM!
OH MY GOSH, THAT WAS— I-I MEAN, TOO BAD WE DIDN'T FIND...
SCORE RANKINGS
UM, YEAH.
WHO WAS THAT GUY IN THE BUNNY SUIT...?
WHOA! HIGH SCORE!!
HNMM??
BWAAH
THERE! THE NEXT SUSPICIOUS LOCATION!!
DINOHAZAR
ANIKI. HEY.
DON'T TELL ME YOU...

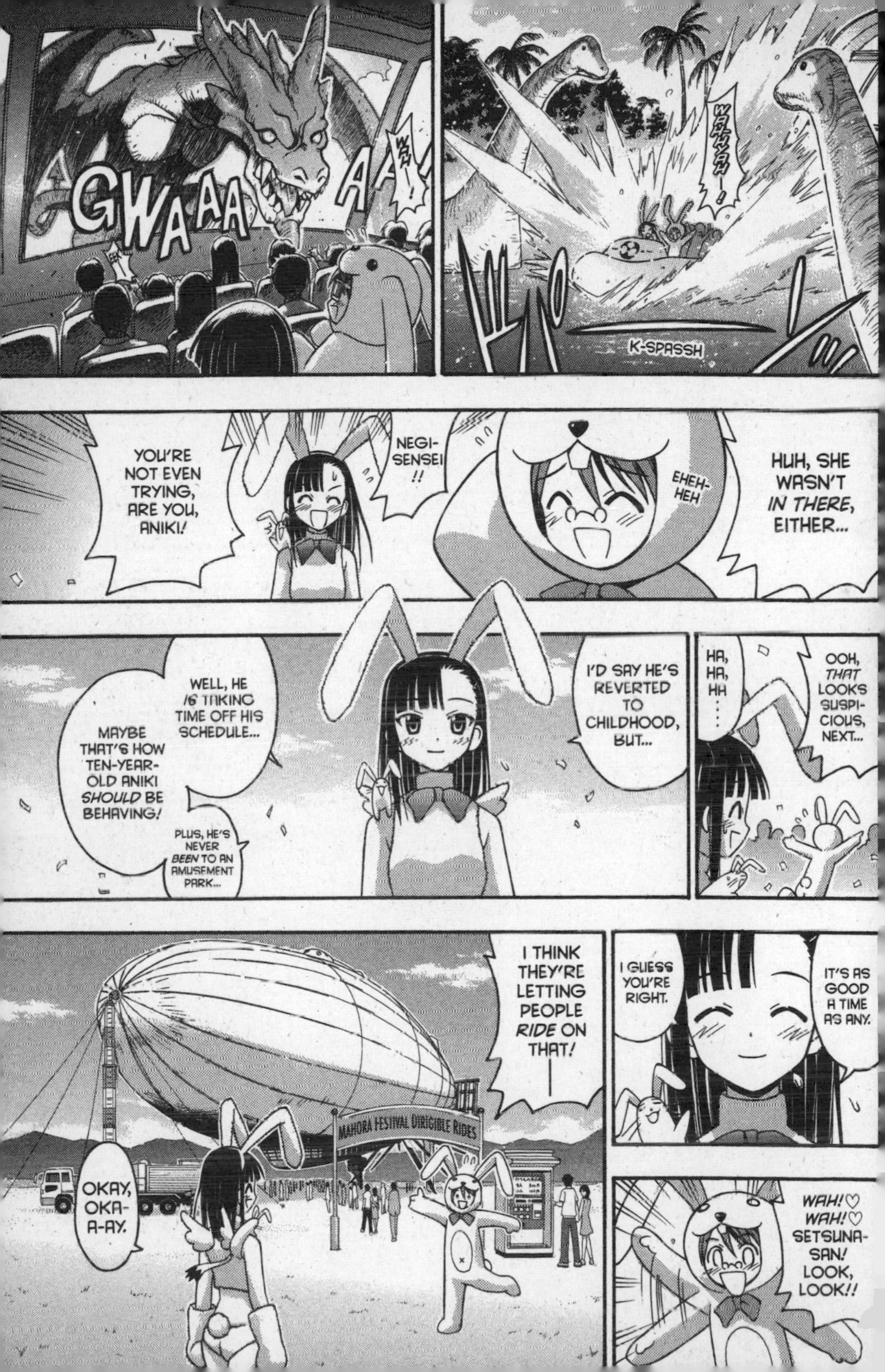
WAHYAAH—!
K-SPASSH
GWAAAAAA
WAH—!
EEK
HUH, SHE WASN'T IN THERE, EITHER...
EHEH-HEH
NEGI-SENSEI!!
YOU'RE NOT EVEN TRYING, ARE YOU, ANIKI!
OOH, THAT LOOKS SUSPI-CIOUS, NEXT...
HA, HA, HH......
I'D SAY HE'S REVERTED TO CHILDHOOD, BUT...
WELL, HE IS TAKING TIME OFF HIS SCHEDULE...
MAYBE THAT'S HOW TEN-YEAR-OLD ANIKI SHOULD BE BEHAVING!
PLUS, HE'S NEVER BEEN TO AN AMUSEMENT PARK...
IT'S AS GOOD A TIME AS ANY.
I GUESS YOU'RE RIGHT.
WAH!♡ WAH!♡ SETSUNA-SAN! LOOK, LOOK!!
I THINK THEY'RE LETTING PEOPLE RIDE ON THAT!
MAHORA FESTIVAL DIRIGIBLE RIDES
OKAY, OKA-A-AY.

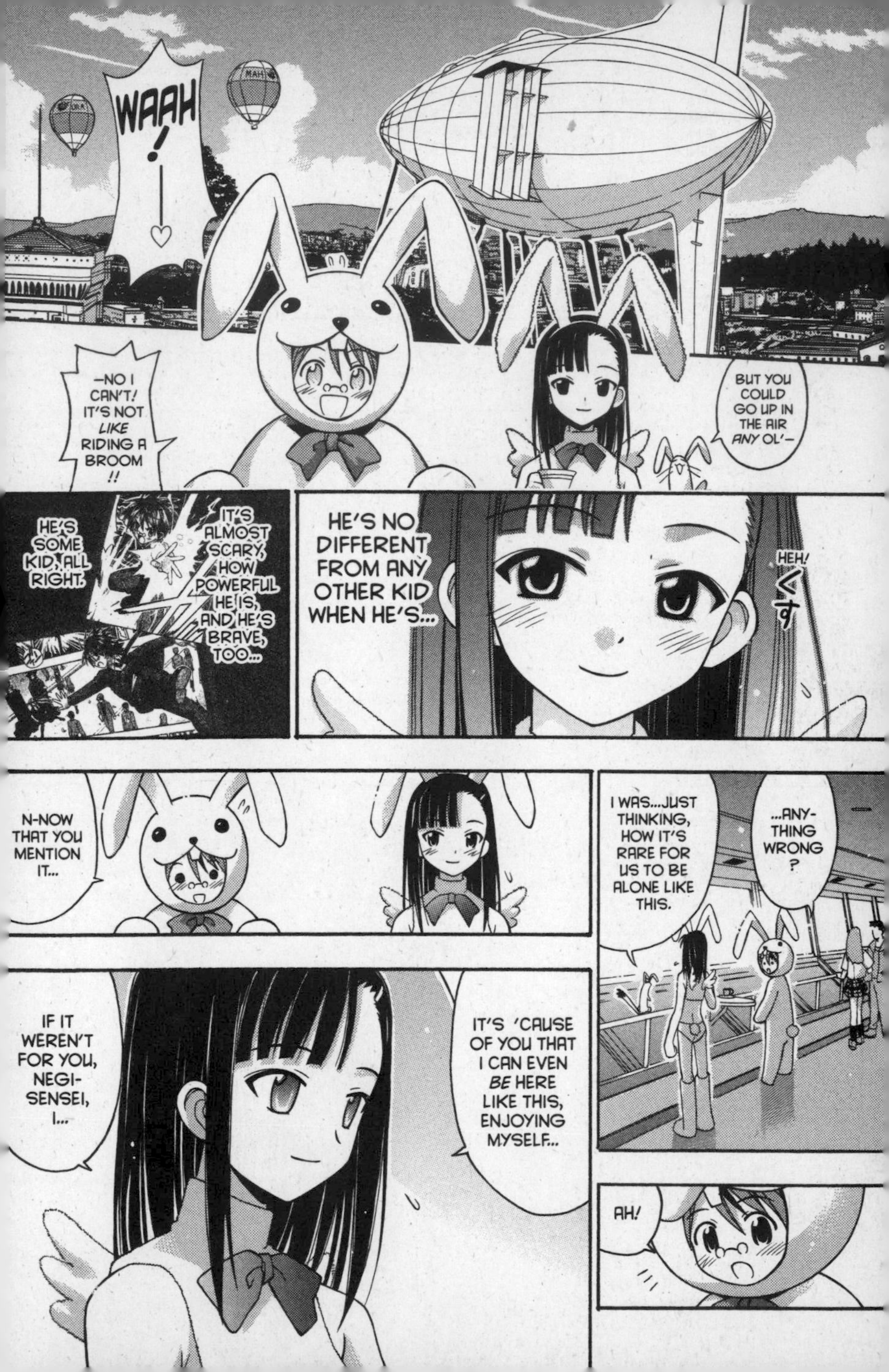
WAAH!
BUT YOU COULD GO UP IN THE AIR *ANY OL'*—
—NO I CAN'T! IT'S NOT *LIKE* RIDING A BROOM!!
HEH! くす
HE'S NO DIFFERENT FROM ANY OTHER KID WHEN HE'S...
IT'S ALMOST SCARY, HOW POWERFUL HE IS, AND HE'S BRAVE, TOO...
HE'S SOME KID, ALL RIGHT.
...ANY-THING WRONG?
I WAS...JUST THINKING, HOW IT'S RARE FOR US TO BE ALONE LIKE THIS.
N-NOW THAT YOU MENTION IT...
IT'S 'CAUSE OF YOU THAT I CAN EVEN *BE* HERE LIKE THIS, ENJOYING MYSELF...
IF IT WEREN'T FOR YOU, NEGI-SENSEI, I...
AH!

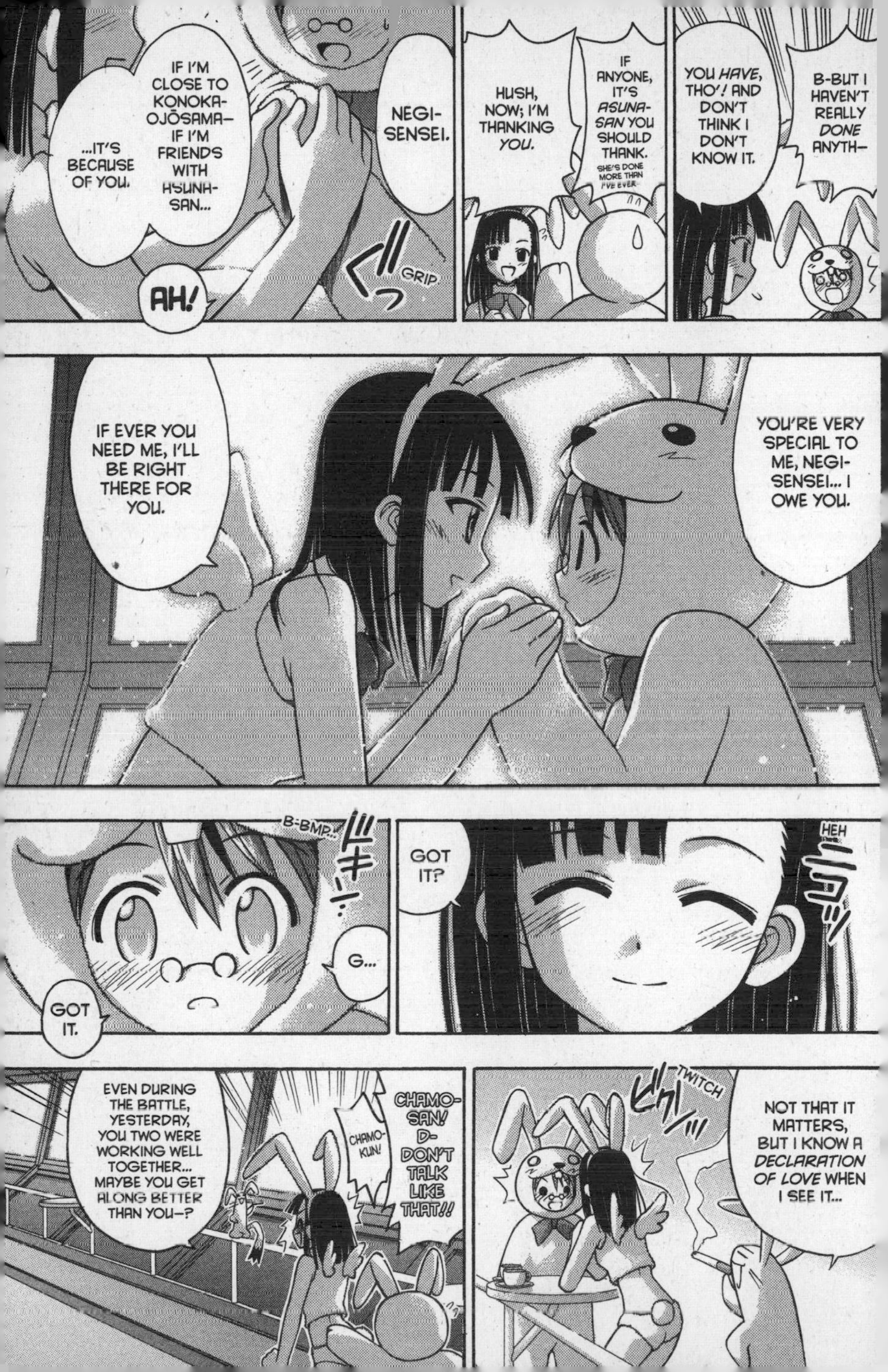
B-BUT I HAVEN'T REALLY *DONE* ANYTH—
YOU *HAVE*, THO'! AND DON'T THINK I DON'T KNOW IT.
IF ANYONE, IT'S *ASUNA-SAN* YOU SHOULD THANK.
SHE'S DONE MORE THAN I'VE EVER
HUSH, NOW; I'M THANKING *YOU*.
NEGI-SENSEI.
IF I'M CLOSE TO KONOKA-OJŌSAMA— IF I'M FRIENDS WITH ASUNA-SAN...
...IT'S BECAUSE OF YOU.
GRIP
AH!
YOU'RE VERY SPECIAL TO ME, NEGI-SENSEI... I OWE YOU.
IF EVER YOU NEED ME, I'LL BE RIGHT THERE FOR YOU.
HEH
GOT IT?
B-BMP...
G...
GOT IT.
TWITCH
NOT THAT IT MATTERS, BUT I KNOW A *DECLARATION OF LOVE* WHEN I SEE IT...
CHAMO-SAN! D-DON'T TALK LIKE THAT!!
CHAMO-KUN!
EVEN DURING THE BATTLE, YESTERDAY, YOU TWO WERE WORKING WELL TOGETHER... MAYBE YOU GET ALONG BETTER THAN YOU—?

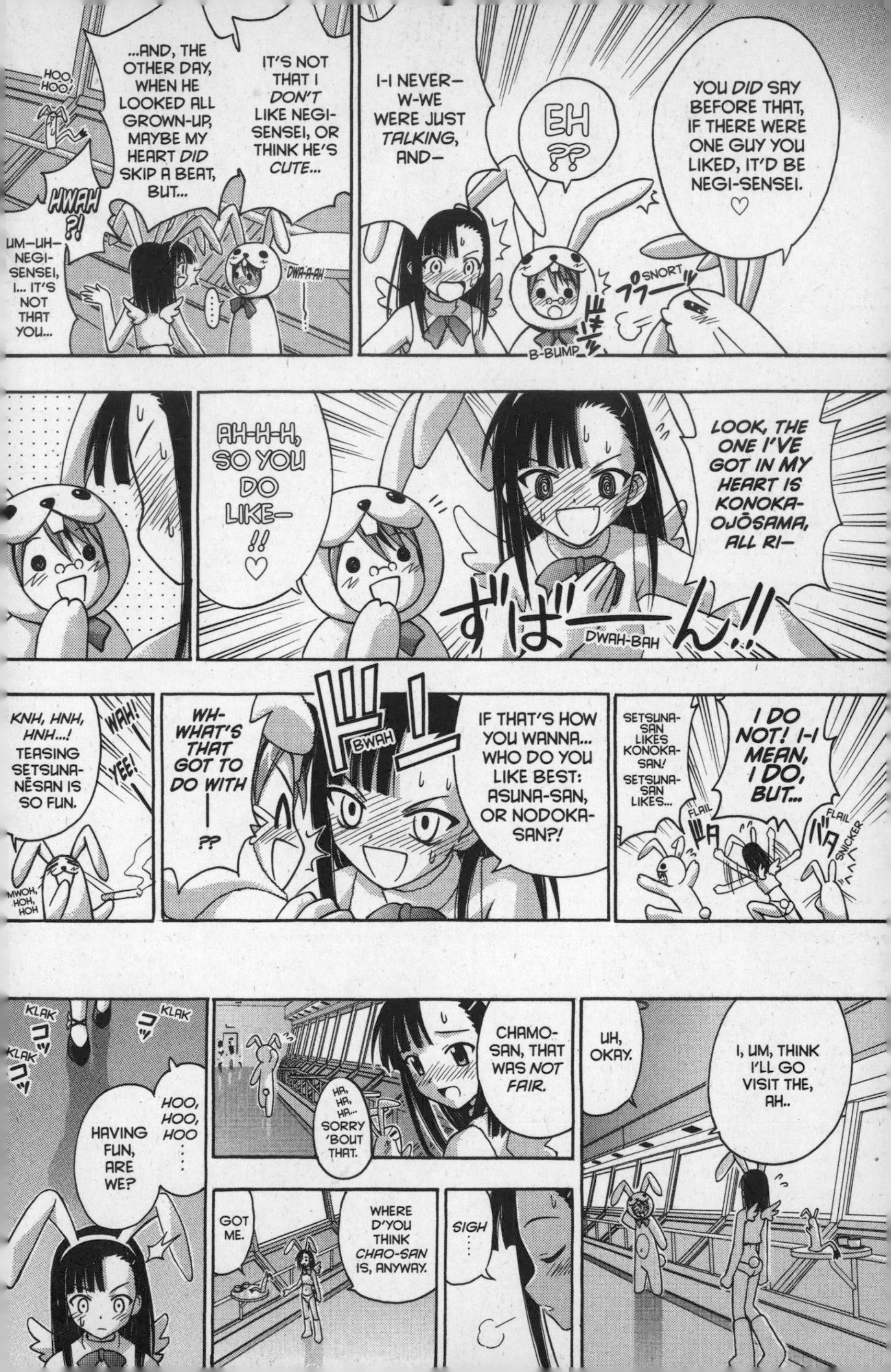
YOU DID SAY BEFORE THAT, IF THERE WERE ONE GUY YOU LIKED, IT'D BE NEGI-SENSEI. ♡
SNORT
EH ??
I-I NEVER— W-WE WERE JUST TALKING, AND—
B-BUMP
IT'S NOT THAT I DON'T LIKE NEGI-SENSEI, OR THINK HE'S CUTE...
...AND, THE OTHER DAY, WHEN HE LOOKED ALL GROWN-UP, MAYBE MY HEART DID SKIP A BEAT, BUT...
HOO, HOO!
HWAH ?!
DWA-A-AH
UM—UH— NEGI-SENSEI, I... IT'S NOT THAT YOU...
LOOK, THE ONE I'VE GOT IN MY HEART IS KONOKA-OJŌSAMA, ALL RI—
AH-H-H, SO YOU DO LIKE— !! ♡
ずばーーん!!
DWAH-BAH
I DO NOT! I-I MEAN, I DO, BUT...
SETSUNA-SAN LIKES KONOKA-SAN! SETSUNA-SAN LIKES...
FLAIL
FLAIL
SNICKER
IF THAT'S HOW YOU WANNA... WHO DO YOU LIKE BEST: ASUNA-SAN, OR NODOKA-SAN?!
BWAH
WH- WHAT'S THAT GOT TO DO WITH— ??
WAH! YEE!
KNH, HNH, HNH...! TEASING SETSUNA-NĒSAN IS SO FUN.
MWOH, HOH, HOH
I, UM, THINK I'LL GO VISIT THE, AH..
UH, OKAY.
CHAMO-SAN, THAT WAS NOT FAIR.
HA, HA, HA... SORRY 'BOUT THAT.
SIGH...
WHERE D'YOU THINK CHAO-SAN IS, ANYWAY.
GOT ME.
KLAK
KLAK
KLAK
HOO, HOO, HOO...
HAVING FUN, ARE WE?

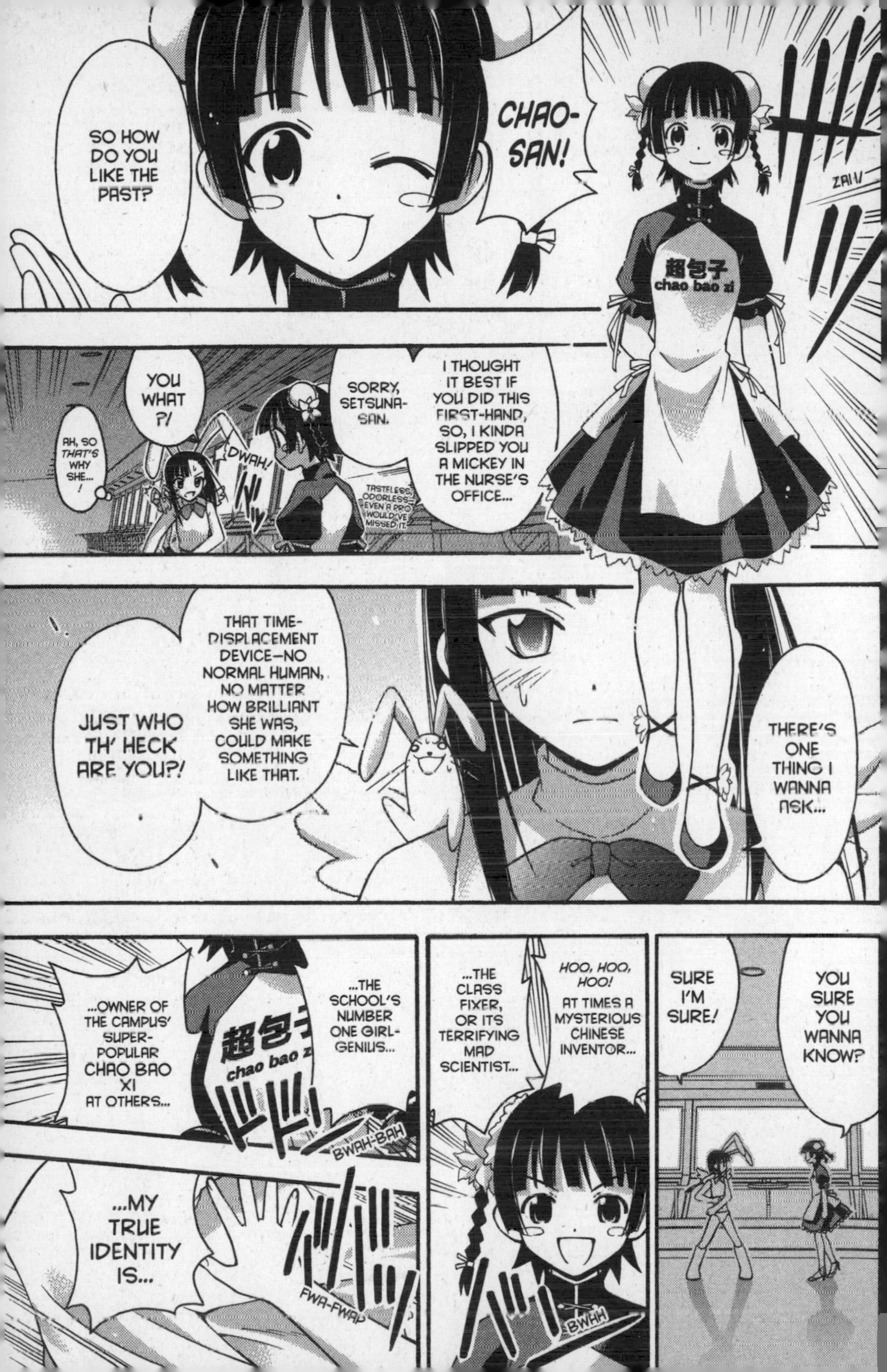
ZAIV
超包子
chao bao zi
CHAO-SAN!
SO HOW DO YOU LIKE THE PAST?
I THOUGHT IT BEST IF YOU DID THIS FIRST-HAND, SO, I KINDA SLIPPED YOU A MICKEY IN THE NURSE'S OFFICE...
SORRY, SETSUNA-SAN.
TASTELESS, ODORLESS— EVEN A PRO WOULD'VE MISSED IT.
YOU WHAT ?!
DWAH!
AH, SO THAT'S WHY SHE... !
THERE'S ONE THING I WANNA ASK...
THAT TIME-DISPLACEMENT DEVICE—NO NORMAL HUMAN, NO MATTER HOW BRILLIANT SHE WAS, COULD MAKE SOMETHING LIKE THAT.
JUST WHO TH' HECK ARE YOU?!
YOU SURE YOU WANNA KNOW?
SURE I'M SURE!
HOO, HOO, HOO! AT TIMES A MYSTERIOUS CHINESE INVENTOR...
...THE CLASS FIXER, OR ITS TERRIFYING MAD SCIENTIST...
BWHH
...THE SCHOOL'S NUMBER ONE GIRL-GENIUS...
...OWNER OF THE CAMPUS' SUPER-POPULAR CHAO BAO XI AT OTHERS...
BWAH-BAH
...MY TRUE IDENTITY IS...
FWA-FWAP

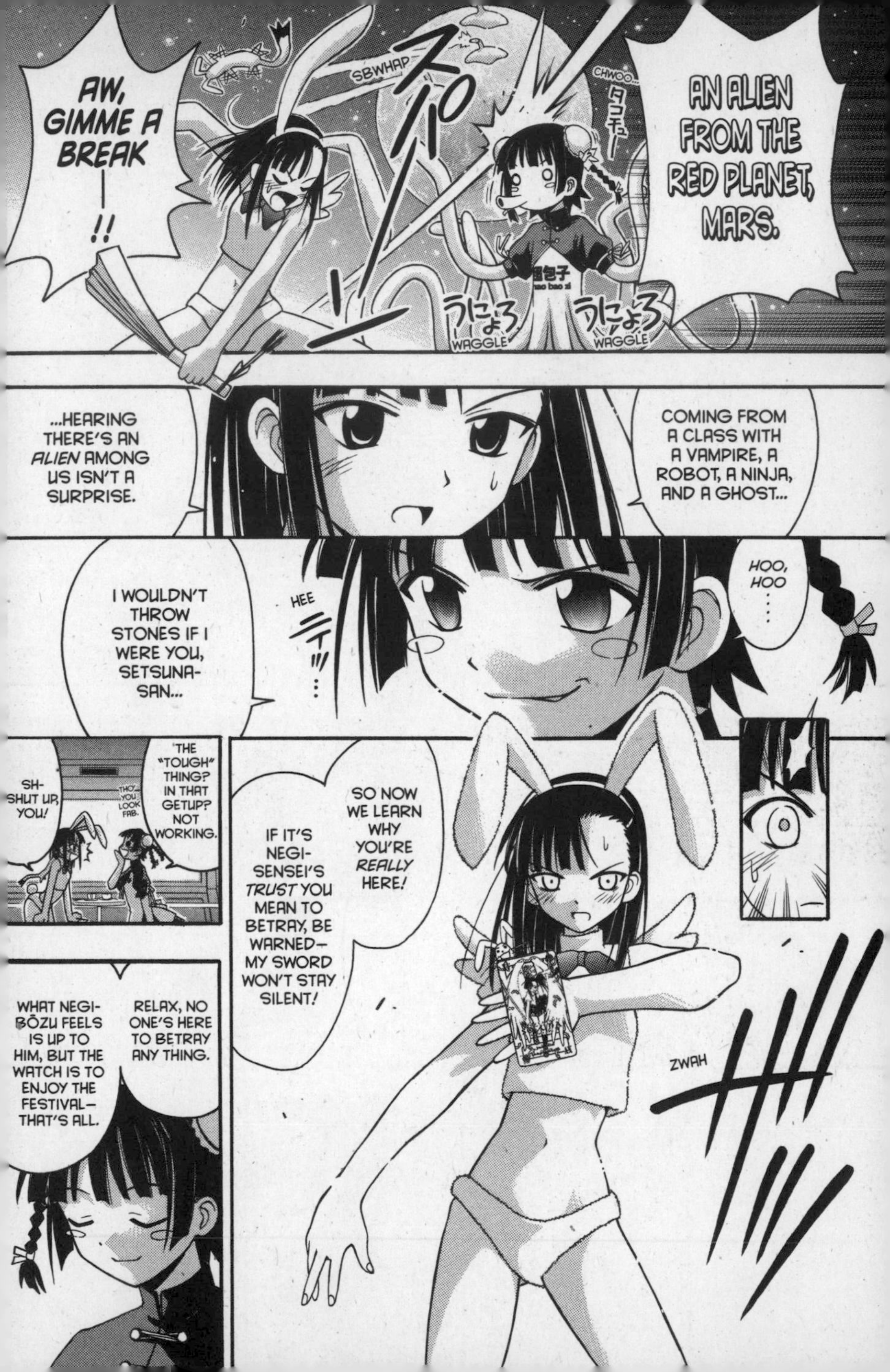
AN ALIEN FROM THE RED PLANET, MARS.
CHWOO...
タコチュー
SBWHAP
AW, GIMME A BREAK—!!
うにょろ
WAGGLE
うにょろ
WAGGLE
COMING FROM A CLASS WITH A VAMPIRE, A ROBOT, A NINJA, AND A GHOST...
...HEARING THERE'S AN *ALIEN* AMONG US ISN'T A SURPRISE.
HOO, HOO ....
HEE
I WOULDN'T THROW STONES IF I WERE YOU, SETSUNA-SAN...
SO NOW WE LEARN WHY YOU'RE *REALLY* HERE!
IF IT'S NEGI-SENSEI'S *TRUST* YOU MEAN TO BETRAY, BE WARNED—MY SWORD WON'T STAY SILENT!
ZWAH
"THE "TOUGH" THING? IN THAT GETUP? NOT WORKING.
THO' YOU LOOK FAB.
SH-SHUT UP, YOU!
RELAX, NO ONE'S HERE TO BETRAY ANY THING.
WHAT NEGI-BŌZU FEELS IS UP TO HIM, BUT THE WATCH IS TO ENJOY THE FESTIVAL—THAT'S ALL.

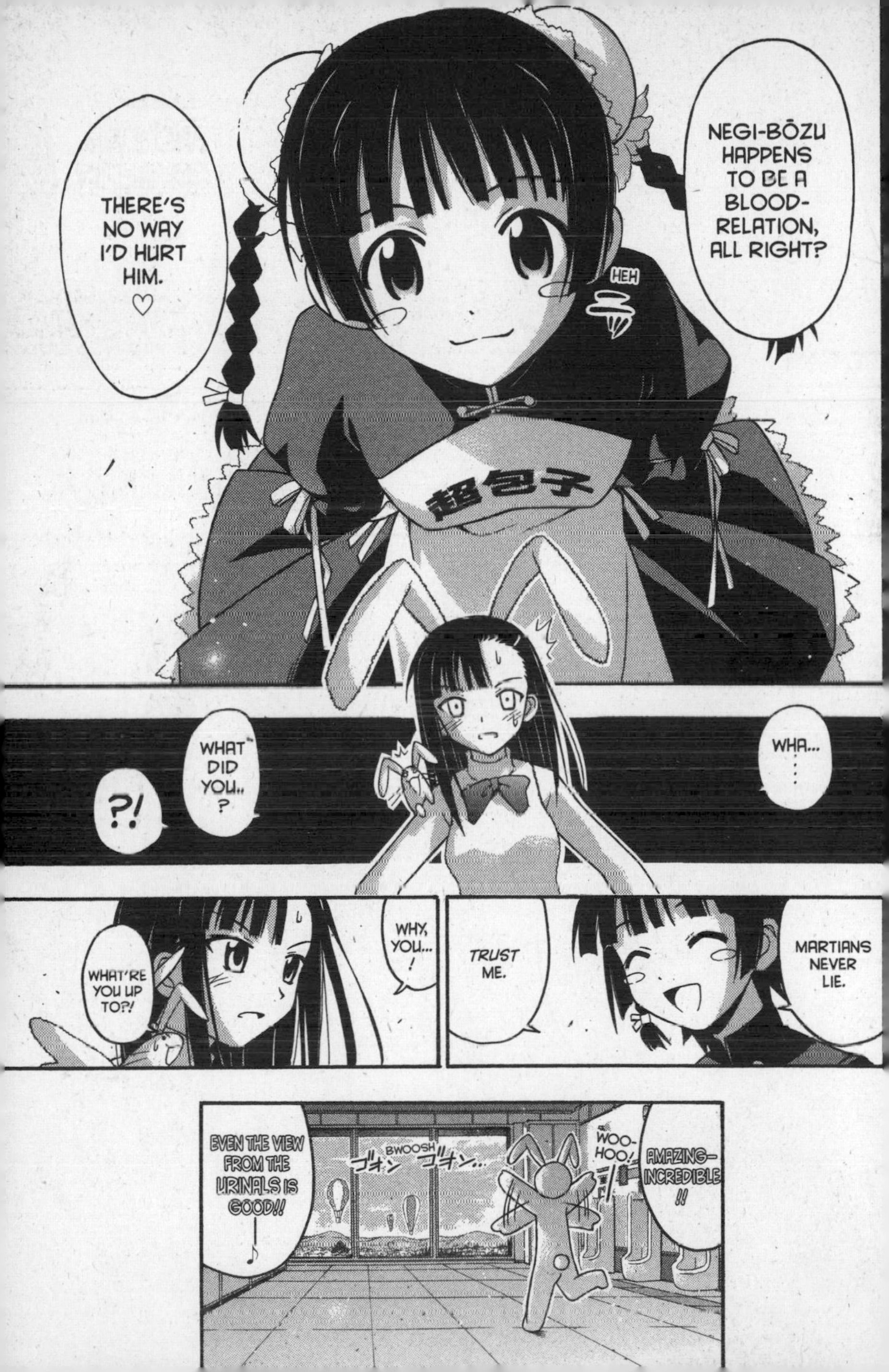
NEGI-BŌZU HAPPENS TO BE A BLOOD-RELATION, ALL RIGHT?
HEH
THERE'S NO WAY I'D HURT HIM. ♡
超包子
WHA... ...
WHAT DID YOU.. ?
?!
MARTIANS NEVER LIE.
TRUST ME.
WHY, YOU... !
WHAT'RE YOU UP TO?!
AMAZING— INCREDIBLE !!
WOO-HOO!
BWOOSH
ゴォン ゴォン...
EVEN THE VIEW FROM THE URINALS IS GOOD!! ♪

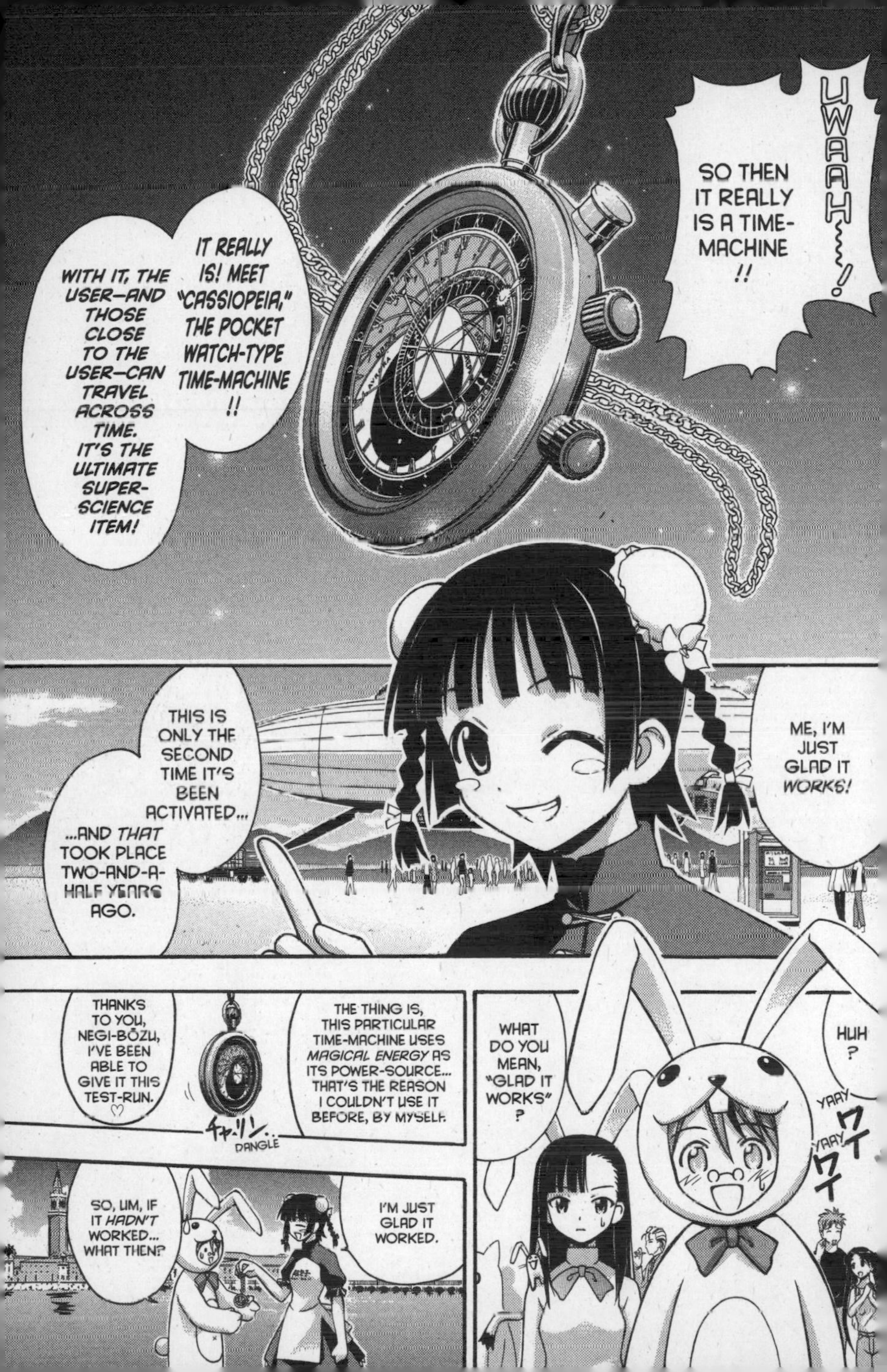
UWAAAH~!
SO THEN IT REALLY IS A TIME-MACHINE!!
IT REALLY IS! MEET "CASSIOPEIA," THE POCKET WATCH-TYPE TIME-MACHINE!!
WITH IT, THE USER—AND THOSE CLOSE TO THE USER—CAN TRAVEL ACROSS TIME. IT'S THE ULTIMATE SUPER-SCIENCE ITEM!
ME, I'M JUST GLAD IT WORKS!
THIS IS ONLY THE SECOND TIME IT'S BEEN ACTIVATED...
...AND THAT TOOK PLACE TWO-AND-A-HALF YEARS AGO.
HUH?
WHAT DO YOU MEAN, "GLAD IT WORKS"?
YAAY ワイ
YAAY ワイ
THE THING IS, THIS PARTICULAR TIME-MACHINE USES MAGICAL ENERGY AS ITS POWER-SOURCE... THAT'S THE REASON I COULDN'T USE IT BEFORE, BY MYSELF.
THANKS TO YOU, NEGI-BŌZU, I'VE BEEN ABLE TO GIVE IT THIS TEST-RUN. ♡
チャリン.. DANGLE
I'M JUST GLAD IT WORKED.
SO, UM, IF IT HADN'T WORKED... WHAT THEN?

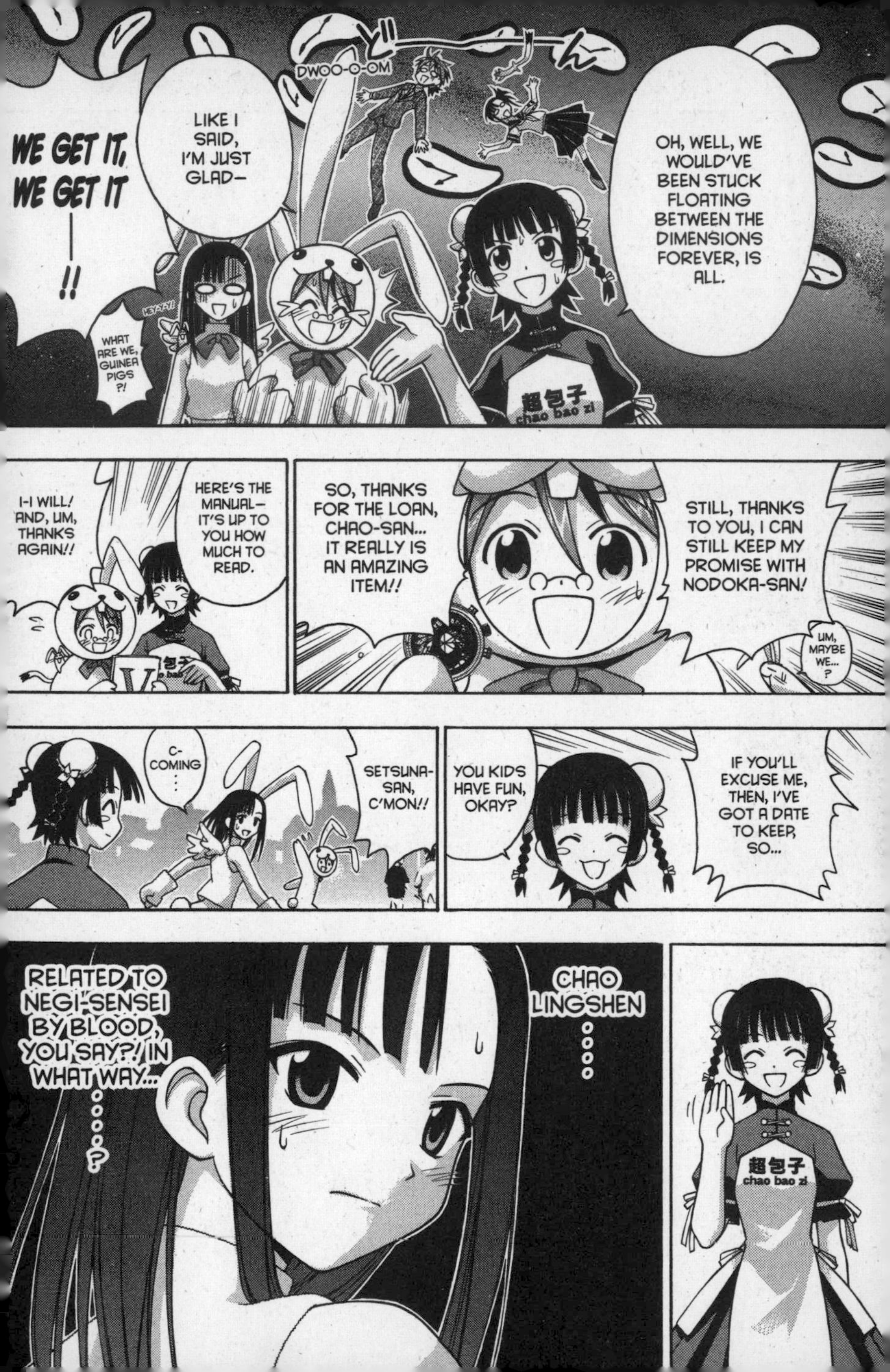
DWOO-O-OM
OH, WELL, WE WOULD'VE BEEN STUCK FLOATING BETWEEN THE DIMENSIONS FOREVER, IS ALL.
LIKE I SAID, I'M JUST GLAD—
WE GET IT, WE GET IT—!!
HEY-Y-Y!
WHAT ARE WE, GUINEA PIGS?!
超包子
chao bao zi
STILL, THANKS TO YOU, I CAN STILL KEEP MY PROMISE WITH NODOKA-SAN!
SO, THANKS FOR THE LOAN, CHAO-SAN... IT REALLY IS AN AMAZING ITEM!!
UM, MAYBE WE...?
HERE'S THE MANUAL—IT'S UP TO YOU HOW MUCH TO READ.
I-I WILL! AND, UM, THANKS AGAIN!!
IF YOU'LL EXCUSE ME, THEN, I'VE GOT A DATE TO KEEP, SO...
YOU KIDS HAVE FUN, OKAY?
SETSUNA-SAN, C'MON!!
C-COMING...
超包子
chao bao zi
CHAO LINGSHEN....
RELATED TO NEGI-SENSEI BY BLOOD, YOU SAY?! IN WHAT WAY.....?

EIGHTY-THIRD PERIOD: DATE WITH A BOOKSTORE ♥

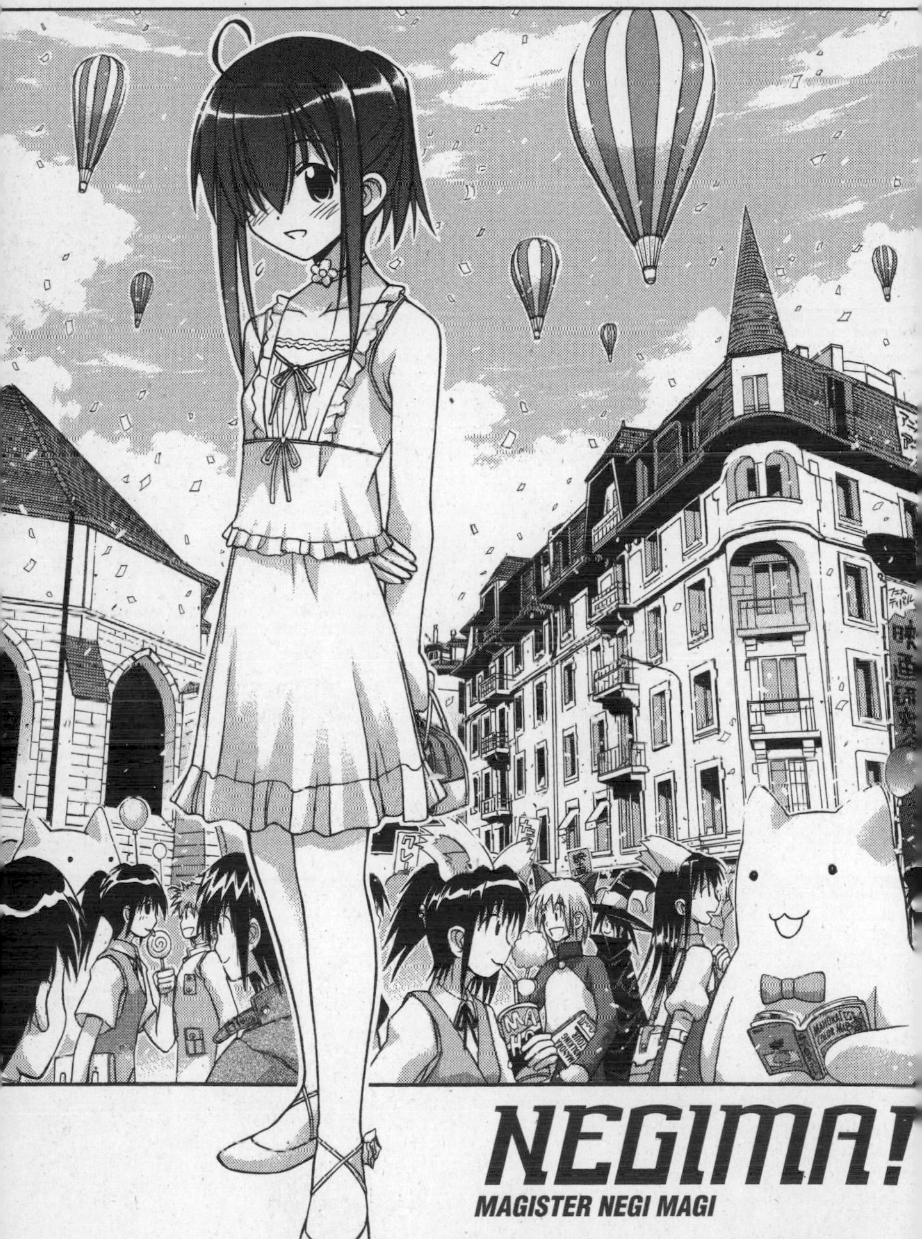

NEGIMA!

MAGISTER NEGI MAGI

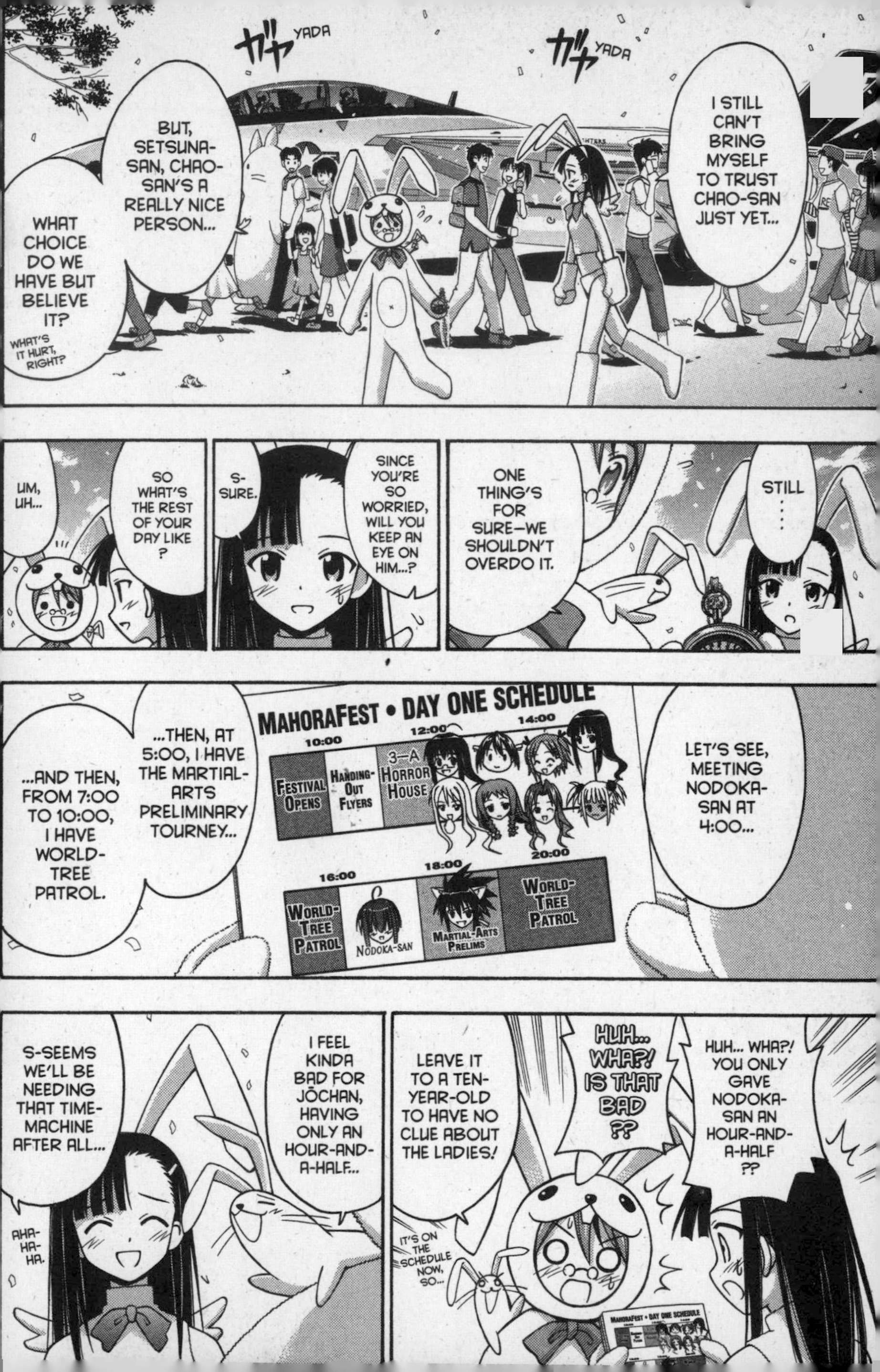
ガヤ YADA
I STILL CAN'T BRING MYSELF TO TRUST CHAO-SAN JUST YET...
ガヤ YADA
BUT, SETSUNA-SAN, CHAO-SAN'S A REALLY NICE PERSON...
WHAT CHOICE DO WE HAVE BUT BELIEVE IT?
WHAT'S IT HURT, RIGHT?
STILL....
ONE THING'S FOR SURE—WE SHOULDN'T OVERDO IT.
SINCE YOU'RE SO WORRIED, WILL YOU KEEP AN EYE ON HIM...?
S-SURE.
SO WHAT'S THE REST OF YOUR DAY LIKE?
UM, UH...
LET'S SEE, MEETING NODOKA-SAN AT 4:00...
MAHORAFEST • DAY ONE SCHEDULE
10:00
12:00
14:00
FESTIVAL OPENS
HANDING-OUT FLYERS
3-A HORROR HOUSE
16:00
18:00
20:00
WORLD-TREE PATROL
NODOKA-SAN
MARTIAL-ARTS PRELIMS
WORLD-TREE PATROL
...THEN, AT 5:00, I HAVE THE MARTIAL-ARTS PRELIMINARY TOURNEY...
...AND THEN, FROM 7:00 TO 10:00, I HAVE WORLD-TREE PATROL.
HUH... WHA?! YOU ONLY GAVE NODOKA-SAN AN HOUR-AND-A-HALF??
HUH... WHA?! IS THAT BAD??
LEAVE IT TO A TEN-YEAR-OLD TO HAVE NO CLUE ABOUT THE LADIES!
IT'S ON THE SCHEDULE NOW, SO...
I FEEL KINDA BAD FOR JŌCHAN, HAVING ONLY AN HOUR-AND-A-HALF...
S-SEEMS WE'LL BE NEEDING THAT TIME-MACHINE AFTER ALL...
AHA-HA-HA.

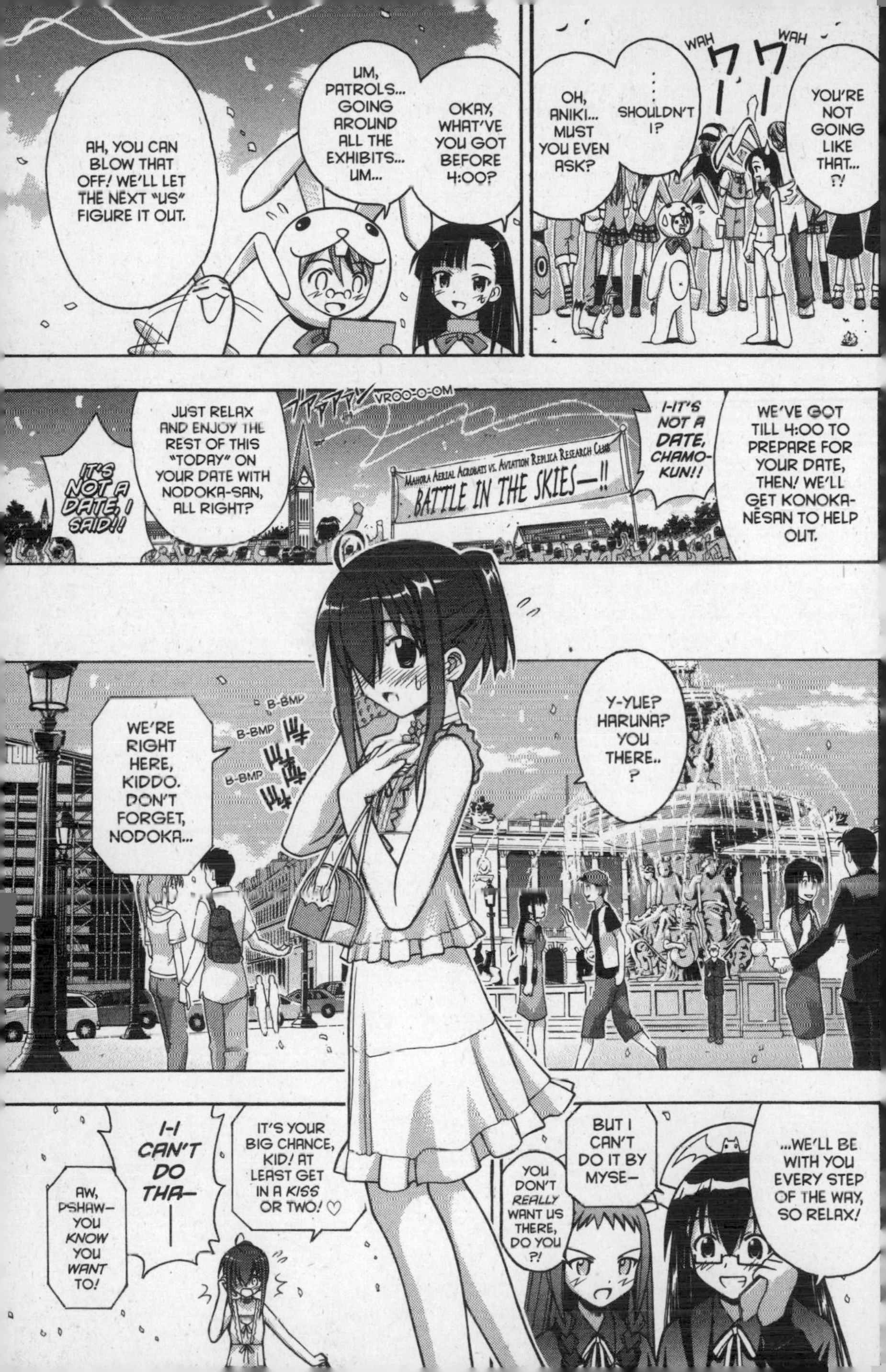
WAH
WAH
YOU'RE NOT GOING LIKE THAT...?!
...SHOULDN'T I?
OH, ANIKI... MUST YOU EVEN ASK?
OKAY, WHAT'VE YOU GOT BEFORE 4:00?
UM, PATROLS... GOING AROUND ALL THE EXHIBITS... UM...
AH, YOU CAN BLOW THAT OFF! WE'LL LET THE NEXT "US" FIGURE IT OUT.
WE'VE GOT TILL 4:00 TO PREPARE FOR YOUR DATE, THEN! WE'LL GET KONOKA-NĒSAN TO HELP OUT.
I-IT'S NOT A DATE, CHAMO-KUN!!
VROO-O-OM
MAHORA AERIAL ACROBATS VS. AVIATION REPLICA RESEARCH CLUB
BATTLE IN THE SKIES—!!
JUST RELAX AND ENJOY THE REST OF THIS "TODAY" ON YOUR DATE WITH NODOKA-SAN, ALL RIGHT?
IT'S NOT A DATE, I SAID!!
Y-YUE? HARUNA? YOU THERE..?
B-BMP
B-BMP
B-BMP
WE'RE RIGHT HERE, KIDDO. DON'T FORGET, NODOKA...
...WE'LL BE WITH YOU EVERY STEP OF THE WAY, SO RELAX!
BUT I CAN'T DO IT BY MYSE—
YOU DON'T *REALLY* WANT US THERE, DO YOU ?!
IT'S YOUR BIG CHANCE, KID! AT LEAST GET IN A *KISS* OR TWO! ♡
I-I CAN'T DO THA—
AW, PSHAW— YOU *KNOW* YOU *WANT* TO!

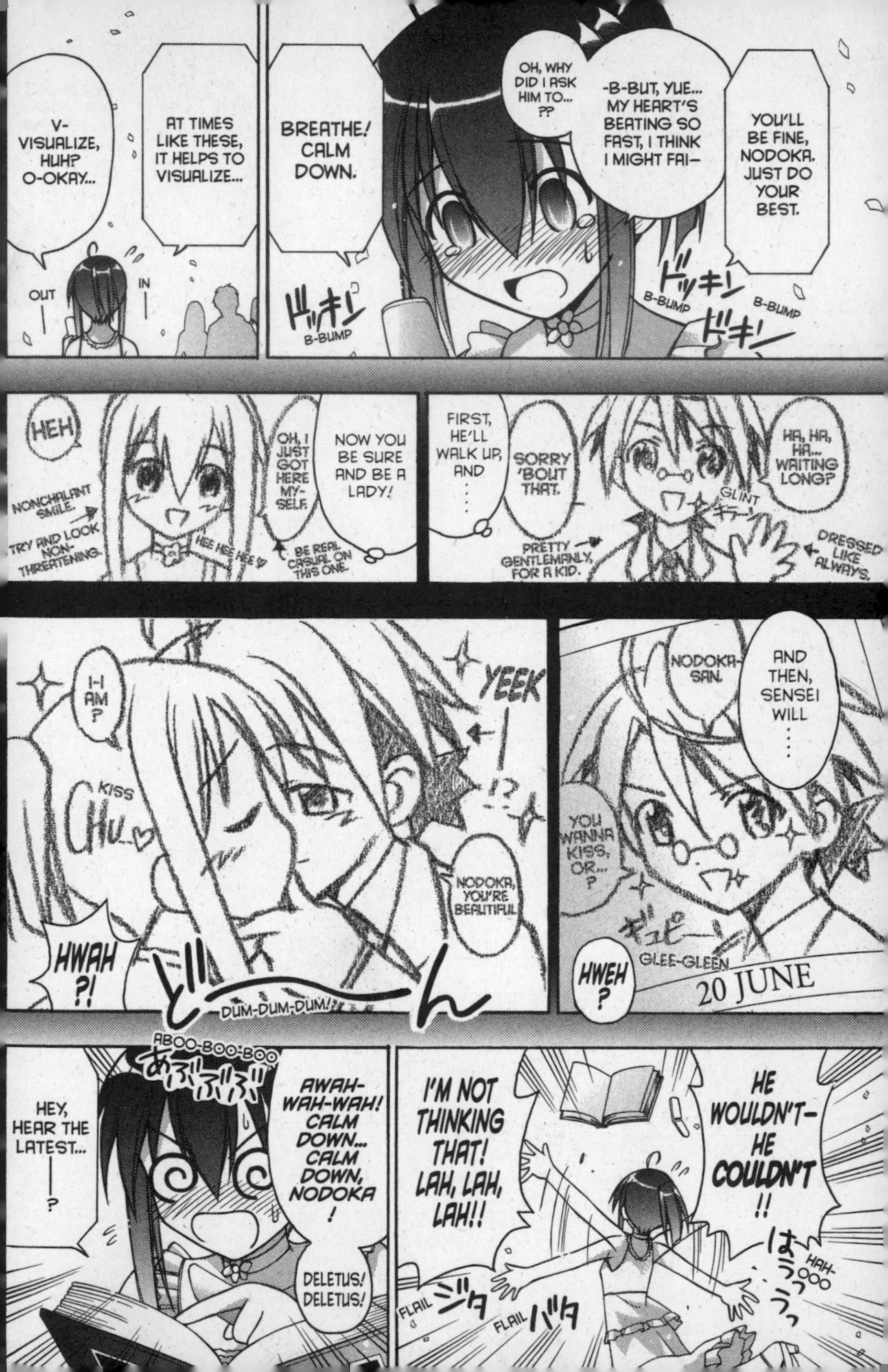

YOU'LL BE FINE, NODOKA. JUST DO YOUR BEST.
B-BUMP
B-BUMP
-B-BUT, YUE... MY HEART'S BEATING SO FAST, I THINK I MIGHT FAI—
OH, WHY DID I ASK HIM TO...??
B-BUMP
BREATHE! CALM DOWN.
AT TIMES LIKE THESE, IT HELPS TO VISUALIZE...
IN
V-VISUALIZE, HUH? O-OKAY...
OUT
HA, HA, HA... WAITING LONG?
GLINT
DRESSED LIKE ALWAYS.
SORRY 'BOUT THAT.
PRETTY GENTLEMANLY, FOR A KID.
FIRST, HE'LL WALK UP, AND ...
NOW YOU BE SURE AND BE A LADY!
OH, I JUST GOT HERE MY-SELF.
BE REAL CASUAL ON THIS ONE.
HEH
NONCHALANT SMILE.
TRY AND LOOK NON-THREATENING.
HEE HEE HEE
AND THEN, SENSEI WILL ...
NODOKA-SAN.
YOU WANNA KISS, OR...?
GLEE-GLEEN
HWEH?
20 JUNE
YEEK !?
NODOKA, YOU'RE BEAUTIFUL
I-I AM?
KISS
CHU
HWAH?!
DUM-DUM-DUM!
HE WOULDN'T-HE COULDN'T!!
HAH-OOO
I'M NOT THINKING THAT! LAH, LAH, LAH!!
FLAIL
FLAIL
ABOO-BOO-BOO
AWAH-WAH-WAH! CALM DOWN... CALM DOWN, NODOKA!
DELETUS! DELETUS!
HEY, HEAR THE LATEST...?

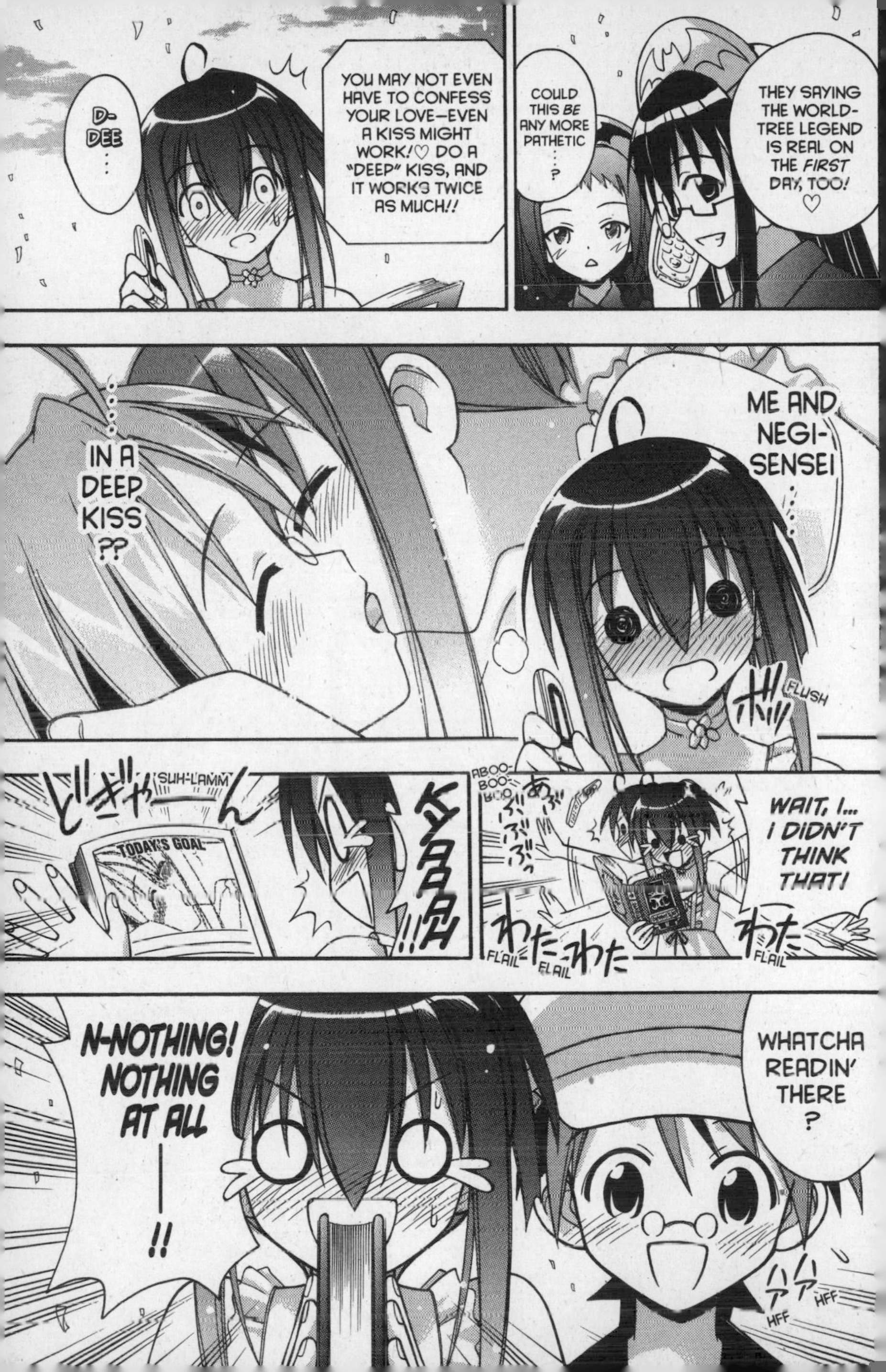
THEY SAYING THE WORLD-TREE LEGEND IS REAL ON THE *FIRST* DAY, TOO! ♡
COULD THIS *BE* ANY MORE PATHETIC ...?
YOU MAY NOT EVEN HAVE TO CONFESS YOUR LOVE—EVEN A KISS MIGHT WORK!♡ DO A "DEEP" KISS, AND IT WORKS TWICE AS MUCH!!
D-DEE ...
ME AND NEGI-SENSEI ...
FLUSH
...IN A DEEP KISS ??
WAIT, I... I DIDN'T THINK THAT!
ABOO-BOO-BOO
FLAIL
FLAIL
FLAIL
SUH-LAMM
TODAY'S GOAL
WHATCHA READIN' THERE ?
HFF
HFF
N-NOTHING! NOTHING AT ALL —!!

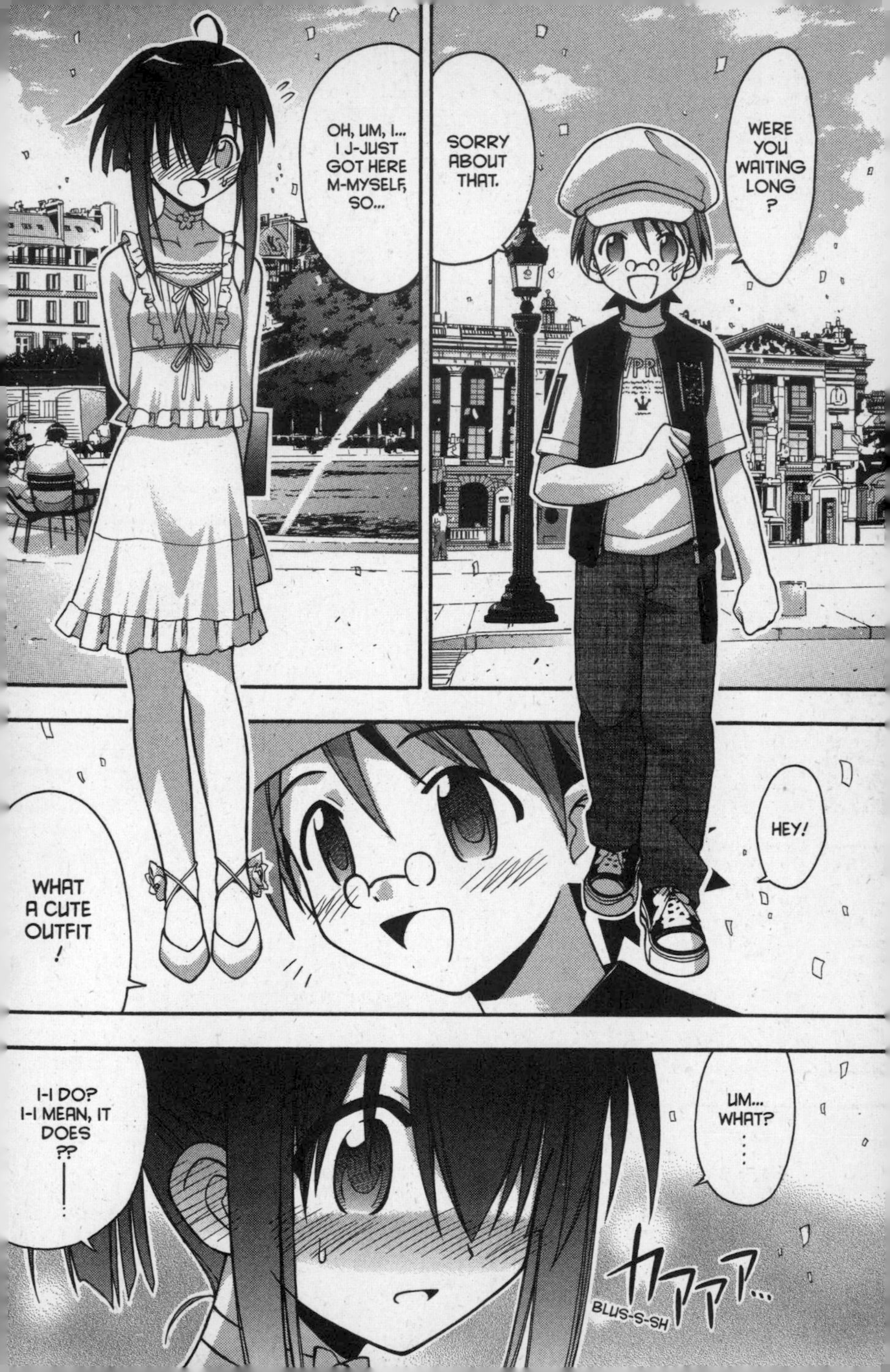
WERE YOU WAITING LONG?
SORRY ABOUT THAT.
OH, UM, I... I J-JUST GOT HERE M-MYSELF, SO...
HEY!
WHAT A CUTE OUTFIT!
UM... WHAT? ...
I-I DO? I-I MEAN, IT DOES??
カァァァ...
BLUS-S-SH

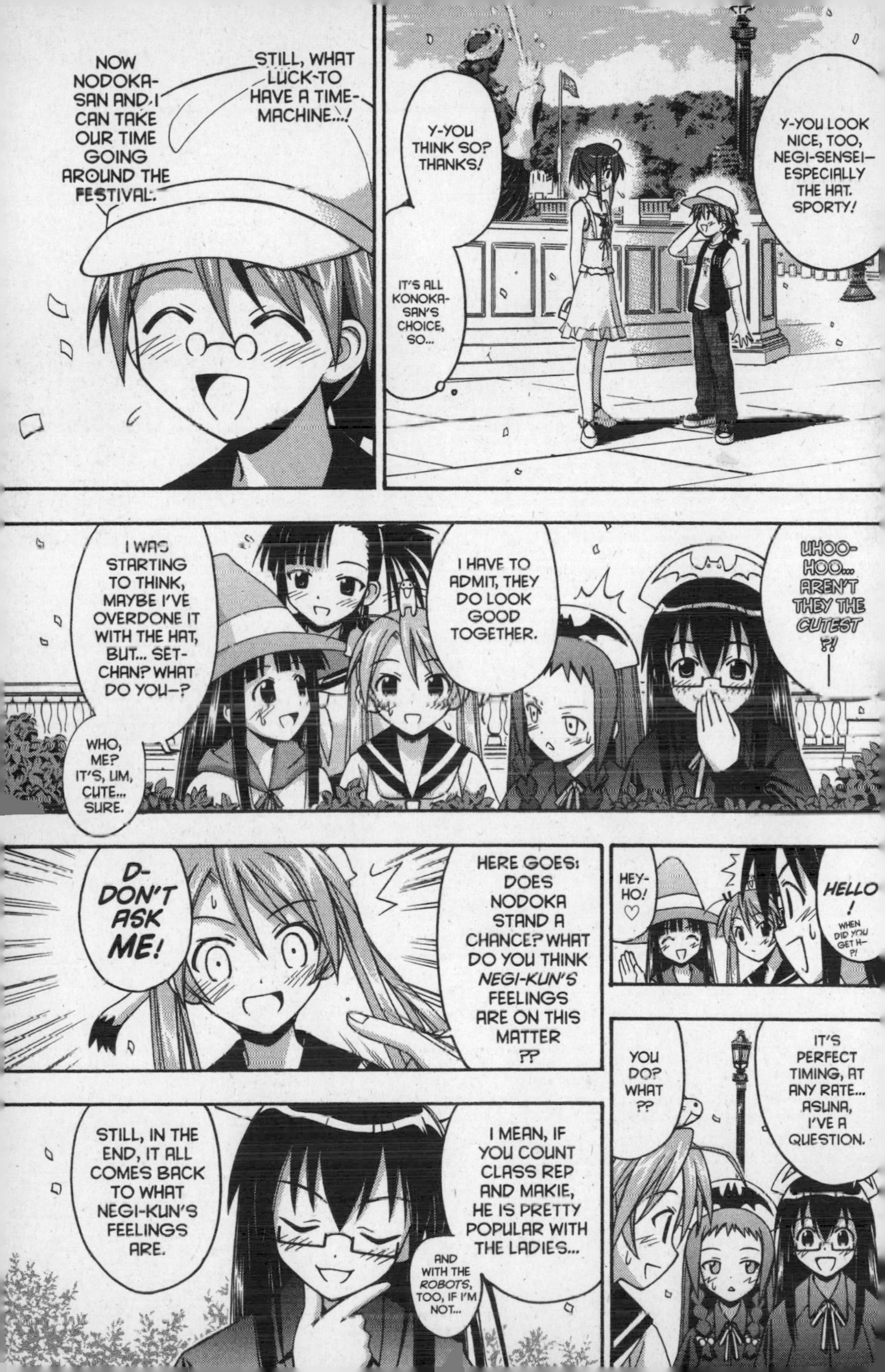
Y-YOU LOOK NICE, TOO, NEGI-SENSEI—ESPECIALLY THE HAT. SPORTY!
Y-YOU THINK SO? THANKS!
IT'S ALL KONOKA-SAN'S CHOICE, SO...
STILL, WHAT LUCK-TO HAVE A TIME-MACHINE...!
NOW NODOKA-SAN AND I CAN TAKE OUR TIME GOING AROUND THE FESTIVAL.
UHOOO-HOO... AREN'T THEY THE CUTEST?!
I HAVE TO ADMIT, THEY DO LOOK GOOD TOGETHER.
I WAS STARTING TO THINK, MAYBE I'VE OVERDONE IT WITH THE HAT, BUT... SET-CHAN? WHAT DO YOU—?
WHO, ME? IT'S, UM, CUTE... SURE.
HELLO!
WHEN DID YOU GET H—?!
HEY-HO! ♡
IT'S PERFECT TIMING, AT ANY RATE... ASUNA, I'VE A QUESTION.
YOU DO? WHAT??
HERE GOES: DOES NODOKA STAND A CHANCE? WHAT DO YOU THINK NEGI-KUN'S FEELINGS ARE ON THIS MATTER??
D-DON'T ASK ME!
I MEAN, IF YOU COUNT CLASS REP AND MAKIE, HE IS PRETTY POPULAR WITH THE LADIES...
AND WITH THE ROBOTS, TOO, IF I'M NOT...
STILL, IN THE END, IT ALL COMES BACK TO WHAT NEGI-KUN'S FEELINGS ARE.

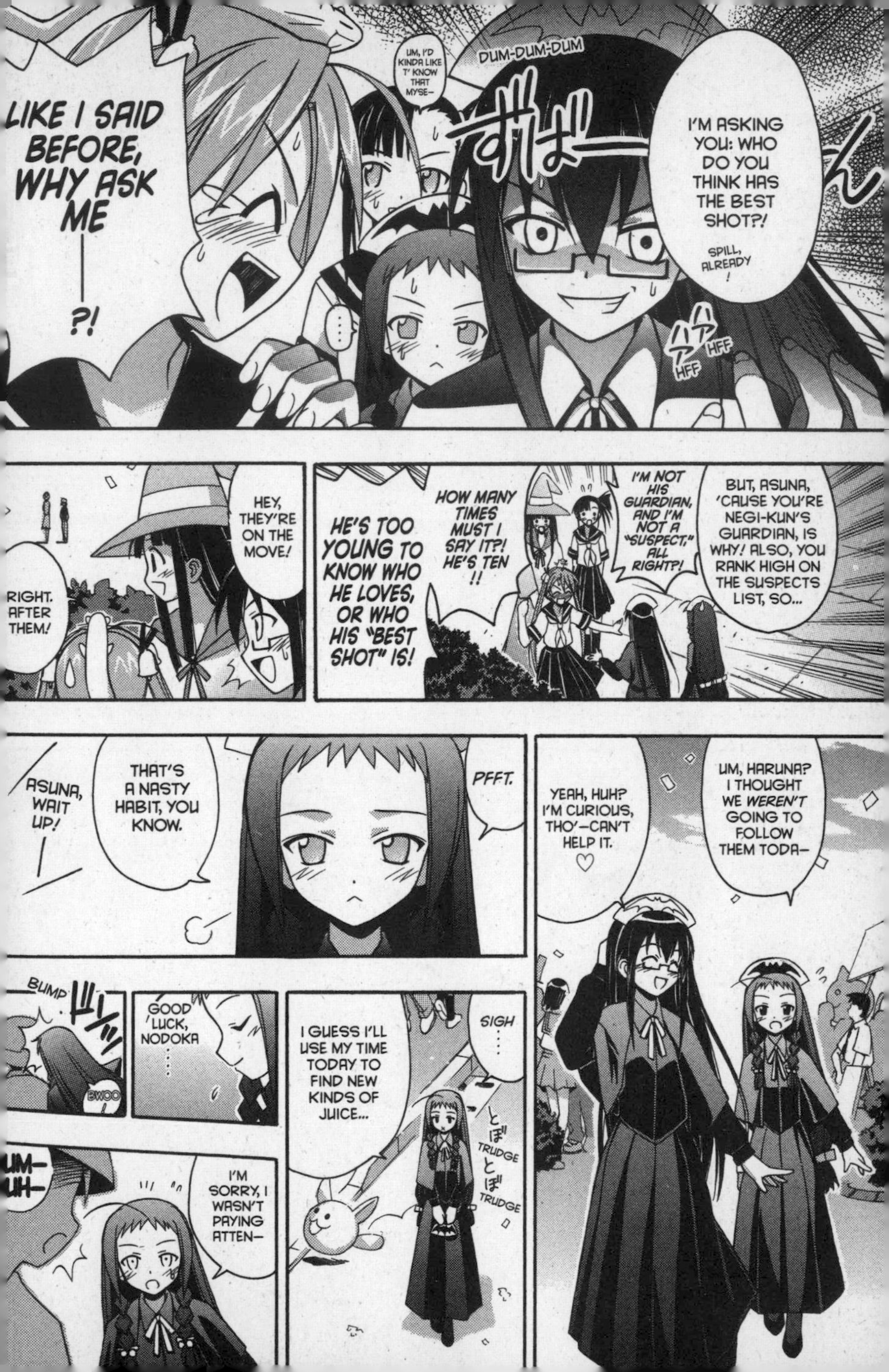
I'M ASKING YOU: WHO DO YOU THINK HAS THE BEST SHOT?!
SPILL, ALREADY!
HFF HFF
ずばーん
DUM-DUM-DUM
UM, I'D KINDA LIKE T' KNOW THAT MYSE—
LIKE I SAID BEFORE, WHY ASK ME—?!
BUT, ASUNA, 'CAUSE YOU'RE NEGI-KUN'S GUARDIAN, IS WHY! ALSO, YOU RANK HIGH ON THE SUSPECTS LIST, SO...
I'M NOT HIS GUARDIAN, AND I'M NOT A "SUSPECT," ALL RIGHT?!
HOW MANY TIMES MUST I SAY IT?! HE'S TEN!!
HE'S TOO YOUNG TO KNOW WHO HE LOVES, OR WHO HIS "BEST SHOT" IS!
HEY, THEY'RE ON THE MOVE!
RIGHT. AFTER THEM!
UM, HARUNA? I THOUGHT WE WEREN'T GOING TO FOLLOW THEM TODA—
YEAH, HUH? I'M CURIOUS, THO'—CAN'T HELP IT. ♡
PFFT.
THAT'S A NASTY HABIT, YOU KNOW.
ASUNA, WAIT UP!
SIGH.....
I GUESS I'LL USE MY TIME TODAY TO FIND NEW KINDS OF JUICE...
とぼ TRUDGE とぼ TRUDGE
GOOD LUCK, NODOKA.....
BUMP
BWOO
I'M SORRY, I WASN'T PAYING ATTEN—
UM— UH—

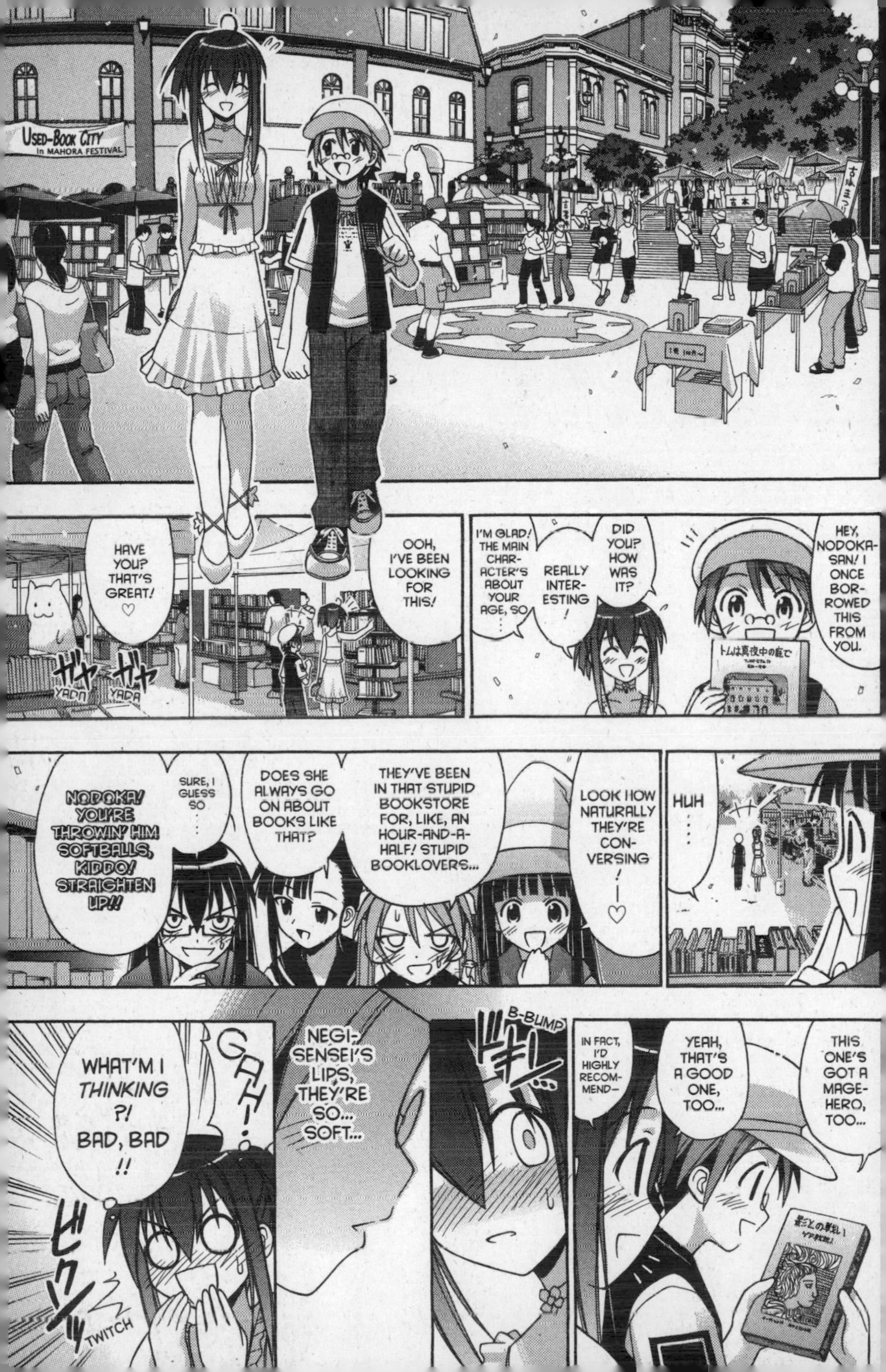
USED-BOOK CITY
In MAHORA FESTIVAL
HEY, NODOKA-SAN! I ONCE BORROWED THIS FROM YOU.
トムは真夜中の庭で
DID YOU? HOW WAS IT?
REALLY INTERESTING!
I'M GLAD! THE MAIN CHARACTER'S ABOUT YOUR AGE, SO...
OOH, I'VE BEEN LOOKING FOR THIS!
HAVE YOU? THAT'S GREAT! ♡
YADA YADA
HUH...
LOOK HOW NATURALLY THEY'RE CONVERSING! ♡
THEY'VE BEEN IN THAT STUPID BOOKSTORE FOR, LIKE, AN HOUR-AND-A-HALF! STUPID BOOKLOVERS...
DOES SHE ALWAYS GO ON ABOUT BOOKS LIKE THAT?
SURE, I GUESS SO...
NODOKA! YOU'RE THROWIN' HIM SOFTBALLS, KIDDO! STRAIGHTEN UP!!
THIS ONE'S GOT A MAGE-HERO, TOO...
影との戦い
YEAH, THAT'S A GOOD ONE, TOO...
IN FACT, I'D HIGHLY RECOMMEND—
B-BUMP
NEGI-SENSEI'S LIPS, THEY'RE SO... SOFT...
GAH!
WHAT'M I THINKING?! BAD, BAD!!
TWITCH

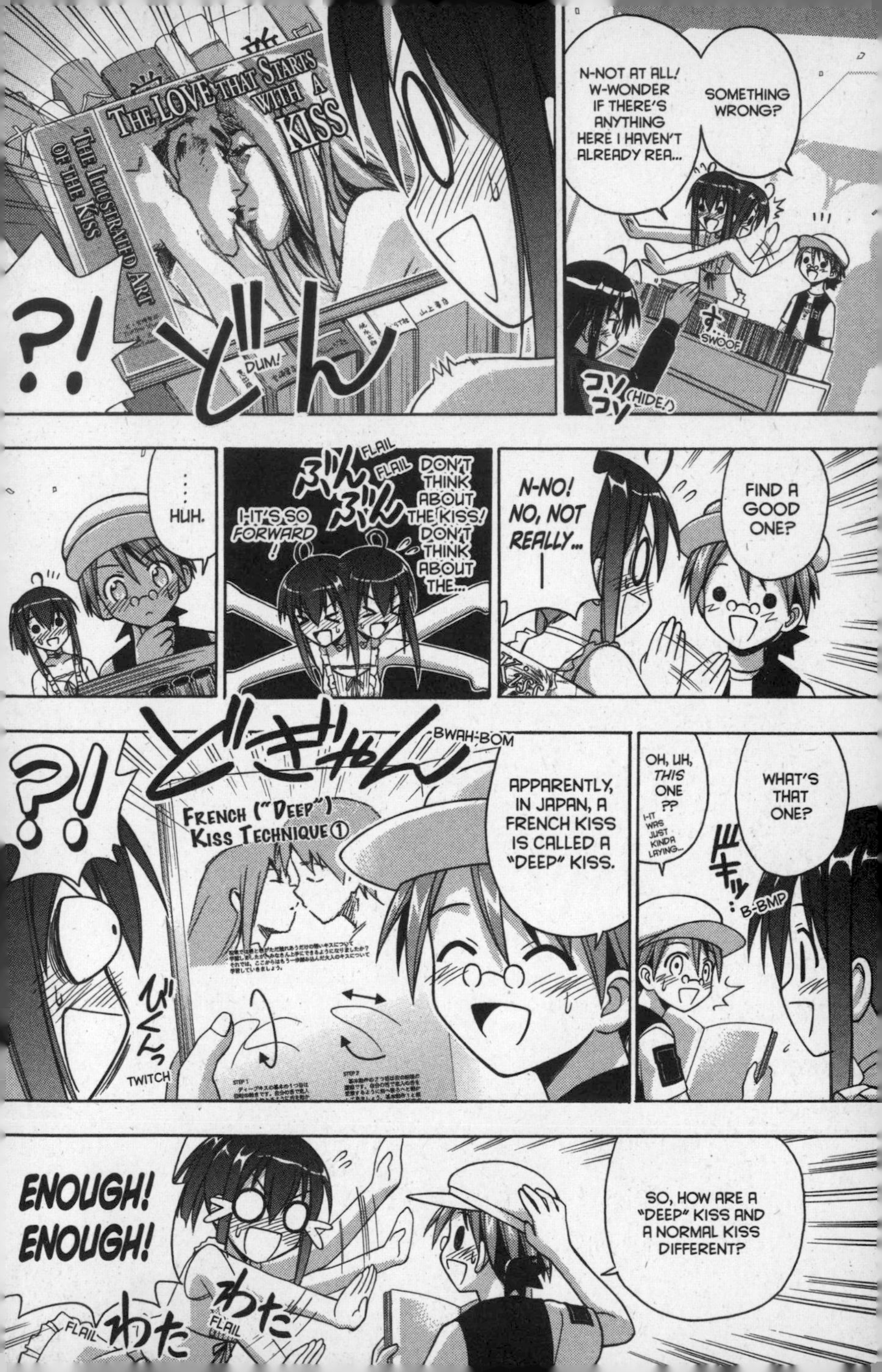
SOMETHING WRONG?
N-NOT AT ALL! W-WONDER IF THERE'S ANYTHING HERE I HAVEN'T ALREADY REA...
SWOOF
(HIDE!)
THE LOVE THAT STARTS WITH A KISS
THE ILLUSTRATED ART OF THE KISS
?!
DUM!
FIND A GOOD ONE?
N-NO! NO, NOT REALLY...
FLAIL FLAIL
DON'T THINK ABOUT THE KISS! DON'T THINK ABOUT THE...
I-IT'S SO FORWARD!
...HUH.
WHAT'S THAT ONE?
OH, UH, THIS ONE ??
I-IT WAS JUST KINDA LAYING...
B-BMP
APPARENTLY, IN JAPAN, A FRENCH KISS IS CALLED A "DEEP" KISS.
BWAH-BOM
?!
FRENCH ("DEEP") KISS TECHNIQUE ①
TWITCH
SO, HOW ARE A "DEEP" KISS AND A NORMAL KISS DIFFERENT?
ENOUGH! ENOUGH!
FLAIL
FLAIL

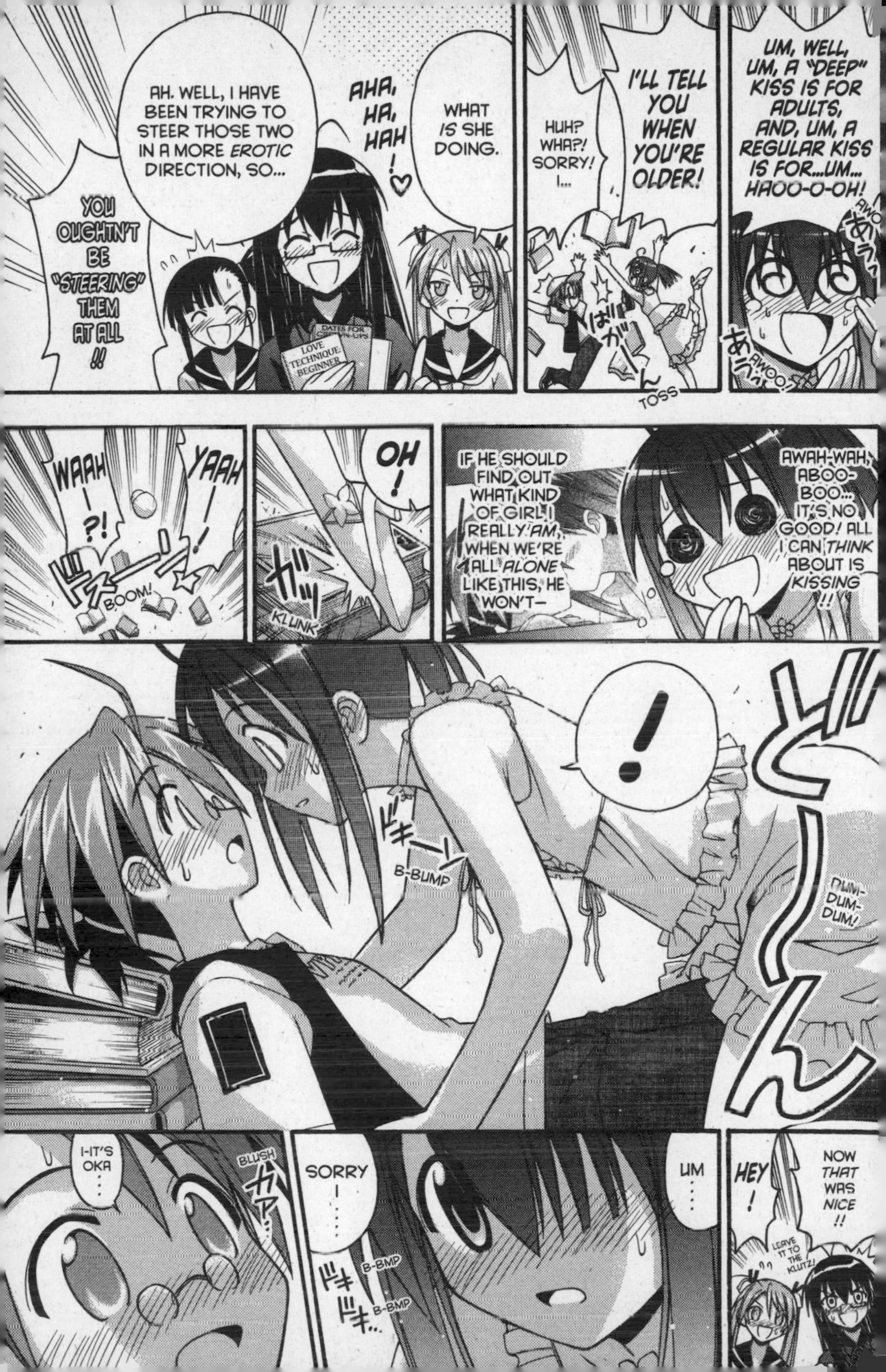
UM, WELL, UM, A "DEEP" KISS IS FOR ADULTS, AND, UM, A REGULAR KISS IS FOR...UM... HAOO-O-OH!
AWOO
AWOO?!
I'LL TELL YOU WHEN YOU'RE OLDER!
HUH? WHA?! SORRY! I...
TOSS
WHAT IS SHE DOING.
AHA, HA, HAH! ♥
AH. WELL, I HAVE BEEN TRYING TO STEER THOSE TWO IN A MORE EROTIC DIRECTION, SO...
DATES FOR GROWN-UPS
LOVE TECHNIQUE: BEGINNER
YOU OUGHTN'T BE "STEERING" THEM AT ALL!!
AWAH-WAH, ABOO-BOO... IT'S NO GOOD! ALL I CAN THINK ABOUT IS KISSING!!
IF HE SHOULD FIND OUT WHAT KIND OF GIRL I REALLY AM, WHEN WE'RE ALL ALONE LIKE THIS, HE WON'T—
OH!
KLUNK
YAAH!
WAAH-?!
BOOM!
!
DUM-DUM-DUM!
B-BUMP
NOW THAT WAS NICE!!
HEY!
LEAVE IT TO THE KLUTZ!
UM...
SORRY!...
B-BMP
B-BMP
BLUSH
I-IT'S OKA...

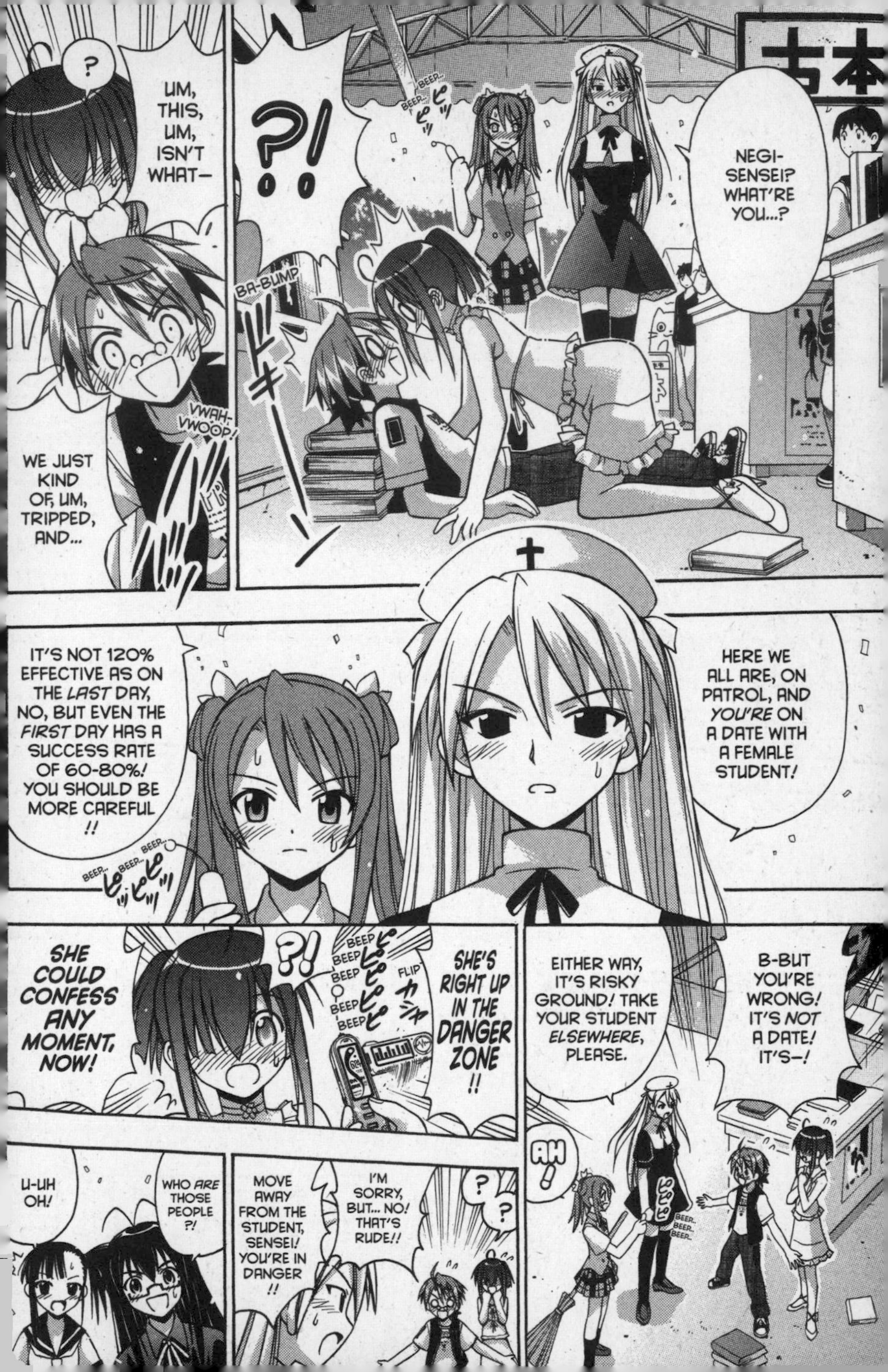
NEGI-SENSEI? WHAT'RE YOU...?
BEEP.. BEEP..
?!
BA-BUMP
VWAH-VWOOP!
?
UM, THIS, UM, ISN'T WHAT—
WE JUST KIND OF, UM, TRIPPED, AND...
HERE WE ALL ARE, ON PATROL, AND *YOU'RE* ON A DATE WITH A FEMALE STUDENT!
IT'S NOT 120% EFFECTIVE AS ON THE *LAST* DAY, NO, BUT EVEN THE *FIRST* DAY HAS A SUCCESS RATE OF 60-80%! YOU SHOULD BE MORE CAREFUL!!
BEEP.. BEEP.. BEEP..
B-BUT YOU'RE WRONG! IT'S *NOT* A DATE! IT'S—!
EITHER WAY, IT'S RISKY GROUND! TAKE YOUR STUDENT *ELSEWHERE*, PLEASE.
AH!
BEEP.. BEEP.. BEEP..
SHE'S RIGHT UP IN THE DANGER ZONE!!
FLIP
BEEP BEEP BEEP BEEP BEEP
?!
SHE COULD CONFESS ANY MOMENT, NOW!
? ?
I'M SORRY, BUT... NO! THAT'S RUDE!!
MOVE AWAY FROM THE STUDENT, SENSEI! YOU'RE IN DANGER!!
WHO *ARE* THOSE PEOPLE?!
U-UH OH!

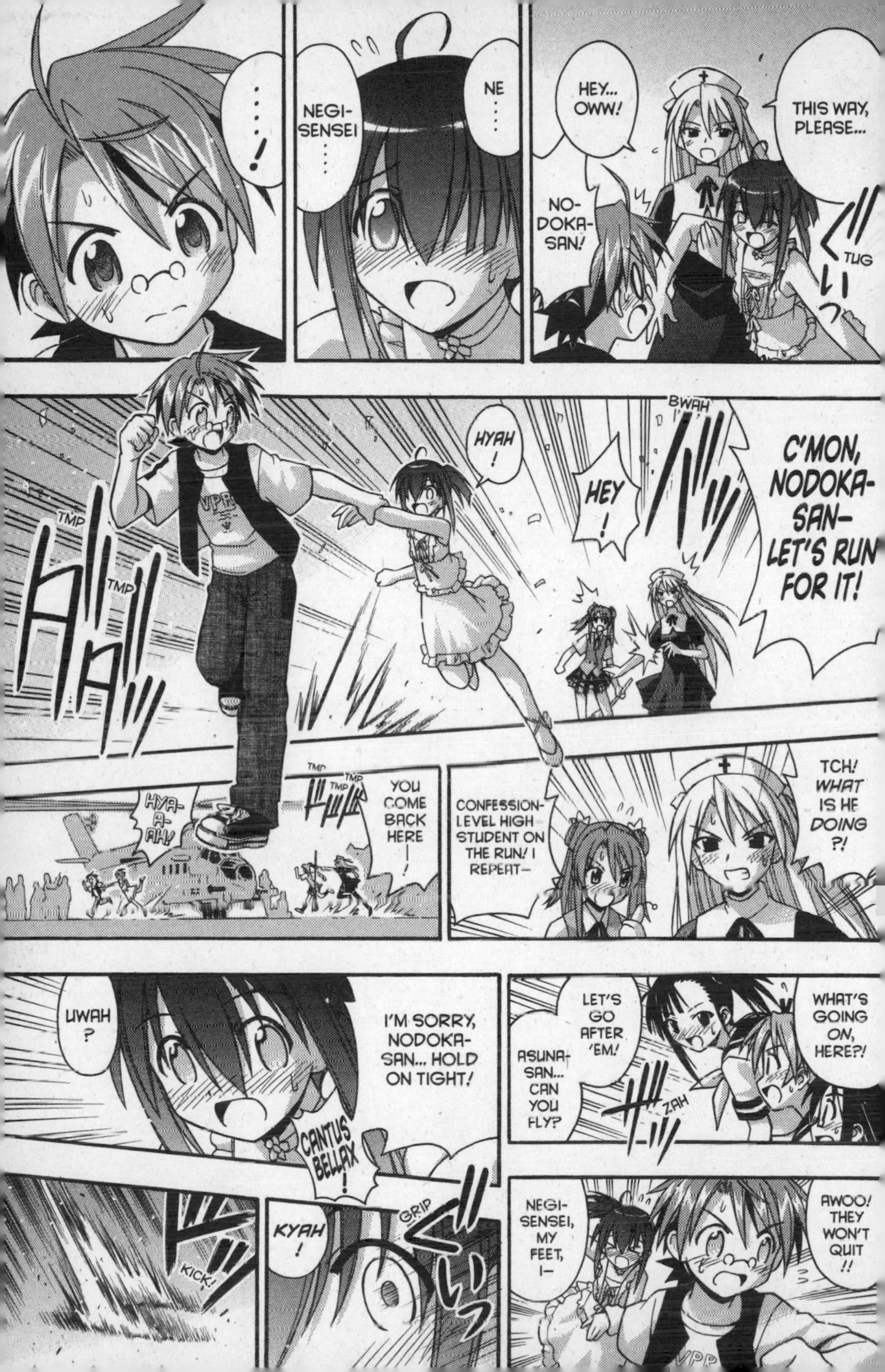
THIS WAY, PLEASE...
HEY... OWW!
NO-DOKA-SAN!
TUG
NE.....
NEGI-SENSEI......
...!
C'MON, NODOKA-SAN— LET'S RUN FOR IT!
BWAH
HEY!
HYAH!
TMP
TMP
TCH! WHAT IS HE DOING?!
CONFESSION-LEVEL HIGH STUDENT ON THE RUN! I REPEAT—
YOU COME BACK HERE!
TMP TMP TMP
HYA-A-AH!
WHAT'S GOING ON, HERE?!
LET'S GO AFTER 'EM!
ASUNA-SAN... CAN YOU FLY?
ZAH
I'M SORRY, NODOKA-SAN... HOLD ON TIGHT!
UWAH?
AWOO! THEY WON'T QUIT!!
NEGI-SENSEI, MY FEET, I—
CANTUS BELLAX!
GRIP
KYAH!
KICK!

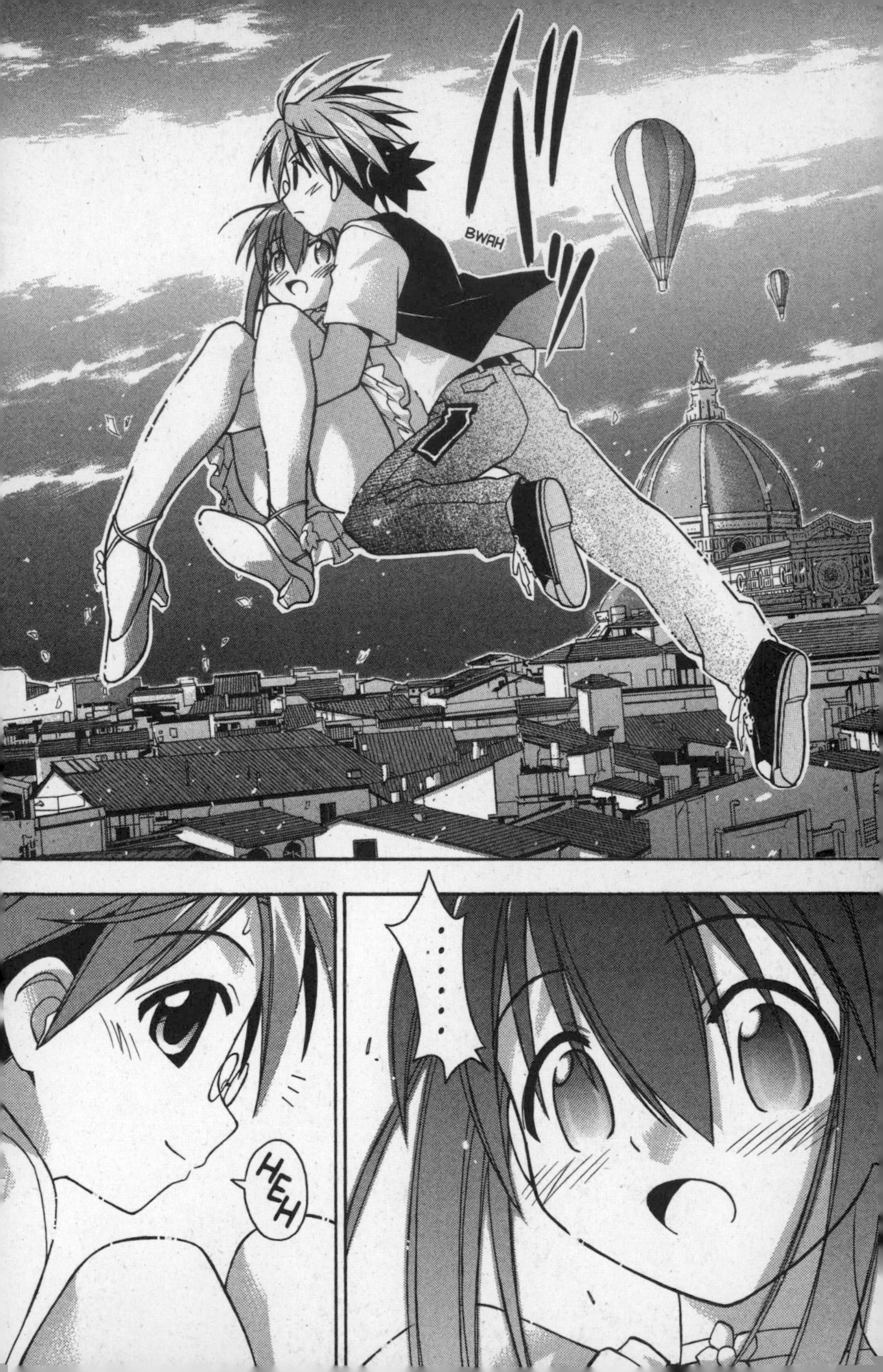
BWAH
......
HEH

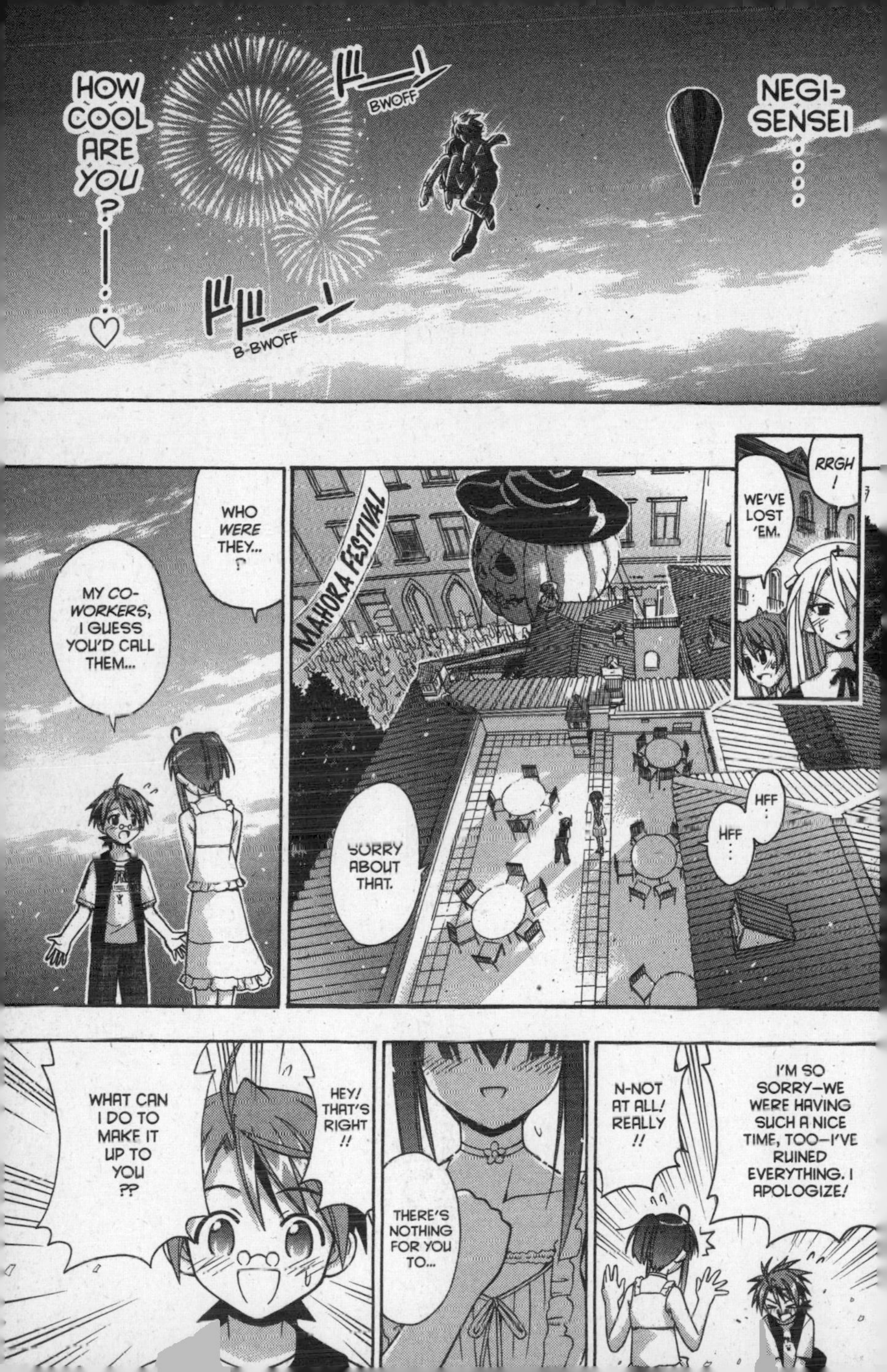
NEGI-SENSEI....
BWOFF
HOW COOL ARE YOU?!...♡
B-BWOFF
RRGH! WE'VE LOST 'EM.
HFF... HFF...
MAHORA FESTIVAL
SORRY ABOUT THAT.
WHO WERE THEY...?
MY CO-WORKERS, I GUESS YOU'D CALL THEM...
I'M SO SORRY—WE WERE HAVING SUCH A NICE TIME, TOO—I'VE RUINED EVERYTHING. I APOLOGIZE!
N-NOT AT ALL! REALLY!!
THERE'S NOTHING FOR YOU TO...
HEY! THAT'S RIGHT!!
WHAT CAN I DO TO MAKE IT UP TO YOU??

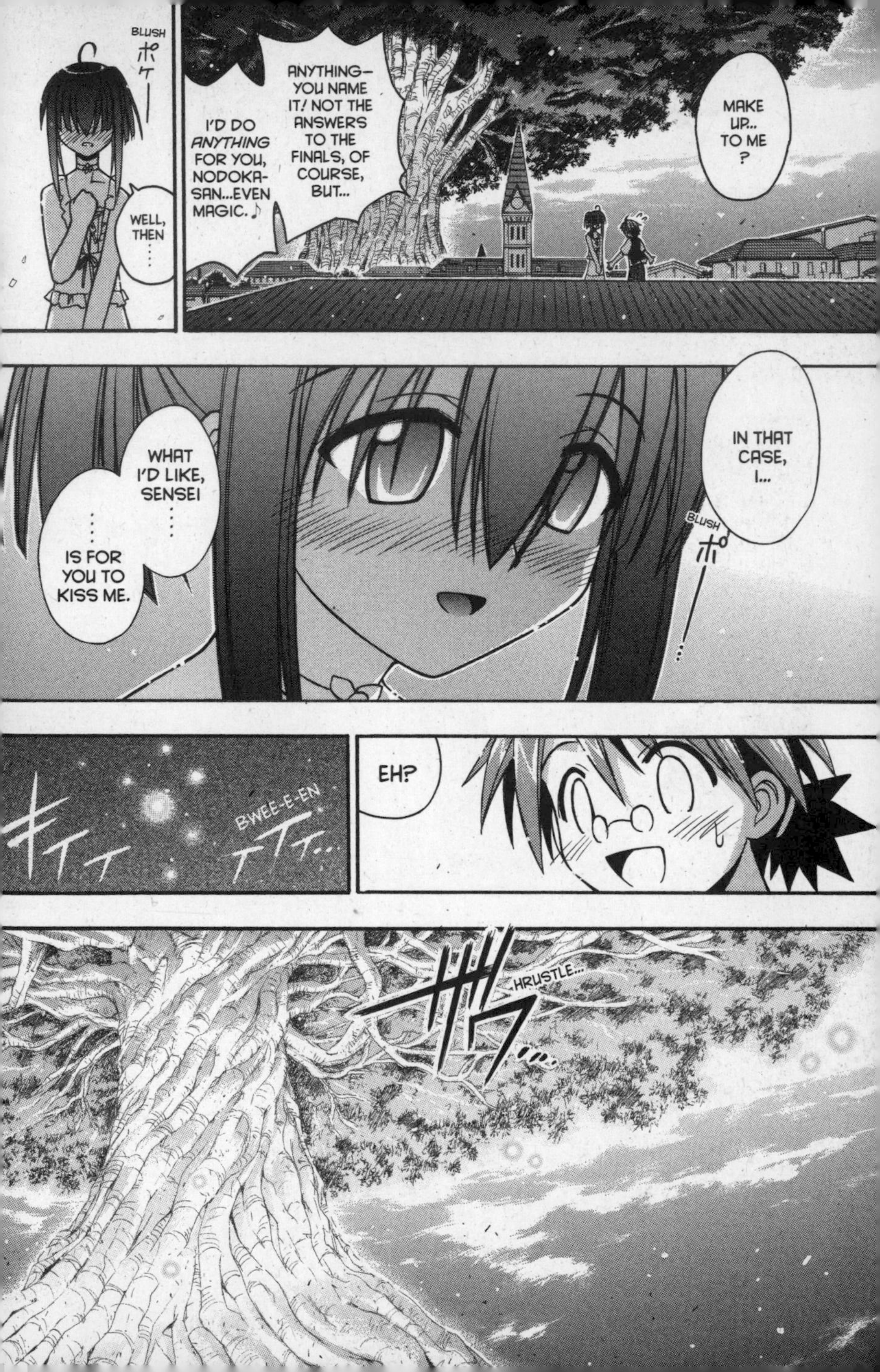
MAKE UP... TO ME ?
ANYTHING— YOU NAME IT! NOT THE ANSWERS TO THE FINALS, OF COURSE, BUT...
I'D DO *ANYTHING* FOR YOU, NODOKA-SAN...EVEN MAGIC.♪
BLUSH
WELL, THEN ....
IN THAT CASE, I...
BLUSH
WHAT I'D LIKE, SENSEI ..... IS FOR YOU TO KISS ME.
EH?
BWEE-E-EN
HRUSTLE...

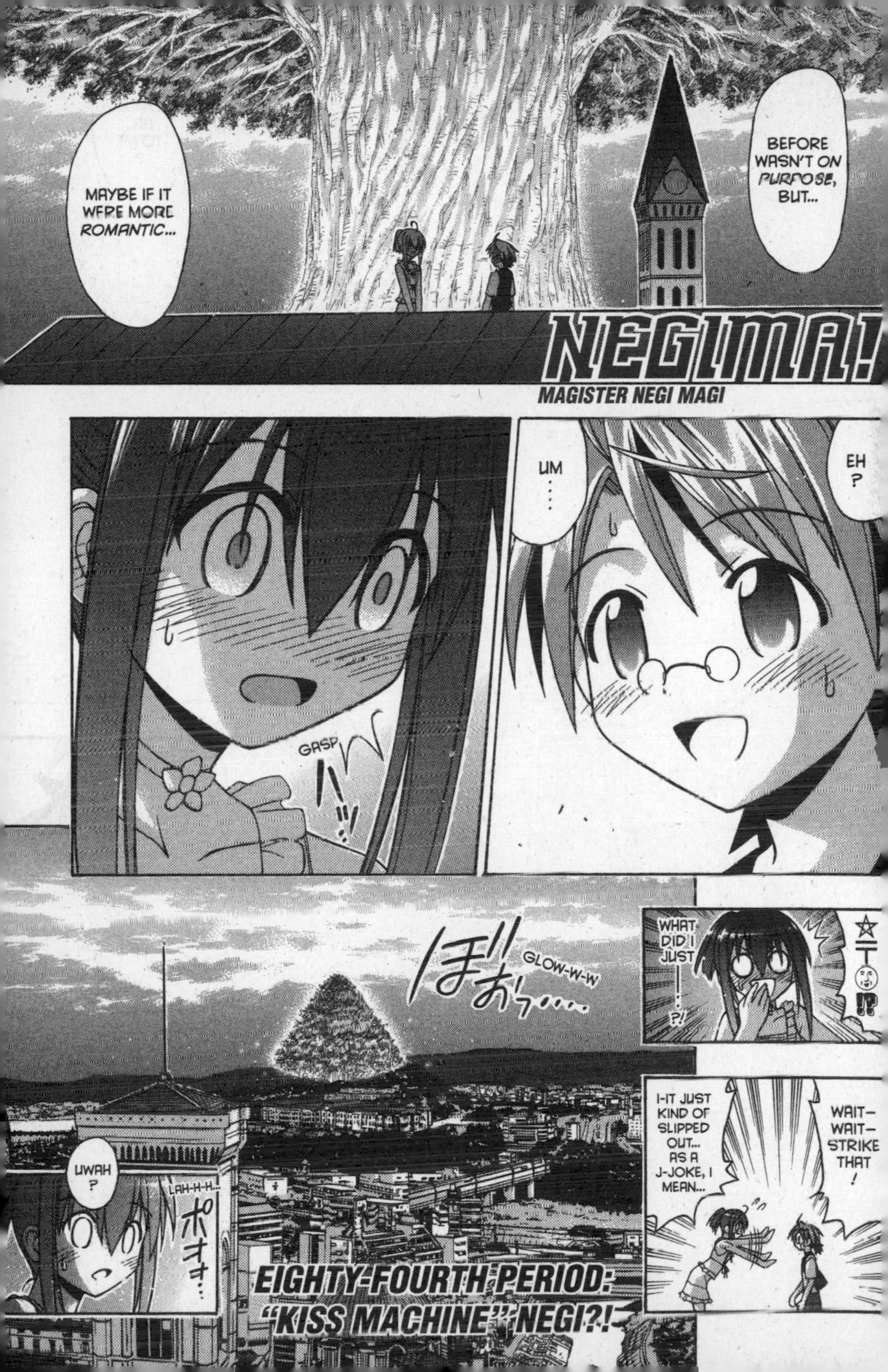
BEFORE WASN'T ON PURPOSE, BUT...
MAYBE IF IT WERE MORE ROMANTIC...
NEGIMA!
MAGISTER NEGI MAGI
EH?
UM....
GASP
WHAT DID I JUST ...?!
!?
WAIT-WAIT-STRIKE THAT!
I-IT JUST KIND OF SLIPPED OUT... AS A J-JOKE, I MEAN...
GLOW-W-W
UWAH?
LAH-H-H...
EIGHTY-FOURTH PERIOD: "KISS MACHINE" NEGI?!

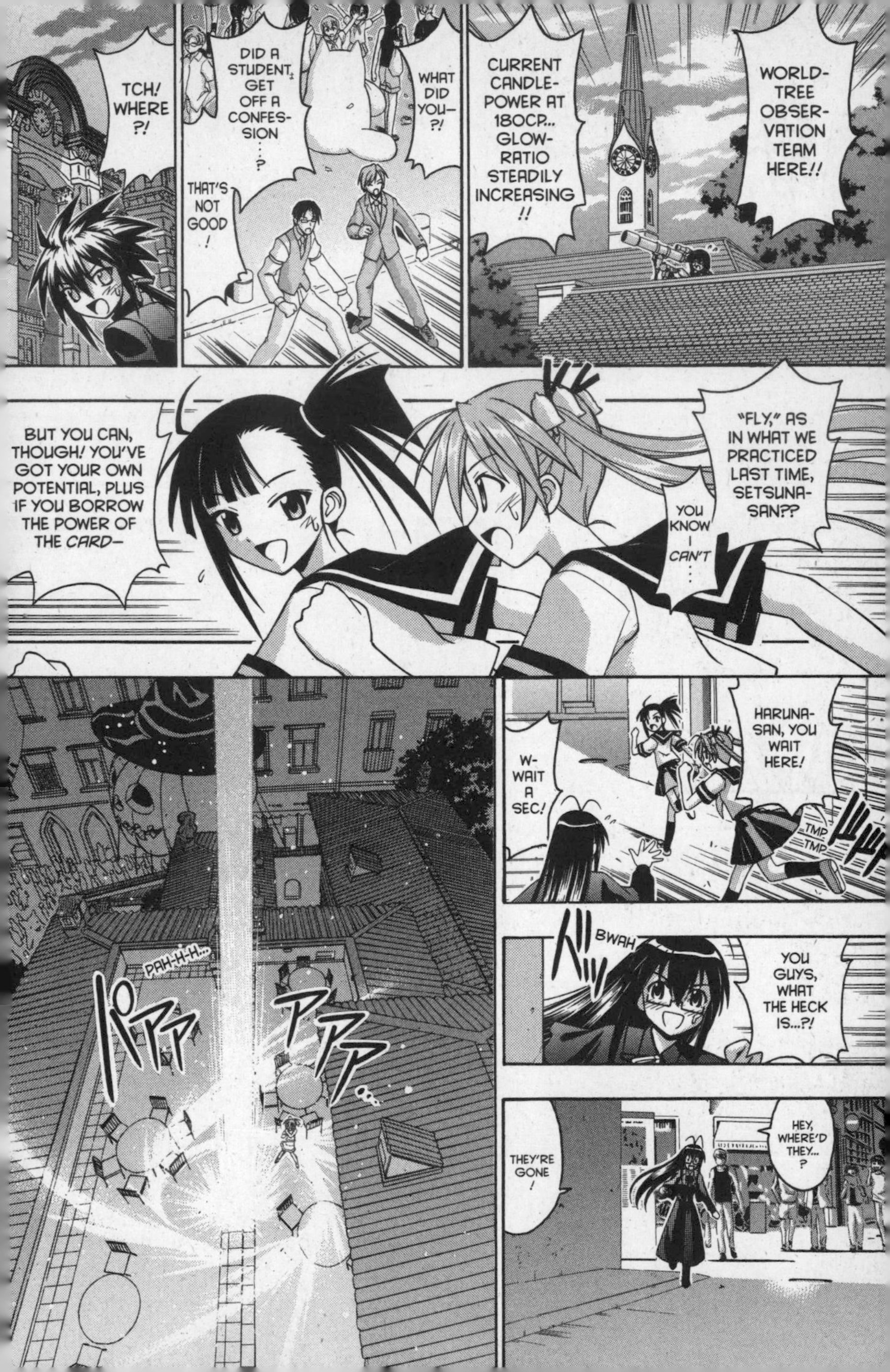

WORLD-TREE OBSERVATION TEAM HERE!!
CURRENT CANDLE-POWER AT 180CP... GLOW-RATIO STEADILY INCREASING!!
WHAT DID YOU—?!
DID A STUDENT GET OFF A CONFESSION...?
THAT'S NOT GOOD!
TCH! WHERE?!
"FLY," AS IN WHAT WE PRACTICED LAST TIME, SETSUNA-SAN??
YOU KNOW I CAN'T...
BUT YOU CAN, THOUGH! YOU'VE GOT YOUR OWN POTENTIAL, PLUS IF YOU BORROW THE POWER OF THE *CARD*—
HARUNA-SAN, YOU WAIT HERE!
TMP TMP
W-WAIT A SEC!
BWAH
YOU GUYS, WHAT THE HECK IS...?!
HEY, WHERE'D THEY...?
THEY'RE GONE!
PAH-H-H...

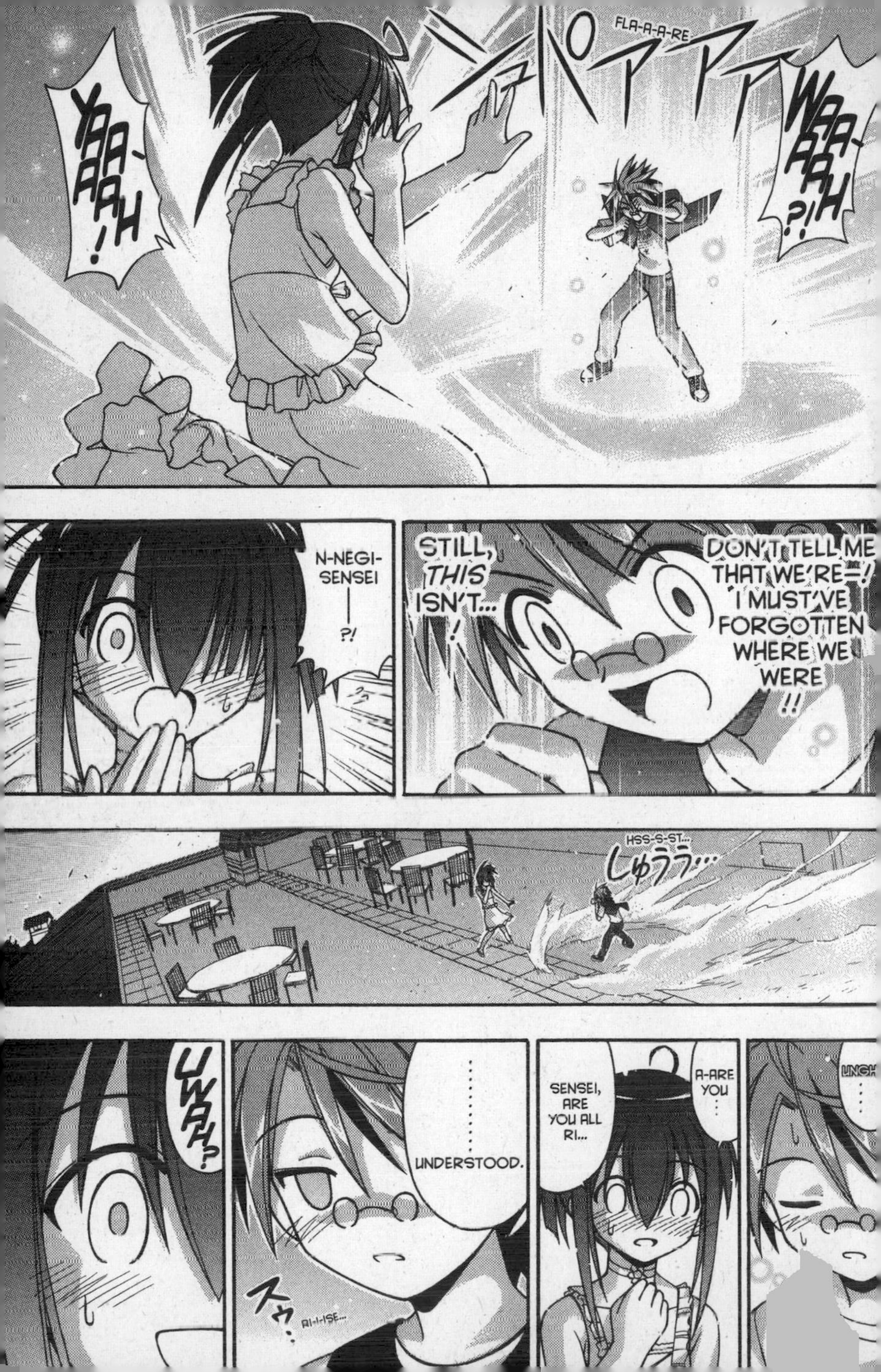
WAA-AAH?!
FLA-A-A-RE
YAAA-AAH!
DON'T TELL ME THAT WE'RE—! I MUST'VE FORGOTTEN WHERE WE WERE!!
STILL, THIS ISN'T...!
N-NEGI-SENSEI—?!
HSS-S-ST...
しゅうう...
UNGH......
A-ARE YOU...
SENSEI, ARE YOU ALL RI...
......UNDERSTOOD.
スゥ...
RI-I-ISE...
UWAH?

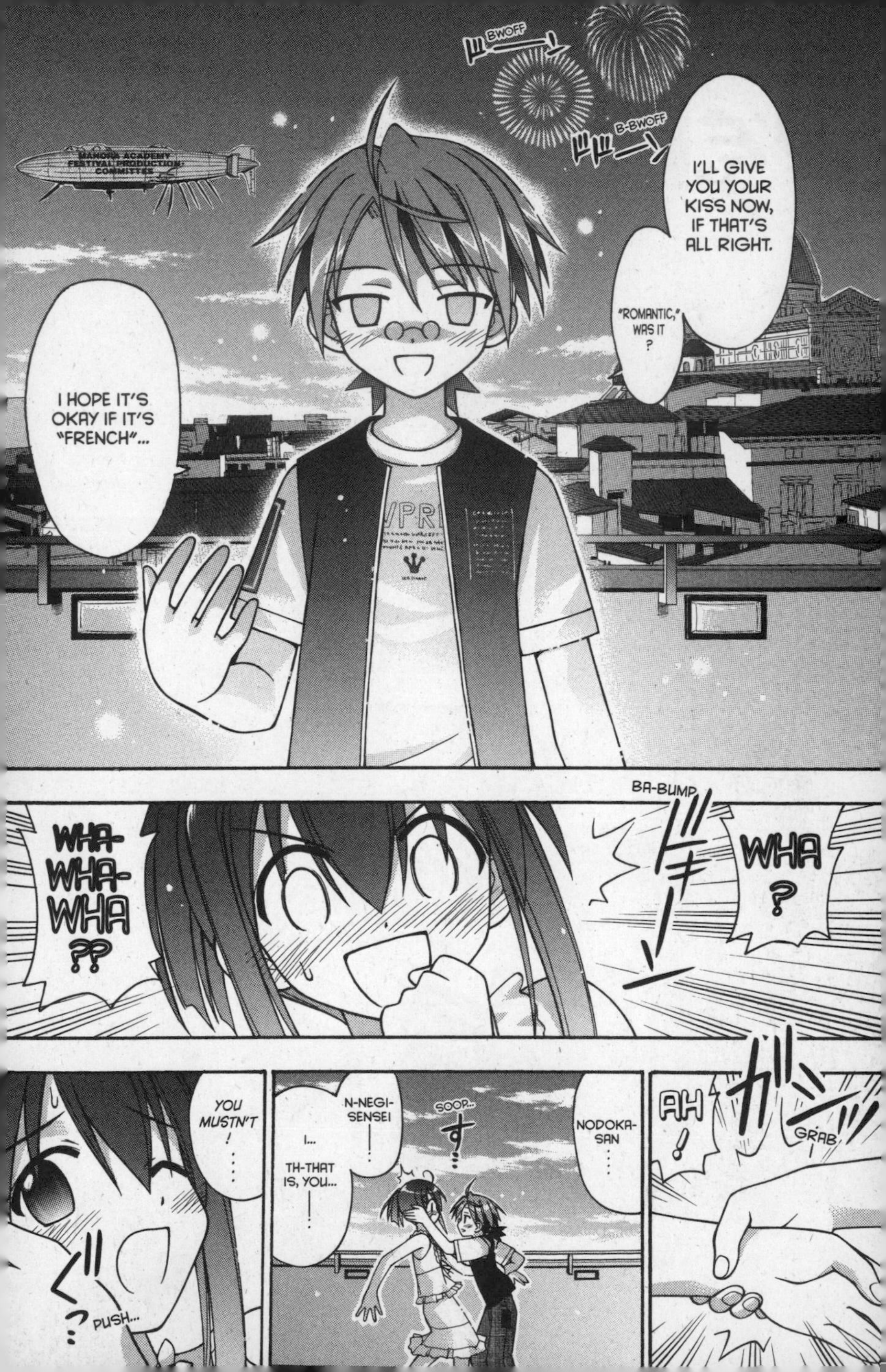
BWOFF
B-BWOFF
I'LL GIVE YOU YOUR KISS NOW, IF THAT'S ALL RIGHT.
"ROMANTIC," WAS IT ?
I HOPE IT'S OKAY IF IT'S "FRENCH"...
BA-BUMP
WHA ?
WHA-WHA-WHA ??
GRAB
AH !
NODOKA-SAN ....
SOOP...
N-NEGI-SENSEI !
I... TH-THAT IS, YOU... !
YOU MUSTN'T ! ....
PUSH...

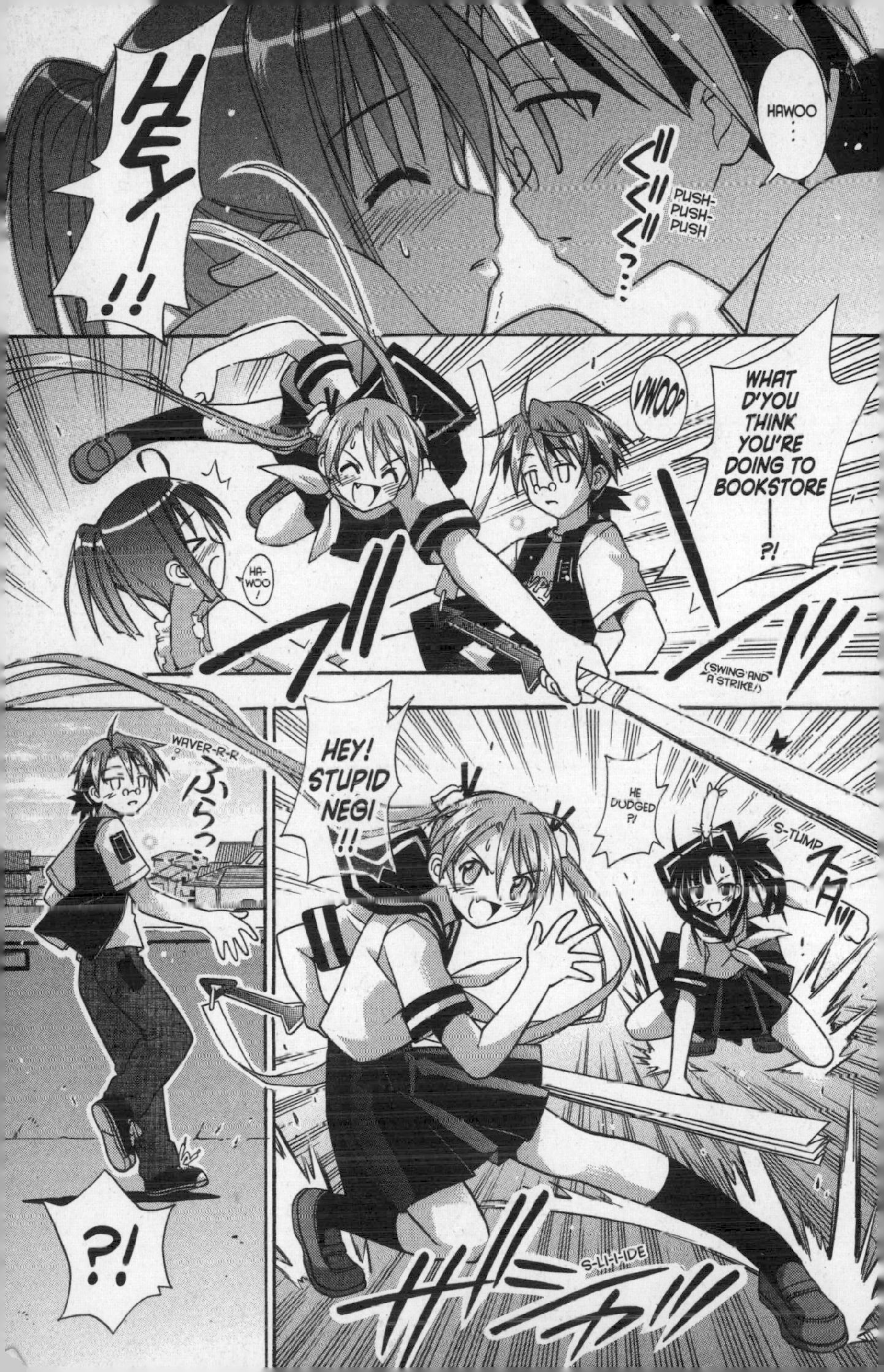
HAWOO...
PUSH-PUSH-PUSH
ぐぐぐっ…
HEY—!!
WHAT D'YOU THINK YOU'RE DOING TO BOOKSTORE—?!
VWOOP
HA-WOO!
(SWING AND A STRIKE!)
HE DUDGED?!
S-TUMP
HEY! STUPID NEGI!!!
S-LI-I-IDE
WAVER-R-R
ふらっ
?!

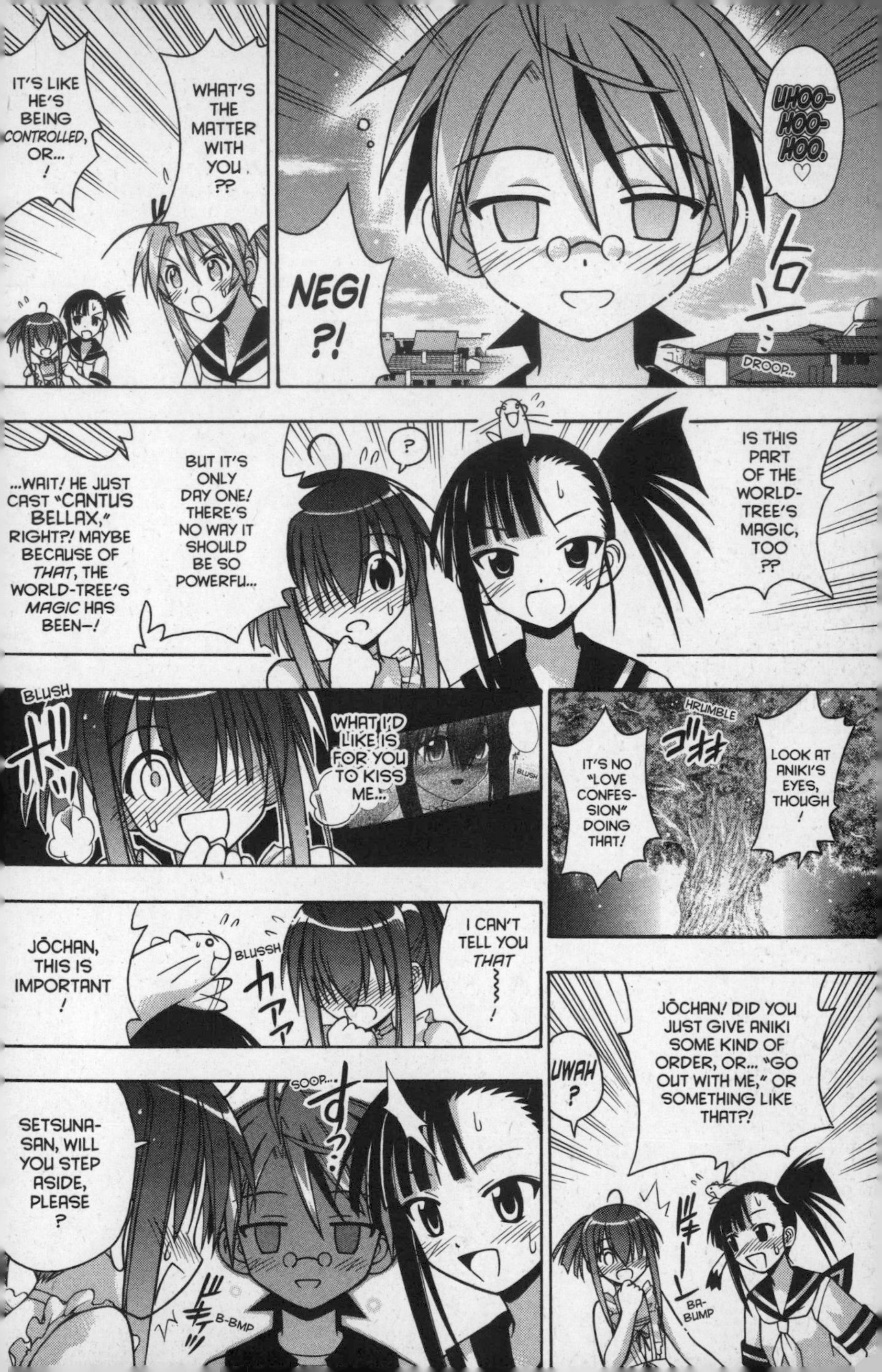
UHOO-HOO-HOO. ♡
DROOP...
NEGI ?!
WHAT'S THE MATTER WITH YOU ??
IT'S LIKE HE'S BEING *CONTROLLED*, OR...!
IS THIS PART OF THE WORLD-TREE'S MAGIC, TOO ??
?
BUT IT'S ONLY DAY ONE! THERE'S NO WAY IT SHOULD BE SO POWERFU...
...WAIT! HE JUST CAST "CANTUS BELLAX," RIGHT?! MAYBE BECAUSE OF *THAT*, THE WORLD-TREE'S *MAGIC* HAS BEEN–!
LOOK AT ANIKI'S EYES, THOUGH!
HRUMBLE
IT'S NO "LOVE CONFESSION" DOING THAT!
WHAT I'D LIKE IS FOR YOU TO KISS ME...
BLUSH
BLUSH
I CAN'T TELL YOU *THAT* ~!
BLUSSH
JŌCHAN, THIS IS IMPORTANT!
JŌCHAN! DID YOU JUST GIVE ANIKI SOME KIND OF ORDER, OR... "GO OUT WITH ME," OR SOMETHING LIKE THAT?!
UWAH ?
BA-BUMP
SOOP...
SETSUNA-SAN, WILL YOU STEP ASIDE, PLEASE ?
B-BMP

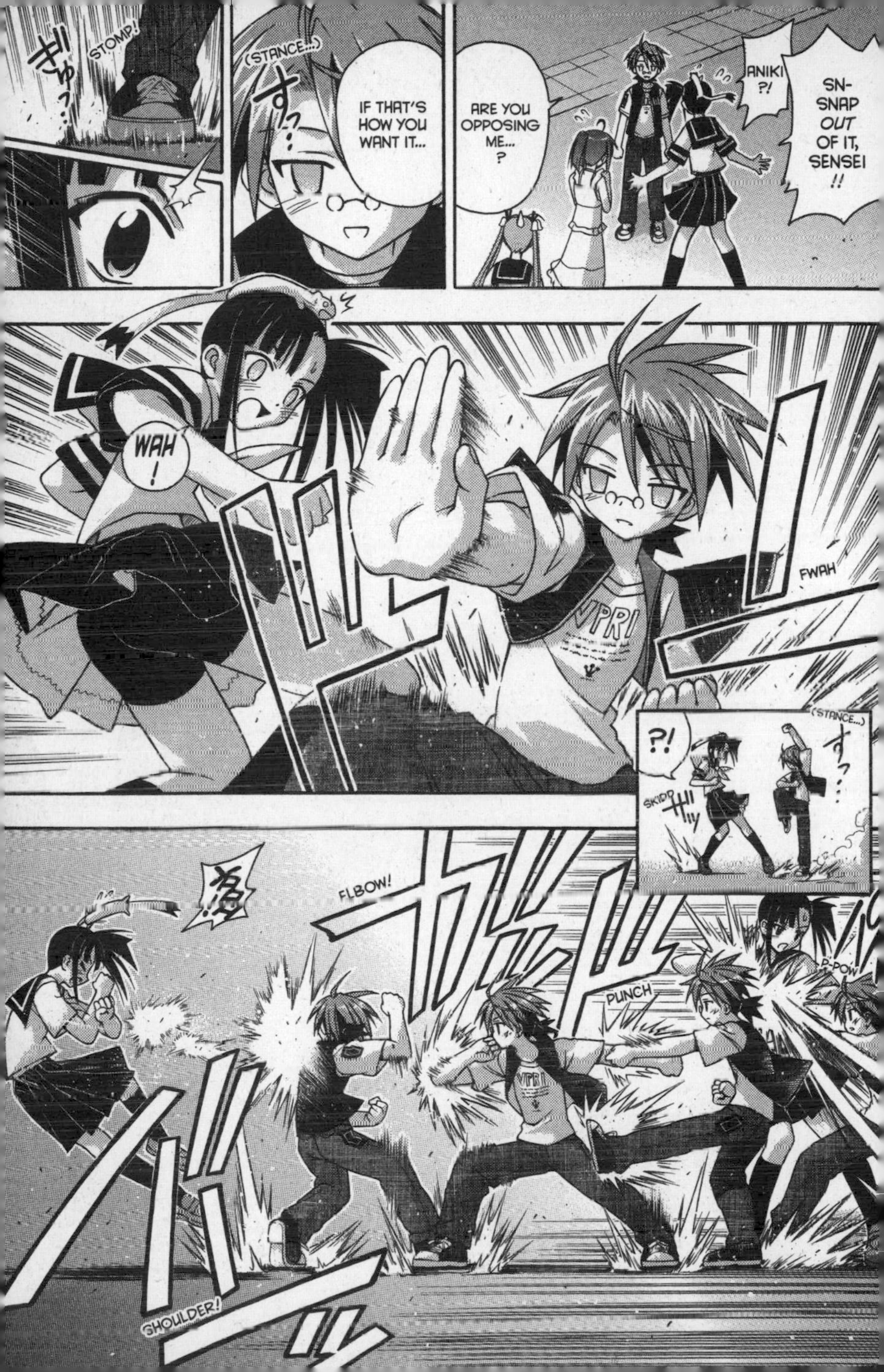

SN-SNAP OUT OF IT, SENSEI!!
ANIKI?!
ARE YOU OPPOSING ME...?
(STANCE...)
すっ
IF THAT'S HOW YOU WANT IT...
STOMP!
ぎゅっ
WAH!
FWAH
(STANCE...)
すっ
?!
SKIDD
ザッ
P-POW
PUNCH
ELBOW!
SHOULDER!

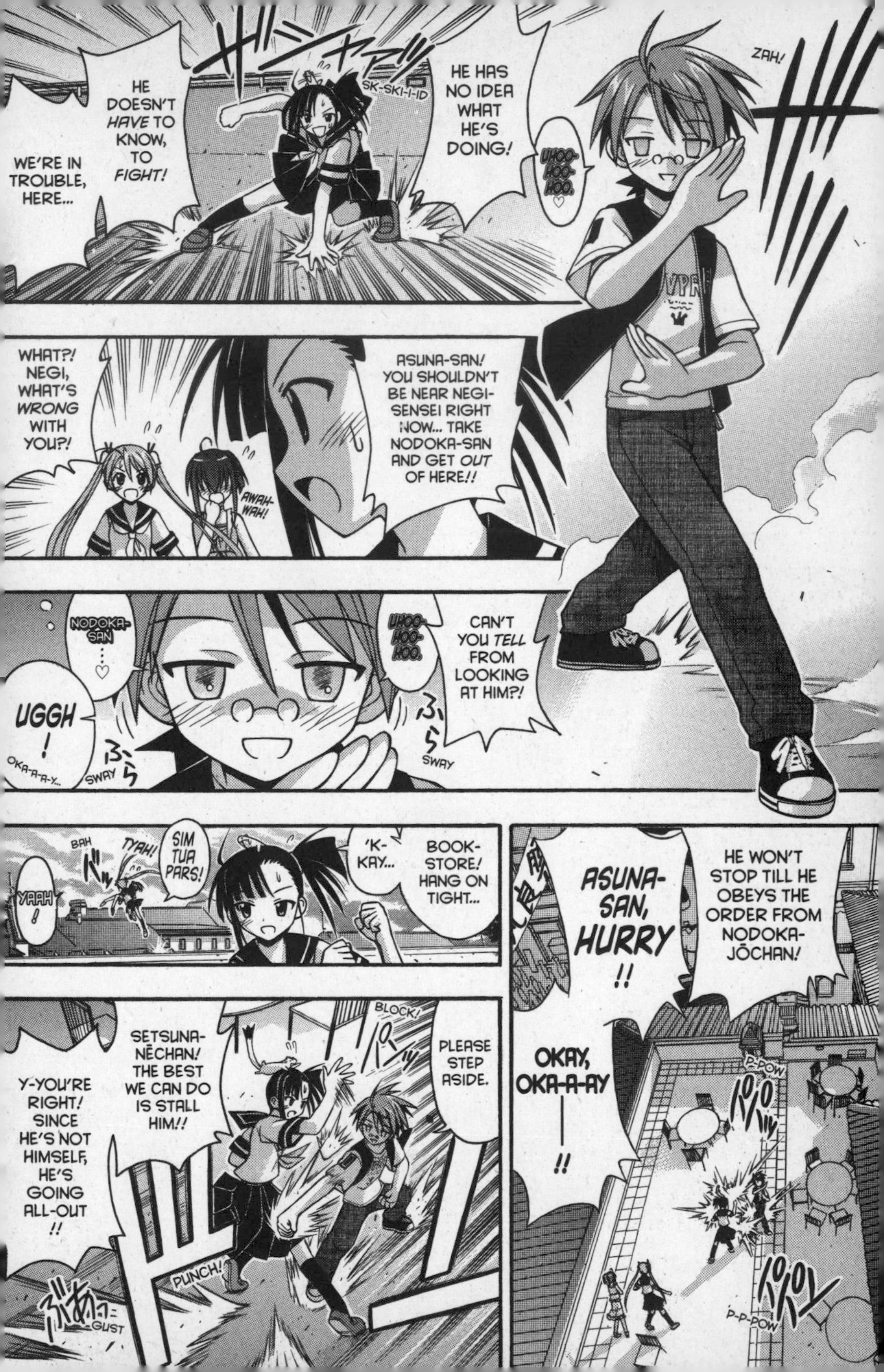
ZAH!
UHOO-HOO-HOO. ♡
HE HAS NO IDEA WHAT HE'S DOING!
SK-SKI-I-ID
HE DOESN'T *HAVE* TO KNOW, TO *FIGHT*!
WE'RE IN TROUBLE, HERE...
ASUNA-SAN! YOU SHOULDN'T BE NEAR NEGI-SENSEI RIGHT NOW... TAKE NODOKA-SAN AND GET *OUT* OF HERE!!
AWAH-WAH!
WHAT?! NEGI, WHAT'S *WRONG* WITH YOU?!
CAN'T YOU *TELL* FROM LOOKING AT HIM?!
UHOO-HOO-HOO.
ふら
SWAY
NODOKA-SAN ... ♡
UGGH!
OKA-A-A-Y...
ふら
SWAY
HE WON'T STOP TILL HE OBEYS THE ORDER FROM NODOKA-JŌCHAN!
ASUNA-SAN, HURRY!!
OKAY, OKA-A-AY—!!
P-POW
P-P-POW
BOOK-STORE! HANG ON TIGHT...
'K-KAY...
SIM TUA PARS!
TYAH!
BAH
YAAAH!
PLEASE STEP ASIDE.
BLOCK!
SETSUNA-NĒCHAN! THE BEST WE CAN DO IS STALL HIM!!
Y-YOU'RE RIGHT! SINCE HE'S NOT HIMSELF, HE'S GOING ALL-OUT!!
PUNCH!
GUST

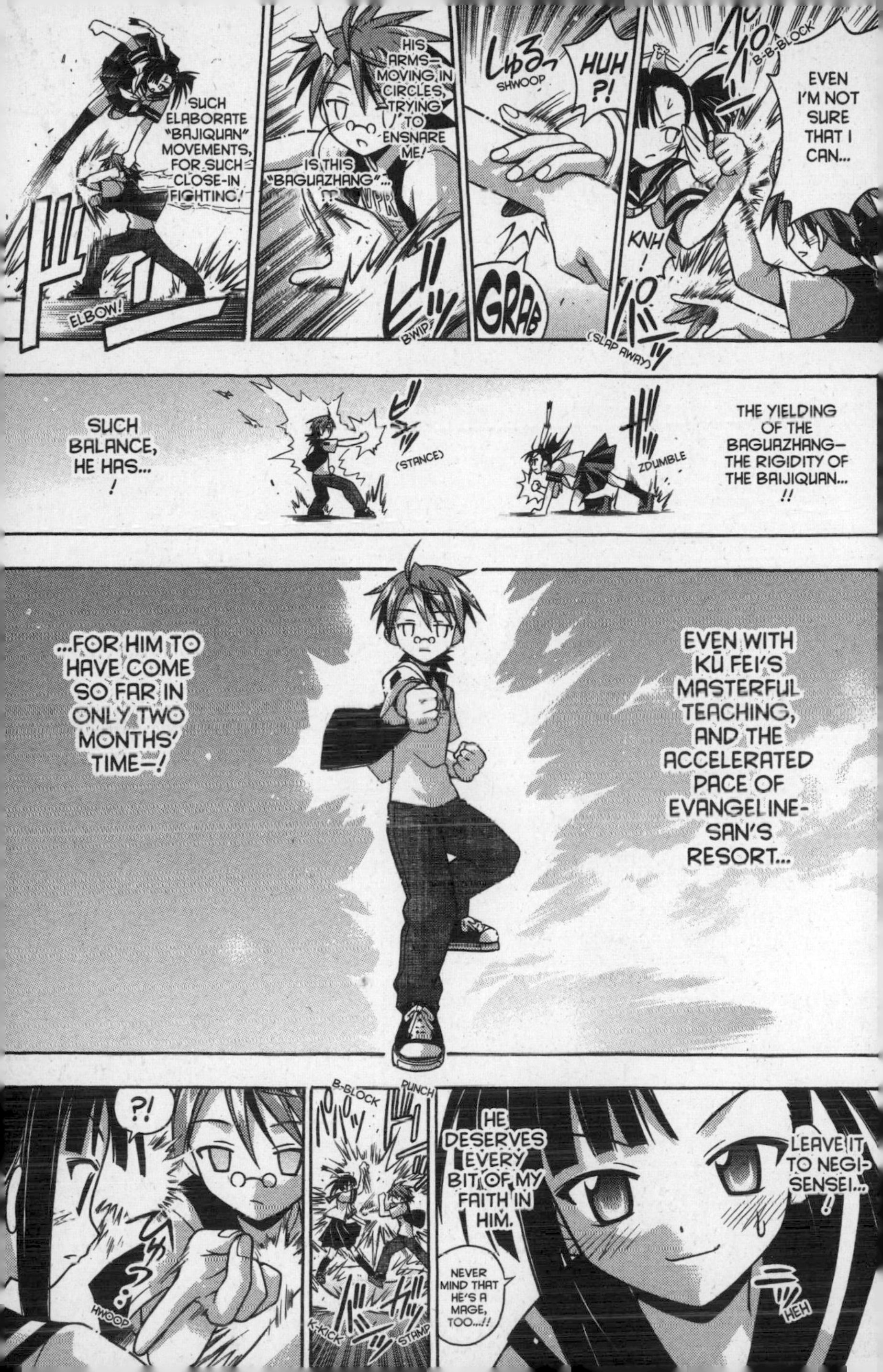
B-B-BLOCK
EVEN I'M NOT SURE THAT I CAN...
KNH!
(SLAP AWAY)
HUH ?!
SHWOOP
GRAB
HIS ARMS— MOVING IN CIRCLES, TRYING TO ENSNARE ME!
IS THIS "BAGUAZHANG"...?!
BWIP
SUCH ELABORATE "BAJIQUAN" MOVEMENTS, FOR SUCH CLOSE-IN FIGHTING!
ELBOW!
THE YIELDING OF THE BAGUAZHANG— THE RIGIDITY OF THE BAIJIQUAN...!!
ZDUMBLE
(STANCE)
SUCH BALANCE, HE HAS...!
EVEN WITH KŪ FEI'S MASTERFUL TEACHING, AND THE ACCELERATED PACE OF EVANGELINE-SAN'S RESORT...
...FOR HIM TO HAVE COME SO FAR IN ONLY TWO MONTHS' TIME—!
LEAVE IT TO NEGI-SENSEI...!
HEH
HE DESERVES EVERY BIT OF MY FAITH IN HIM.
NEVER MIND THAT HE'S A MAGE, TOO...!!
PUNCH
B-BLOCK
K-KICK
STAMP
?!
HWOOP

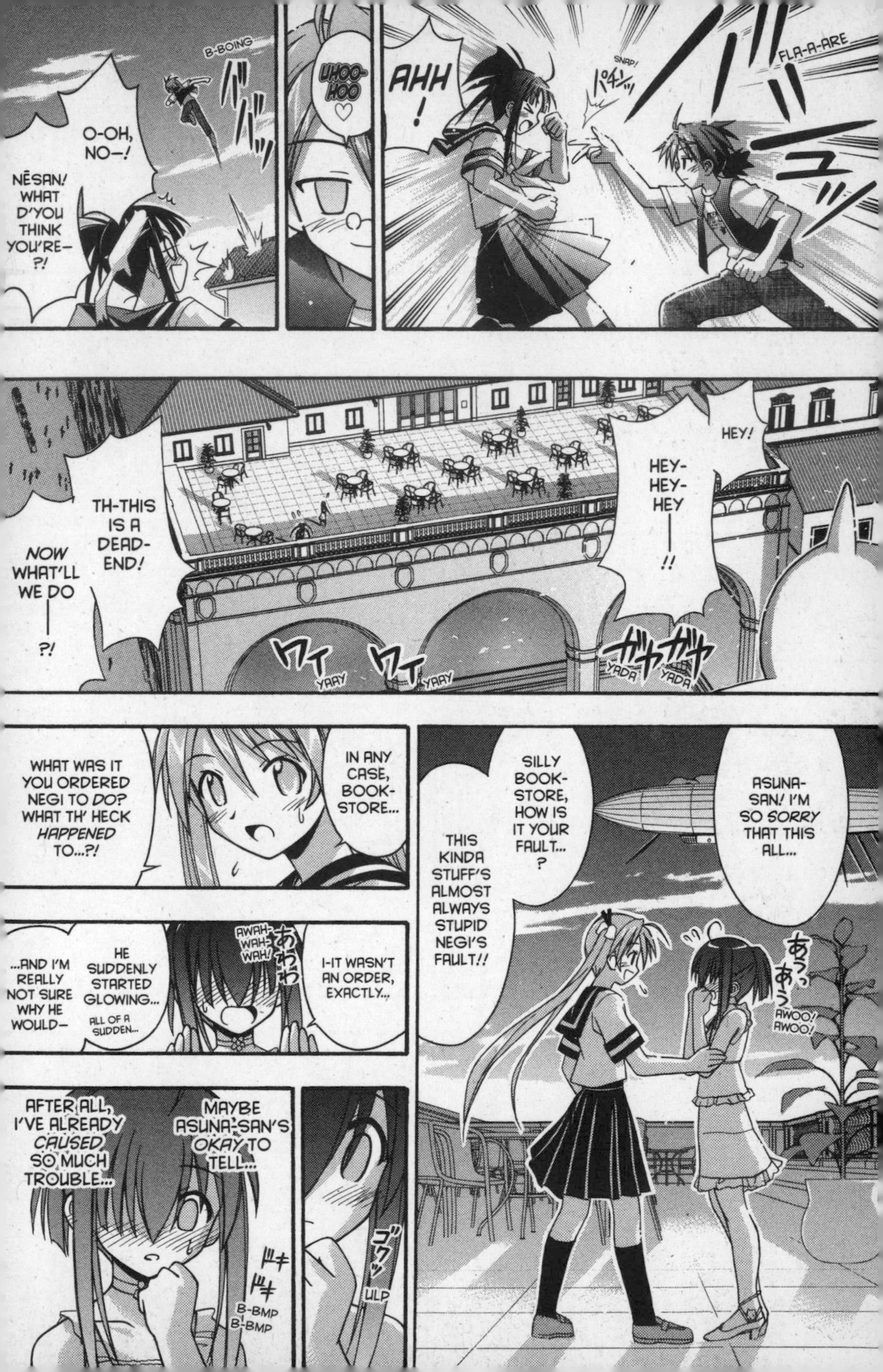
FLA-A-ARE
パチンッ
SNAP!
AHH!
UHOO-HOO ♡
B-BOING
O-OH, NO—!
NĒSAN! WHAT D'YOU THINK YOU'RE—?!
HEY!
HEY-HEY-HEY—!!
TH-THIS IS A DEAD-END!
NOW WHAT'LL WE DO—?!
ガヤガヤ
YADA YADA
ワイワイ
YAAY YAAY
ASUNA-SAN! I'M SO SORRY THAT THIS ALL...
SILLY BOOKSTORE, HOW IS IT YOUR FAULT...?
THIS KINDA STUFF'S ALMOST ALWAYS STUPID NEGI'S FAULT!!
あうっあうっ
AWOO! AWOO!
IN ANY CASE, BOOKSTORE...
WHAT WAS IT YOU ORDERED NEGI TO DO? WHAT TH' HECK HAPPENED TO...?!
I-IT WASN'T AN ORDER, EXACTLY...
あわわ
AWAH-WAH-WAH!
HE SUDDENLY STARTED GLOWING...
ALL OF A SUDDEN...
...AND I'M REALLY NOT SURE WHY HE WOULD—
ゴクッ
ULP
MAYBE ASUNA-SAN'S OKAY TO TELL...
AFTER ALL, I'VE ALREADY CAUSED SO MUCH TROUBLE...
ドキドキ
B-BMP B-BMP

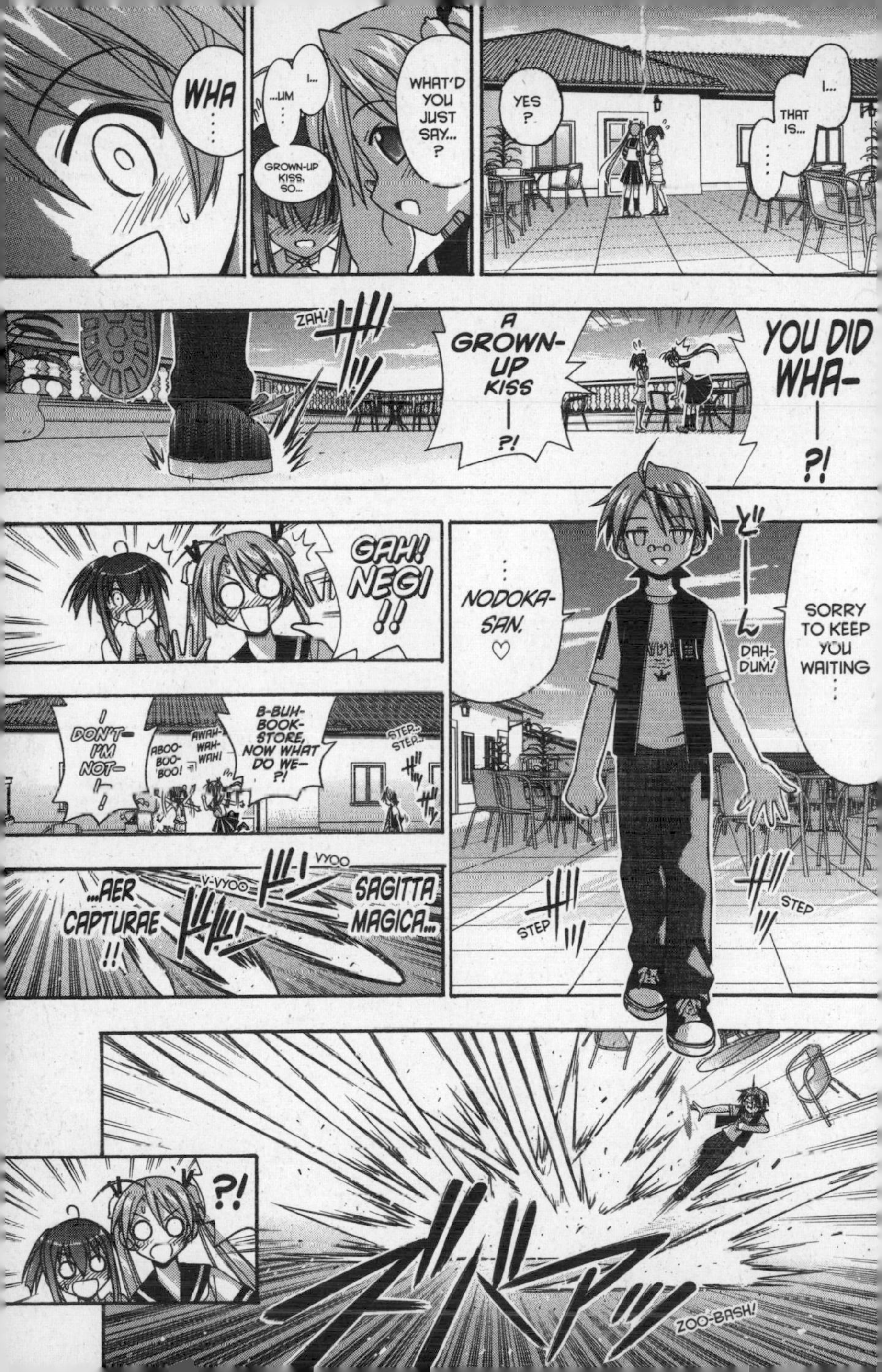
I...
THAT IS...
...
YES?
WHAT'D YOU JUST SAY...?
I...
...UM
...
GROWN-UP KISS, SO...
WHA......
YOU DID WHA——?!
A GROWN-UP KISS—?!
ZAH!
SORRY TO KEEP YOU WAITING...
DAH-DUM!
...NODOKA-SAN. ♡
STEP
STEP
GAH! NEGI!!
B-BUH-BOOKSTORE, NOW WHAT DO WE—?!
STEP... STEP...
AWAH-WAH-WAH!
ABOO-BOO-BOO!
I DON'T— I'M NOT—!
SAGITTA MAGICA...
VYOO
V-VYOO
...AER CAPTURAE!!
ZOO-BASH!
?!

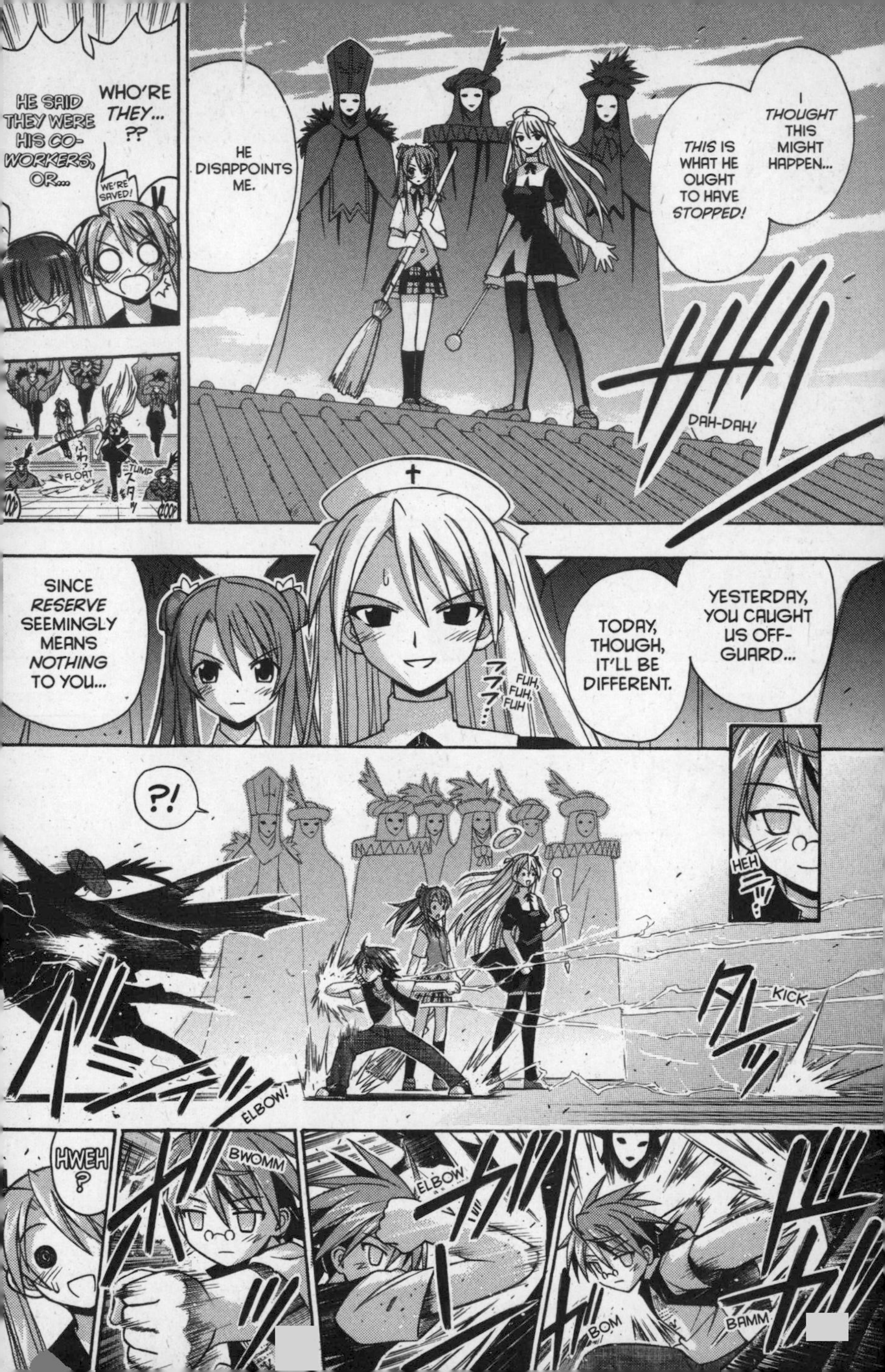
I *THOUGHT* THIS MIGHT HAPPEN...
THIS IS WHAT HE OUGHT TO HAVE *STOPPED!*
HE DISAPPOINTS ME.
DAH-DAH!
WHO'RE *THEY*...??
HE SAID THEY WERE HIS CO-WORKERS, OR...
WE'RE SAVED!
FLOAT
TUMP
ZOOP
ZOOP
YESTERDAY, YOU CAUGHT US OFF-GUARD...
TODAY, THOUGH, IT'LL BE DIFFERENT.
FUH, FUH, FUH
SINCE *RESERVE* SEEMINGLY MEANS *NOTHING* TO YOU...
HEH
KICK
?!
ELBOW!
BAMM
BOM
ELBOW
BWOMM
HWEH?

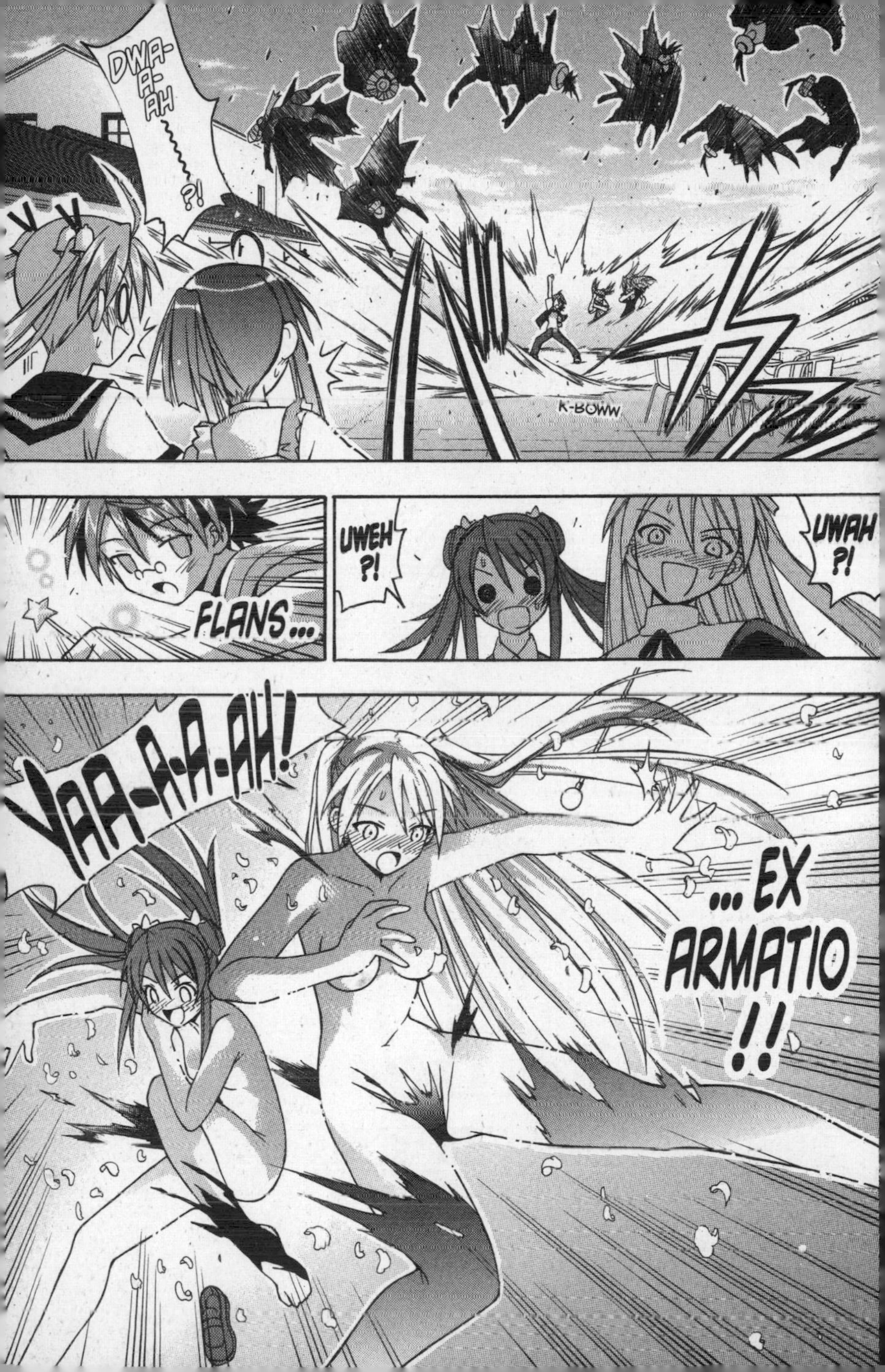
DWA-A-AH ~~~
?!
K-BOWW
UWAH ?!
UWEH ?!
FLANS...
...EX ARMATIO !!
YAA-A-A-AH!

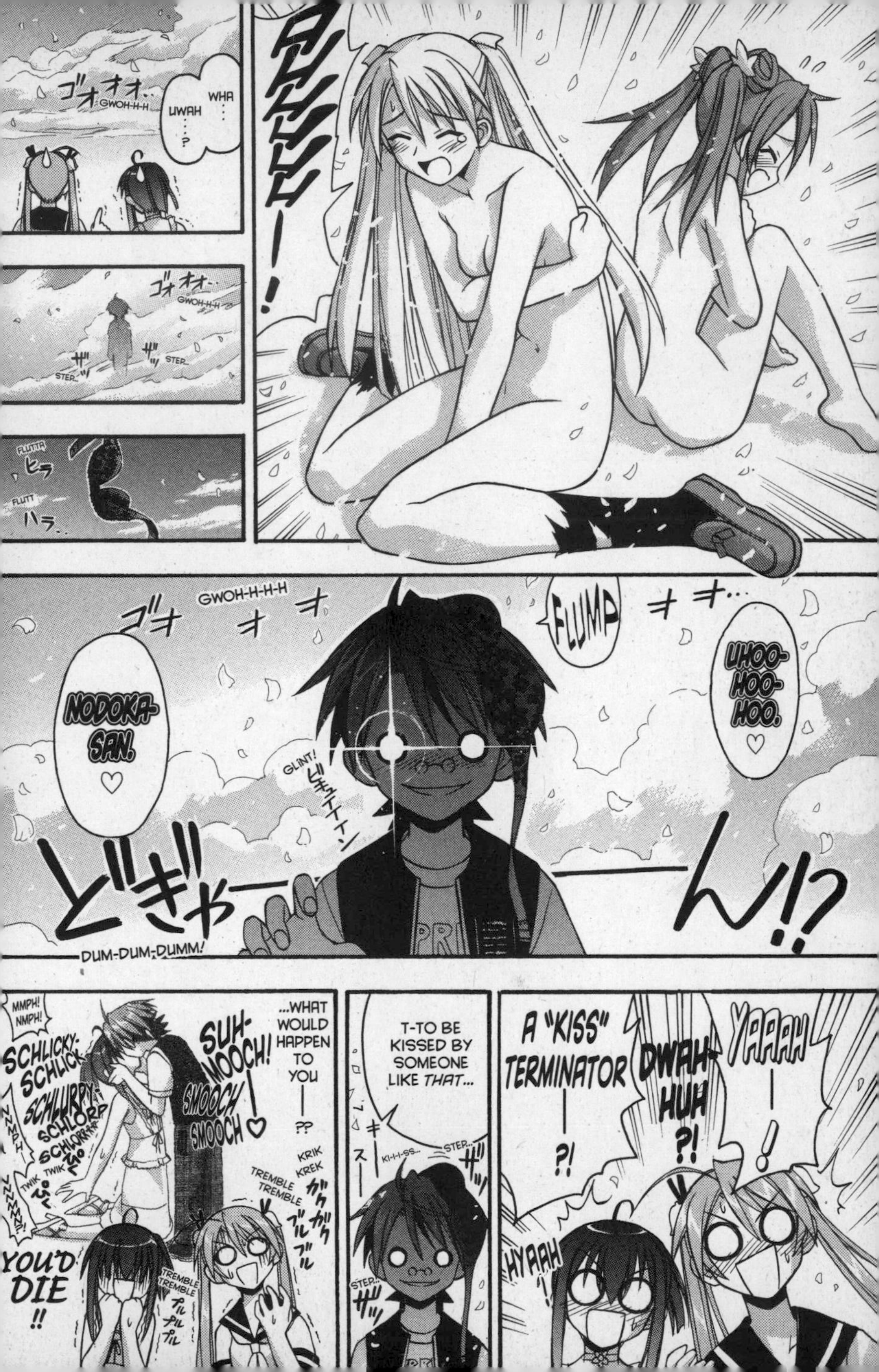

タルンルンルンルンー!!
WHA . . .
UWAH . . . ?
ゴォオオ… GWOH-H-H
ゴォオオー GWOH-H-H
ザッ STEP...
ザッ STEP...
ヒラ FLUTTA
ハラ… FLUTT
FLUMP
ォォ…
UHOO-HOO-HOO. ♡
ゴォ ォ ォ GWOH-H-H-H
NODOKA-SAN. ♡
GLINT! ビキィィイン
どぎゃーーーん!?
DUM-DUM-DUMM!
YAAAH—!
DWAH-HUH?!
A "KISS" TERMINATOR—?!
HYAAH!
T-TO BE KISSED BY SOMEONE LIKE THAT...
キスー KI-I-I-SS...
ザッ STEP...
ザッ STEP...
...WHAT WOULD HAPPEN TO YOU—??
KRIK KREK ガクガク
TREMBLE TREMBLE ブルブル
SUH-MOOCH!
SMOOCH SMOOCH ♡
MMPH! NMPH!
SCHLICKY-SCHLICK
SCHLURPY-SCHLORP
SCHLORRRRR
TWIK TWIK
TWIK
NNMPH
NNNMM!?
YOU'D DIE!!
TREMBLE TREMBLE プルプルプル

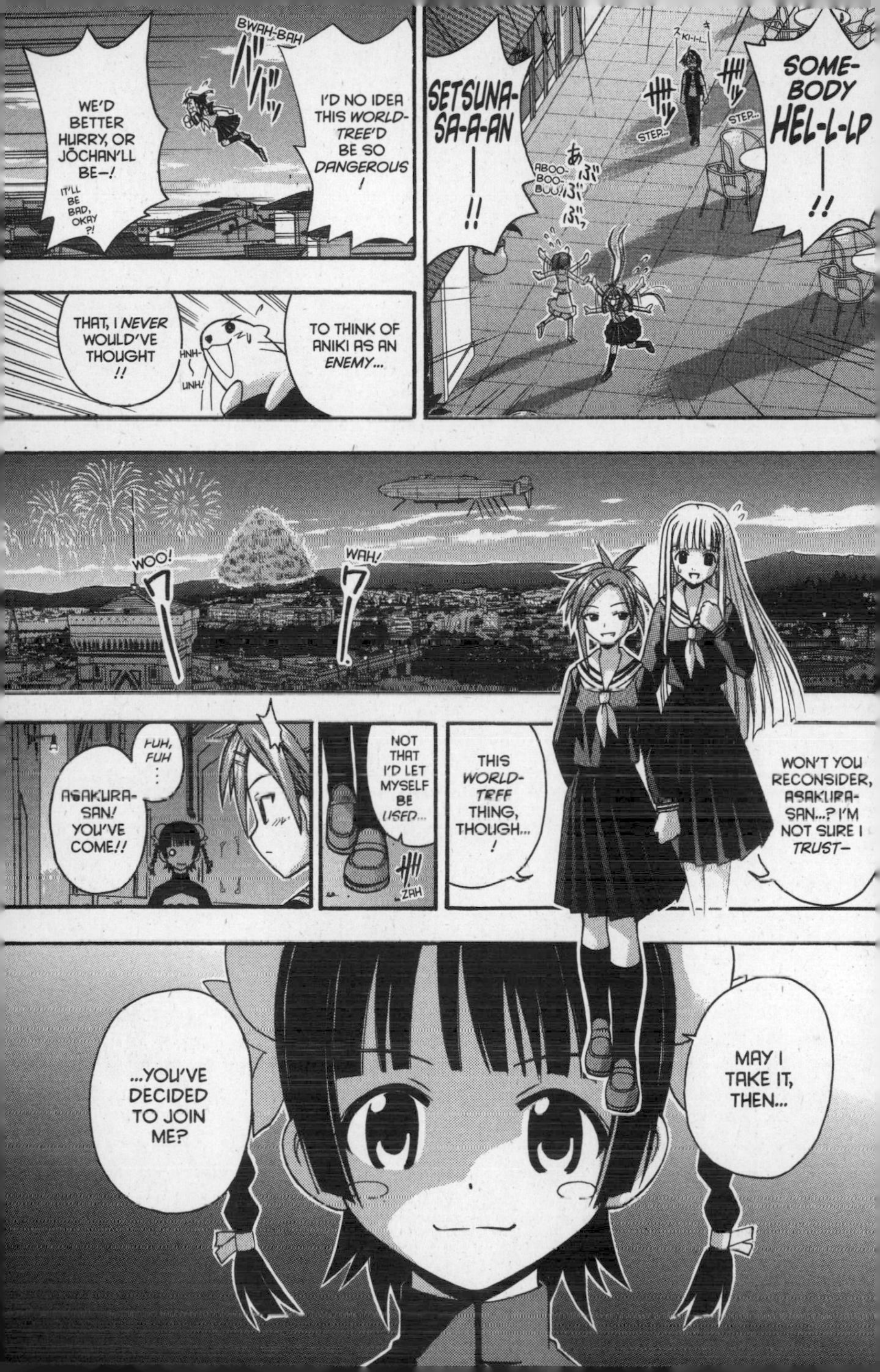
SKI-I-I...
STEP...
STEP...
SOMEBODY HEL-L-LP—!!
ABOO-BOO-BOO!!
あぶぶぶ
SETSUNA-SA-A-AN—!!
BWAH-BAH
I'D NO IDEA THIS WORLD-TREE'D BE SO DANGEROUS!
WE'D BETTER HURRY, OR JŌCHAN'LL BE—!
IT'LL BE BAD, OKAY?!
TO THINK OF ANIKI AS AN ENEMY...
HNH-UNH!
THAT, I NEVER WOULD'VE THOUGHT!!
WAH!
WOO!
WON'T YOU RECONSIDER, ASAKURA-SAN...? I'M NOT SURE I TRUST—
THIS WORLD-TREE THING, THOUGH...!
NOT THAT I'D LET MYSELF BE USED...
ZAH
FUH, FUH...
ASAKURA-SAN! YOU'VE COME!!
MAY I TAKE IT, THEN...
...YOU'VE DECIDED TO JOIN ME?

NEGIMA!
MAGISTER NEGI MAGI

EIGHTY-FOURTH PERIOD: LEXICON NEGIMARIUM

■「シム・トゥア・パルス」

SIM TUA PARS

Spell that allows the Minister/Ministra (say, Asuna) to receive magical power from the Magic User (for example, Negi) with whom he or she has performed a *Pactio*. Unlike times when *Sim Mea Pars* ("May You Be a Part of Me") is cast by the Magic User to increase the magical power of the Ministra, *Sim Tua Pars* ("May I Be a Part of You") may be cast by the Ministra independently.

In the event the Magic User is asleep, or incapacitated in battle, he or she will obviously be unable to actively provide power to his or her Ministra. Even in those cases, however, the Ministra who has performed the Pactio with the Magic User is still obliged to defend them. This, then, is a spell designed to provide the Ministra with magical support—within certain limitations.

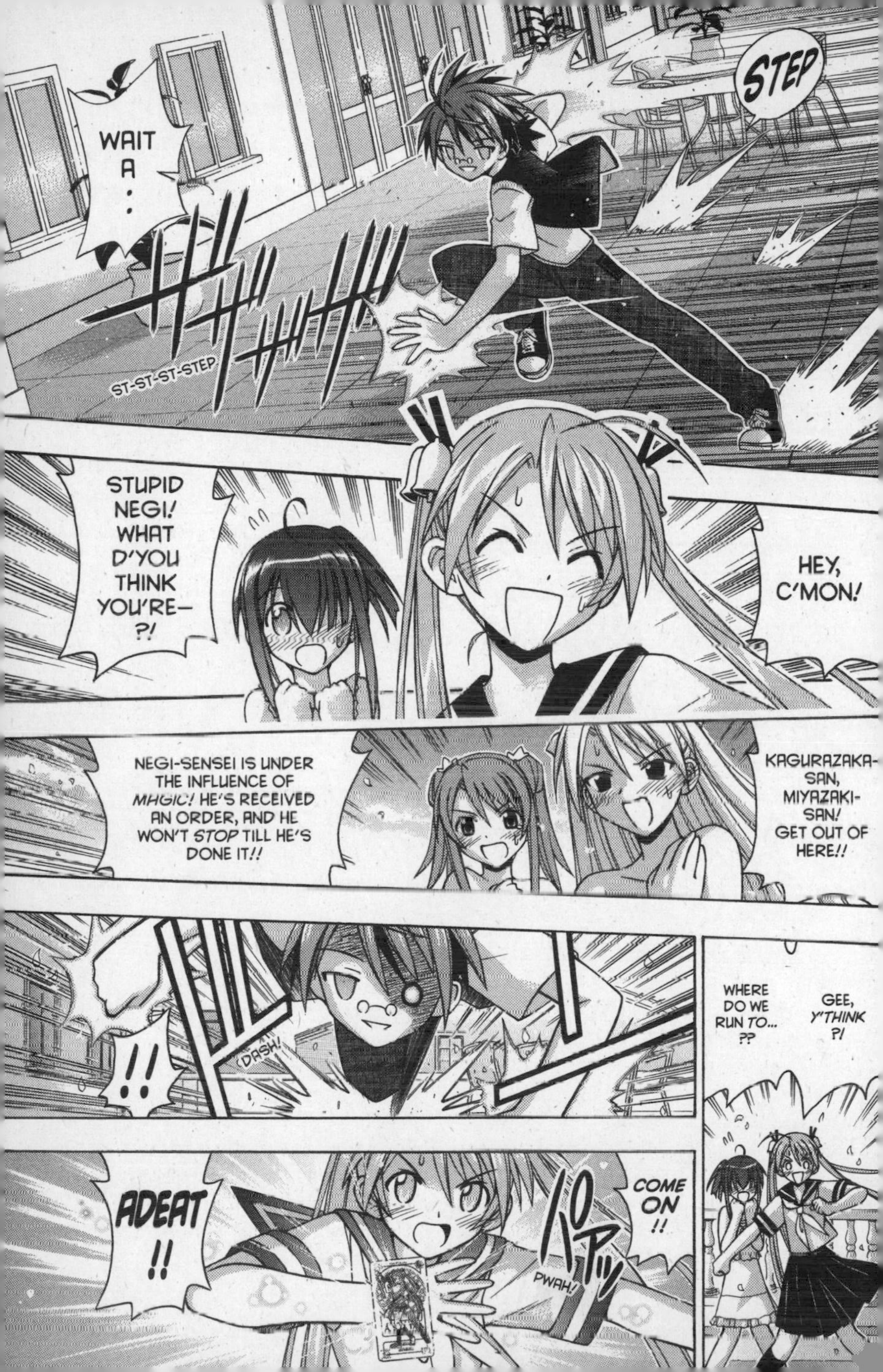
STEP
WAIT A . .
ST-ST-ST-STEP
HEY, C'MON!
STUPID NEGI! WHAT D'YOU THINK YOU'RE—?!
KAGURAZAKA-SAN, MIYAZAKI-SAN! GET OUT OF HERE!!
NEGI-SENSEI IS UNDER THE INFLUENCE OF *MAGIC*! HE'S RECEIVED AN ORDER, AND HE WON'T *STOP* TILL HE'S DONE IT!!
GEE, Y'THINK ?!
WHERE DO WE RUN *TO*... ??
DASH!
!!
COME ON !!
PWAH!
ADEAT !!

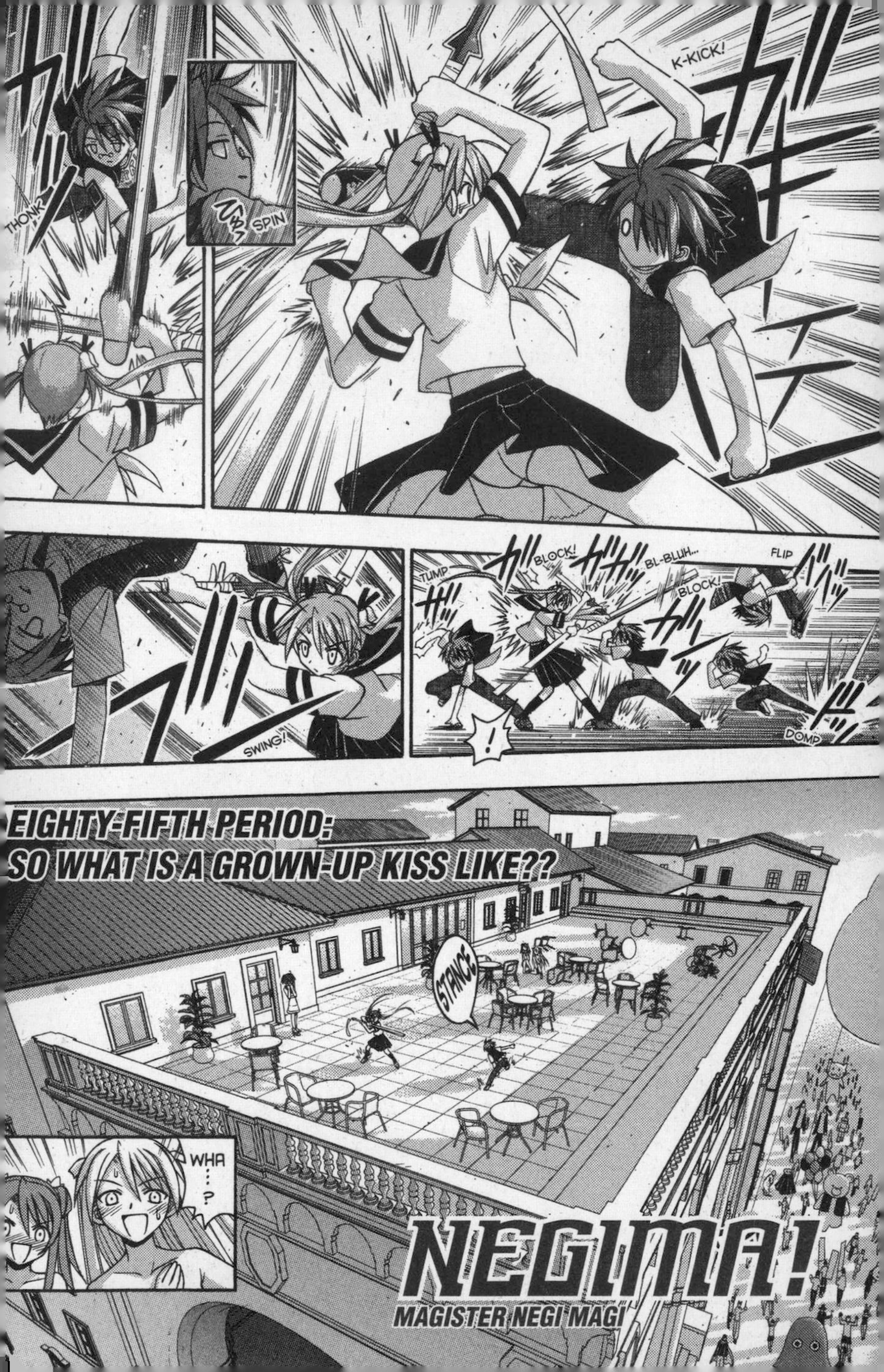

K-KICK!
SPIN
THONK
FLIP
BL-BLUH...
BLOCK!
BLOCK!
TUMP
DOMP
!
SWING!
EIGHTY-FIFTH PERIOD:
SO WHAT IS A GROWN-UP KISS LIKE??
STANCE
NEGIMA!
MAGISTER NEGI MAGI
WHA...?

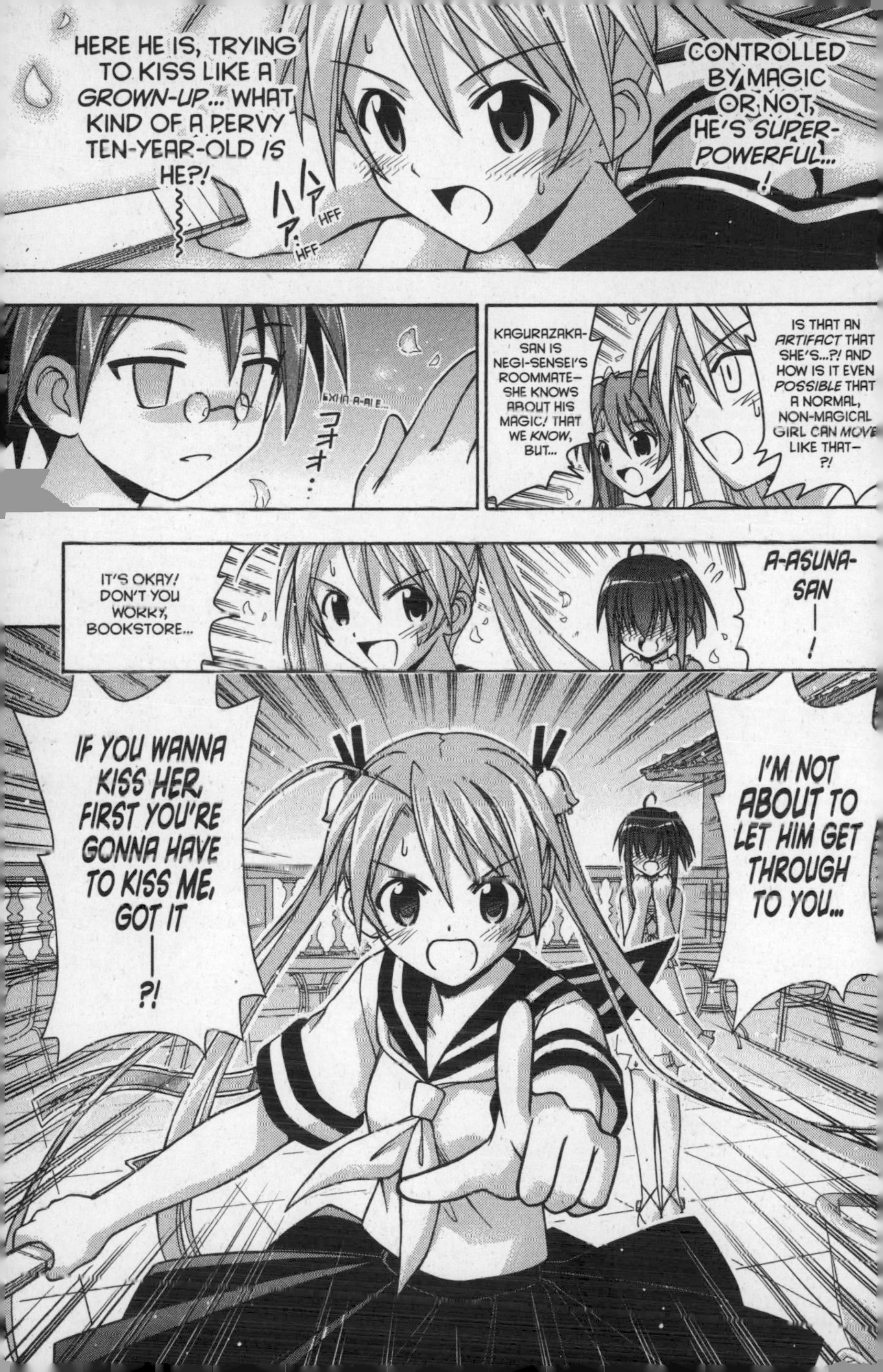
CONTROLLED BY MAGIC OR NOT, HE'S SUPER-POWERFUL...!
HERE HE IS, TRYING TO KISS LIKE A GROWN-UP... WHAT KIND OF A PERVY TEN-YEAR-OLD IS HE?!
ハア ハア
HFF HFF
IS THAT AN ARTIFACT THAT SHE'S...?! AND HOW IS IT EVEN POSSIBLE THAT A NORMAL, NON-MAGICAL GIRL CAN MOVE LIKE THAT—?!
KAGURAZAKA-SAN IS NEGI-SENSEI'S ROOMMATE—SHE KNOWS ABOUT HIS MAGIC! THAT WE KNOW, BUT...
EXHA-A-ALE...
フオオ…
A-ASUNA-SAN—!
IT'S OKAY! DON'T YOU WORRY, BOOKSTORE...
I'M NOT ABOUT TO LET HIM GET THROUGH TO YOU...
IF YOU WANNA KISS HER, FIRST YOU'RE GONNA HAVE TO KISS ME, GOT IT—?!

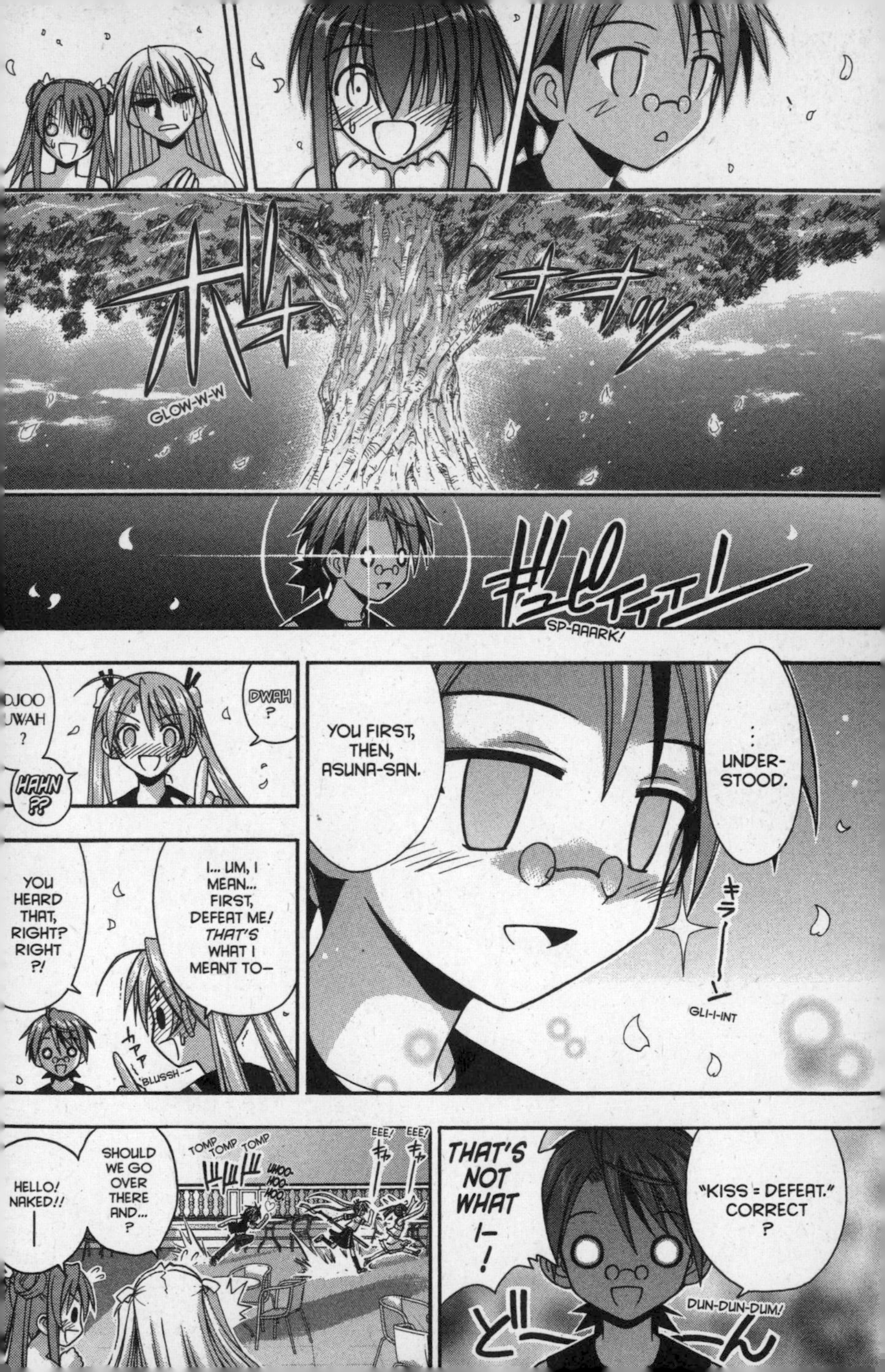
GLOW-W-W
SP-AAARK!
... UNDER-STOOD.
YOU FIRST, THEN, ASUNA-SAN.
GLI-I-INT
DWAH ?
DJOO UWAH ?
HAHN ??
I... UM, I MEAN... FIRST, DEFEAT ME! THAT'S WHAT I MEANT TO—
YOU HEARD THAT, RIGHT? RIGHT ?!
BLUSSH—
"KISS = DEFEAT." CORRECT ?
THAT'S NOT WHAT I— !
DUN-DUN-DUM!
EEE! EEE!
UHOO-HOO-HOO
TOMP TOMP TOMP
SHOULD WE GO OVER THERE AND... ?
HELLO! NAKED!!

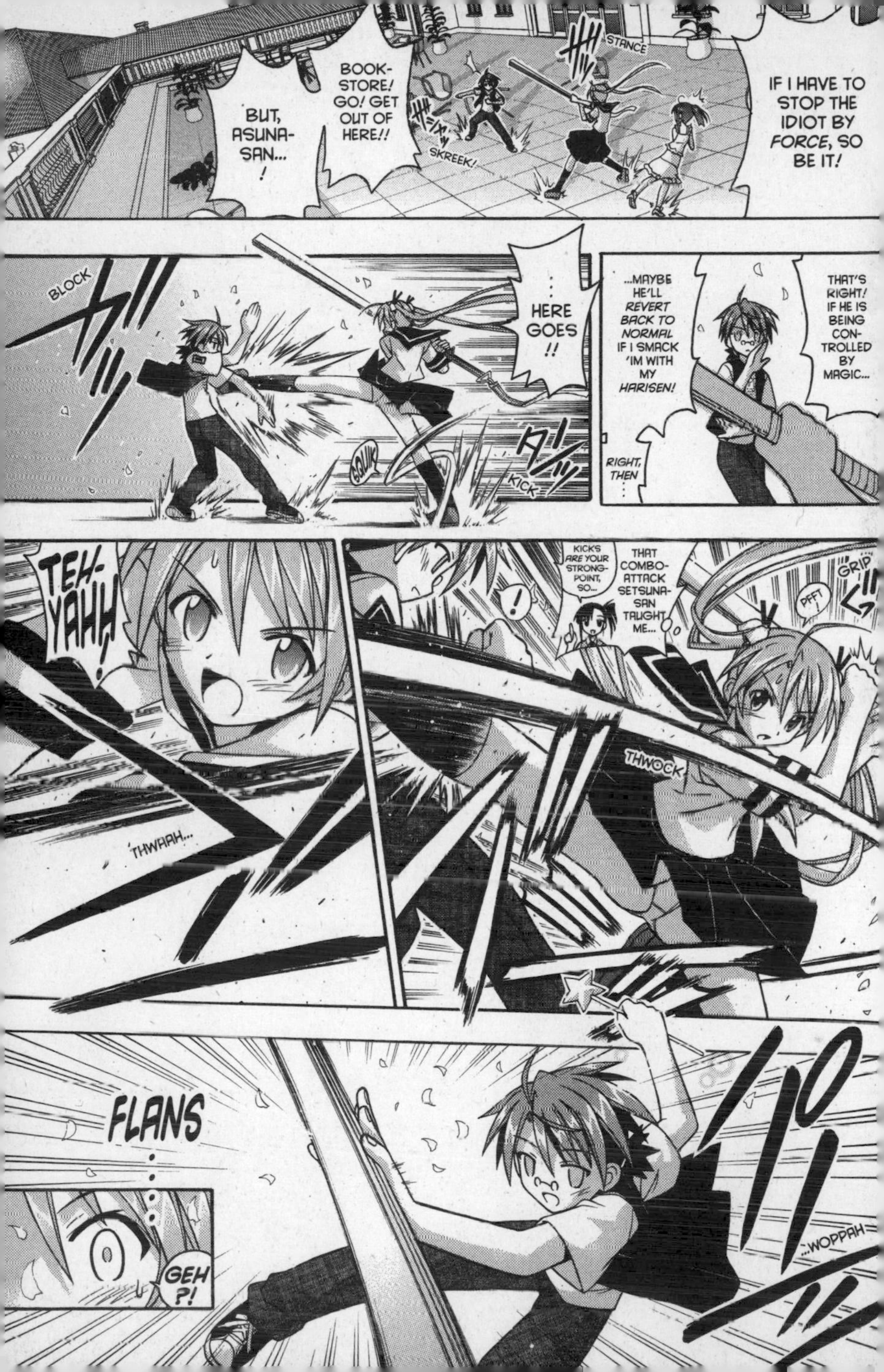
IF I HAVE TO STOP THE IDIOT BY *FORCE*, SO BE IT!
STANCE
BOOK-STORE! GO! GET OUT OF HERE!!
SKREEK!
BUT, ASUNA-SAN...!
THAT'S RIGHT! IF HE IS BEING CON-TROLLED BY MAGIC...
...MAYBE HE'LL *REVERT BACK TO NORMAL* IF I SMACK 'IM WITH MY *HARISEN!*
RIGHT, THEN...
...HERE GOES!!
KICK
SQUIK
BLOCK
GRIP
PFFT!
THAT COMBO-ATTACK SETSUNA-SAN TAUGHT ME...
KICKS *ARE* YOUR STRONG-POINT, SO...
!
THWOCK
TEH-YAHH!
THWAAH...
...WOPPAH
FLANS...
GEH?!

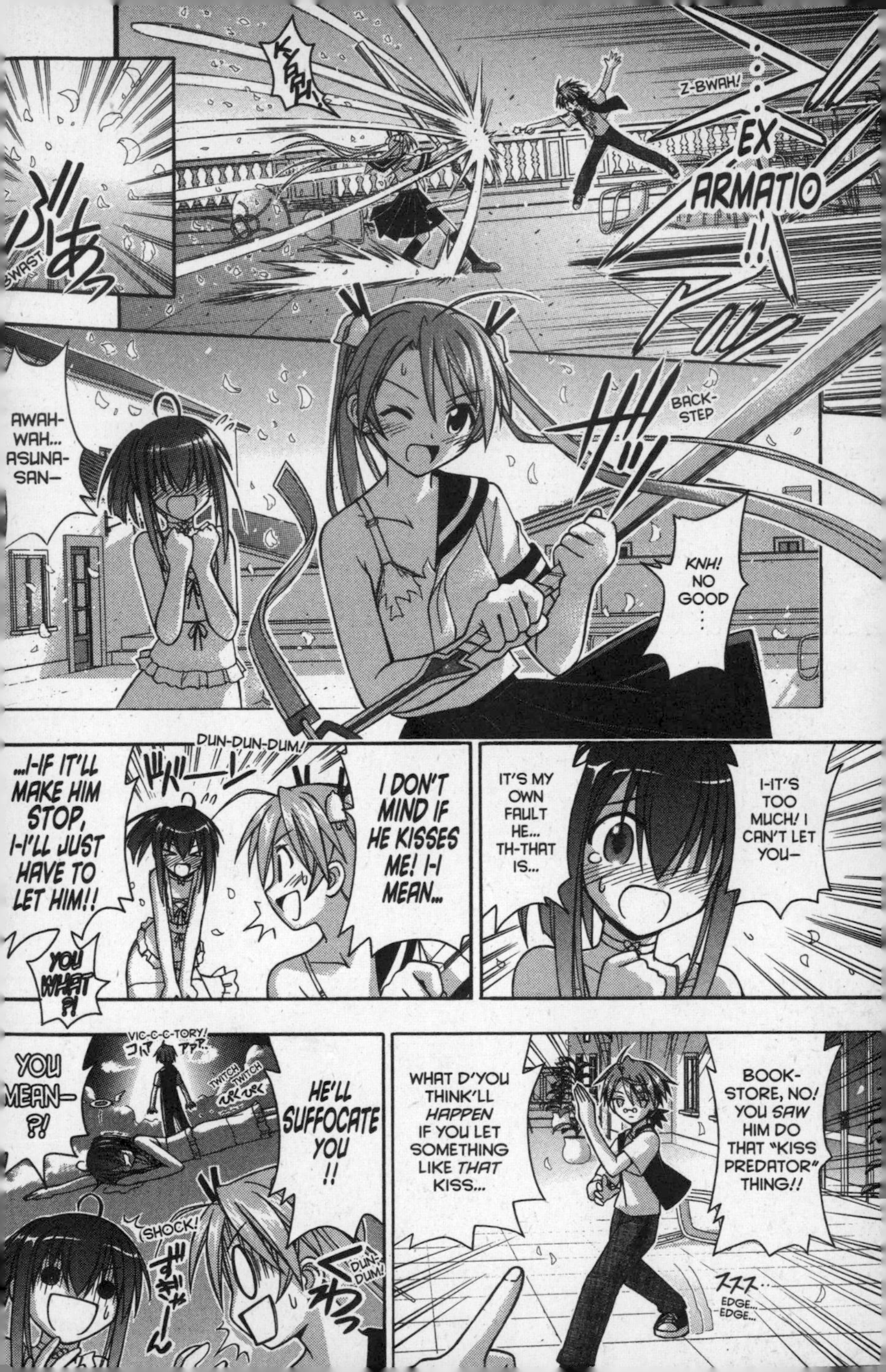
Z-BWAH!
EX ARMATIO!!
K-BOOM!
SWAST
BACK-STEP
KNH! NO GOOD...
AWAH-WAH... ASUNA-SAN—
I-IT'S TOO MUCH! I CAN'T LET YOU—
IT'S MY OWN FAULT HE... TH-THAT IS...
I DON'T MIND IF HE KISSES ME! I-I MEAN...
DUN-DUN-DUM!
...I-IF IT'LL MAKE HIM STOP, I-I'LL JUST HAVE TO LET HIM!!
YOU WHAT?!
BOOK-STORE, NO! YOU SAW HIM DO THAT "KISS PREDATOR" THING!!
WHAT D'YOU THINK'LL HAPPEN IF YOU LET SOMETHING LIKE THAT KISS...
EDGE... EDGE...
HE'LL SUFFOCATE YOU!!
VIC-C-C-TORY!
TWITCH TWITCH
YOU MEAN—?!
SHOCK!
DUN-DUM!

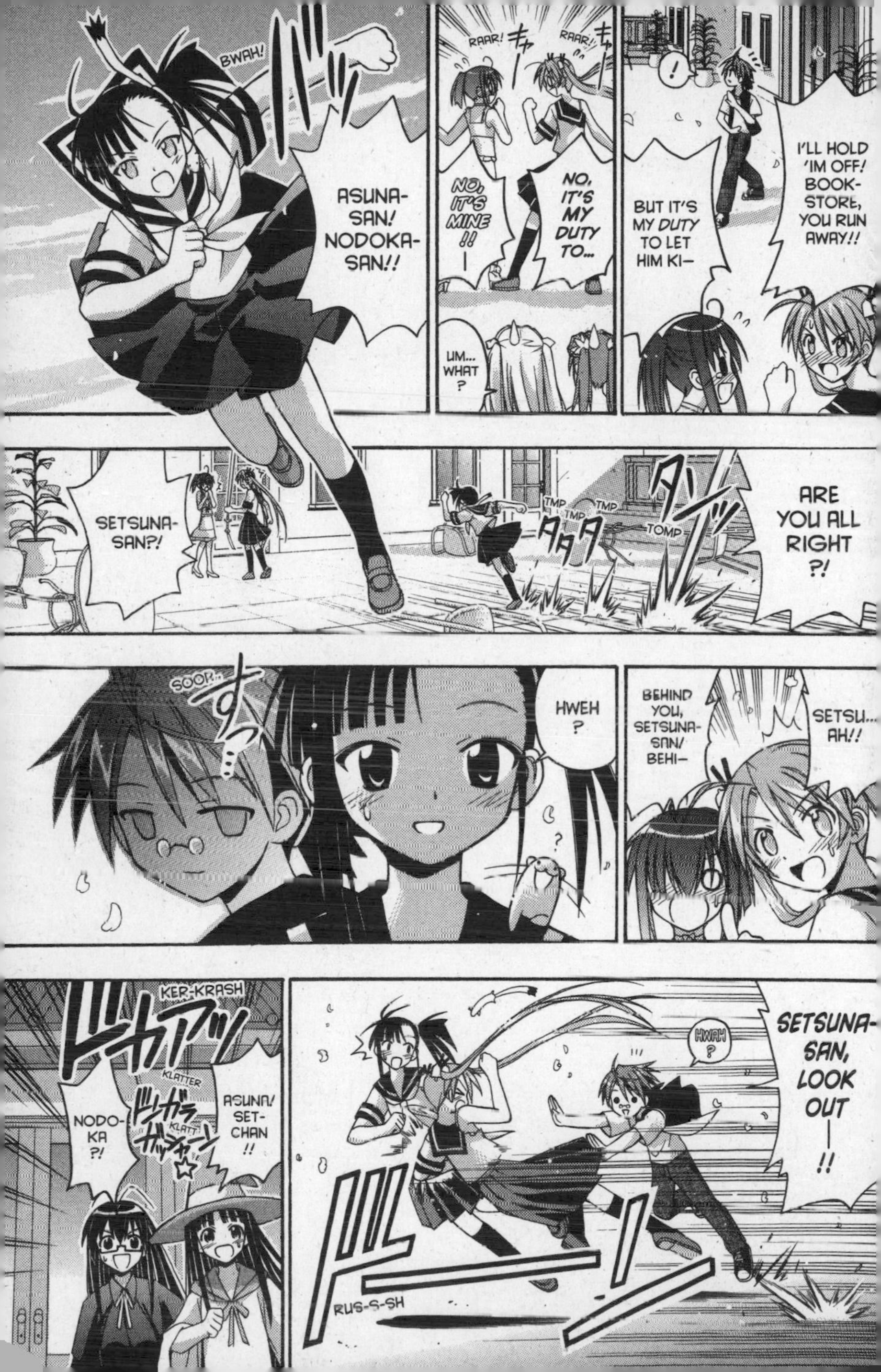
!
I'LL HOLD 'IM OFF! BOOK-STORE, YOU RUN AWAY!!
BUT IT'S MY DUTY TO LET HIM KI—
RAAR!
RAAR!
NO, IT'S MY DUTY TO...
NO, IT'S MINE!! —
UM... WHAT?
BWAH!
ASUNA-SAN! NODOKA-SAN!!
ARE YOU ALL RIGHT ?!
TOMP
TMP TMP TMP
SETSUNA-SAN?!
SETSU... AH!!
BEHIND YOU, SETSUNA-SAN! BEHI—
HWEH ?
SOOR..
SETSUNA-SAN, LOOK OUT —!!
HWAH ?
RUS-S-SH
KER-KRASH
ASUNA! SET-CHAN !!
KLATTER
KLATT
NODOKA ?!

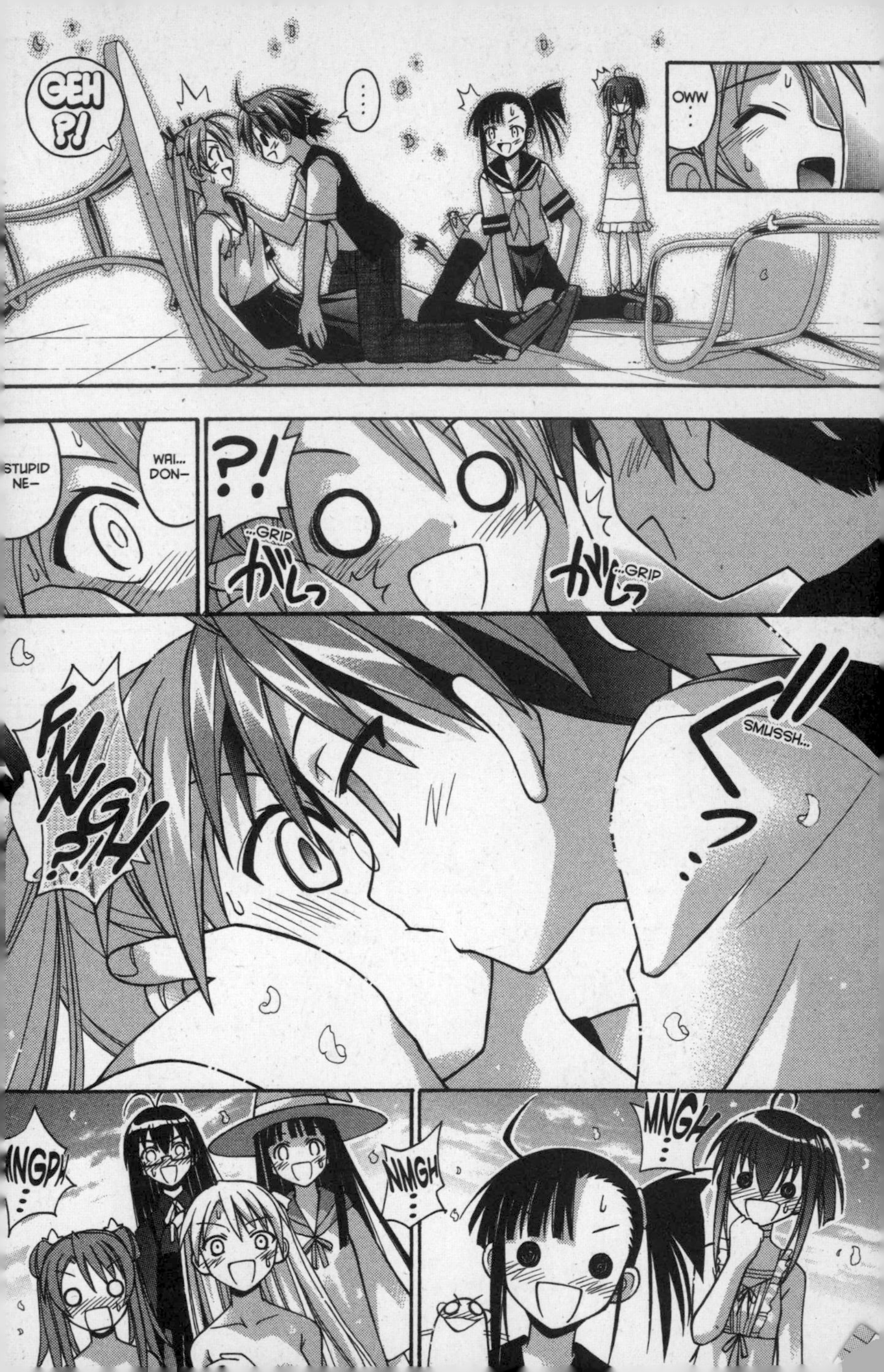

OWW...
....
GEH P!
がしっ
...GRIP
?!
がしっ
...GRIP
WAI... DON–
STUPID NE–
SMUSSH...
FMNGH ?!
MNGH...
NMGH
MNGPH...

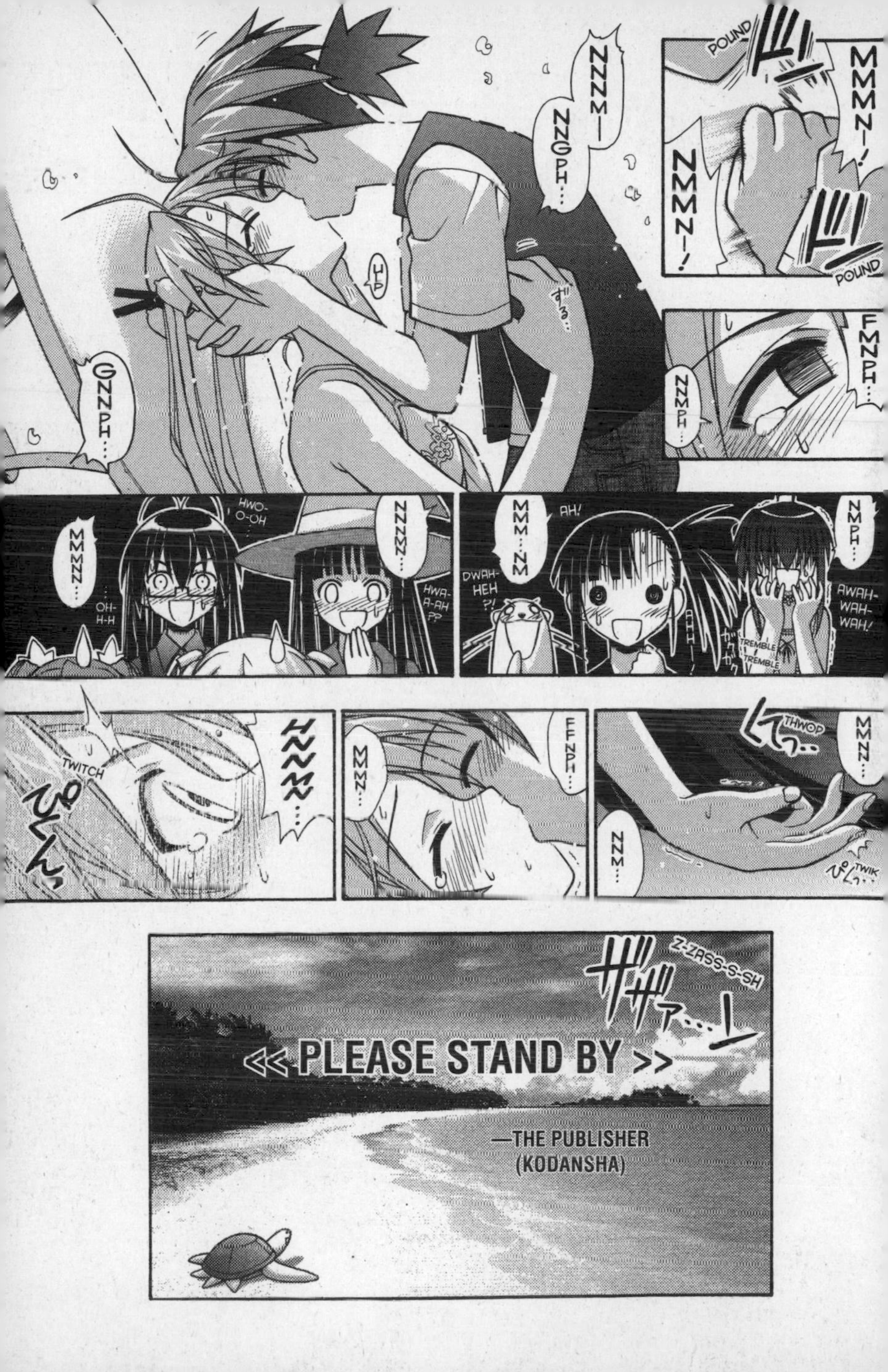
POUND
MMMNI—!
NMMNI—!
POUND
FMNPH...
NNMPH...
NNNMI—
NNGPH...
UP
ずる...
GNNPH...
NMPH...
AWAH-WAH-WAH!
TREMBLE
TREMBLE
MMM...NM
AH!
DWAH-HEH?!
NNNMN...
HWA-A-AH??
HWO-O-OH
MMMNN...
OH-H-H
MMN...
THWOP
NNM...
TWIK
FFNPH...
MMMN...
HNNMN...
TWITCH
Z-ZASS-S-SH
<< PLEASE STAND BY >>
—THE PUBLISHER
(KODANSHA)

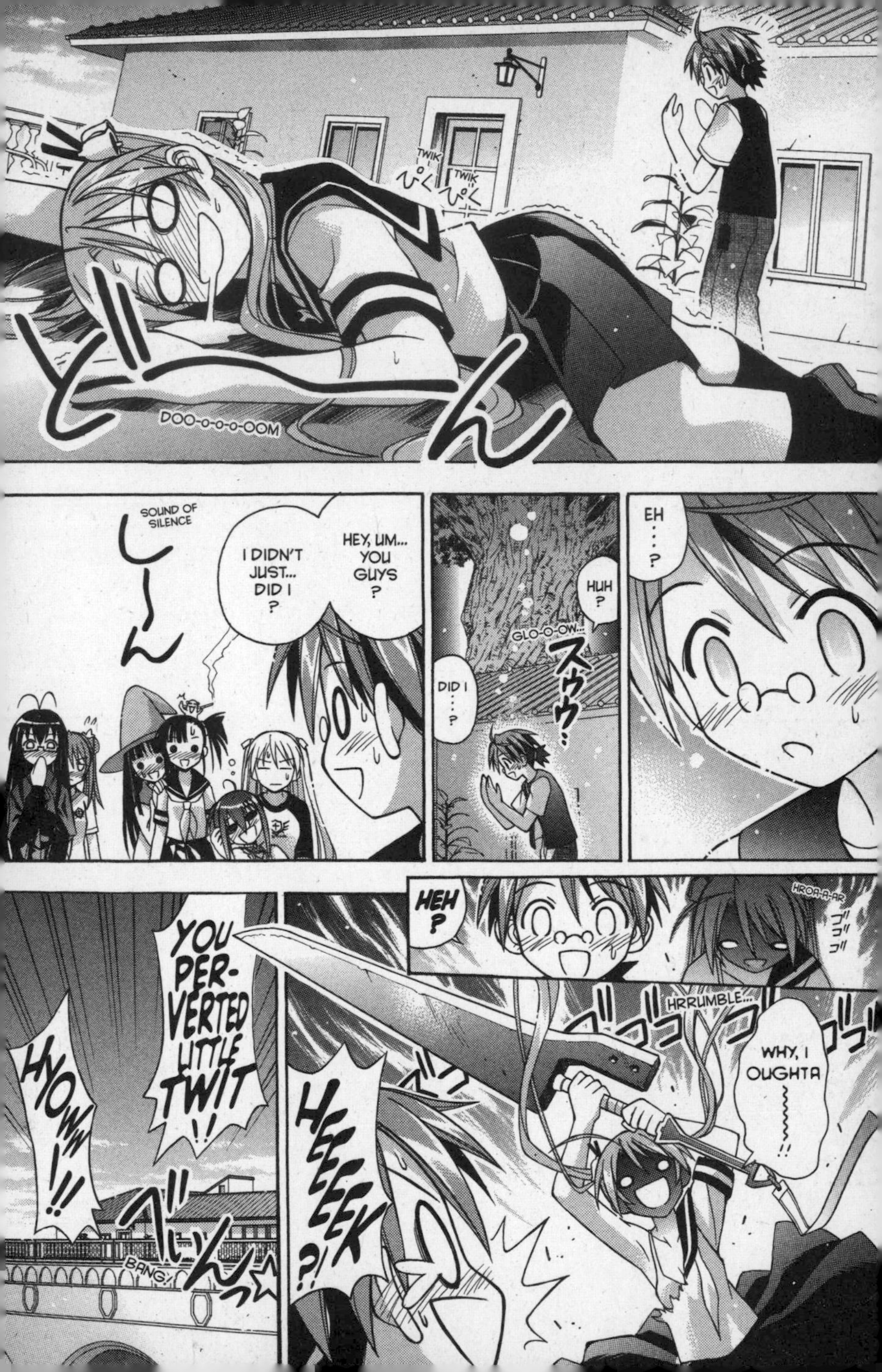
TWIK TWIK
DOO-o-o-o-OOM
EH...?
HUH?
GLO-O-OW...
DID I...?
HEY, UM... YOU GUYS?
I DIDN'T JUST... DID I?
SOUND OF SILENCE
HROA-A-AR
HEH?
HRRUMBLE...
WHY, I OUGHTA~~!!
HEEEEK?!
YOU PERVERTED LITTLE TWIT!!
KYOWW!!!
BANG!

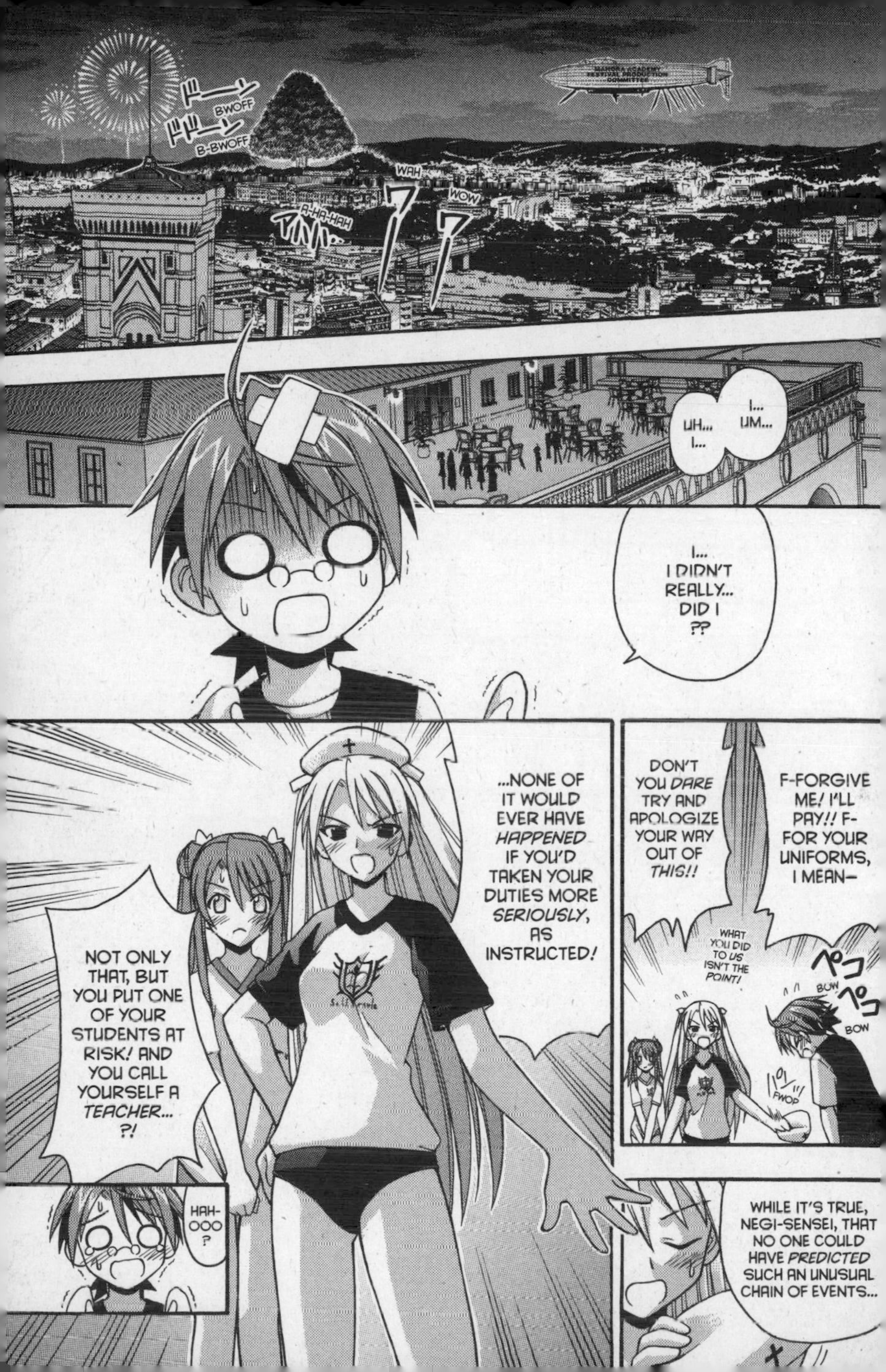
MAHORA ACADEMY FESTIVAL PRODUCTION COMMITTEE
ドーン
BWOFF
ドドーン
B-BWOFF
ワ
WAH
ワ
WOW
A-HA-HAH
I... UM...
UH... I...
I... I DIDN'T REALLY... DID I ??
F-FORGIVE ME! I'LL PAY!! F-FOR YOUR UNIFORMS, I MEAN—
DON'T YOU *DARE* TRY AND APOLOGIZE YOUR WAY OUT OF *THIS!!*
WHAT YOU DID TO US ISN'T THE *POINT!*
ペコ
BOW
ペコ
BOW
FWOP
...NONE OF IT WOULD EVER HAVE *HAPPENED* IF YOU'D TAKEN YOUR DUTIES MORE *SERIOUSLY,* AS INSTRUCTED!
NOT ONLY THAT, BUT YOU PUT ONE OF YOUR STUDENTS AT RISK! AND YOU CALL YOURSELF A *TEACHER...* ?!
WHILE IT'S TRUE, NEGI-SENSEI, THAT NO ONE COULD HAVE *PREDICTED* SUCH AN UNUSUAL CHAIN OF EVENTS...
HAH-OOO?

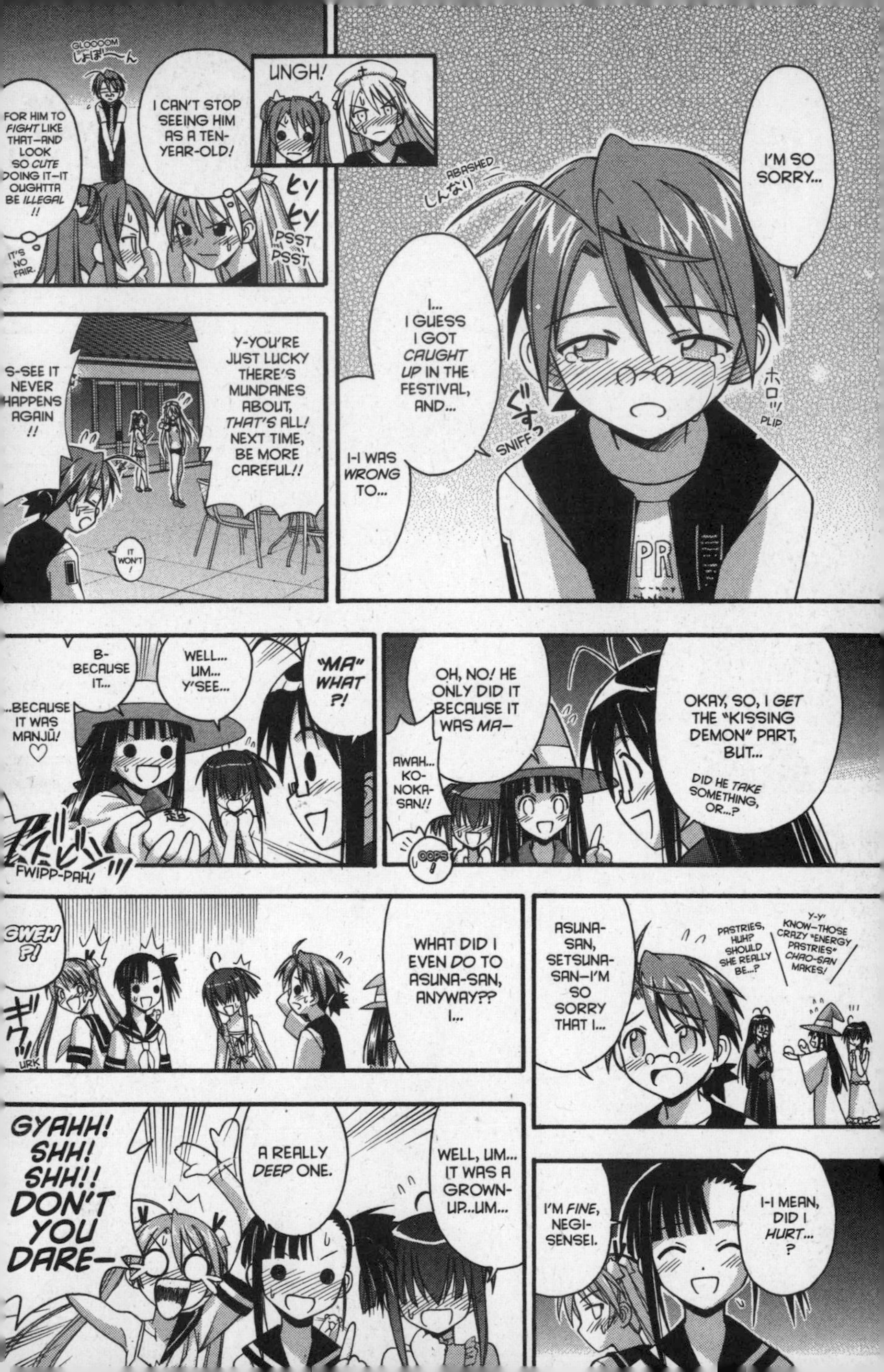
I'M SO SORRY...
ABASHED
しんなり
I... I GUESS I GOT CAUGHT UP IN THE FESTIVAL, AND...
I-I WAS WRONG TO...
ぐすっ
SNIFF
ホロッ
PLIP
UNGH!
I CAN'T STOP SEEING HIM AS A TEN-YEAR-OLD!
とソ とソ
PSST PSST
GLOOOOM
しょぼ〜ん
FOR HIM TO FIGHT LIKE THAT—AND LOOK SO CUTE DOING IT—IT OUGHTTA BE ILLEGAL!!
IT'S NO FAIR.
Y-YOU'RE JUST LUCKY THERE'S MUNDANES ABOUT, THAT'S ALL! NEXT TIME, BE MORE CAREFUL!!
S-SEE IT NEVER HAPPENS AGAIN!!
IT WON'T!
OKAY, SO, I GET THE "KISSING DEMON" PART, BUT...
DID HE TAKE SOMETHING, OR...?
OH, NO! HE ONLY DID IT BECAUSE IT WAS MA—
AWAH... KONOKA-SAN!!
OOPS
"MA" WHAT?!
WELL... UM... Y'SEE...
B-BECAUSE IT...
...BECAUSE IT WAS MANJŪ! ♡
FWIPP-PAH!
Y-Y'KNOW—THOSE CRAZY "ENERGY PASTRIES" CHAO-SAN MAKES!
PASTRIES, HUH? SHOULD SHE REALLY BE...?
ASUNA-SAN, SETSUNA-SAN—I'M SO SORRY THAT I...
WHAT DID I EVEN DO TO ASUNA-SAN, ANYWAY?? I...
SWEH?!
ギクッ
URK
I-I MEAN, DID I HURT...?
I'M FINE, NEGI-SENSEI.
WELL, UM... IT WAS A GROWN-UP...UM...
A REALLY DEEP ONE.
GYAHH! SHH! SHH!! DON'T YOU DARE—

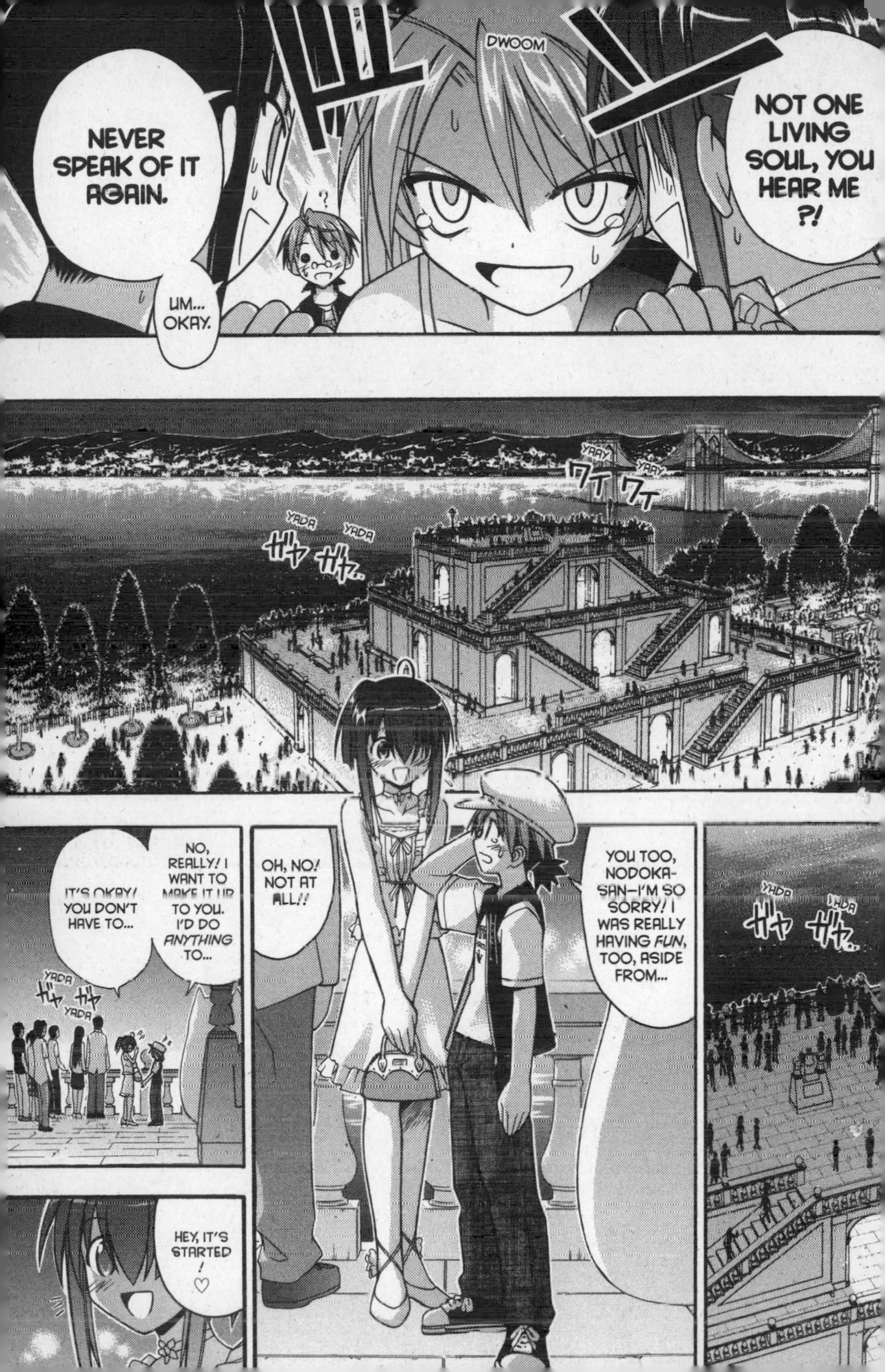
DWOOM
NOT ONE LIVING SOUL, YOU HEAR ME ?!
NEVER SPEAK OF IT AGAIN.
UM... OKAY.
YAAY YAAY
ワイ ワイ
YADA YADA
ガヤ ガヤ..
YADA YADA
ガヤ ガヤ..
YOU TOO, NODOKA-SAN—I'M SO SORRY! I WAS REALLY HAVING FUN, TOO, ASIDE FROM...
OH, NO! NOT AT ALL!!
NO, REALLY! I WANT TO MAKE IT UP TO YOU. I'D DO ANYTHING TO...
IT'S OKAY! YOU DON'T HAVE TO...
YADA YADA
ガヤ ガヤ
HEY, IT'S STARTED! ♡

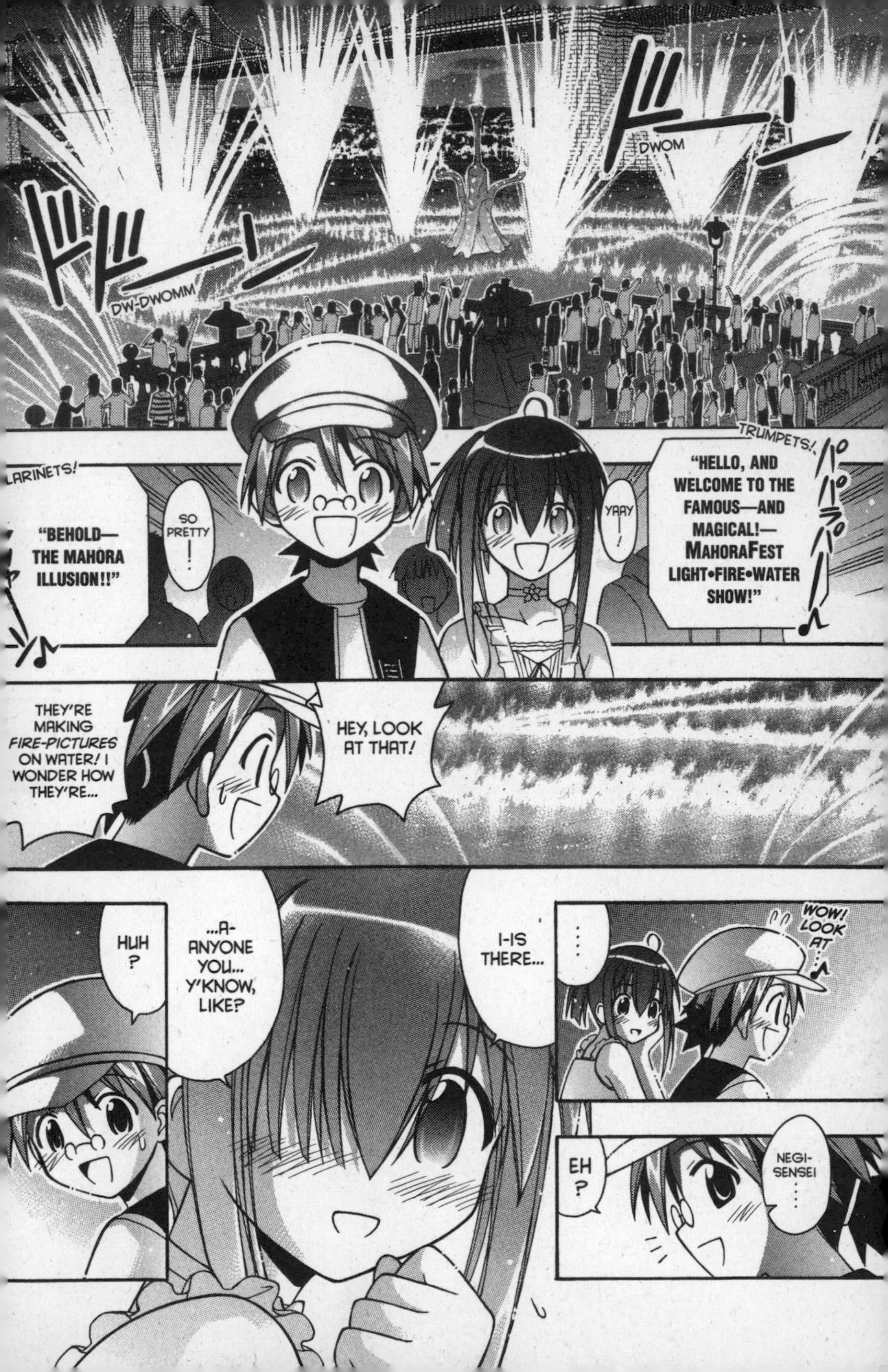
DWOM
DW-DWOMM
TRUMPETS!
"HELLO, AND WELCOME TO THE FAMOUS—AND MAGICAL!—MAHORAFEST LIGHT•FIRE•WATER SHOW!"
YAAY—!
SO PRETTY—!
LARINETS!
"BEHOLD—THE MAHORA ILLUSION!!"
HEY, LOOK AT THAT!
THEY'RE MAKING FIRE-PICTURES ON WATER! I WONDER HOW THEY'RE...
WOW! LOOK AT...
...
NEGI-SENSEI...
EH?
I-IS THERE...
...A-ANYONE YOU... Y'KNOW, LIKE?
HUH?

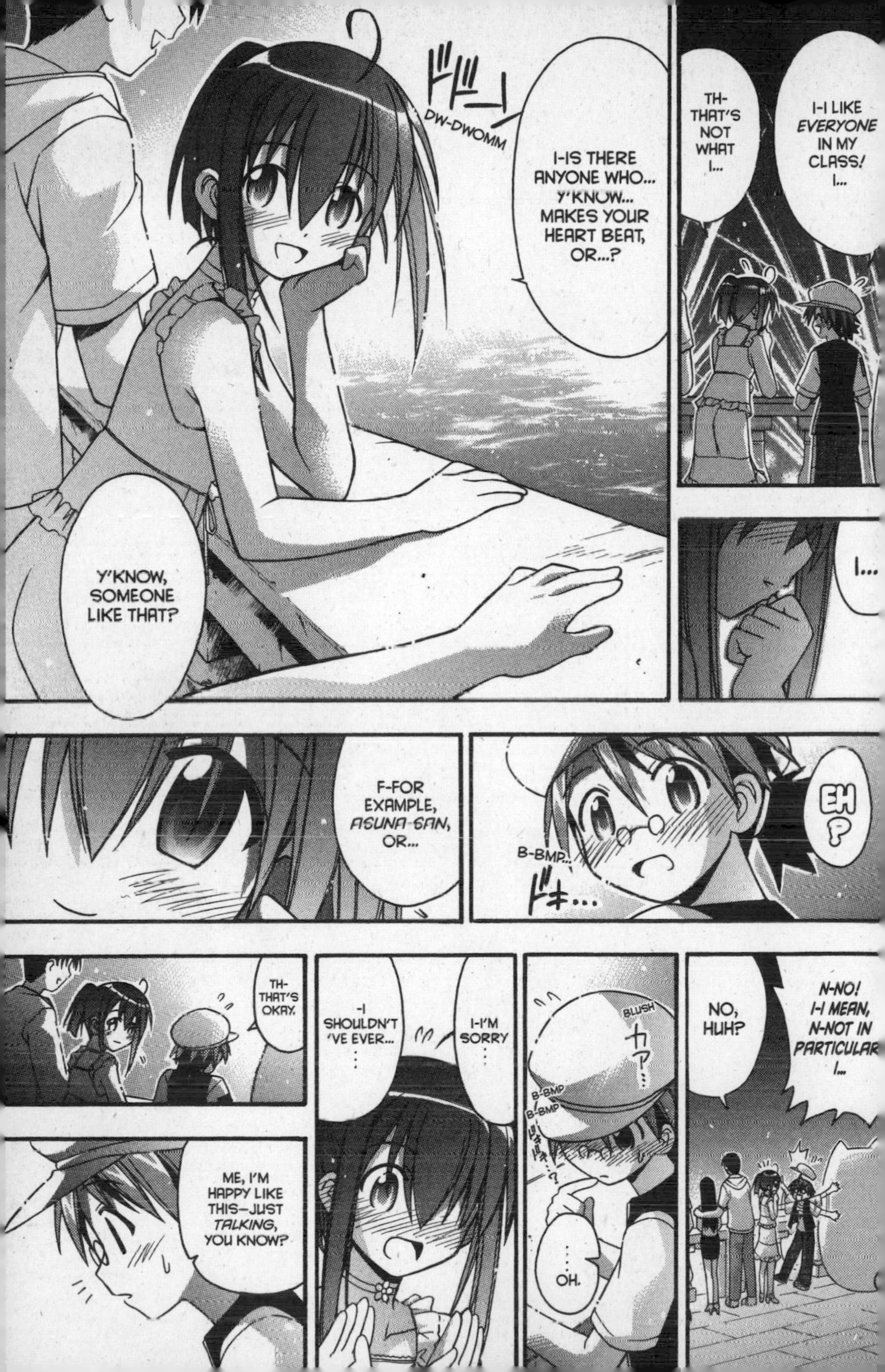
I-I LIKE *EVERYONE* IN MY CLASS! I...
TH-THAT'S NOT WHAT I...
I...
ドドーン
DW-DWOMM
I-IS THERE ANYONE WHO... Y'KNOW... MAKES YOUR HEART BEAT, OR...?
Y'KNOW, SOMEONE LIKE THAT?
EH?
B-BMP...
ドキ...
F-FOR EXAMPLE, *ASUNA-SAN*, OR...
N-NO! I-I MEAN, N-NOT IN PARTICULAR I...
NO, HUH?
BLUSH
カァ...
B-BMP B-BMP
...OH.
I-I'M SORRY...
-I SHOULDN'T 'VE EVER...
TH-THAT'S OKAY.
ME, I'M HAPPY LIKE THIS—JUST *TALKING*, YOU KNOW?

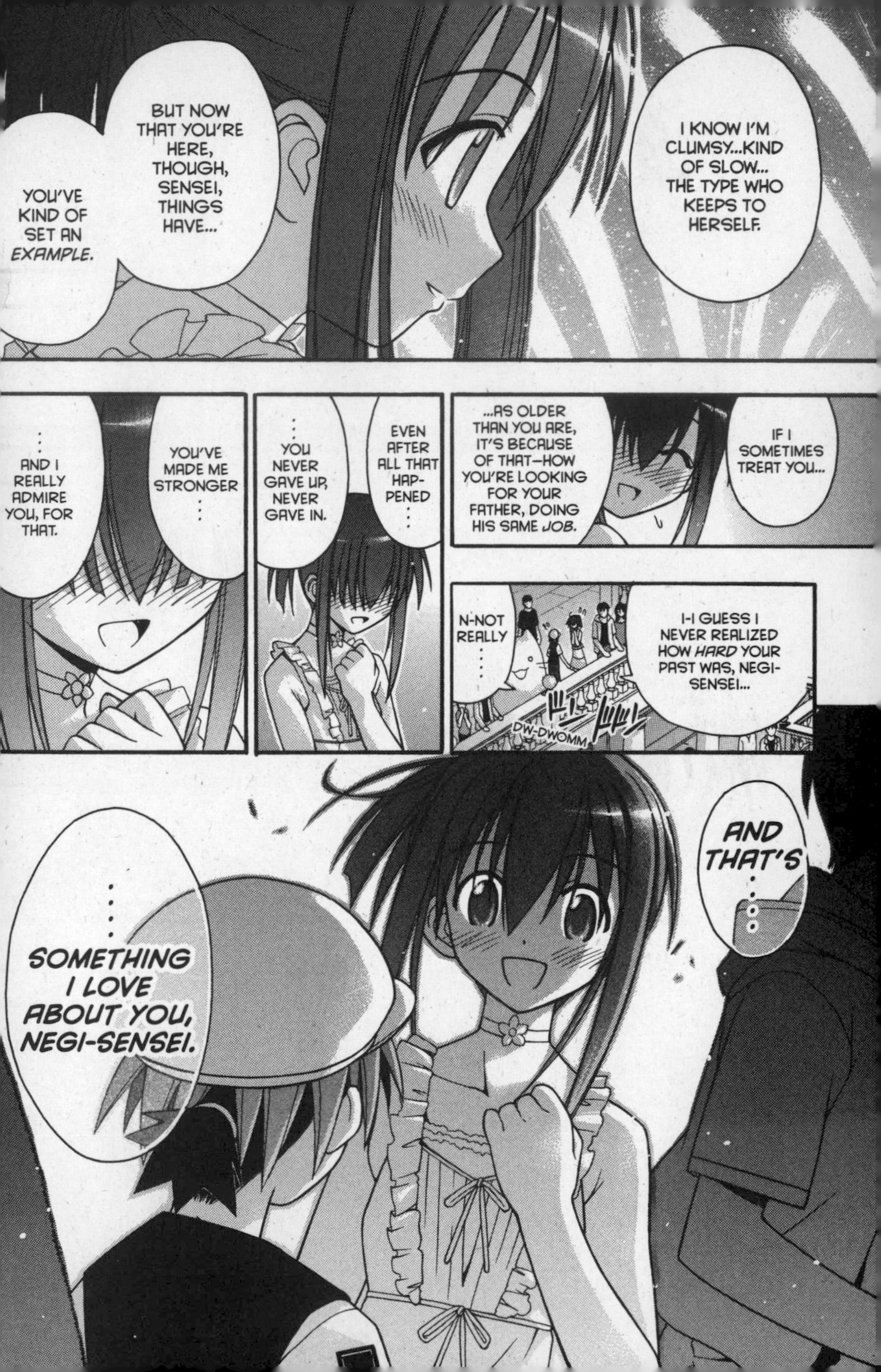

I KNOW I'M CLUMSY...KIND OF SLOW... THE TYPE WHO KEEPS TO HERSELF.
BUT NOW THAT YOU'RE HERE, THOUGH, SENSEI, THINGS HAVE...
YOU'VE KIND OF SET AN *EXAMPLE*.
IF I SOMETIMES TREAT YOU...
...AS OLDER THAN YOU ARE, IT'S BECAUSE OF THAT—HOW YOU'RE LOOKING FOR YOUR FATHER, DOING HIS SAME *JOB*.
I-I GUESS I NEVER REALIZED HOW *HARD* YOUR PAST WAS, NEGI-SENSEI...
N-NOT REALLY...
DW-DWOMM
EVEN AFTER ALL THAT HAPPENED...
...YOU NEVER GAVE UP, NEVER GAVE IN.
YOU'VE MADE ME STRONGER...
...AND I REALLY ADMIRE YOU, FOR THAT.
AND THAT'S...
...SOMETHING I LOVE ABOUT YOU, NEGI-SENSEI.

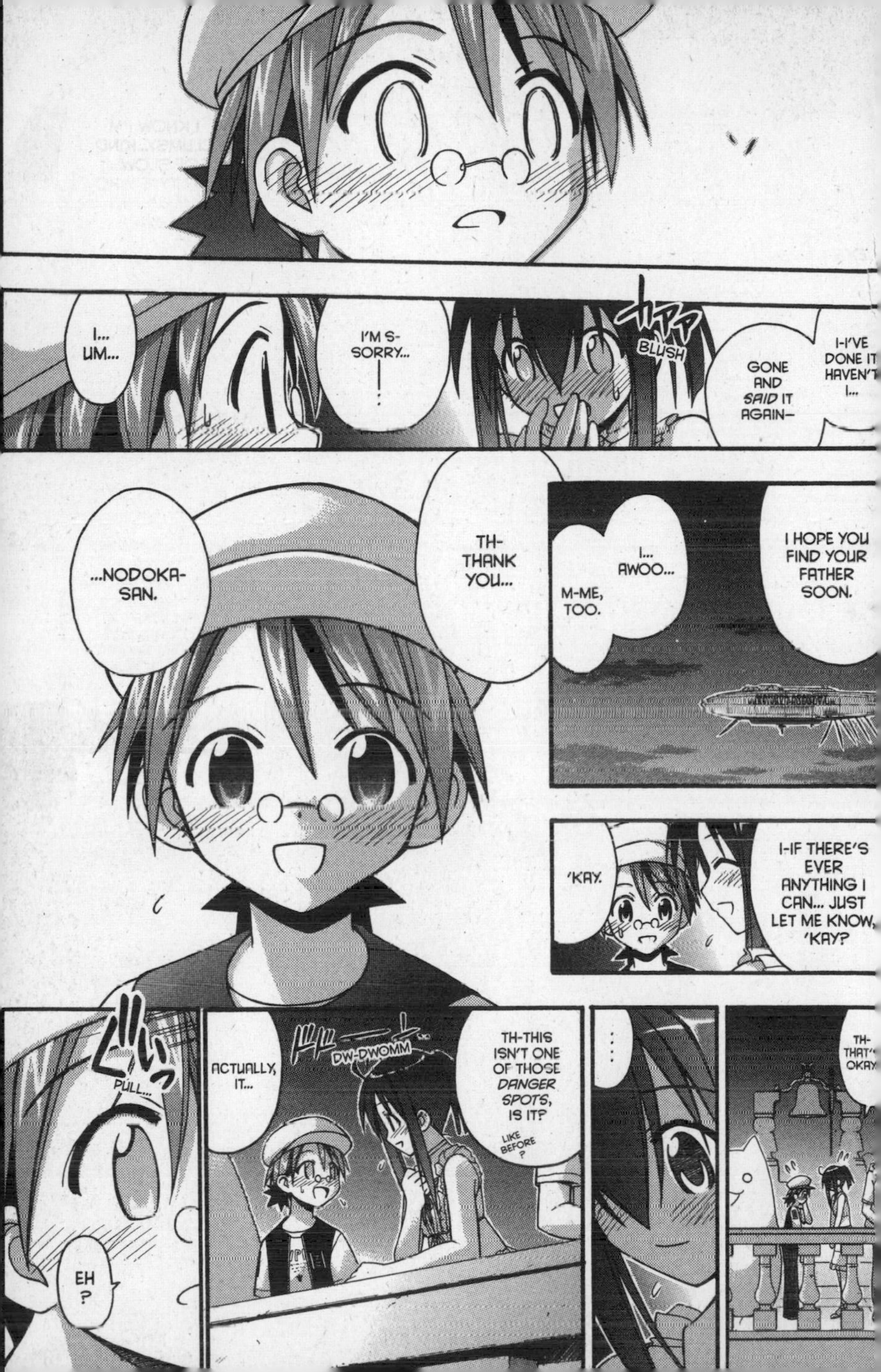
I-I'VE DONE IT HAVEN'T I...
GONE AND *SAID* IT AGAIN—
BLUSH
I'M S-SORRY...
I... UM...
I HOPE YOU FIND YOUR FATHER SOON.
I... AWOO...
M-ME, TOO.
I-IF THERE'S EVER ANYTHING I CAN... JUST LET ME KNOW, 'KAY?
'KAY.
TH-THANK YOU...
...NODOKA-SAN.
TH-THAT'S OKAY
....
TH-THIS ISN'T ONE OF THOSE *DANGER SPOTS*, IS IT?
LIKE BEFORE?
DW-DWOMM
ACTUALLY, IT...
PULL...
EH?

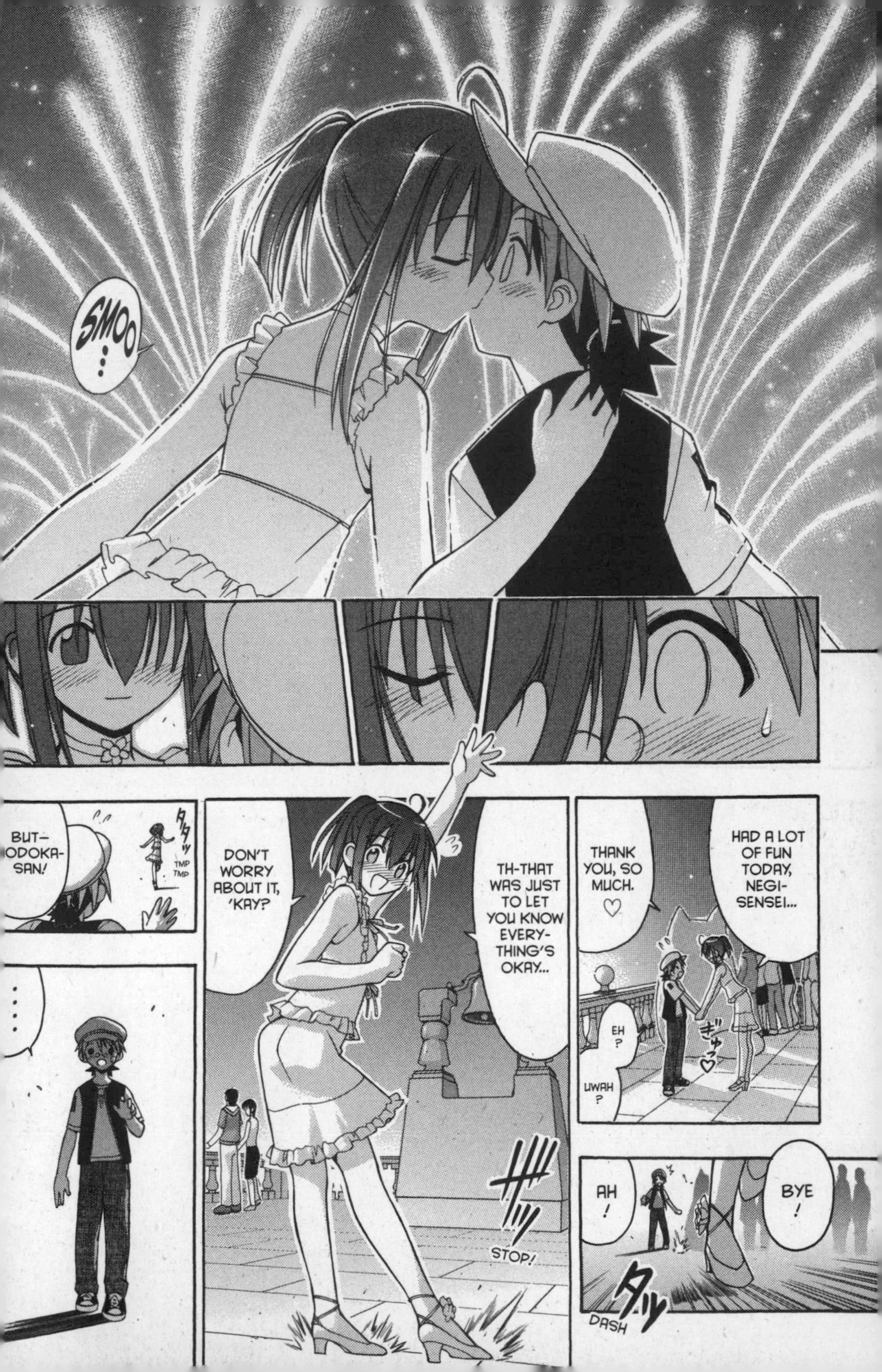
SMOO...
HAD A LOT OF FUN TODAY, NEGI-SENSEI...
THANK YOU, SO MUCH. ♡
EH?
UWAH?
ぎゅっ♡
BYE!
AH!
DASH
TH-THAT WAS JUST TO LET YOU KNOW EVERYTHING'S OKAY...
DON'T WORRY ABOUT IT, 'KAY?
STOP!
BUT– ODOKA-SAN!
TMP TMP
....

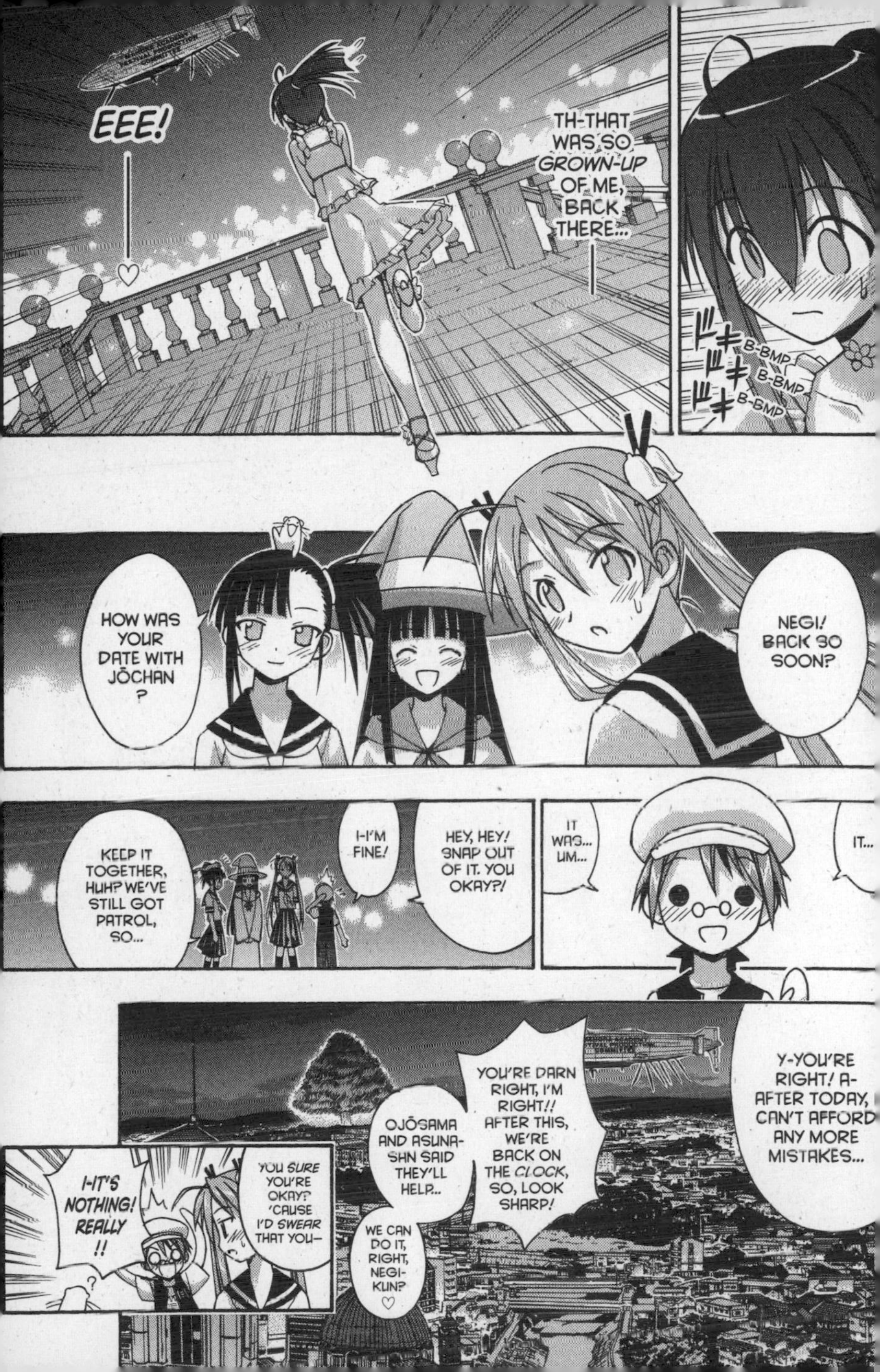
ドキ B-BMP
ドキ B-BMP
ドキ B-BMP
TH-THAT WAS SO GROWN-UP OF ME, BACK THERE...
EEE! ♡
NEGI! BACK SO SOON?
HOW WAS YOUR DATE WITH JŌCHAN?
IT...
IT WAS... UM...
HEY, HEY! SNAP OUT OF IT. YOU OKAY?!
I-I'M FINE!
KEEP IT TOGETHER, HUH? WE'VE STILL GOT PATROL, SO...
Y-YOU'RE RIGHT! A-AFTER TODAY, CAN'T AFFORD ANY MORE MISTAKES...
YOU'RE DARN RIGHT, I'M RIGHT!! AFTER THIS, WE'RE BACK ON THE CLOCK, SO, LOOK SHARP!
OJŌSAMA AND ASUNA-SAN SAID THEY'LL HELP...
WE CAN DO IT, RIGHT, NEGI-KUN? ♡
YOU SURE YOU'RE OKAY? 'CAUSE I'D SWEAR THAT YOU—
I-IT'S NOTHING! REALLY!!
?

STUDENT NUMBER 18
TATSUMIYA, MANA
BORN: 17 NOVEMBER 1988
BLOODTYPE: A
LIKES: DARTS, BILLIARDS, "ANMITSU"
      JAPANESE DESSERT, PUPPIES
DISLIKES: OKRA, SHRIMP
AFFILIATIONS: BIATHLON
      (UNIVERSITY-LEVEL)

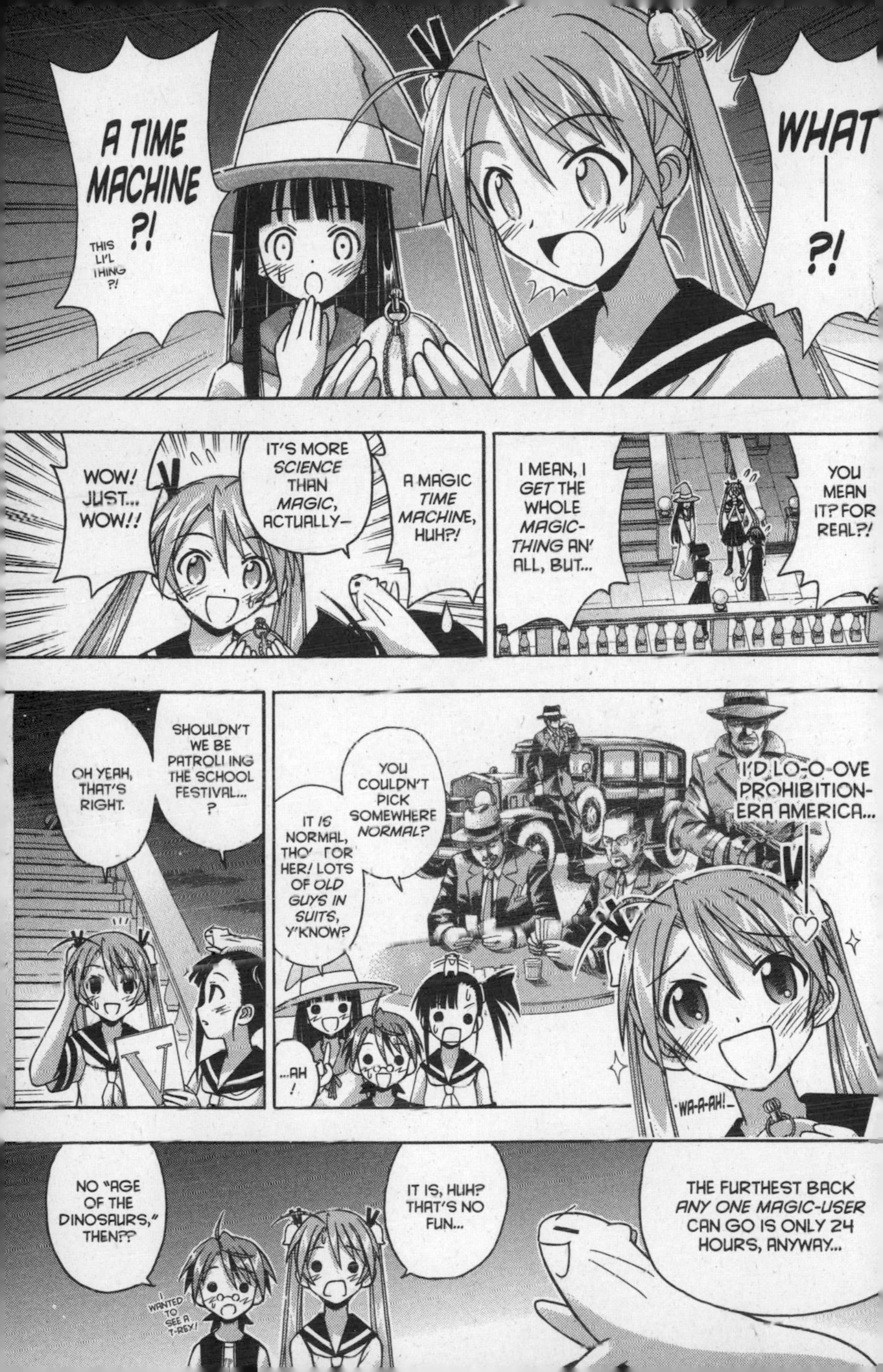
WHAT —— ?!
A TIME MACHINE ?!
THIS LI'L THING ?!
YOU MEAN IT? FOR REAL?!
I MEAN, I GET THE WHOLE MAGIC-THING AN' ALL, BUT...
A MAGIC TIME MACHINE, HUH?!
IT'S MORE SCIENCE THAN MAGIC, ACTUALLY—
WOW! JUST... WOW!!
I'D LO-O-OVE PROHIBITION-ERA AMERICA...
YOU COULDN'T PICK SOMEWHERE NORMAL?
IT IS NORMAL, THO' FOR HER! LOTS OF OLD GUYS IN SUITS, Y'KNOW?
...AH !
WA-A-AH!
SHOULDN'T WE BE PATROLLING THE SCHOOL FESTIVAL... ?
OH YEAH, THAT'S RIGHT.
THE FURTHEST BACK ANY ONE MAGIC-USER CAN GO IS ONLY 24 HOURS, ANYWAY...
IT IS, HUH? THAT'S NO FUN...
NO "AGE OF THE DINOSAURS," THEN??
I WANTED TO SEE A T-REX!

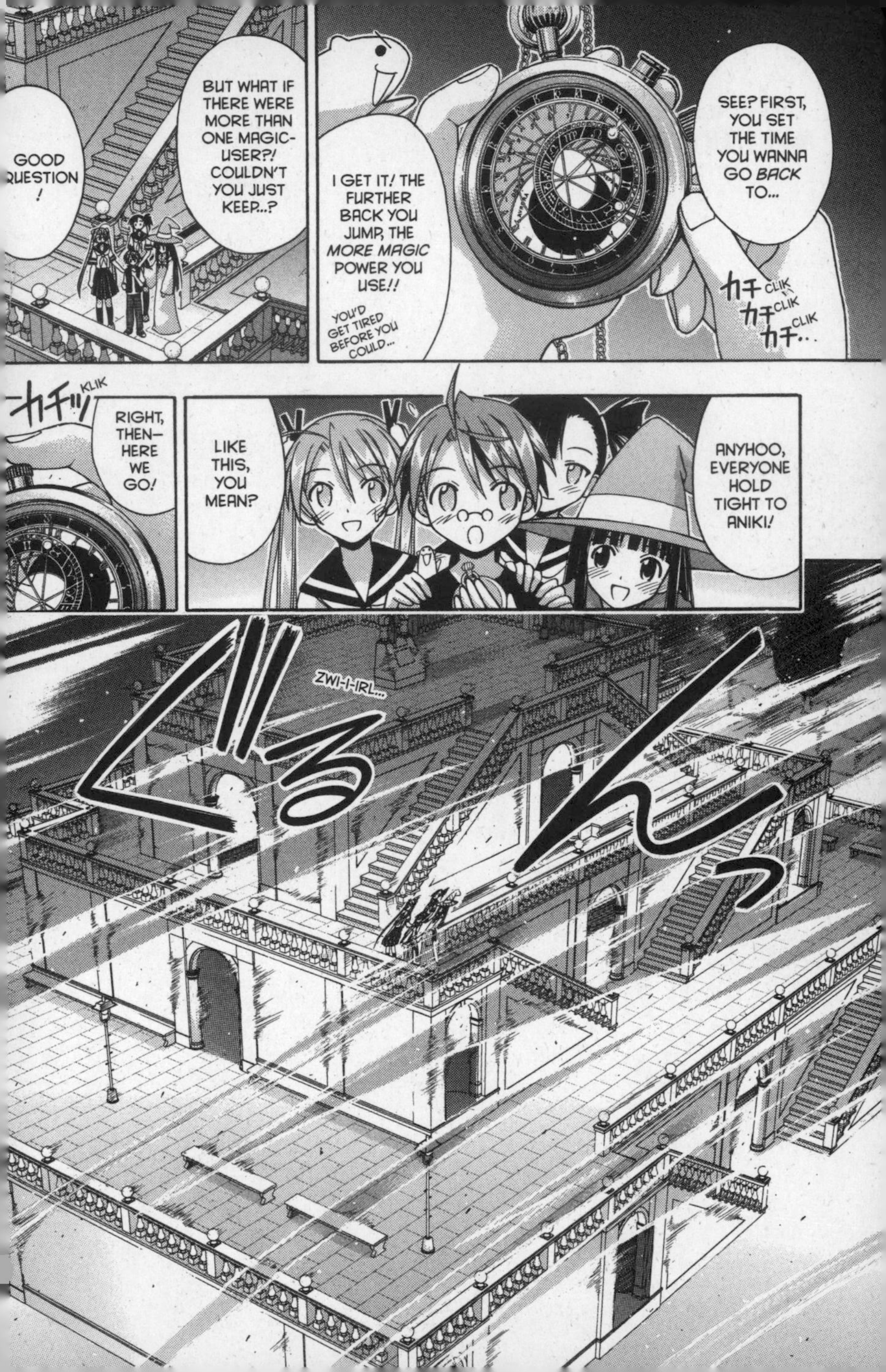
SEE? FIRST, YOU SET THE TIME YOU WANNA GO *BACK* TO...
カチ CLIK
カチ CLIK
カチ... CLIK
I GET IT! THE FURTHER BACK YOU JUMP, THE *MORE MAGIC* POWER YOU USE!!
YOU'D GET TIRED BEFORE YOU COULD...
BUT WHAT IF THERE WERE MORE THAN ONE MAGIC-USER?! COULDN'T YOU JUST KEEP...?
GOOD QUESTION!
ANYHOO, EVERYONE HOLD TIGHT TO ANIKI!
LIKE THIS, YOU MEAN?
RIGHT, THEN— HERE WE GO!
カチッ KLIK
ぐるん
ZWI-I-IRL...

NEGIMA!

MAGISTER NEGI MAGI

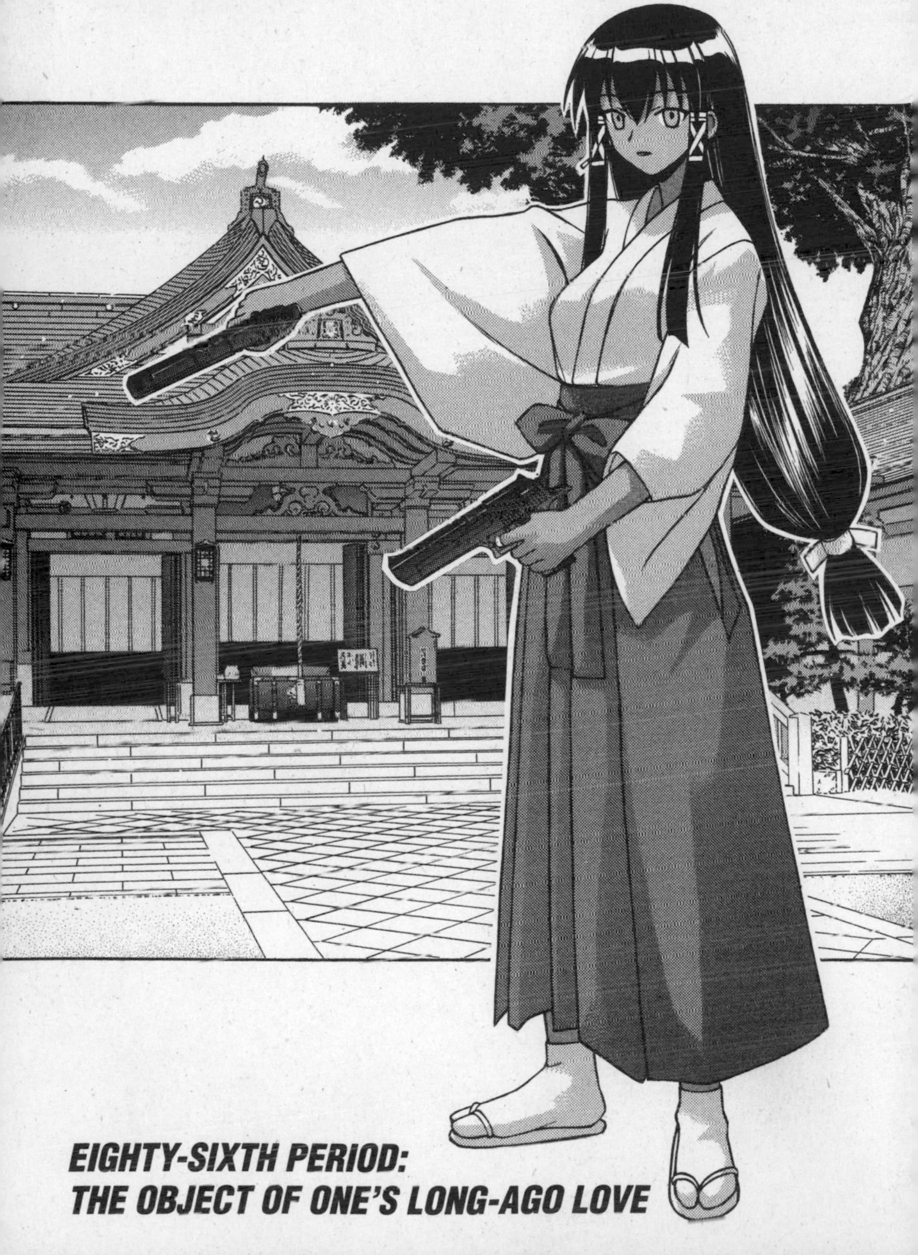

EIGHTY-SIXTH PERIOD: THE OBJECT OF ONE'S LONG-AGO LOVE

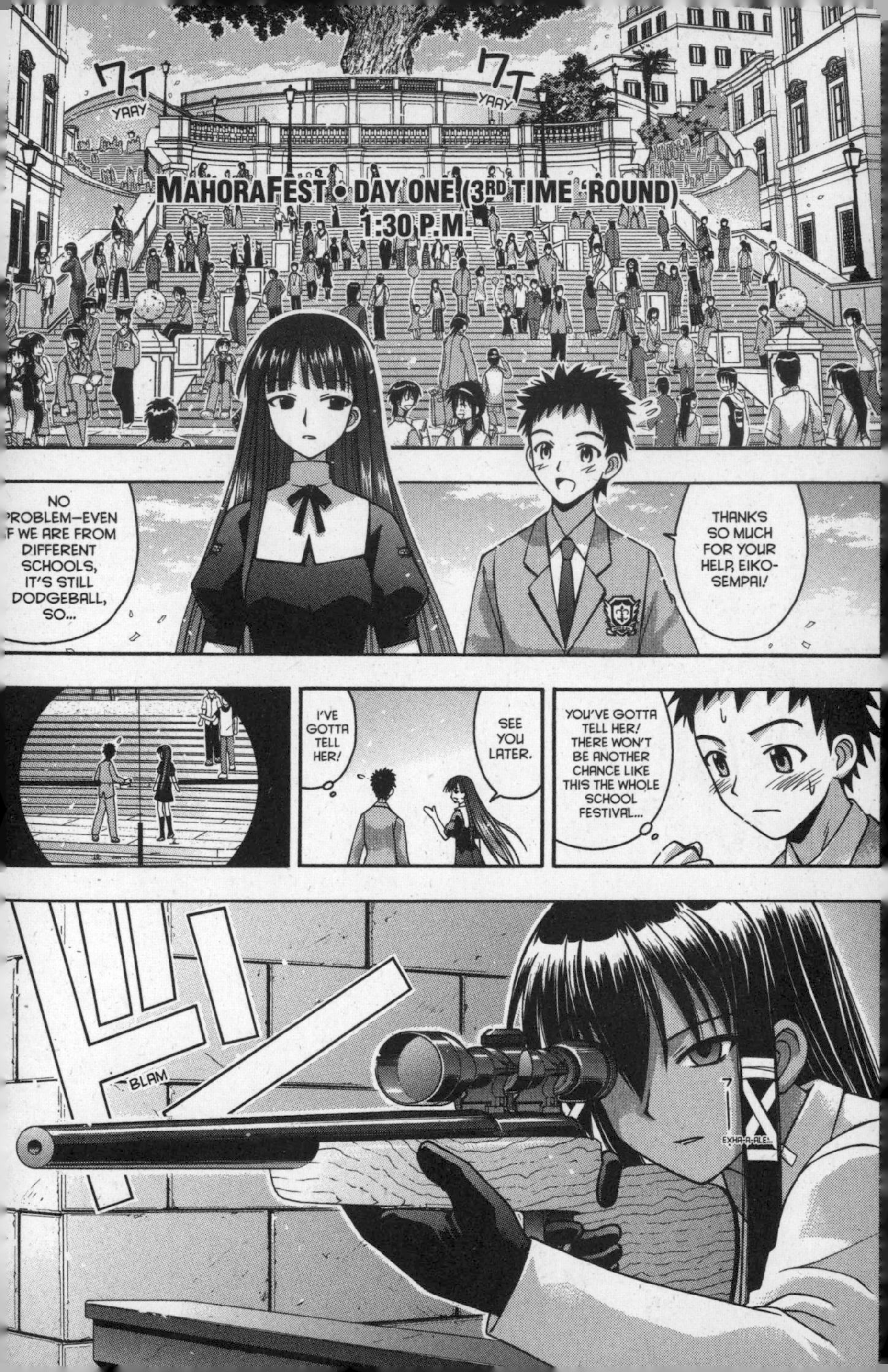
MAHORAFEST • DAY ONE (3RD TIME 'ROUND)
1:30 P.M.
YAAY
YAAY
THANKS SO MUCH FOR YOUR HELP, EIKO-SEMPAI!
NO PROBLEM—EVEN IF WE ARE FROM DIFFERENT SCHOOLS, IT'S STILL DODGEBALL, SO...
YOU'VE GOTTA TELL HER! THERE WON'T BE ANOTHER CHANCE LIKE THIS THE WHOLE SCHOOL FESTIVAL...
SEE YOU LATER.
I'VE GOTTA TELL HER!
EXHA-A-ALE...
BLAM

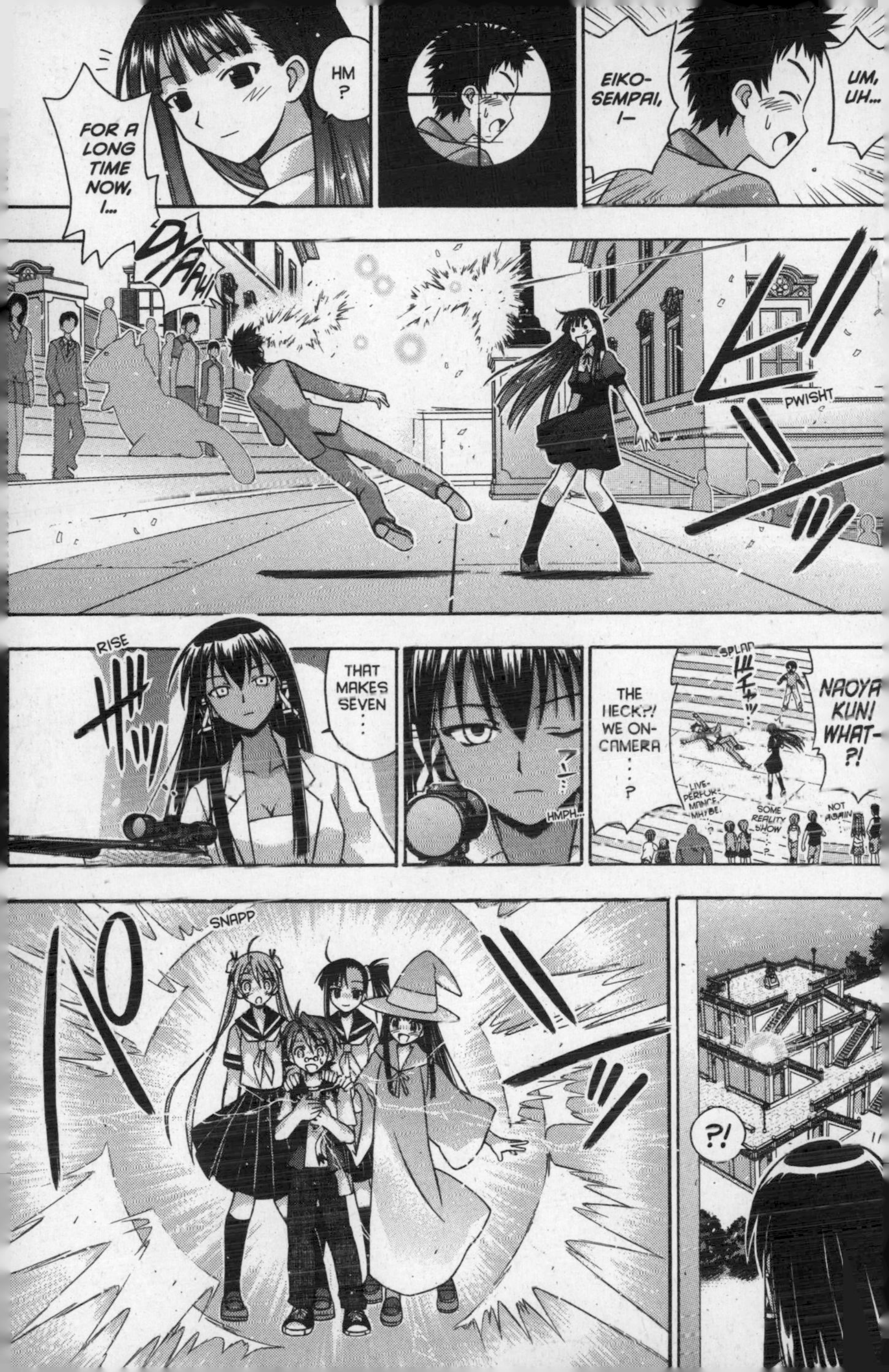

UM, UH...
EIKO-SEMPAI, I—
HM ?
FOR A LONG TIME NOW, I...
PWISHT
DYAAH!
NAOYA KUN! WHAT-?!
SPLAD
THE HECK?! WE ON-CAMERA . . . ?
NOT AGAIN
SOME REALITY SHOW . . . ?
LIVE-PERFORMANCE, MAYBE . . . ?
HMPH...
THAT MAKES SEVEN . . .
RISE
?!
SNAPP

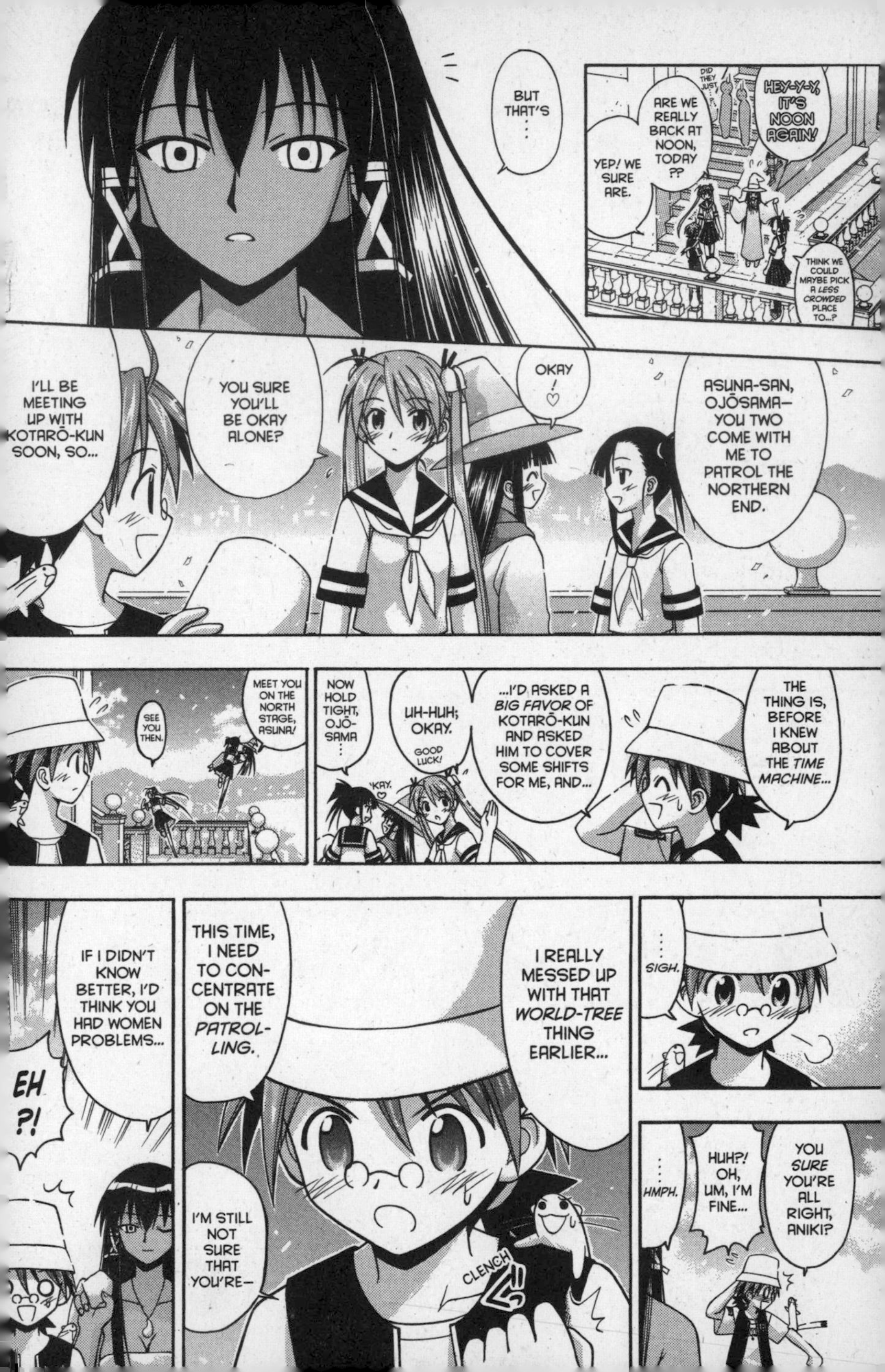

HEY-Y-Y, IT'S NOON AGAIN!
DID THEY JUST...?
ARE WE REALLY BACK AT NOON, TODAY??
YEP! WE SURE ARE.
THINK WE COULD MAYBE PICK A LESS CROWDED PLACE TO...?
BUT THAT'S...
ASUNA-SAN, OJŌSAMA— YOU TWO COME WITH ME TO PATROL THE NORTHERN END.
OKAY! ♡
YOU SURE YOU'LL BE OKAY ALONE?
I'LL BE MEETING UP WITH KOTARŌ-KUN SOON, SO...
THE THING IS, BEFORE I KNEW ABOUT THE TIME MACHINE...
...I'D ASKED A BIG FAVOR OF KOTARŌ-KUN AND ASKED HIM TO COVER SOME SHIFTS FOR ME, AND...
UH-HUH; OKAY.
GOOD LUCK!
NOW HOLD TIGHT, OJŌ-SAMA...
'KAY. ♡
MEET YOU ON THE NORTH STAGE, ASUNA!
SEE YOU THEN.
...SIGH.
YOU SURE YOU'RE ALL RIGHT, ANIKI?
HUH?! OH, UM, I'M FINE...
...HMPH.
I REALLY MESSED UP WITH THAT WORLD-TREE THING EARLIER...
THIS TIME, I NEED TO CONCENTRATE ON THE PATROLLING.
I'M STILL NOT SURE THAT YOU'RE—
CLENCH
IF I DIDN'T KNOW BETTER, I'D THINK YOU HAD WOMEN PROBLEMS...
EH?!

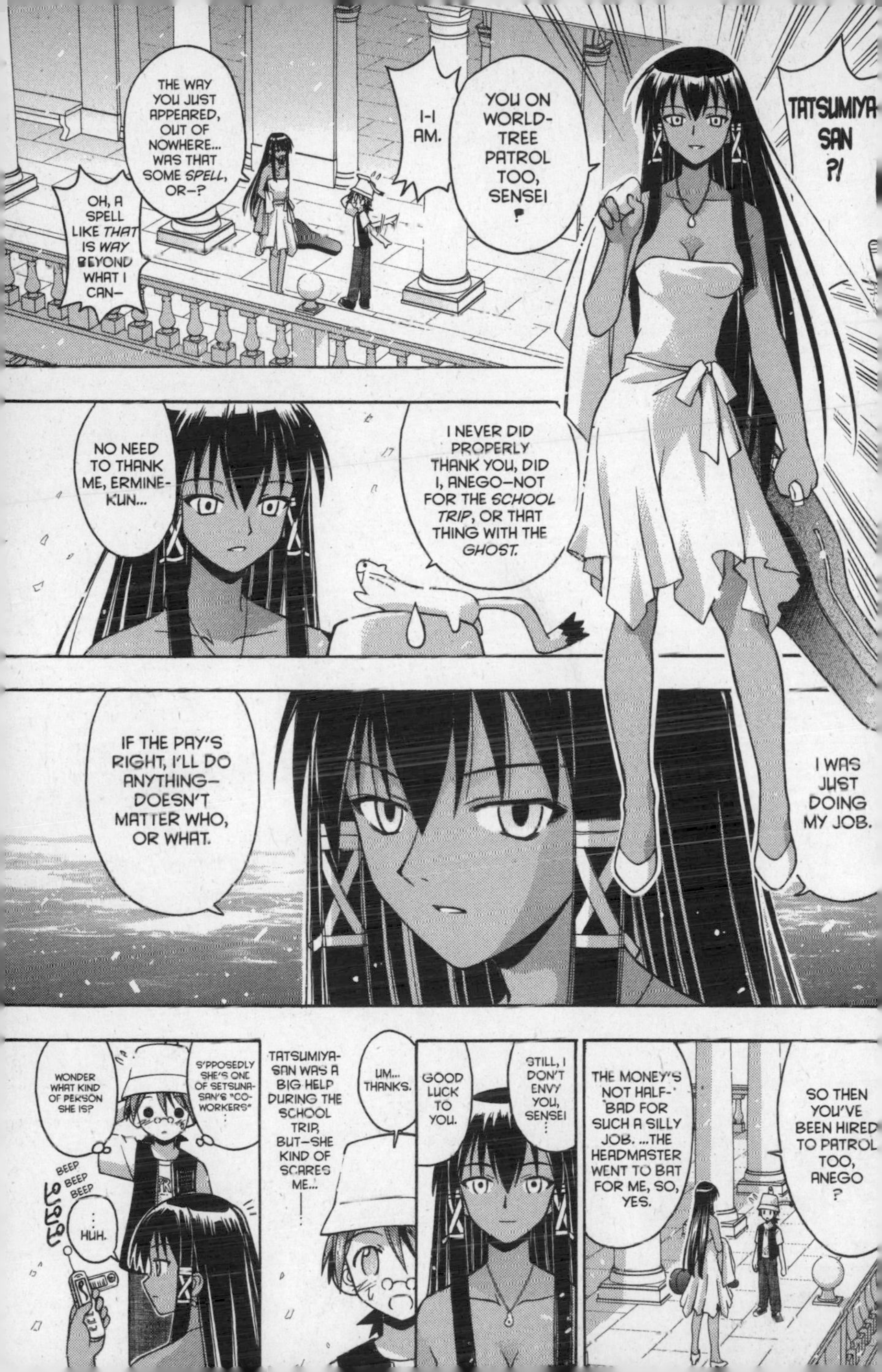
TATSUMIYA SAN ?!
YOU ON WORLD-TREE PATROL TOO, SENSEI ?
I-I AM.
THE WAY YOU JUST APPEARED, OUT OF NOWHERE... WAS THAT SOME *SPELL*, OR—?
OH, A SPELL LIKE *THAT* IS *WAY* BEYOND WHAT I CAN—
I NEVER DID PROPERLY THANK YOU, DID I, ANEGO—NOT FOR THE *SCHOOL TRIP*, OR THAT THING WITH THE *GHOST.*
NO NEED TO THANK ME, ERMINE-KUN...
I WAS JUST DOING MY JOB.
IF THE PAY'S RIGHT, I'LL DO ANYTHING—DOESN'T MATTER WHO, OR WHAT.
SO THEN YOU'VE BEEN HIRED TO PATROL TOO, ANEGO ?
THE MONEY'S NOT HALF-BAD FOR SUCH A SILLY JOB. ...THE HEADMASTER WENT TO BAT FOR ME, SO, YES.
STILL, I DON'T ENVY YOU, SENSEI ...
GOOD LUCK TO YOU.
UM... THANKS.
TATSUMIYA-SAN WAS A BIG HELP DURING THE SCHOOL TRIP, BUT—SHE KIND OF SCARES ME...
S'PPOSEDLY SHE'S ONE OF SETSUNA-SAN'S "CO-WORKERS" ...
WONDER WHAT KIND OF PERSON SHE IS?
BEEP BEEP BEEP
... HUH.

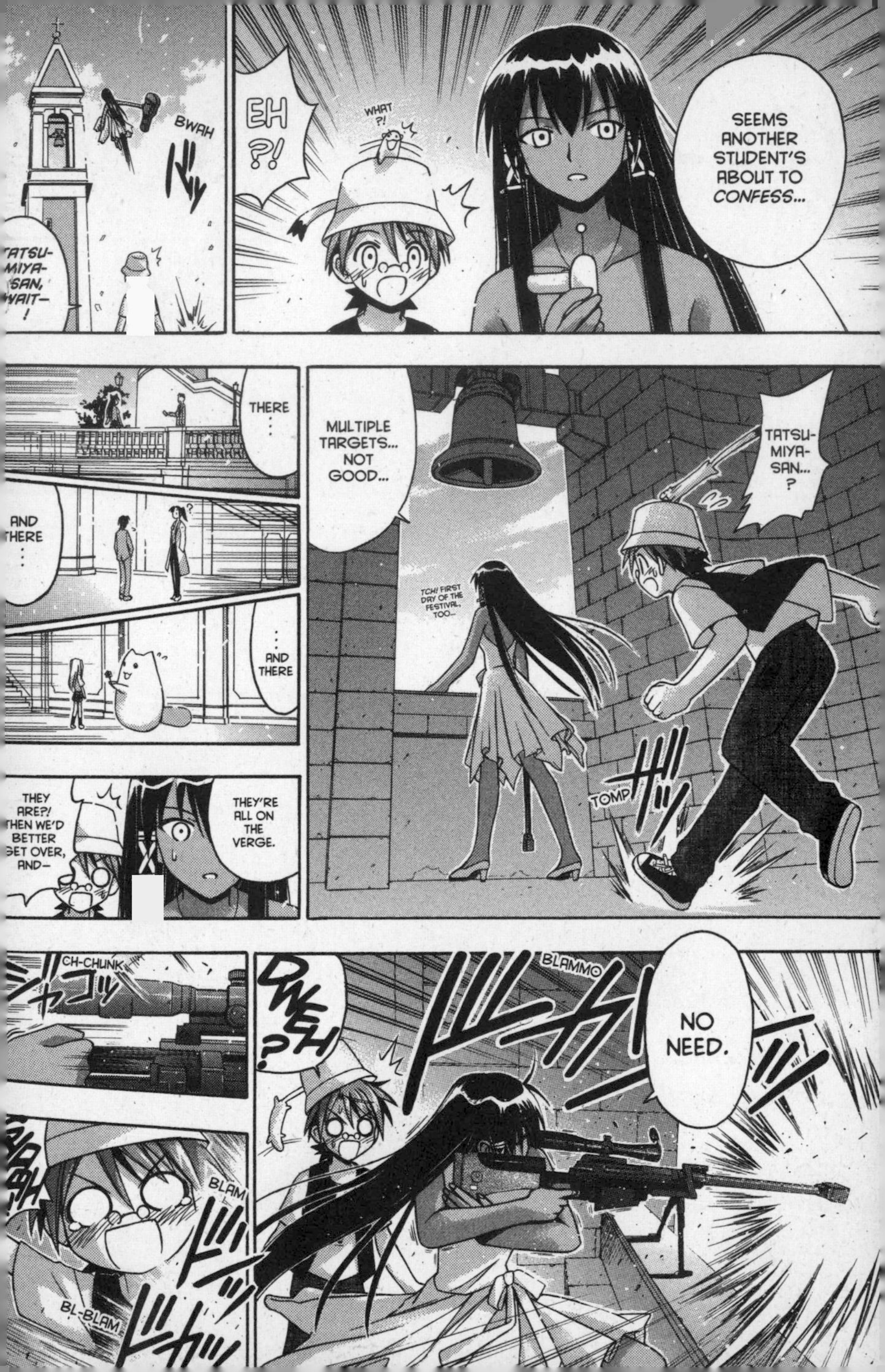
SEEMS ANOTHER STUDENT'S ABOUT TO CONFESS...
EH?!
WHAT?!
BWAH
TATSU-MIYA-SAN, WAIT—!
TATSU-MIYA-SAN...?
MULTIPLE TARGETS... NOT GOOD...
TCH! FIRST DAY OF THE FESTIVAL, TOO...
TOMP
THERE...
AND THERE...
...AND THERE
THEY'RE ALL ON THE VERGE.
THEY ARE?! THEN WE'D BETTER GET OVER, AND—
NO NEED.
BLAMMO
DWEH?
CH-CHUNK
BLAM
BL-BLAM

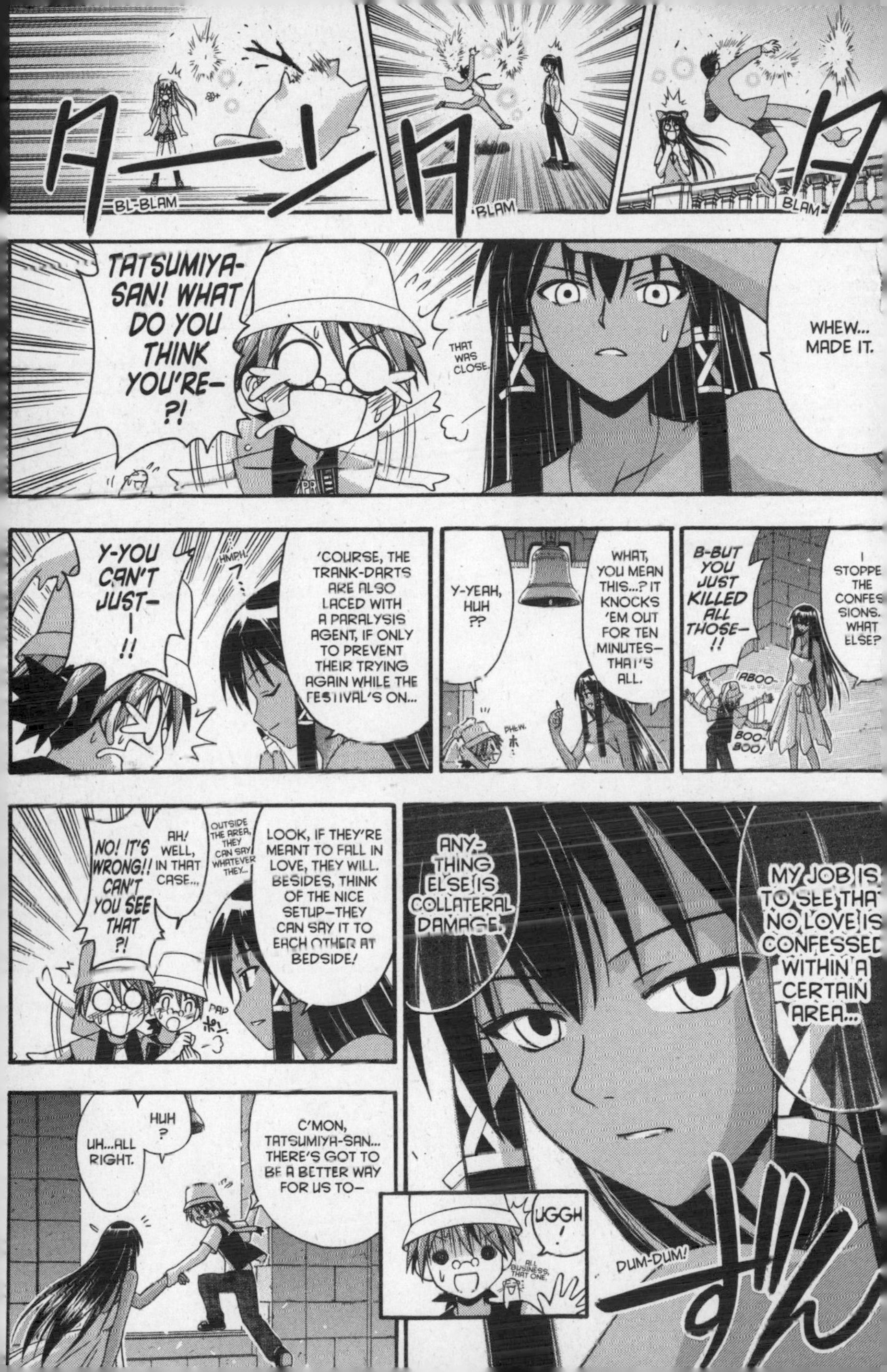
BLAM
BLAM
BL-BLAM
WHEW... MADE IT.
THAT WAS CLOSE.
TATSUMIYA-SAN! WHAT DO YOU THINK YOU'RE-?!
I STOPPE THE CONFES- SIONS. WHAT ELSE?
B-BUT YOU JUST KILLED ALL THOSE-!!
BOO-BOO!
WHAT, YOU MEAN THIS...? IT KNOCKS 'EM OUT FOR TEN MINUTES—THAT'S ALL.
Y-YEAH, HUH ??
PHEW.
'COURSE, THE TRANK-DARTS ARE ALSO LACED WITH A PARALYSIS AGENT, IF ONLY TO PREVENT THEIR TRYING AGAIN WHILE THE FESTIVAL'S ON...
HMPH!
Y-YOU CAN'T JUST- !!
MY JOB IS TO SEE THAT NO LOVE IS CONFESSED WITHIN A CERTAIN AREA...
ANYTHING ELSE IS COLLATERAL DAMAGE.
DUM-DUM!
LOOK, IF THEY'RE MEANT TO FALL IN LOVE, THEY WILL. BESIDES, THINK OF THE NICE SETUP—THEY CAN SAY IT TO EACH OTHER AT BEDSIDE!
OUTSIDE THE AREA, THEY CAN SAY WHATEVER THEY...
AH! WELL, IN THAT CASE...
NO! IT'S WRONG!! CAN'T YOU SEE THAT ?!
C'MON, TATSUMIYA-SAN... THERE'S GOT TO BE A BETTER WAY FOR US TO—
HUH ?
UH...ALL RIGHT.
UGGH !
ALL BUSINESS, THAT ONE.

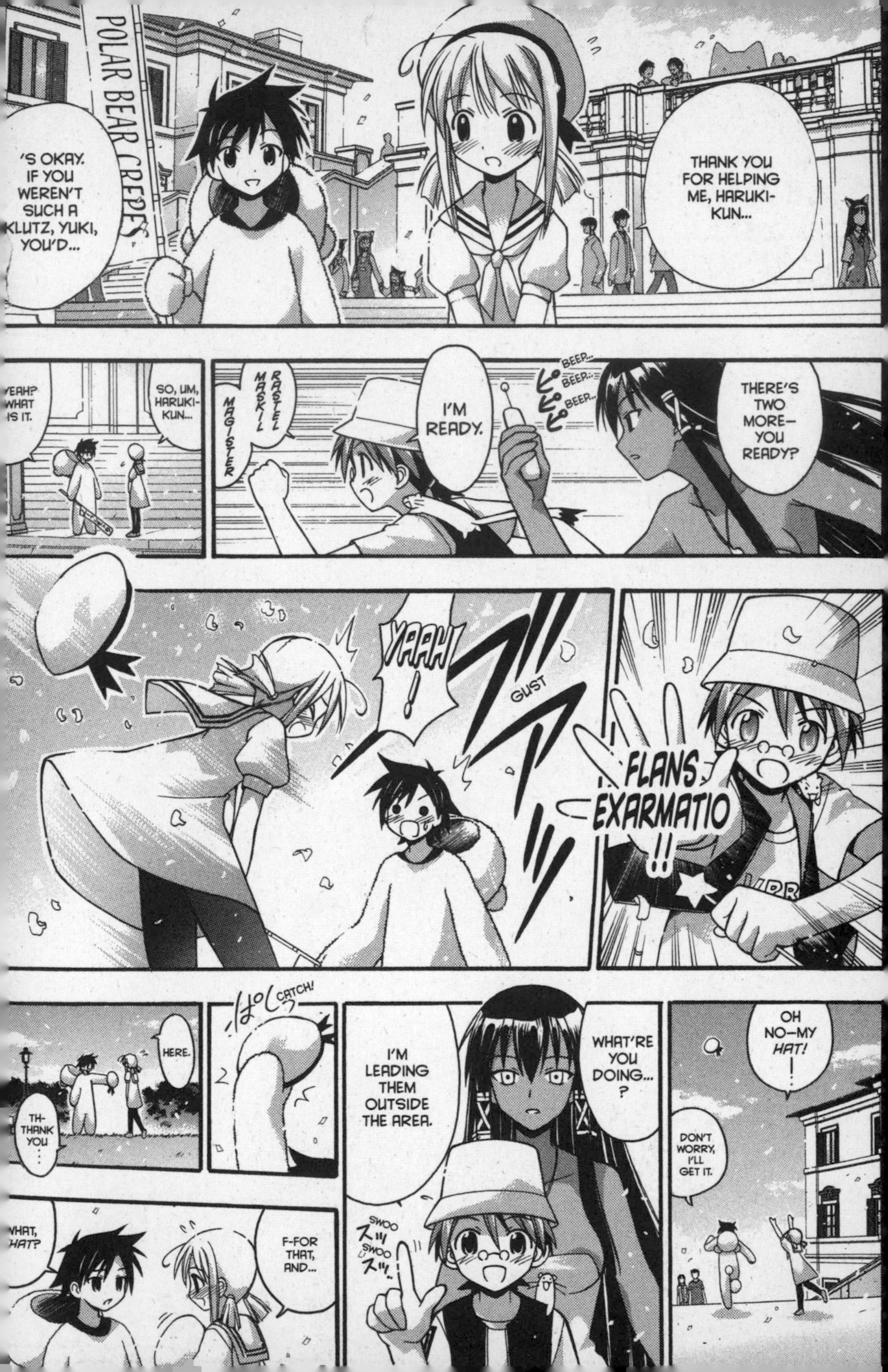
THANK YOU FOR HELPING ME, HARUKI-KUN...
POLAR BEAR CREPES
'S OKAY. IF YOU WEREN'T SUCH A KLUTZ, YUKI, YOU'D...
THERE'S TWO MORE— YOU READY?
BEEP... BEEP... BEEP...
I'M READY.
RASTEL MASKIL MAGISTER
SO, UM, HARUKI-KUN...
YEAH? WHAT IS IT.
FLANS EXARMATIO!!
GUST
YAAH!
OH NO—MY HAT!
DON'T WORRY, I'LL GET IT.
WHAT'RE YOU DOING...?
I'M LEADING THEM OUTSIDE THE AREA.
SWOO SWOO
CATCH!
HERE.
TH-THANK YOU...
F-FOR THAT, AND...
WHAT, THAT?

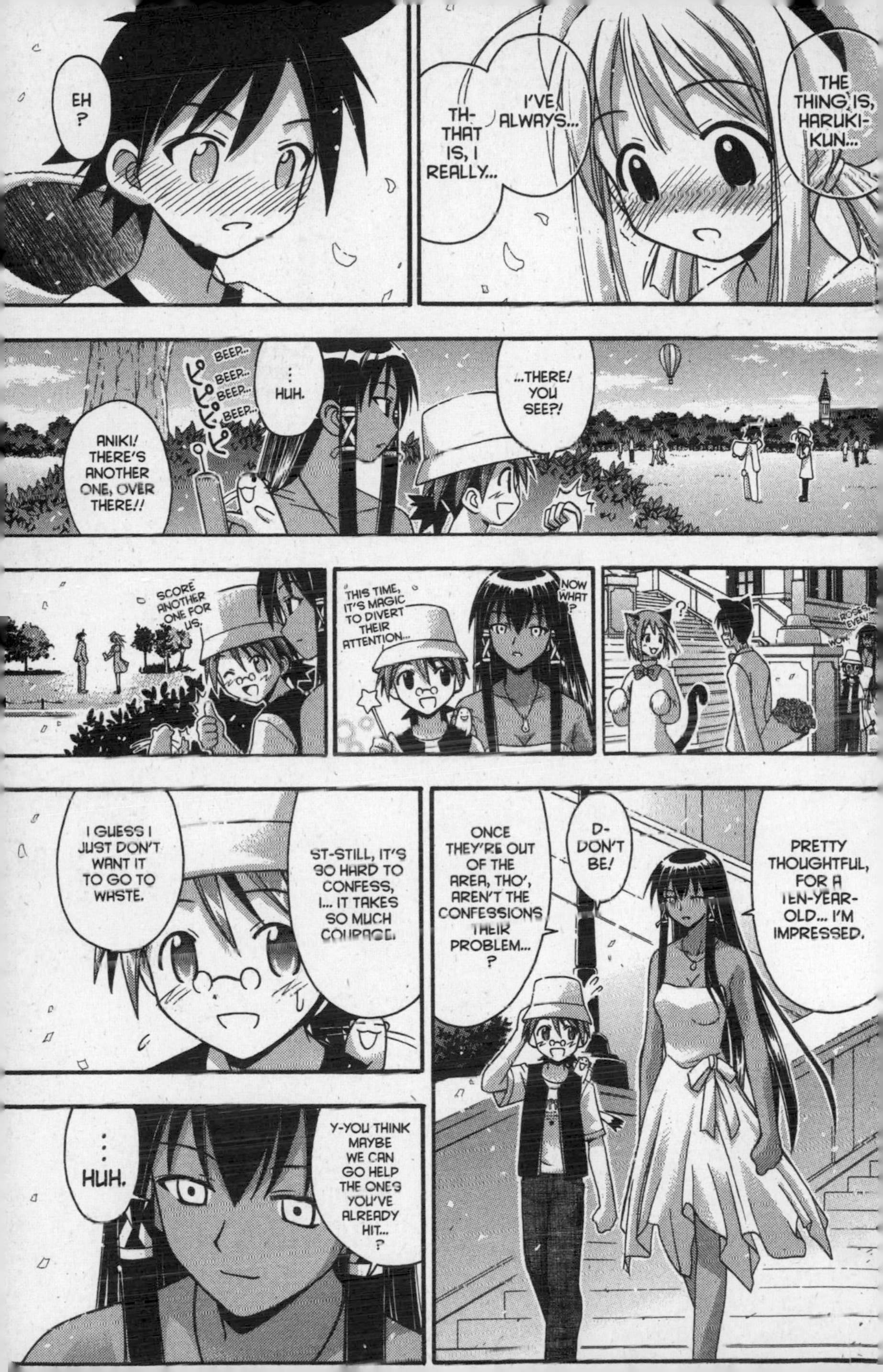
THE THING IS, HARUKI-KUN...
I'VE ALWAYS...
TH-THAT IS, I REALLY...
EH ?
...THERE! YOU SEE?!
... HUH.
BEEP... BEEP... BEEP... BEEP...
ピピピピ
ANIKI! THERE'S ANOTHER ONE, OVER THERE!!
ROSES, EVEN!
WOW.
NOW WHAT ?
THIS TIME, IT'S MAGIC TO DIVERT THEIR ATTENTION...
SCORE ANOTHER ONE FOR US.
PRETTY THOUGHTFUL, FOR A TEN-YEAR-OLD... I'M IMPRESSED.
D-DON'T BE!
ONCE THEY'RE OUT OF THE AREA, THO', AREN'T THE CONFESSIONS THEIR PROBLEM... ?
ST-STILL, IT'S SO HARD TO CONFESS, I... IT TAKES SO MUCH COURAGE.
I GUESS I JUST DON'T WANT IT TO GO TO WASTE.
Y-YOU THINK MAYBE WE CAN GO HELP THE ONES YOU'VE ALREADY HIT... ?
... HUH.

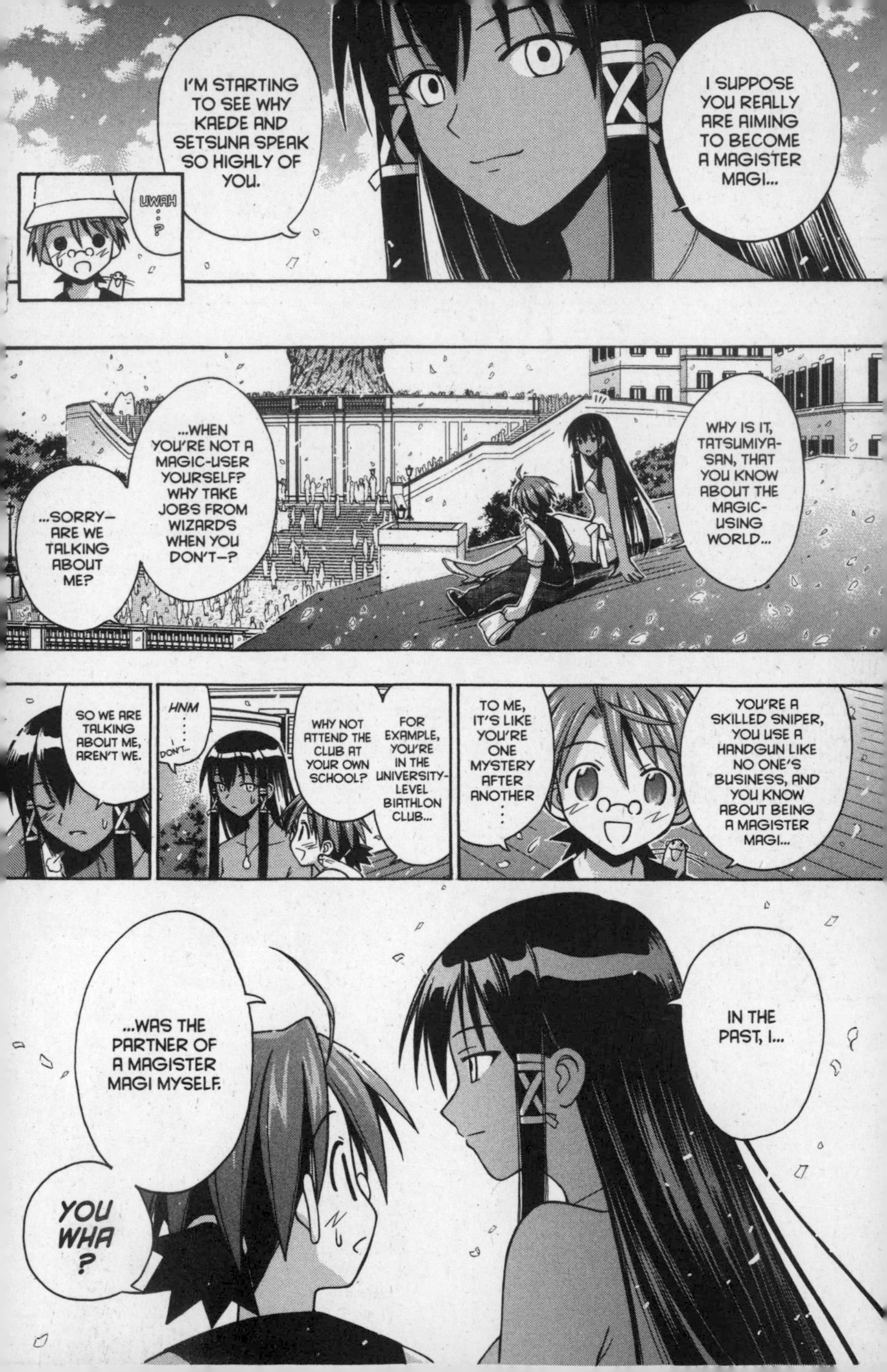
I SUPPOSE YOU REALLY ARE AIMING TO BECOME A MAGISTER MAGI...
I'M STARTING TO SEE WHY KAEDE AND SETSUNA SPEAK SO HIGHLY OF YOU.
UWAH...?
WHY IS IT, TATSUMIYA-SAN, THAT YOU KNOW ABOUT THE MAGIC-USING WORLD...
...WHEN YOU'RE NOT A MAGIC-USER YOURSELF? WHY TAKE JOBS FROM WIZARDS WHEN YOU DON'T-?
...SORRY-ARE WE TALKING ABOUT ME?
YOU'RE A SKILLED SNIPER, YOU USE A HANDGUN LIKE NO ONE'S BUSINESS, AND YOU KNOW ABOUT BEING A MAGISTER MAGI...
TO ME, IT'S LIKE YOU'RE ONE MYSTERY AFTER ANOTHER...
FOR EXAMPLE, YOU'RE IN THE UNIVERSITY-LEVEL BIATHLON CLUB...
WHY NOT ATTEND THE CLUB AT YOUR OWN SCHOOL?
HNM...
I DON'T...
SO WE ARE TALKING ABOUT ME, AREN'T WE.
IN THE PAST, I...
...WAS THE PARTNER OF A MAGISTER MAGI MYSELF.
YOU WHA?

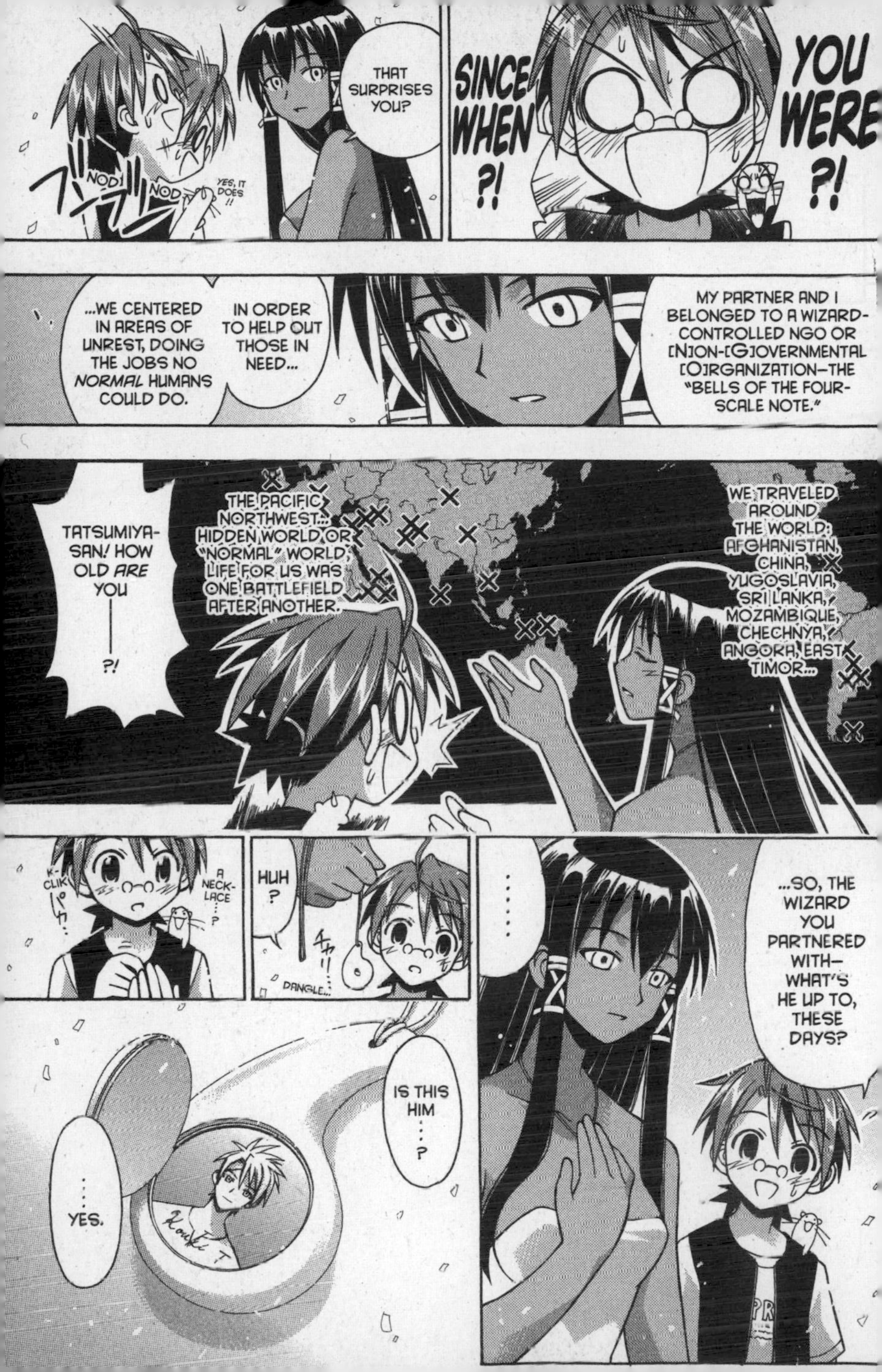
YOU WERE ?!
SINCE WHEN ?!
THAT SURPRISES YOU?
NOD NOD
YES, IT DOES !!
MY PARTNER AND I BELONGED TO A WIZARD-CONTROLLED NGO OR [N]ON-[G]OVERNMENTAL [O]RGANIZATION—THE "BELLS OF THE FOUR-SCALE NOTE."
IN ORDER TO HELP OUT THOSE IN NEED...
...WE CENTERED IN AREAS OF UNREST, DOING THE JOBS NO *NORMAL* HUMANS COULD DO.
WE TRAVELED AROUND THE WORLD: AFGHANISTAN, CHINA, YUGOSLAVIA, SRI LANKA, MOZAMBIQUE, CHECHNYA, ANGORA, EAST TIMOR...
THE PACIFIC NORTHWEST... HIDDEN WORLD OR "NORMAL" WORLD, LIFE FOR US WAS ONE BATTLEFIELD AFTER ANOTHER.
TATSUMIYA-SAN! HOW OLD *ARE* YOU——?!
...SO, THE WIZARD YOU PARTNERED WITH—WHAT'S HE UP TO, THESE DAYS?
......
HUH?
DANGLE...
A NECKLACE...?
K-CLIK
IS THIS HIM...?
...YES.

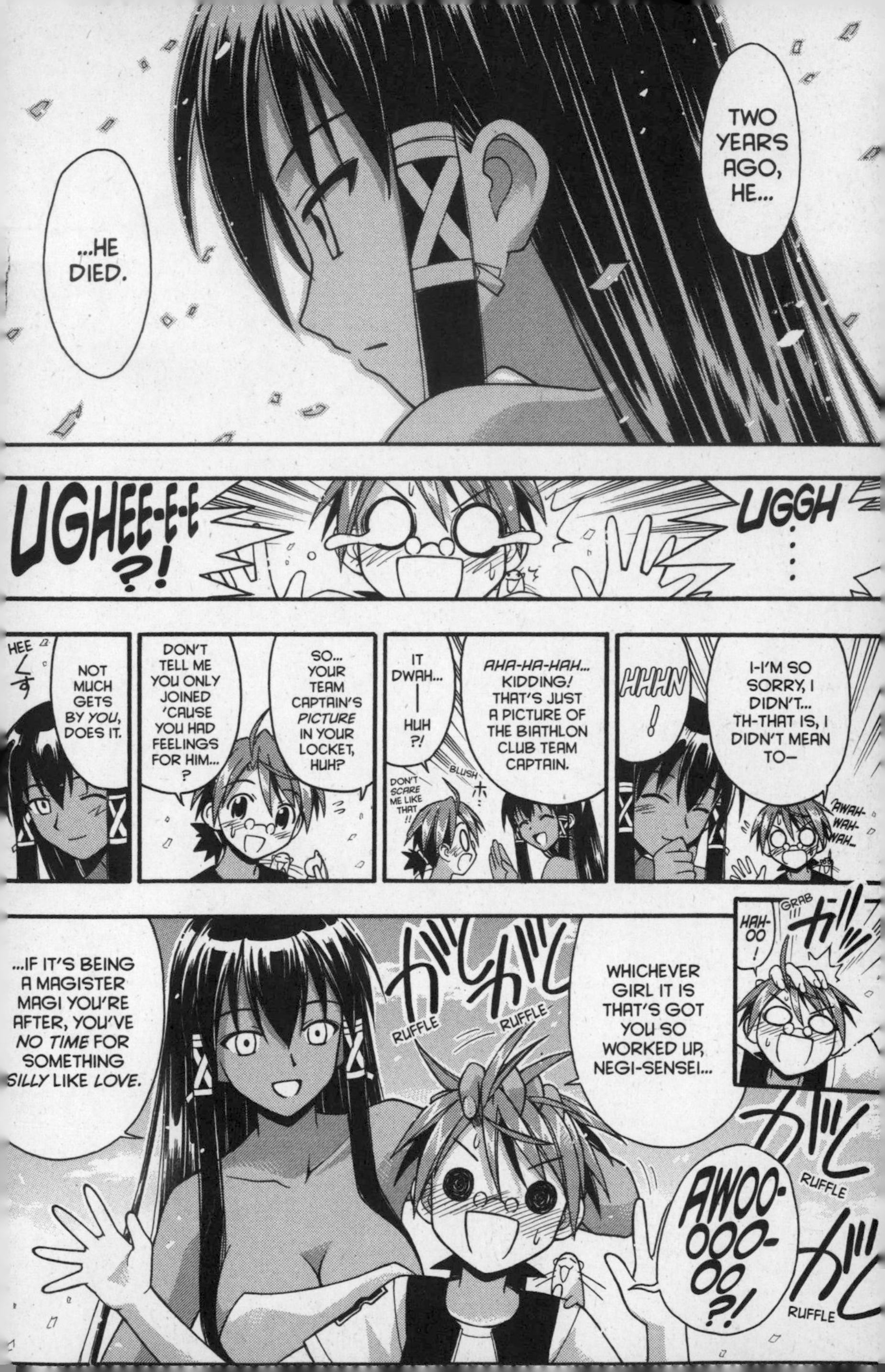
TWO YEARS AGO, HE...
...HE DIED.
UGGH ....
UGHEE-E-E ?!
I-I'M SO SORRY, I DIDN'T... TH-THAT IS, I DIDN'T MEAN TO—
HHHN !
AWAH-WAH-WAH...
AHA-HA-HAH... KIDDING! THAT'S JUST A PICTURE OF THE BIATHLON CLUB TEAM CAPTAIN.
IT DWAH... — HUH ?!
BLUSH
DON'T *SCARE* ME LIKE THAT !!
SO... YOUR TEAM CAPTAIN'S *PICTURE* IN YOUR LOCKET, HUH?
DON'T TELL ME YOU ONLY JOINED 'CAUSE YOU HAD FEELINGS FOR HIM... ?
NOT MUCH GETS BY *YOU*, DOES IT.
HEE くす
GRAB ガッ
HAH-OO !
WHICHEVER GIRL IT IS THAT'S GOT YOU SO WORKED UP, NEGI-SENSEI...
RUFFLE
RUFFLE
...IF IT'S BEING A MAGISTER MAGI YOU'RE AFTER, YOU'VE *NO TIME* FOR SOMETHING *SILLY* LIKE *LOVE*.
RUFFLE
AWOO-OOO-OOO ?!
RUFFLE

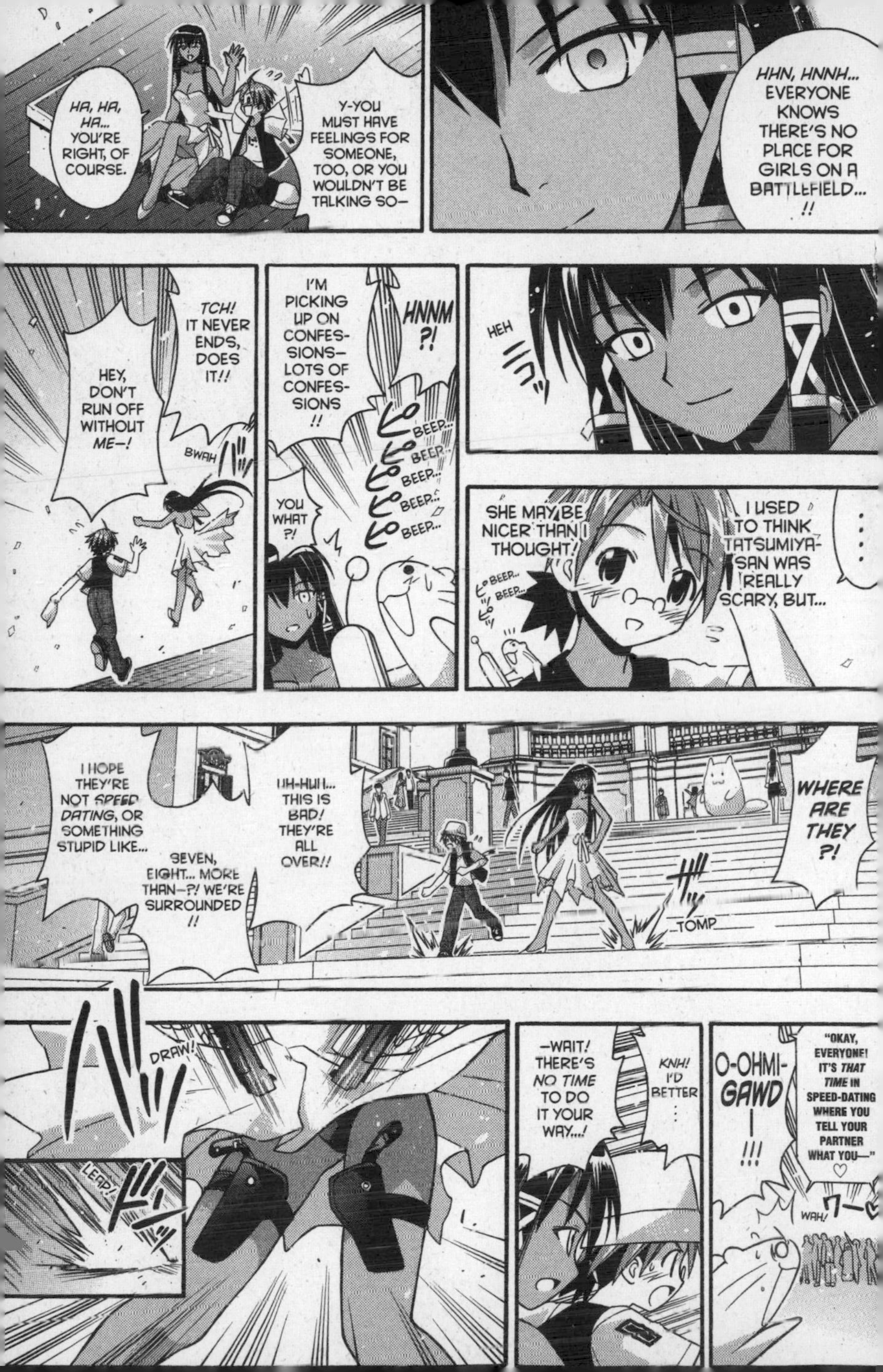
HHN, HNNH... EVERYONE KNOWS THERE'S NO PLACE FOR GIRLS ON A BATTLEFIELD... !!
Y-YOU MUST HAVE FEELINGS FOR SOMEONE, TOO, OR YOU WOULDN'T BE TALKING SO—
HA, HA, HA... YOU'RE RIGHT, OF COURSE.
HEH
. . . .
I USED TO THINK TATSUMIYA-SAN WAS REALLY SCARY, BUT...
SHE MAY BE NICER THAN I THOUGHT!
BEEP... BEEP...
HNNM ?!
I'M PICKING UP ON CONFESSIONS— LOTS OF CONFESSIONS !!
BEEP... BEEP... BEEP... BEEP... BEEP...
YOU WHAT ?!
TCH! IT NEVER ENDS, DOES IT!!
HEY, DON'T RUN OFF WITHOUT ME—!
BWAH
WHERE ARE THEY ?!
TOMP
UH-HUH... THIS IS BAD! THEY'RE ALL OVER!!
SEVEN, EIGHT... MORE THAN—?! WE'RE SURROUNDED !!
I HOPE THEY'RE NOT SPEED DATING, OR SOMETHING STUPID LIKE...
"OKAY, EVERYONE! IT'S THAT TIME IN SPEED-DATING WHERE YOU TELL YOUR PARTNER WHAT YOU—" ♡
O-OHMI-GAWD !!!
WAH!
KNH! I'D BETTER...
—WAIT! THERE'S NO TIME TO DO IT YOUR WAY...!
DRAW!
LEAP!

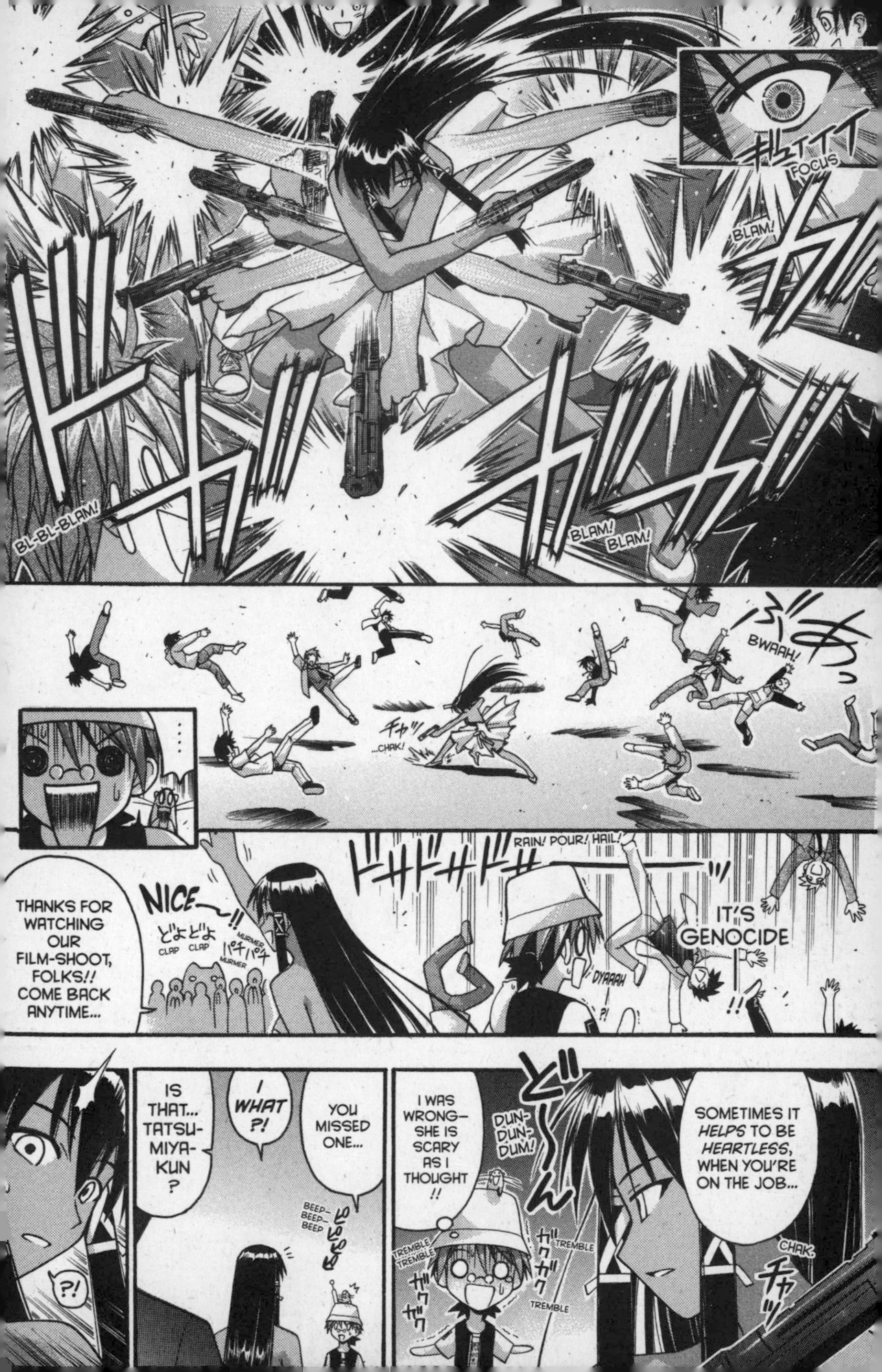
FOCUS
BLAM!
BLAM! BLAM!
BL-BL-BLAM!
BWAAH!
...CHAK!
....
IT'S GENOCIDE!!
DYAAAH!?!
RAIN! POUR! HAIL!
NICE~!!
CLAP CLAP
MURMER MURMER
THANKS FOR WATCHING OUR FILM-SHOOT, FOLKS!! COME BACK ANYTIME...
SOMETIMES IT *HELPS* TO BE *HEARTLESS*, WHEN YOU'RE ON THE JOB...
CHAK.
DUN-DUN-DUM!
I WAS WRONG— SHE IS SCARY AS I THOUGHT!!
TREMBLE TREMBLE
TREMBLE
TREMBLE
YOU MISSED ONE...
I *WHAT*?!
IS THAT... TATSU-MIYA-KUN?
BEEP-BEEP-BEEP
?!

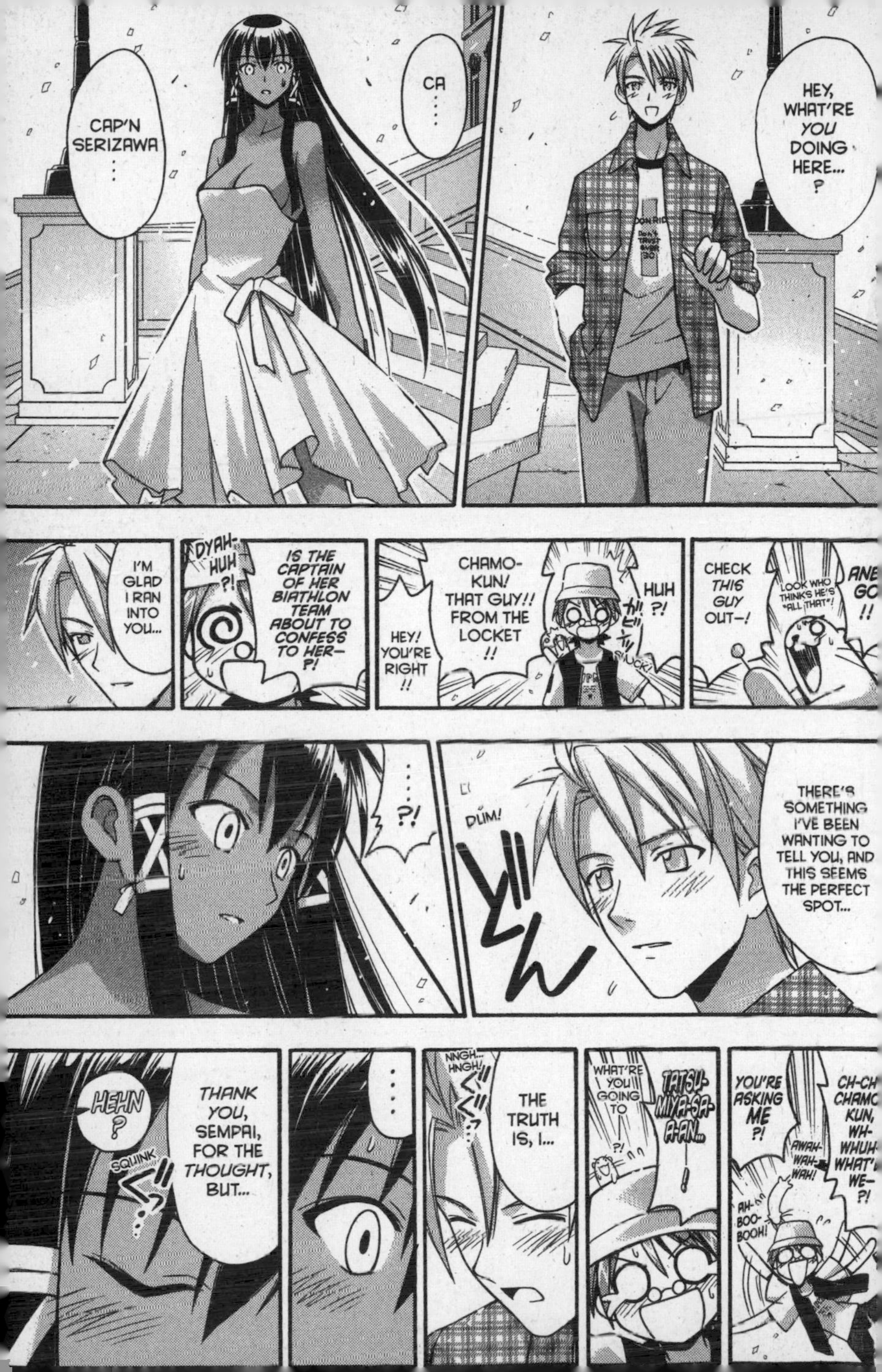
HEY, WHAT'RE YOU DOING HERE...?
CA ....
CAP'N SERIZAWA ...
ANEGO!!
LOOK WHO THINKS HE'S "ALL THAT"!
CHECK THIS GUY OUT—!
HUH ?!
CHAMO-KUN! THAT GUY!! FROM THE LOCKET!!
HEY! YOU'RE RIGHT!!
IS THE CAPTAIN OF HER BIATHLON TEAM ABOUT TO CONFESS TO HER—?!
DYAH-HUH ?!
I'M GLAD I RAN INTO YOU...
THERE'S SOMETHING I'VE BEEN WANTING TO TELL YOU, AND THIS SEEMS THE PERFECT SPOT...
DUM!
....?!
CH-CH CHAMO KUN, WH-WHUH-WHAT' WE-?!
YOU'RE ASKING ME?!
AWAH-WAH-WAH!
AH-BOO-BOOH!
TATSU-MIYA-SA-A-AN...
WHAT'RE YOU GOING TO ?!
THE TRUTH IS, I...
NNGH... HNGH!
....
THANK YOU, SEMPAI, FOR THE THOUGHT, BUT...
HEHN ?
SQUINK

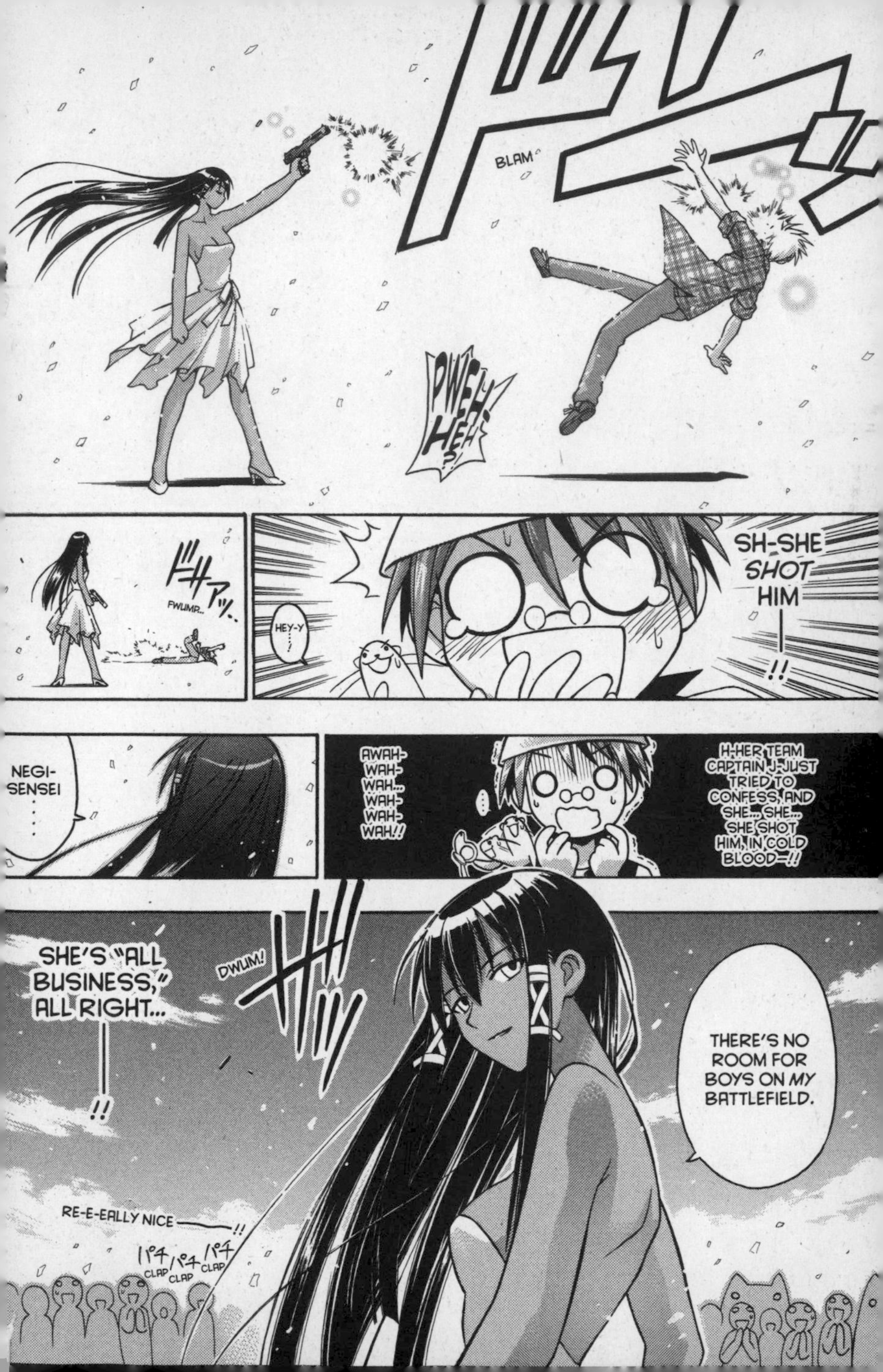
BLAM
PWEH HEH?
SH-SHE SHOT HIM —!!
HEY-Y...!
ドサアッ..
FWUMP..
H-HER TEAM CAPTAIN J-JUST TRIED TO CONFESS, AND SHE... SHE... SHE SHOT HIM, IN COLD BLOOD—!!
AWAH-WAH-WAH... WAH-WAH-WAH!!
...
NEGI-SENSEI......
THERE'S NO ROOM FOR BOYS ON MY BATTLEFIELD.
DWUM!
SHE'S "ALL BUSINESS," ALL RIGHT... —!!
RE-E-EALLY NICE——!!
パチ パチ パチ
CLAP CLAP CLAP

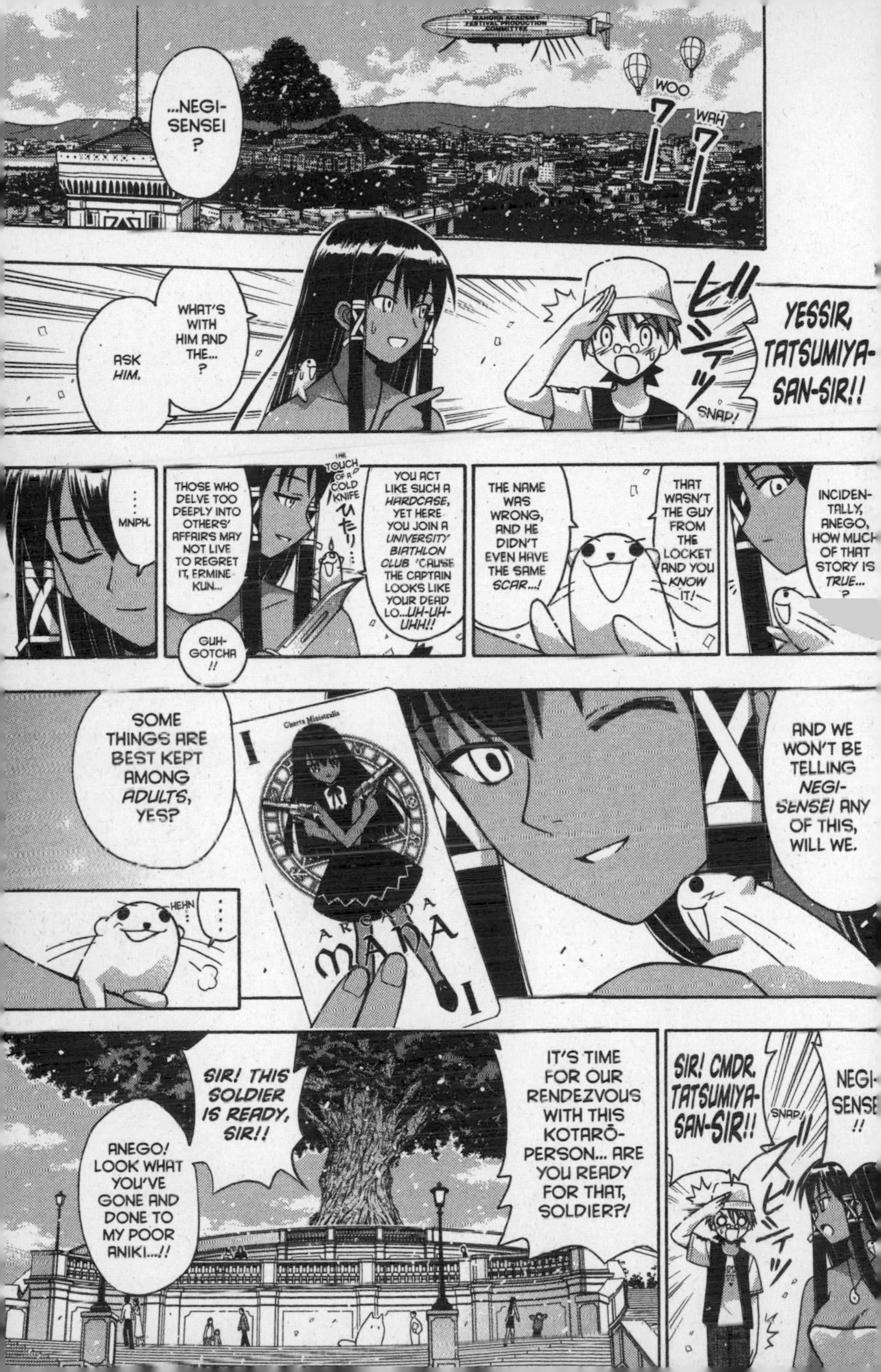
MAHORA ACADEMY FESTIVAL PRODUCTION COMMITTEE
WOO
WAH
...NEGI-SENSEI?
YESSIR, TATSUMIYA-SAN-SIR!!
SNAP!
WHAT'S WITH HIM AND THE...?
ASK HIM.
INCIDENTALLY, ANEGO, HOW MUCH OF THAT STORY IS TRUE...?
THAT WASN'T THE GUY FROM THE LOCKET AND YOU KNOW IT!
THE NAME WAS WRONG, AND HE DIDN'T EVEN HAVE THE SAME SCAR...!
YOU ACT LIKE SUCH A HARDCASE, YET HERE YOU JOIN A UNIVERSITY BIATHLON CLUB 'CAUSE THE CAPTAIN LOOKS LIKE YOUR DEAD LO...UH-UH-UHH!!
THE TOUCH OF A COLD KNIFE
THOSE WHO DELVE TOO DEEPLY INTO OTHERS' AFFAIRS MAY NOT LIVE TO REGRET IT, ERMINE-KUN...
GUH-GOTCHA!!
......MNPH.
AND WE WON'T BE TELLING NEGI-SENSEI ANY OF THIS, WILL WE.
Charta Ministralis
ARCANA MANA
SOME THINGS ARE BEST KEPT AMONG ADULTS, YES?
HEHN
......
NEGI-SENSE!!
SIR! CMDR. TATSUMIYA-SAN-SIR!!
SNAP!
IT'S TIME FOR OUR RENDEZVOUS WITH THIS KOTARŌ-PERSON... ARE YOU READY FOR THAT, SOLDIER?!
SIR! THIS SOLDIER IS READY, SIR!!
ANEGO! LOOK WHAT YOU'VE GONE AND DONE TO MY POOR ANIKI...!!

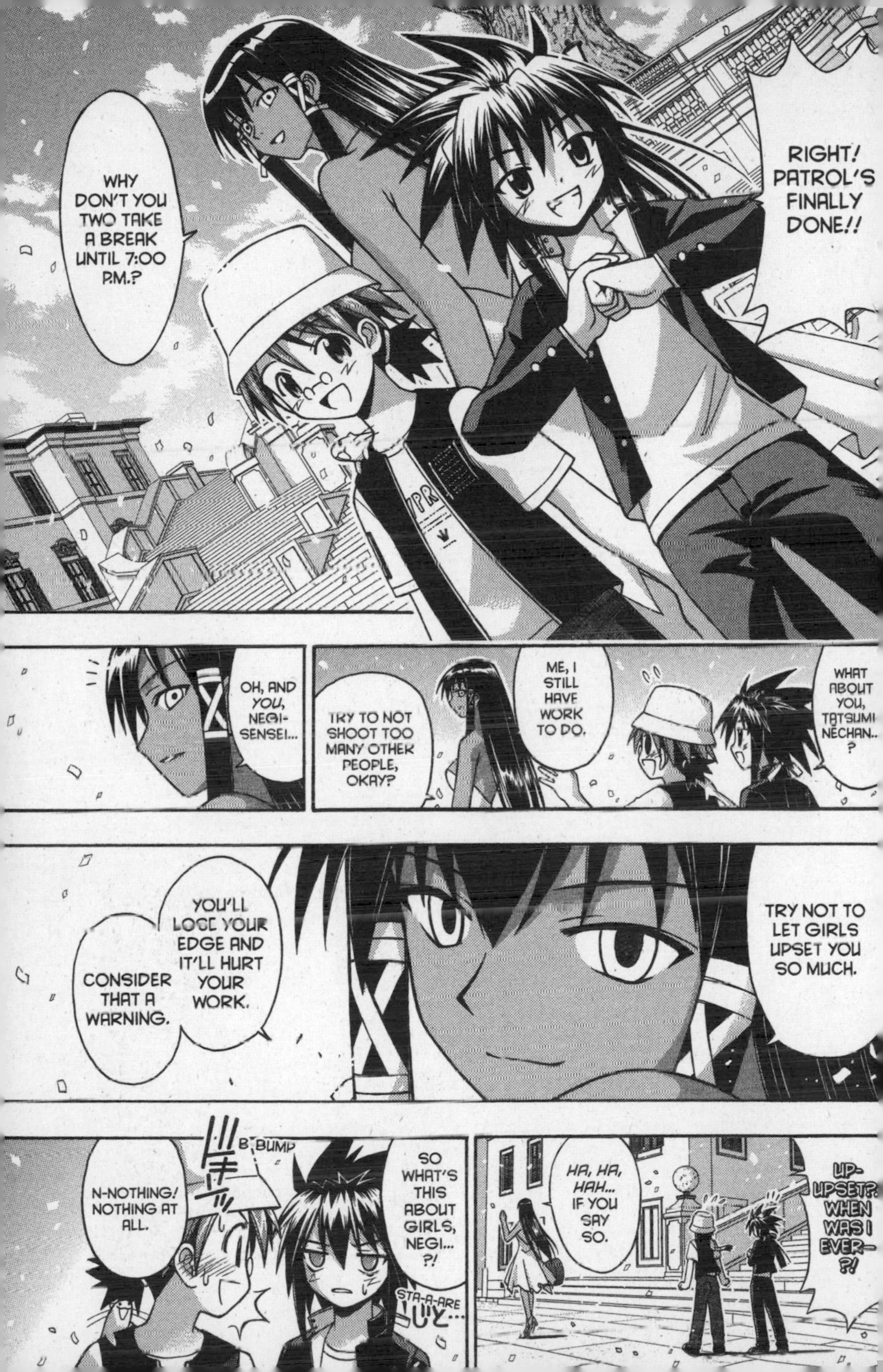
RIGHT! PATROL'S FINALLY DONE!!
WHY DON'T YOU TWO TAKE A BREAK UNTIL 7:00 P.M.?
WHAT ABOUT YOU, TATSUMI NECHAN...?
ME, I STILL HAVE WORK TO DO.
TRY TO NOT SHOOT TOO MANY OTHER PEOPLE, OKAY?
OH, AND YOU, NEGI-SENSEI...
TRY NOT TO LET GIRLS UPSET YOU SO MUCH.
YOU'LL LOSE YOUR EDGE AND IT'LL HURT YOUR WORK.
CONSIDER THAT A WARNING.
UP-UPSET?! WHEN WAS I EVER-?!
HA, HA, HAH... IF YOU SAY SO.
SO WHAT'S THIS ABOUT GIRLS, NEGI...?!
B-BUMP
N-NOTHING! NOTHING AT ALL.
STA-A-ARE

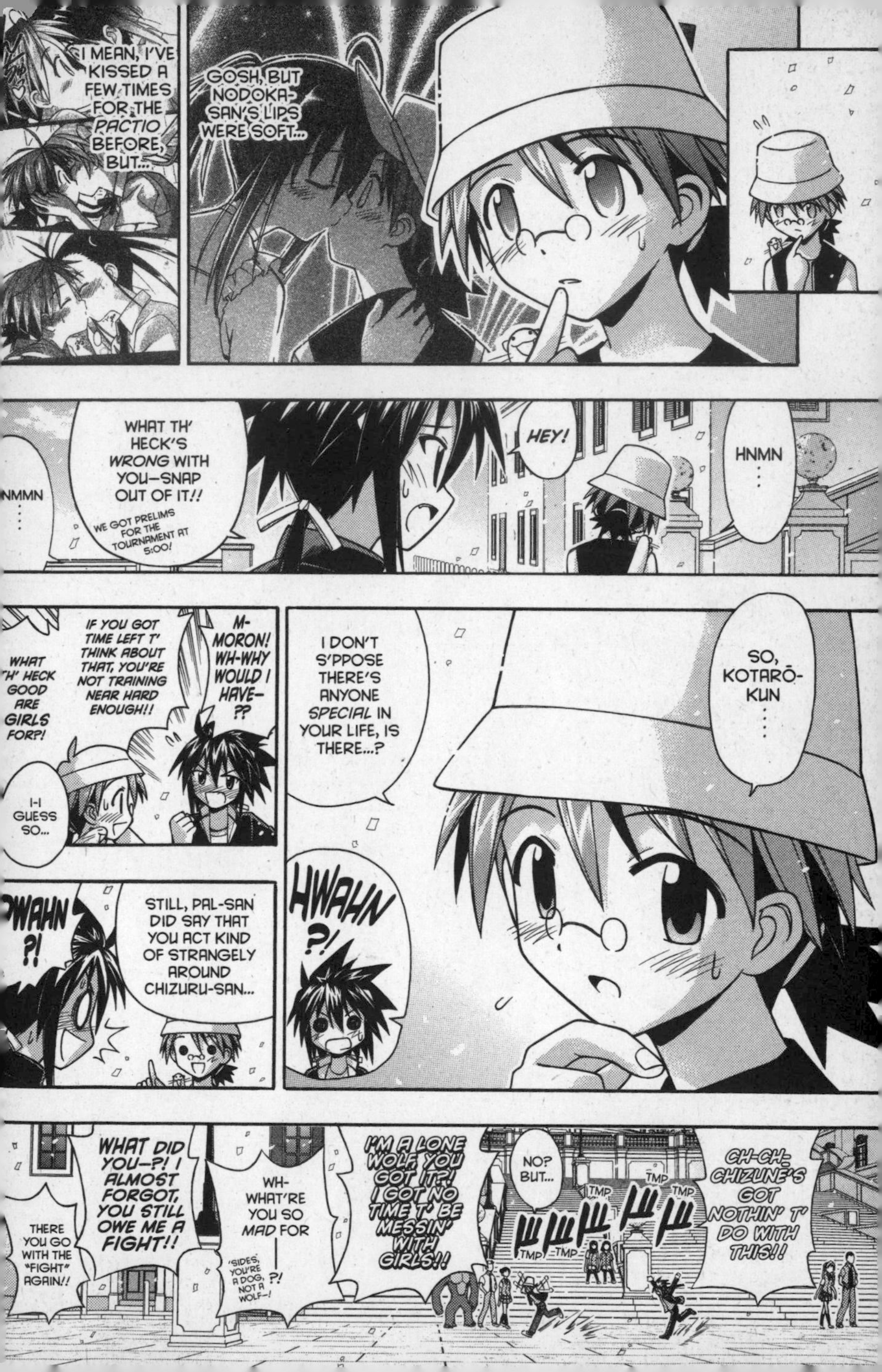
GOSH, BUT NODOKA-SAN'S LIPS WERE SOFT...
I MEAN, I'VE KISSED A FEW TIMES FOR THE PACTIO BEFORE, BUT...
HNMN ...
HEY!
WHAT TH' HECK'S WRONG WITH YOU—SNAP OUT OF IT!!
WE GOT PRELIMS FOR THE TOURNAMENT AT 5:00!
NMMN ...
SO, KOTARŌ-KUN ...
I DON'T S'PPOSE THERE'S ANYONE SPECIAL IN YOUR LIFE, IS THERE...?
HWAHN ?!
M-MORON! WH-WHY WOULD I HAVE—??
IF YOU GOT TIME LEFT T' THINK ABOUT THAT, YOU'RE NOT TRAINING NEAR HARD ENOUGH!!
WHAT TH' HECK GOOD ARE GIRLS FOR?!
I-I GUESS SO...
STILL, PAL-SAN DID SAY THAT YOU ACT KIND OF STRANGELY AROUND CHIZURU-SAN...
WAHN ?!
CH-CH-CHIZUNE'S GOT NOTHIN' T' DO WITH THIS!!
NO? BUT...
TMP TMP TMP TMP TMP
I'M A LONE WOLF, YOU GOT IT?! I GOT NO TIME T' BE MESSIN' WITH GIRLS!!
WH-WHAT'RE YOU SO MAD FOR—?!
'SIDES, YOU'RE A DOG, NOT A WOLF—!
WHAT DID YOU—?! I ALMOST FORGOT, YOU STILL OWE ME A FIGHT!!
THERE YOU GO WITH THE "FIGHT" AGAIN!!

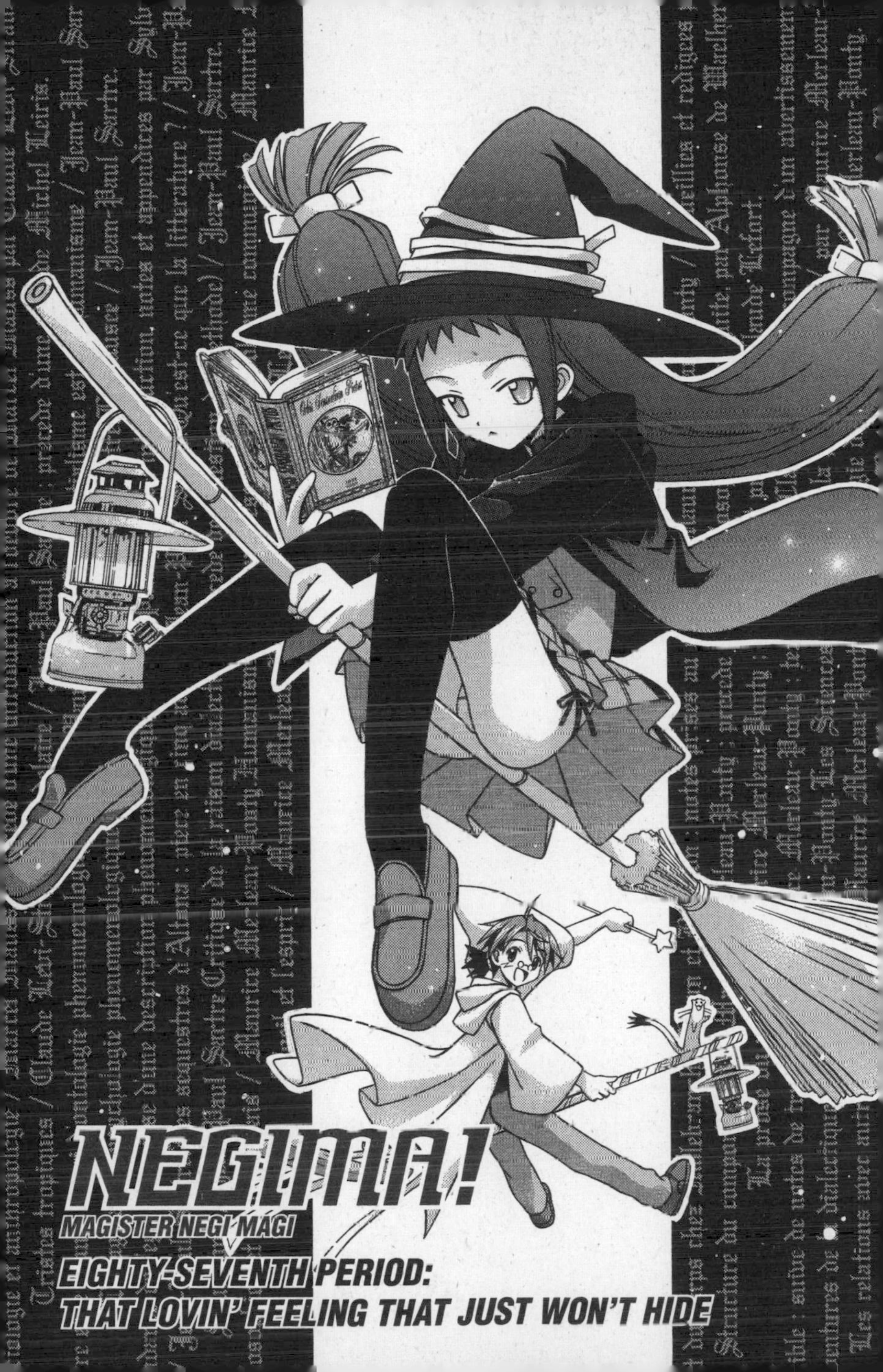
NEGIMA!
MAGISTER NEGI MAGI
EIGHTY-SEVENTH PERIOD:
THAT LOVIN' FEELING THAT JUST WON'T HIDE

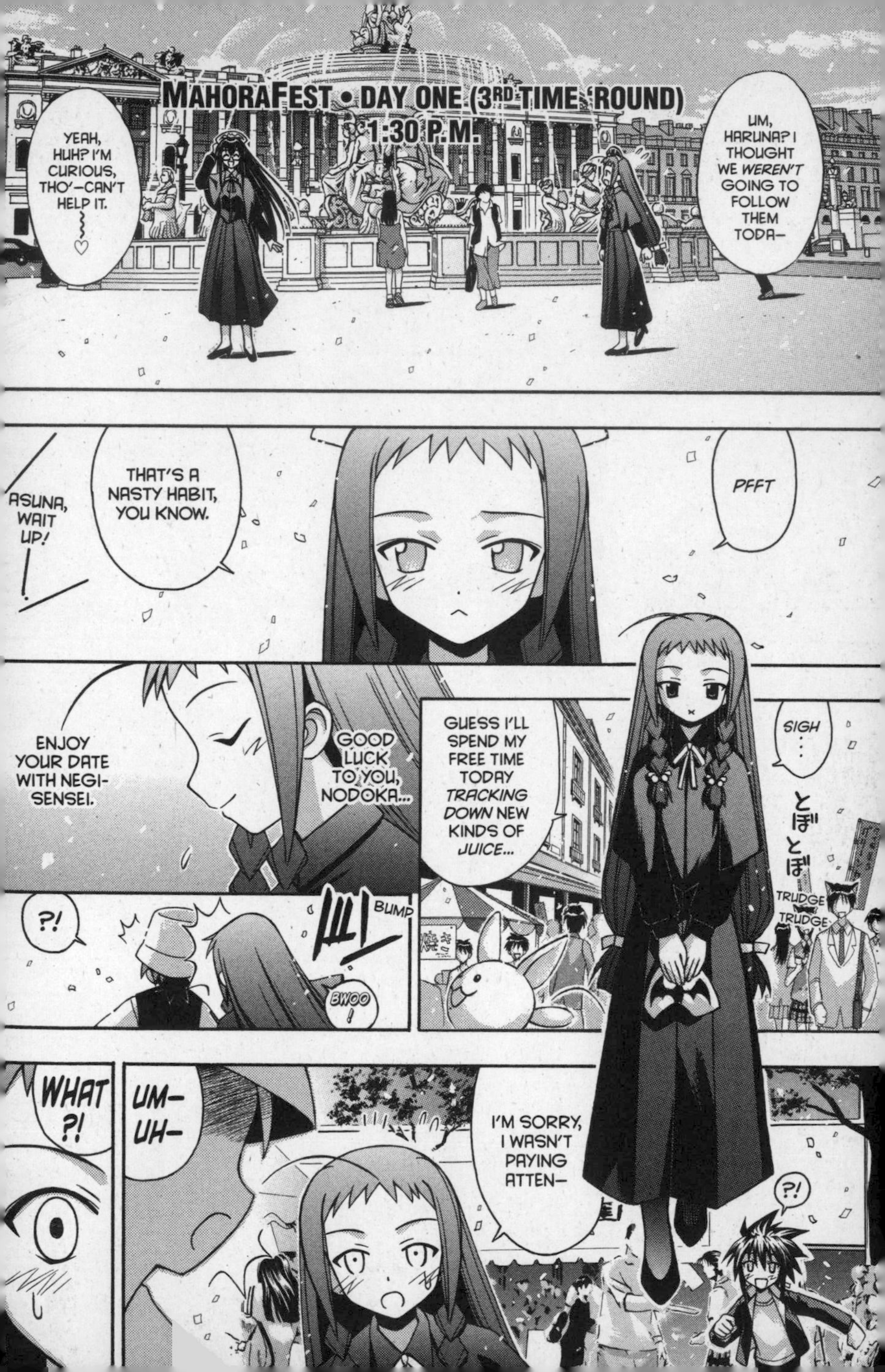
MAHORAFEST • DAY ONE (3RD TIME 'ROUND)
1:30 P.M.
UM, HARUNA? I THOUGHT WE *WEREN'T* GOING TO FOLLOW THEM TODA—
YEAH, HUH? I'M CURIOUS, THO'—CAN'T HELP IT. ♡
PFFT
THAT'S A NASTY HABIT, YOU KNOW.
ASUNA, WAIT UP!
SIGH...
とぼとぼ
TRUDGE TRUDGE
GUESS I'LL SPEND MY FREE TIME TODAY *TRACKING DOWN* NEW KINDS OF *JUICE*...
GOOD LUCK TO YOU, NODOKA...
ENJOY YOUR DATE WITH NEGI-SENSEI.
BUMP
BWOO!
?!
I'M SORRY, I WASN'T PAYING ATTEN—
?!
UM—UH—
WHAT?!

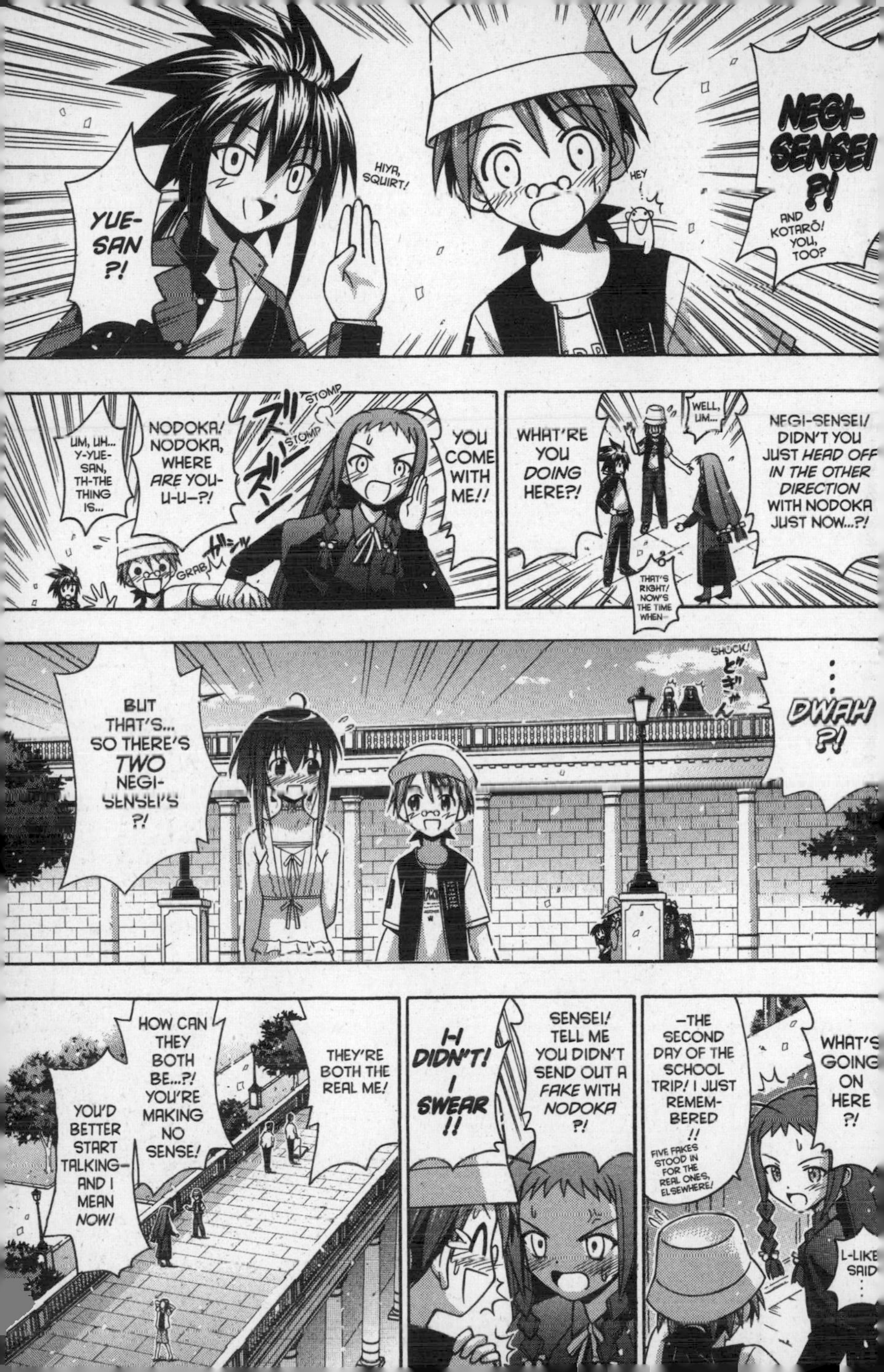
NEGI-SENSEI ?!
AND KOTARŌ! YOU, TOO?
HEY
HIYA, SQUIRT!
YUE-SAN ?!
NEGI-SENSEI! DIDN'T YOU JUST *HEAD OFF IN THE OTHER DIRECTION* WITH NODOKA JUST NOW...?!
WELL, UM...
WHAT'RE YOU *DOING* HERE?!
THAT'S RIGHT! NOW'S THE TIME WHEN—
YOU COME WITH ME!!
STOMP
STOMP
NODOKA! NODOKA, WHERE *ARE* YOU-U-U—?!
UM, UH... Y-YUE-SAN, TH-THE THING IS...
GRAB
...DWAH ?!
SHUCK!
BUT THAT'S... SO THERE'S *TWO* NEGI-SENSEI'S ?!
WHAT'S GOING ON HERE ?!
—THE SECOND DAY OF THE SCHOOL TRIP! I JUST REMEMBERED !!
FIVE FAKES STOOD IN FOR THE REAL ONES, ELSEWHERE!
L-LIKE I SAID...
SENSEI! TELL ME YOU DIDN'T SEND OUT A *FAKE* WITH *NODOKA* ?!
I-I DIDN'T! I SWEAR !!
THEY'RE BOTH THE REAL ME!
HOW CAN THEY BOTH BE...?! YOU'RE MAKING NO SENSE!
YOU'D BETTER START TALKING—AND I MEAN *NOW*!

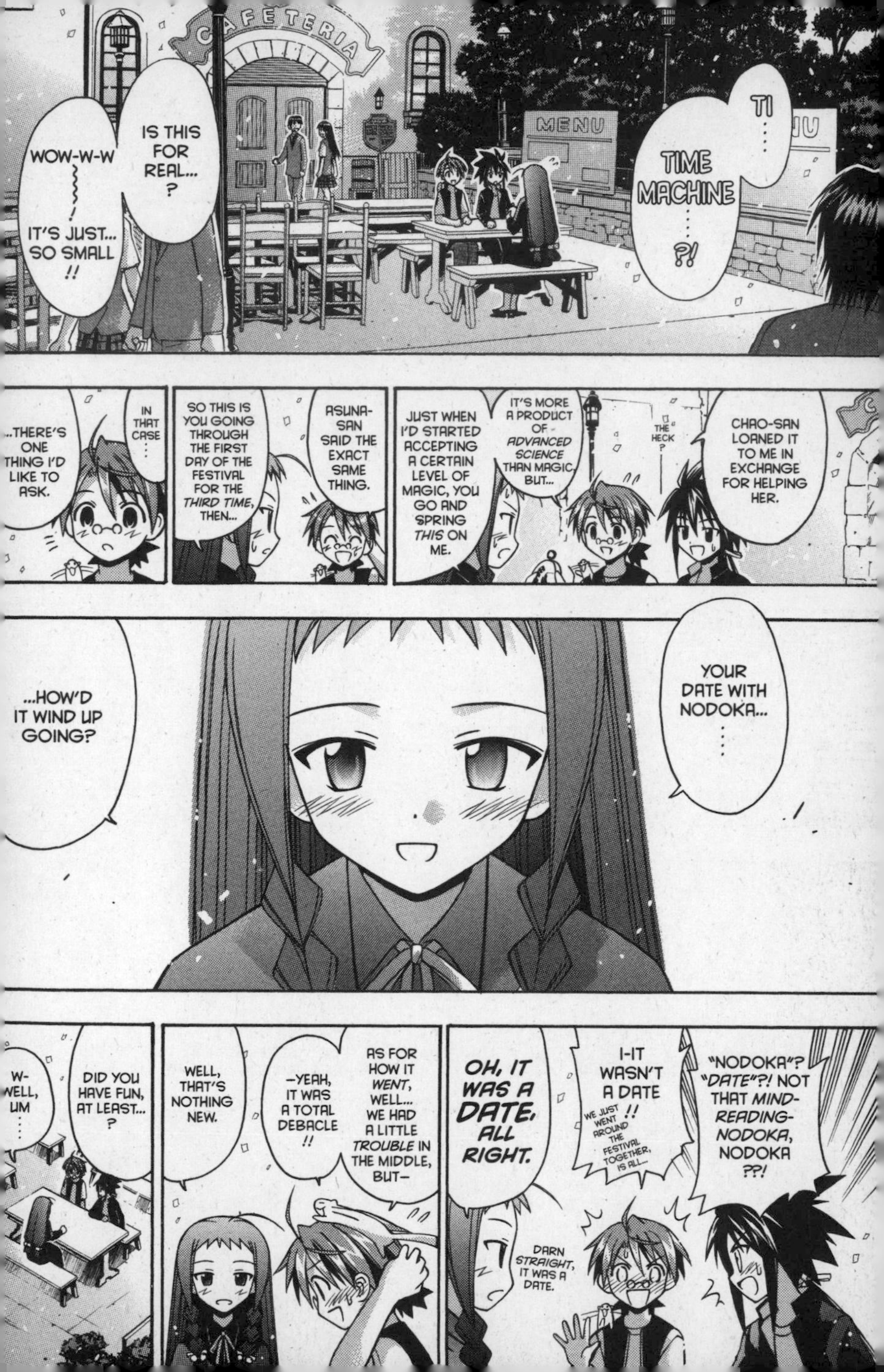

TI.... TIME MACHINE......?!
IS THIS FOR REAL...?
WOW-W-W~~~! IT'S JUST... SO SMALL!!
CHAO-SAN LOANED IT TO ME IN EXCHANGE FOR HELPING HER.
THE HECK?
IT'S MORE A PRODUCT OF ADVANCED SCIENCE THAN MAGIC, BUT...
JUST WHEN I'D STARTED ACCEPTING A CERTAIN LEVEL OF MAGIC, YOU GO AND SPRING THIS ON ME.
ASUNA-SAN SAID THE EXACT SAME THING.
SO THIS IS YOU GOING THROUGH THE FIRST DAY OF THE FESTIVAL FOR THE THIRD TIME, THEN...
IN THAT CASE...
...THERE'S ONE THING I'D LIKE TO ASK.
YOUR DATE WITH NODOKA......
...HOW'D IT WIND UP GOING?
"NODOKA"? "DATE"?! NOT THAT MIND-READING-NODOKA, NODOKA??!
I-IT WASN'T A DATE!!
WE JUST WENT AROUND THE FESTIVAL TOGETHER, IS ALL...
OH, IT WAS A DATE, ALL RIGHT.
DARN STRAIGHT, IT WAS A DATE.
AS FOR HOW IT WENT, WELL... WE HAD A LITTLE TROUBLE IN THE MIDDLE, BUT—
—YEAH, IT WAS A TOTAL DEBACLE!!
WELL, THAT'S NOTHING NEW.
DID YOU HAVE FUN, AT LEAST...?
W-WELL, UM....

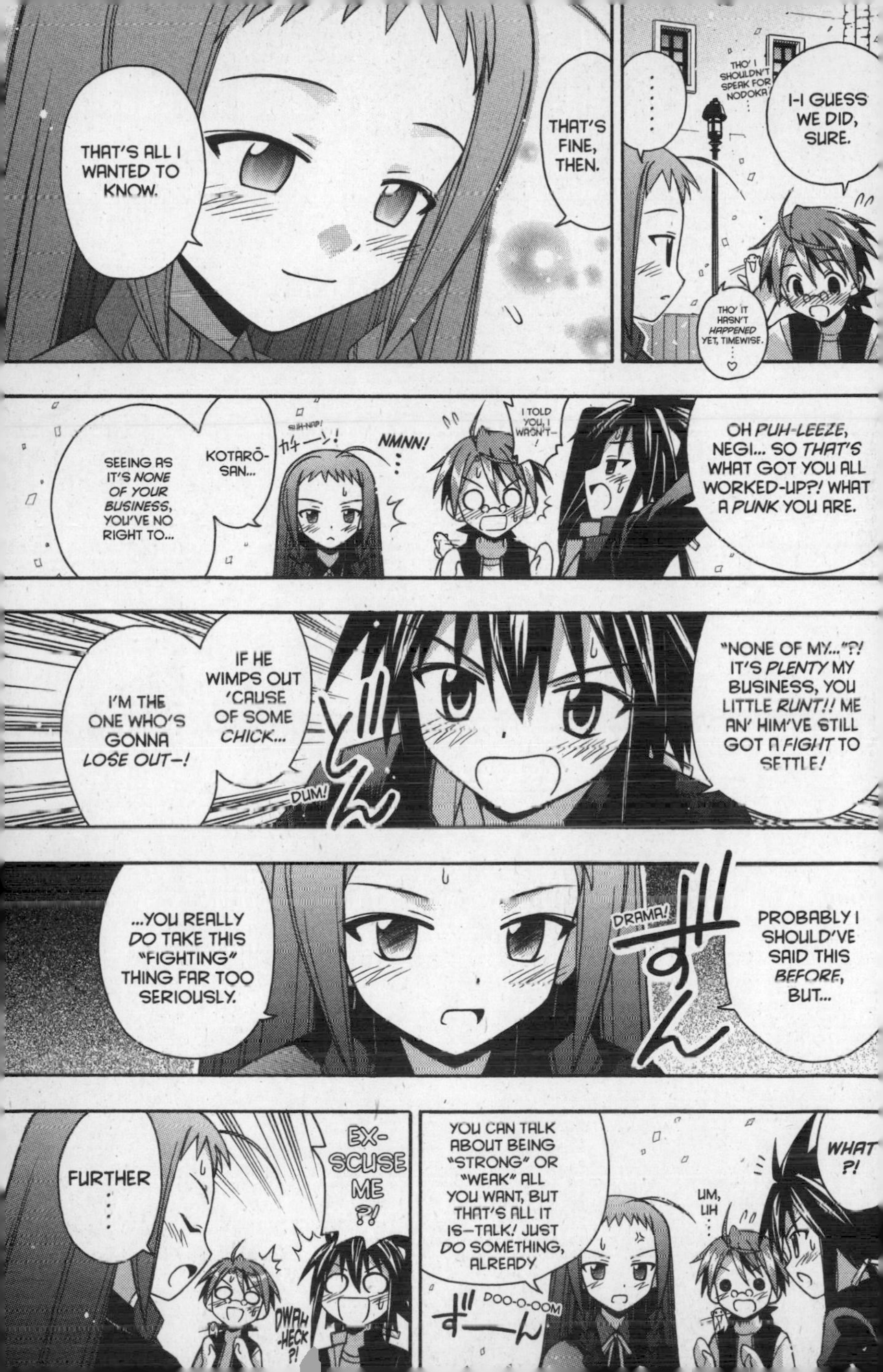
I-I GUESS WE DID, SURE.
THO' I SHOULDN'T SPEAK FOR NODOKA!
THO' IT HASN'T HAPPENED YET, TIMEWISE. ... ♡
......
THAT'S FINE, THEN.
THAT'S ALL I WANTED TO KNOW.
OH PUH-LEEZE, NEGI... SO THAT'S WHAT GOT YOU ALL WORKED-UP?! WHAT A PUNK YOU ARE.
I TOLD YOU, I WASN'T—!
NMNN! ...
SHH-NAP!
カチーン!
KOTARŌ-SAN...
SEEING AS IT'S NONE OF YOUR BUSINESS, YOU'VE NO RIGHT TO...
"NONE OF MY..."?! IT'S PLENTY MY BUSINESS, YOU LITTLE RUNT!! ME AN' HIM'VE STILL GOT A FIGHT TO SETTLE!
DUM!
IF HE WIMPS OUT 'CAUSE OF SOME CHICK...
I'M THE ONE WHO'S GONNA LOSE OUT—!
PROBABLY I SHOULD'VE SAID THIS BEFORE, BUT...
DRAMA!
...YOU REALLY DO TAKE THIS "FIGHTING" THING FAR TOO SERIOUSLY.
WHAT?!
UM, UH ...
YOU CAN TALK ABOUT BEING "STRONG" OR "WEAK" ALL YOU WANT, BUT THAT'S ALL IT IS—TALK! JUST DO SOMETHING, ALREADY
DOO-O-OOM
ずーん
EX-SCUSE ME ?!
FURTHER ...
DWAH-HECK ?!

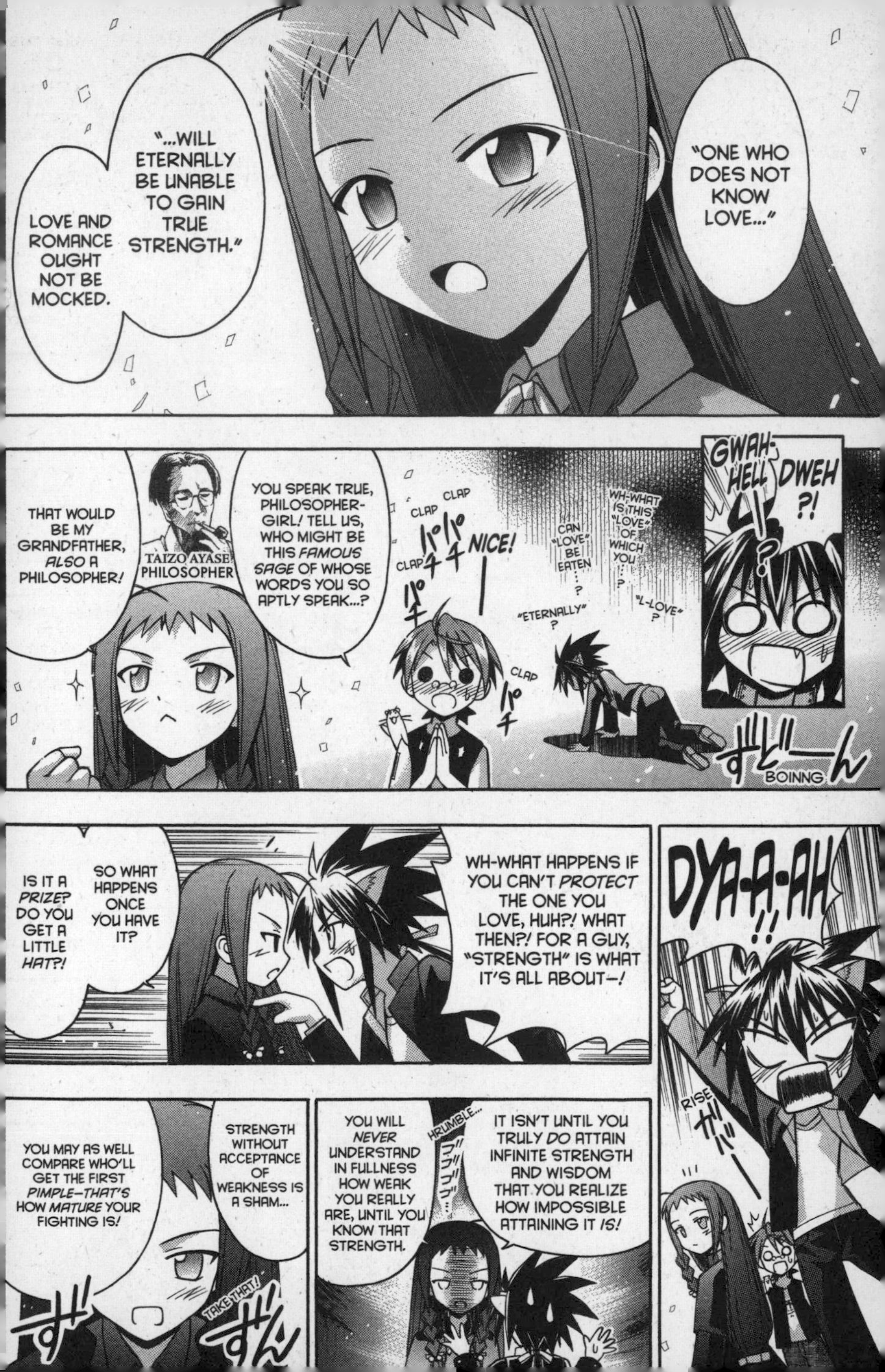
"ONE WHO DOES NOT KNOW LOVE..."
"...WILL ETERNALLY BE UNABLE TO GAIN TRUE STRENGTH."
LOVE AND ROMANCE OUGHT NOT BE MOCKED.
GWAH-HELL DWEH ?!
!?
WH-WHAT IS THIS "LOVE" OF WHICH YOU...?
CAN "LOVE" BE EATEN...?
"L-LOVE"?
"ETERNALLY"?
BOINNG
CLAP CLAP
CLAP
NICE!
CLAP
YOU SPEAK TRUE, PHILOSOPHER-GIRL! TELL US, WHO MIGHT BE THIS *FAMOUS SAGE* OF WHOSE WORDS YOU SO APTLY SPEAK...?
TAIZO AYASE PHILOSOPHER
THAT WOULD BE MY GRANDFATHER, *ALSO* A PHILOSOPHER!
DYA-A-AH !!
RISE
WH-WHAT HAPPENS IF YOU CAN'T *PROTECT* THE ONE YOU LOVE, HUH?! WHAT THEN?! FOR A GUY, "STRENGTH" IS WHAT IT'S ALL ABOUT—!
SO WHAT HAPPENS ONCE YOU HAVE IT?
IS IT A *PRIZE*? DO YOU GET A LITTLE *HAT*?!
IT ISN'T UNTIL YOU TRULY *DO* ATTAIN INFINITE STRENGTH AND WISDOM THAT YOU REALIZE HOW IMPOSSIBLE ATTAINING IT *IS*!
HRUMBLE...
YOU WILL *NEVER* UNDERSTAND IN FULLNESS HOW WEAK YOU REALLY ARE, UNTIL YOU KNOW THAT STRENGTH.
STRENGTH WITHOUT ACCEPTANCE OF WEAKNESS IS A SHAM...
YOU MAY AS WELL COMPARE WHO'LL GET THE FIRST *PIMPLE*—THAT'S HOW *MATURE* YOUR FIGHTING IS!
TAKE THAT!

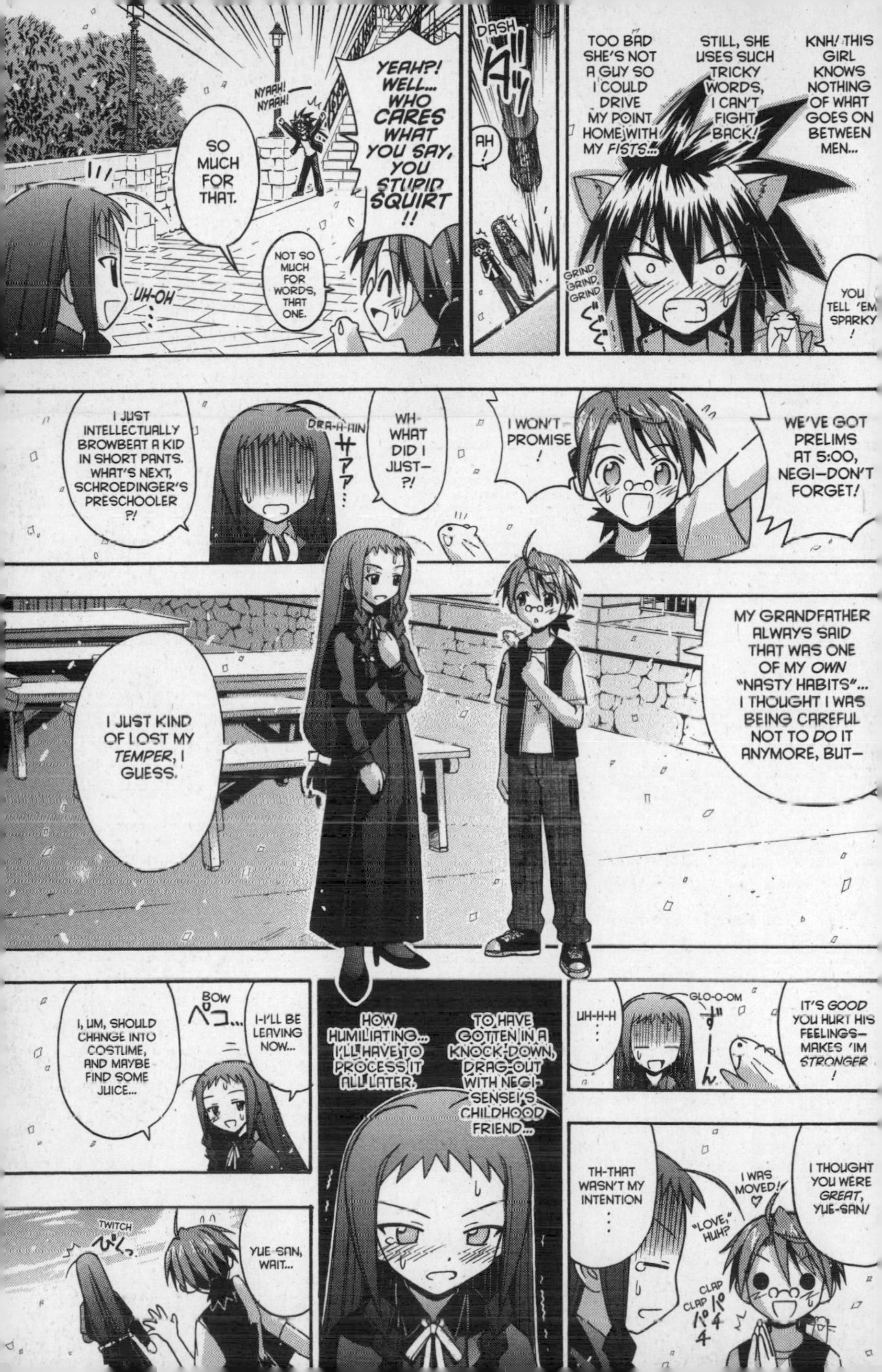
KNH! THIS GIRL KNOWS NOTHING OF WHAT GOES ON BETWEEN MEN...
STILL, SHE USES SUCH TRICKY WORDS, I CAN'T FIGHT BACK!
TOO BAD SHE'S NOT A GUY SO I COULD DRIVE MY POINT HOME WITH MY *FISTS*...
GRIND GRIND GRIND
YOU TELL 'EM SPARKY!
DASH
AH!
YEAH?! WELL... WHO CARES WHAT YOU SAY, YOU STUPID SQUIRT!!
NYAAH! NYAAH!
SO MUCH FOR THAT.
NOT SO MUCH FOR WORDS, THAT ONE.
UH-OH...
WE'VE GOT PRELIMS AT 5:00, NEGI—DON'T FORGET!
I WON'T PROMISE!
WH-WHAT DID I JUST—?!
DRA-A-AIN
I JUST INTELLECTUALLY BROWBEAT A KID IN SHORT PANTS. WHAT'S NEXT, SCHROEDINGER'S PRESCHOOLER?!
MY GRANDFATHER ALWAYS SAID THAT WAS ONE OF MY *OWN* "NASTY HABITS"... I THOUGHT I WAS BEING CAREFUL NOT TO *DO* IT ANYMORE, BUT—
I JUST KIND OF LOST MY *TEMPER*, I GUESS.
IT'S *GOOD* YOU HURT HIS FEELINGS—MAKES 'IM *STRONGER*!
GLO-O-OM
UH-H-H...
I THOUGHT YOU WERE *GREAT*, YUE-SAN!
I WAS MOVED! ♡
"LOVE," HUH?
TH-THAT WASN'T MY INTENTION...
CLAP CLAP
TO HAVE GOTTEN IN A KNOCK-DOWN, DRAG-OUT WITH NEGI-SENSEI'S CHILDHOOD FRIEND...
HOW HUMILIATING... I'LL HAVE TO PROCESS IT ALL LATER.
I-I'LL BE LEAVING NOW...
BOW
I, UM, SHOULD CHANGE INTO COSTUME, AND MAYBE FIND SOME JUICE...
YUE-SAN, WAIT...
TWITCH

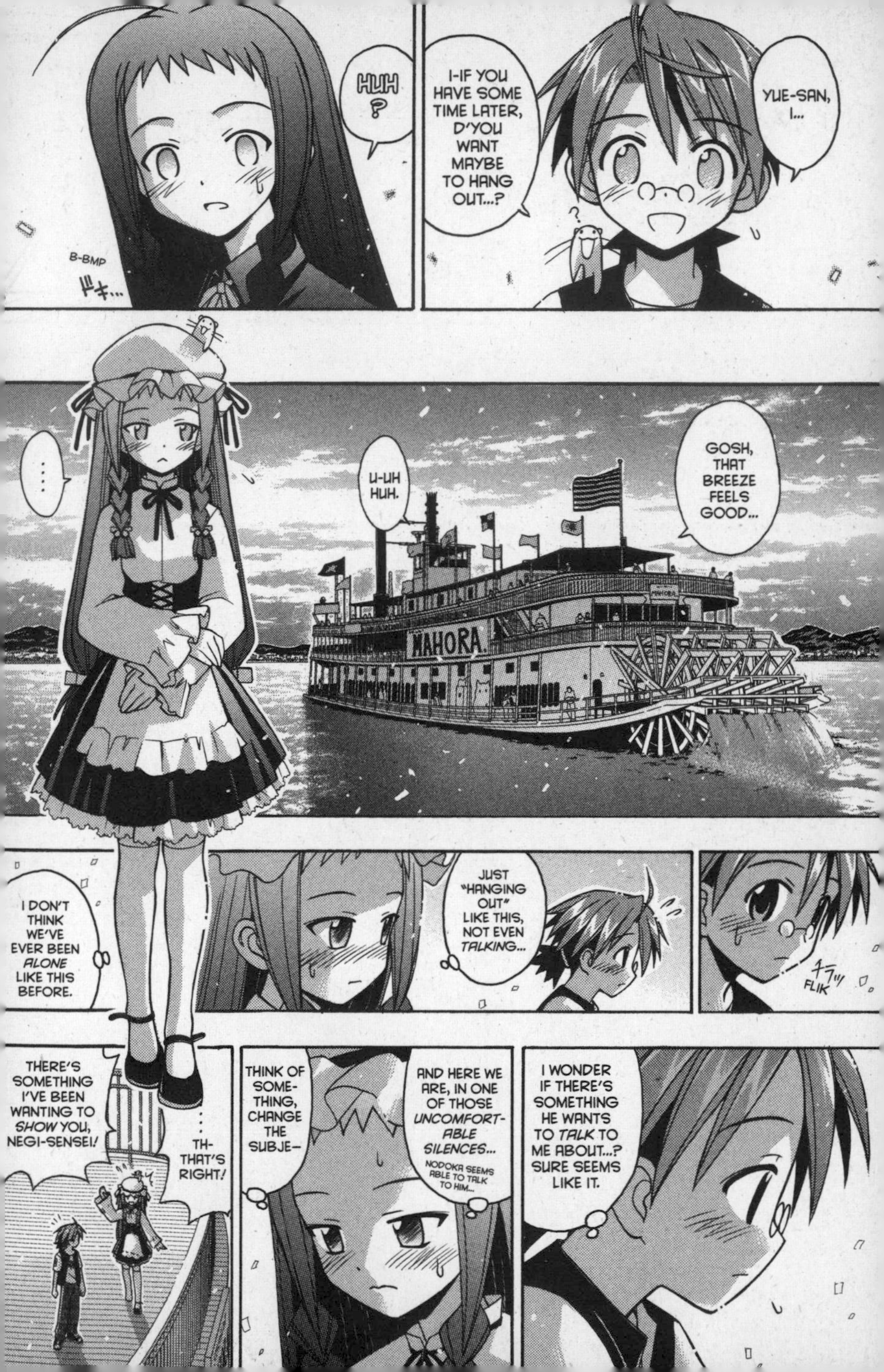
YUE-SAN, I...
I-IF YOU HAVE SOME TIME LATER, D'YOU WANT MAYBE TO HANG OUT...?
HUH ?
B-BMP
ドキ…
GOSH, THAT BREEZE FEELS GOOD...
U-UH HUH.
......
MAHORA
チラッ
FLIK
JUST "HANGING OUT" LIKE THIS, NOT EVEN TALKING...
I DON'T THINK WE'VE EVER BEEN ALONE LIKE THIS BEFORE.
I WONDER IF THERE'S SOMETHING HE WANTS TO TALK TO ME ABOUT...? SURE SEEMS LIKE IT.
AND HERE WE ARE, IN ONE OF THOSE UNCOMFORTABLE SILENCES...
NODOKA SEEMS ABLE TO TALK TO HIM...
THINK OF SOMETHING, CHANGE THE SUBJE—
...TH-THAT'S RIGHT!
THERE'S SOMETHING I'VE BEEN WANTING TO SHOW YOU, NEGI-SENSEI!

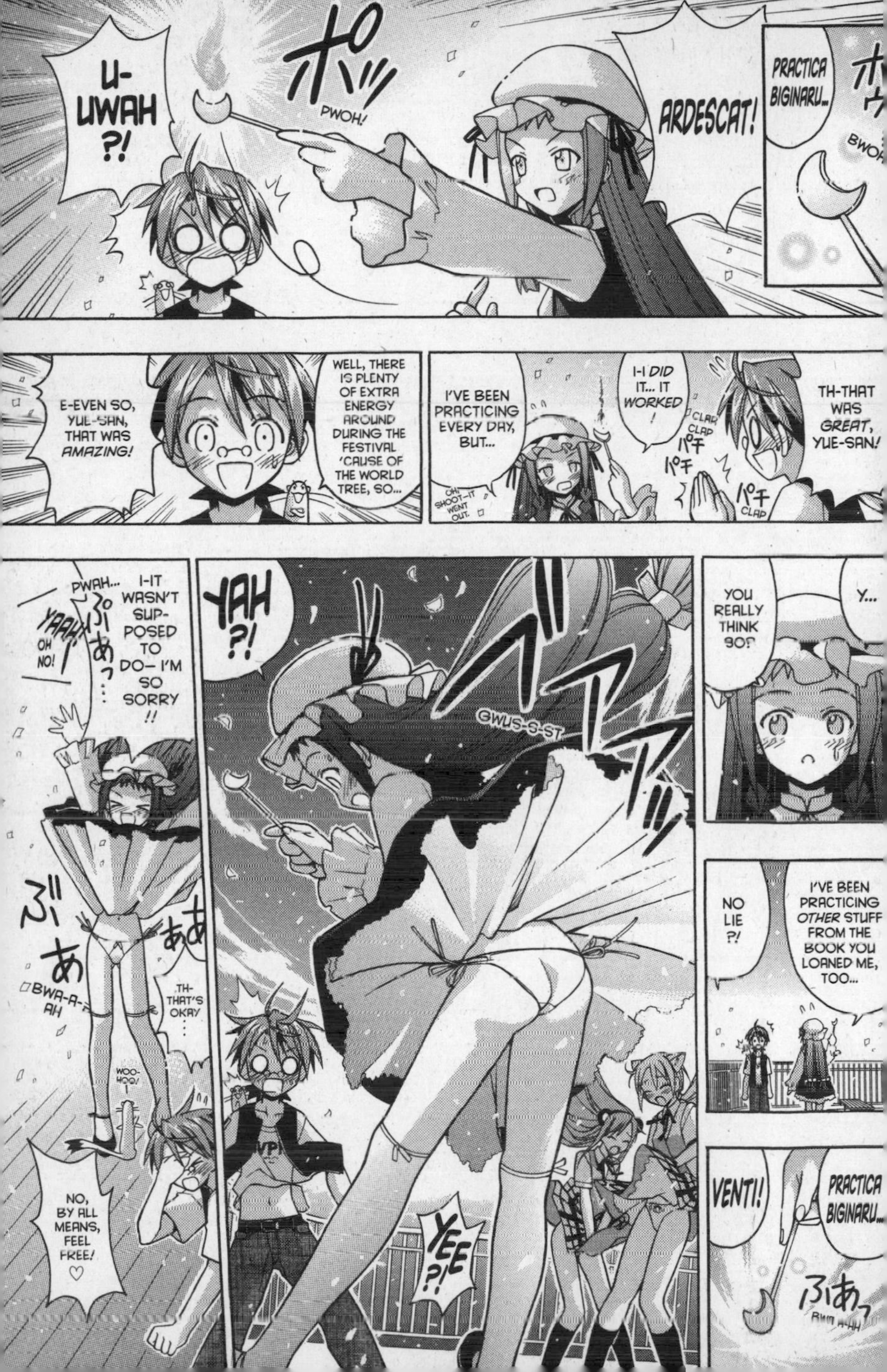
PRACTICA BIGINARU...
ホウ
BWOH
ARDESCAT!
ポッ
PWOH!
U-UWAH?!
TH-THAT WAS GREAT, YUE-SAN!
I-I DID IT... IT WORKED!
CLAP CLAP
パチ パチ
パチ
CLAP
I'VE BEEN PRACTICING EVERY DAY, BUT...
OH! SHOOT—IT WENT OUT.
WELL, THERE IS PLENTY OF EXTRA ENERGY AROUND DURING THE FESTIVAL 'CAUSE OF THE WORLD TREE, SO...
E-EVEN SO, YUE-SAN, THAT WAS AMAZING!
Y...
YOU REALLY THINK SO?
I'VE BEEN PRACTICING OTHER STUFF FROM THE BOOK YOU LOANED ME, TOO...
NO LIE?!
PRACTICA BIGINARU...
VENTI!
ふあっ
BWA-AH
YAH?!
GWUS-S-ST
YEE?!
TH-THAT'S OKAY...
WOO-HOO!
PWAH...
ぷあっ...
I-IT WASN'T SUPPOSED TO DO— I'M SO SORRY!!
YAAH! OH NO!
ぶあ
ああ
BWA-A-AH
NO, BY ALL MEANS, FEEL FREE! ♡

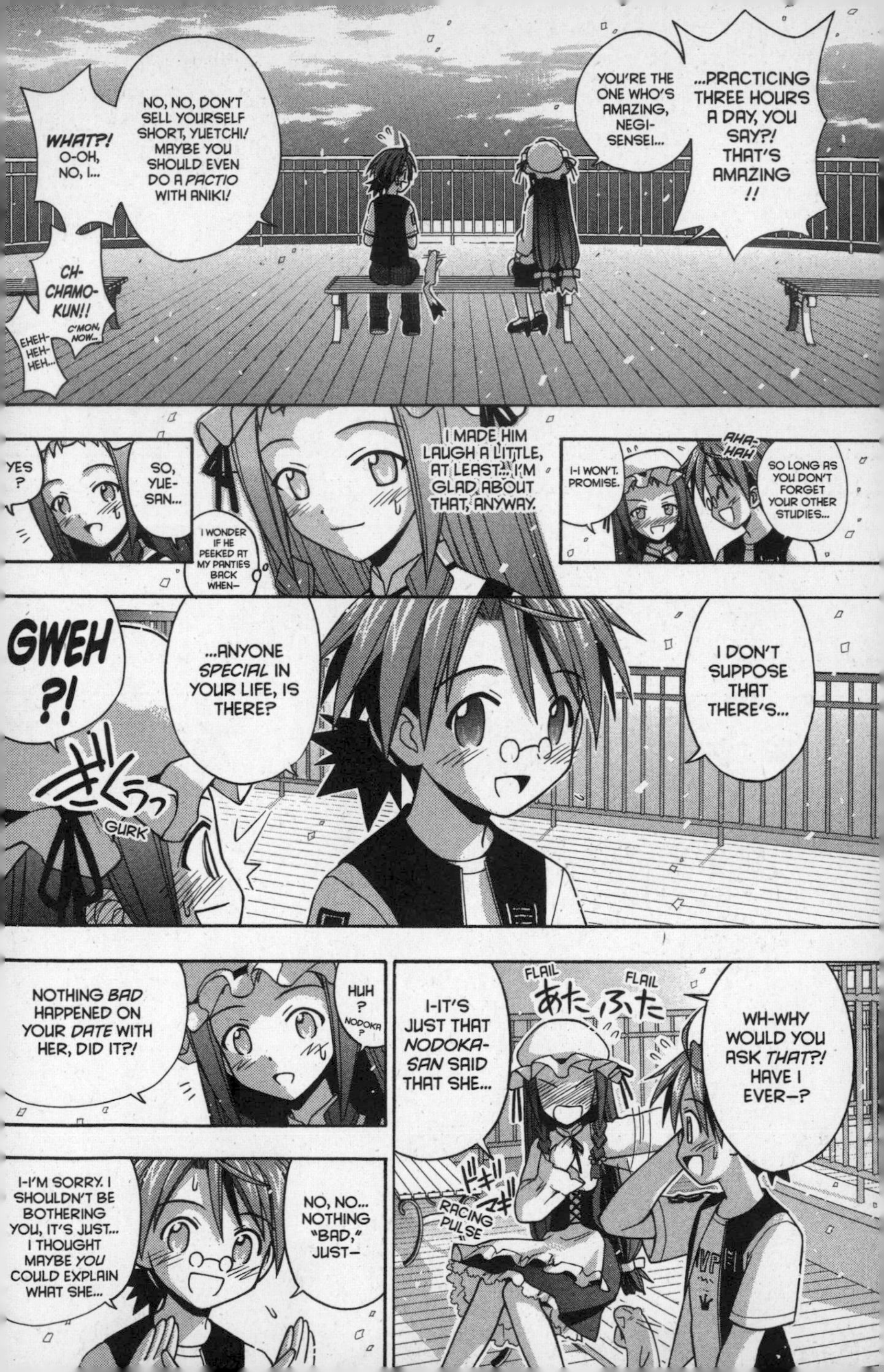

...PRACTICING THREE HOURS A DAY, YOU SAY?! THAT'S AMAZING!!
YOU'RE THE ONE WHO'S AMAZING, NEGI-SENSEI...
NO, NO, DON'T SELL YOURSELF SHORT, YUETCHI! MAYBE YOU SHOULD EVEN DO A PACTIO WITH ANIKI!
WHAT?! O-OH, NO, I...
CH-CHAMO-KUN!!
C'MON, NOW...
EHEH-HEH-HEH...
AHA-HAH
SO LONG AS YOU DON'T FORGET YOUR OTHER STUDIES...
I-I WON'T. PROMISE.
I MADE HIM LAUGH A LITTLE, AT LEAST... I'M GLAD ABOUT THAT, ANYWAY.
I WONDER IF HE PEEKED AT MY PANTIES BACK WHEN—
SO, YUE-SAN...
YES?
I DON'T SUPPOSE THAT THERE'S...
...ANYONE SPECIAL IN YOUR LIFE, IS THERE?
GWEH?!
ぎくうっ
GURK
WH-WHY WOULD YOU ASK THAT?! HAVE I EVER—?
FLAIL
FLAIL
あたふた
I-IT'S JUST THAT NODOKA-SAN SAID THAT SHE...
ドキマギ
RACING PULSE
HUH? NODOKA?
NOTHING BAD HAPPENED ON YOUR DATE WITH HER, DID IT?!
NO, NO... NOTHING "BAD," JUST—
I-I'M SORRY. I SHOULDN'T BE BOTHERING YOU, IT'S JUST... I THOUGHT MAYBE YOU COULD EXPLAIN WHAT SHE...

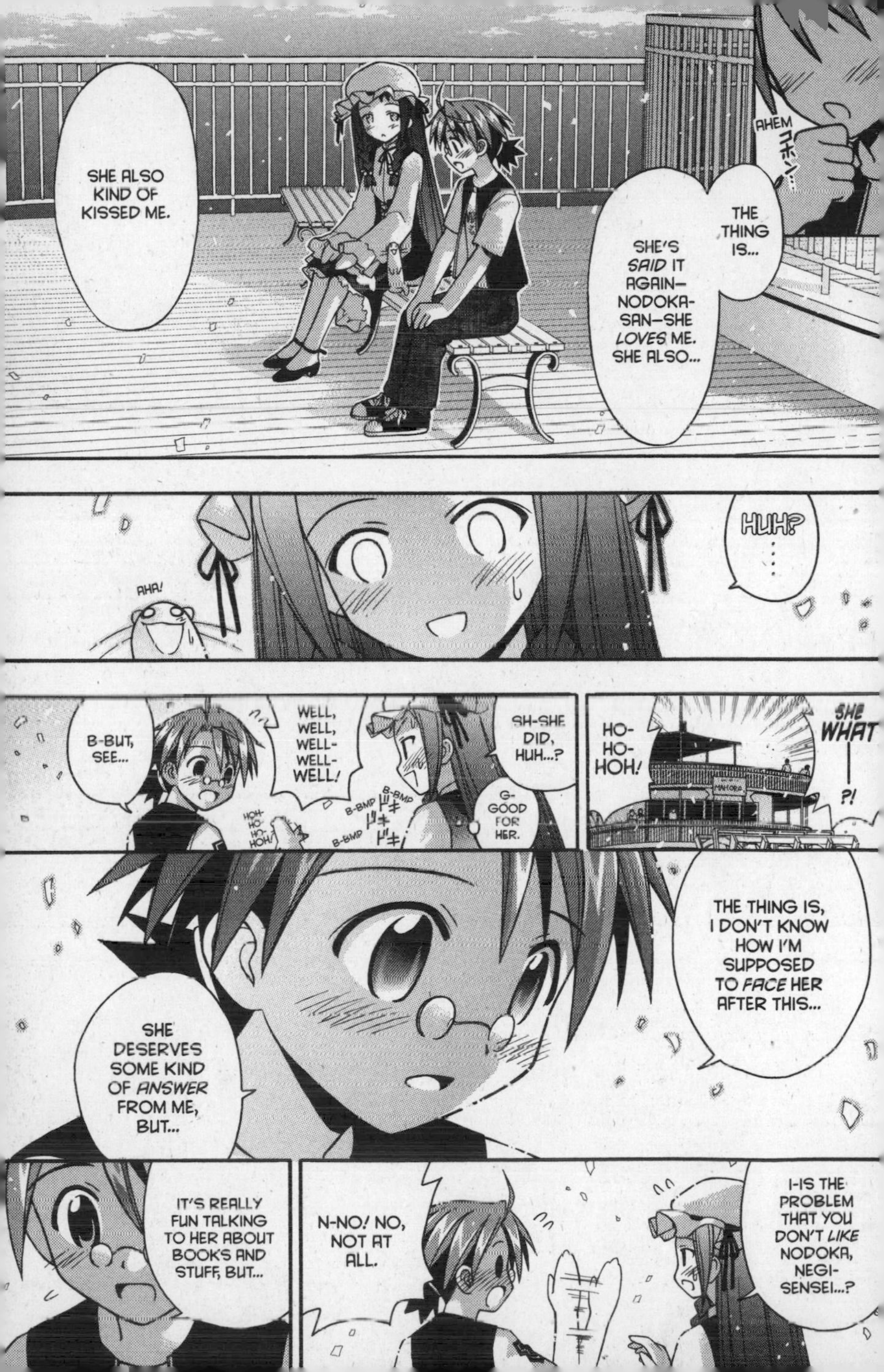
AHEM
コホン…
THE THING IS...
SHE'S *SAID* IT AGAIN—NODOKA-SAN—SHE *LOVES* ME. SHE ALSO...
SHE ALSO KIND OF KISSED ME.
HUH? ......
AHA!
SHE WHAT ?!
HO-HO-HOH!
SH-SHE DID, HUH...?
G-GOOD FOR HER.
B-BMP B-BMP B-BMP
ドキドキドキ
WELL, WELL, WELL-WELL-WELL!
HOH-HO-HO-HOH!
B-BUT, SEE...
THE THING IS, I DON'T KNOW HOW I'M SUPPOSED TO *FACE* HER AFTER THIS...
SHE DESERVES SOME KIND OF *ANSWER* FROM ME, BUT...
I-IS THE PROBLEM THAT YOU DON'T *LIKE* NODOKA, NEGI-SENSEI...?
N-NO! NO, NOT AT ALL.
IT'S REALLY FUN TALKING TO HER ABOUT BOOKS AND STUFF, BUT...

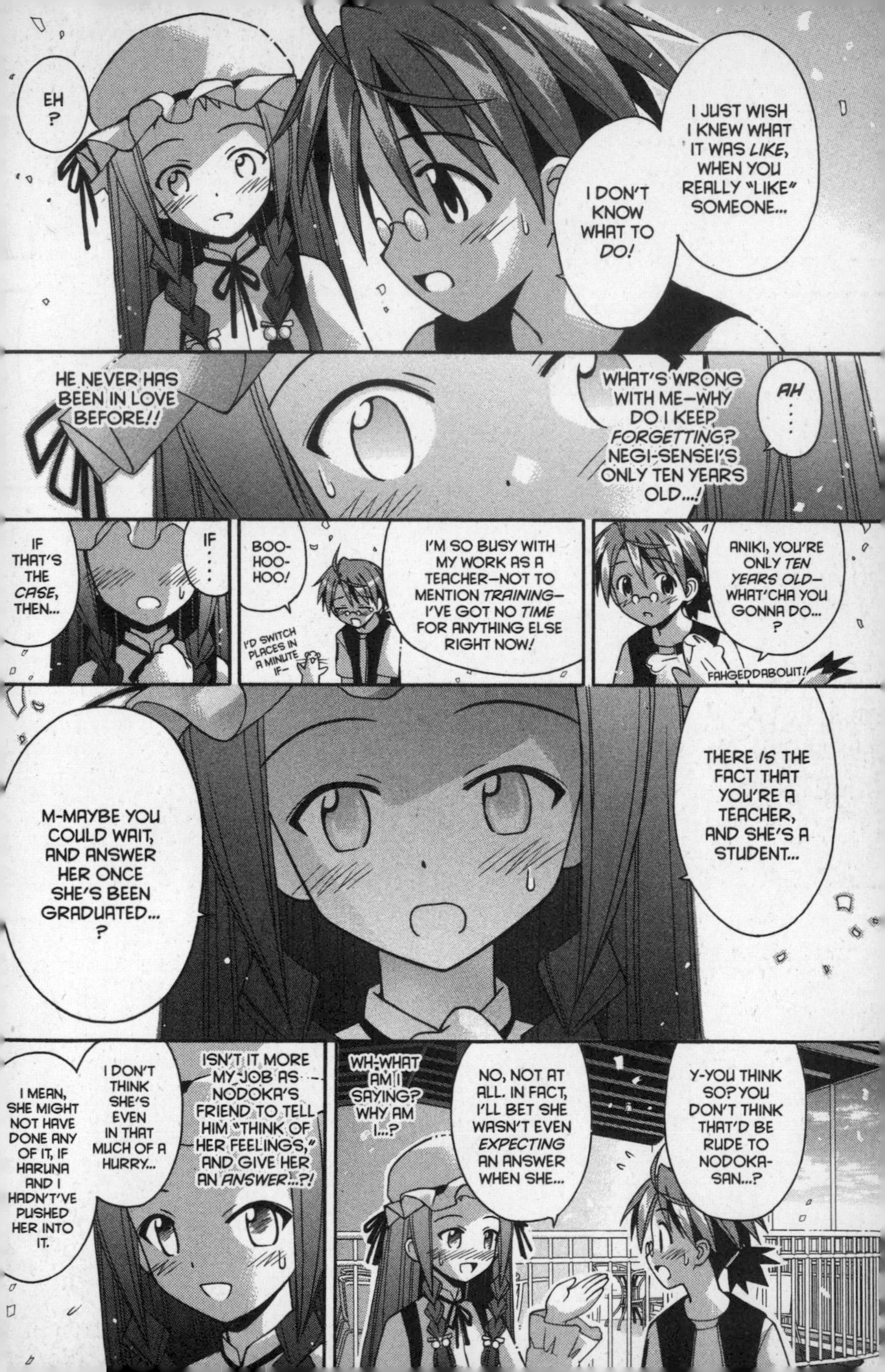
I JUST WISH I KNEW WHAT IT WAS *LIKE*, WHEN YOU REALLY "LIKE" SOMEONE...
I DON'T KNOW WHAT TO *DO*!
EH?
AH...
WHAT'S WRONG WITH ME—WHY DO I KEEP *FORGETTING*? NEGI-SENSEI'S ONLY TEN YEARS OLD...!
HE NEVER HAS BEEN IN LOVE BEFORE!!
ANIKI, YOU'RE ONLY *TEN YEARS OLD*—WHAT'CHA YOU GONNA DO...?
FAHGEDDABOUIT!
I'M SO BUSY WITH MY WORK AS A TEACHER—NOT TO MENTION *TRAINING*—I'VE GOT NO *TIME* FOR ANYTHING ELSE RIGHT NOW!
BOO-HOO-HOO!
I'D SWITCH PLACES IN A MINUTE IF—
IF...
IF THAT'S THE *CASE*, THEN...
THERE *IS* THE FACT THAT YOU'RE A TEACHER, AND SHE'S A STUDENT...
M-MAYBE YOU COULD WAIT, AND ANSWER HER ONCE SHE'S BEEN GRADUATED...?
Y-YOU THINK SO? YOU DON'T THINK THAT'D BE RUDE TO NODOKA-SAN...?
NO, NOT AT ALL. IN FACT, I'LL BET SHE WASN'T EVEN *EXPECTING* AN ANSWER WHEN SHE...
WH-WHAT AM I SAYING? WHY AM I...?
ISN'T IT MORE MY JOB AS NODOKA'S FRIEND TO TELL HIM "THINK OF HER FEELINGS," AND GIVE HER AN *ANSWER*...?!
I DON'T THINK SHE'S EVEN IN THAT MUCH OF A HURRY...
I MEAN, SHE MIGHT NOT HAVE DONE ANY OF IT, IF HARUNA AND I HADN'T'VE PUSHED HER INTO IT.

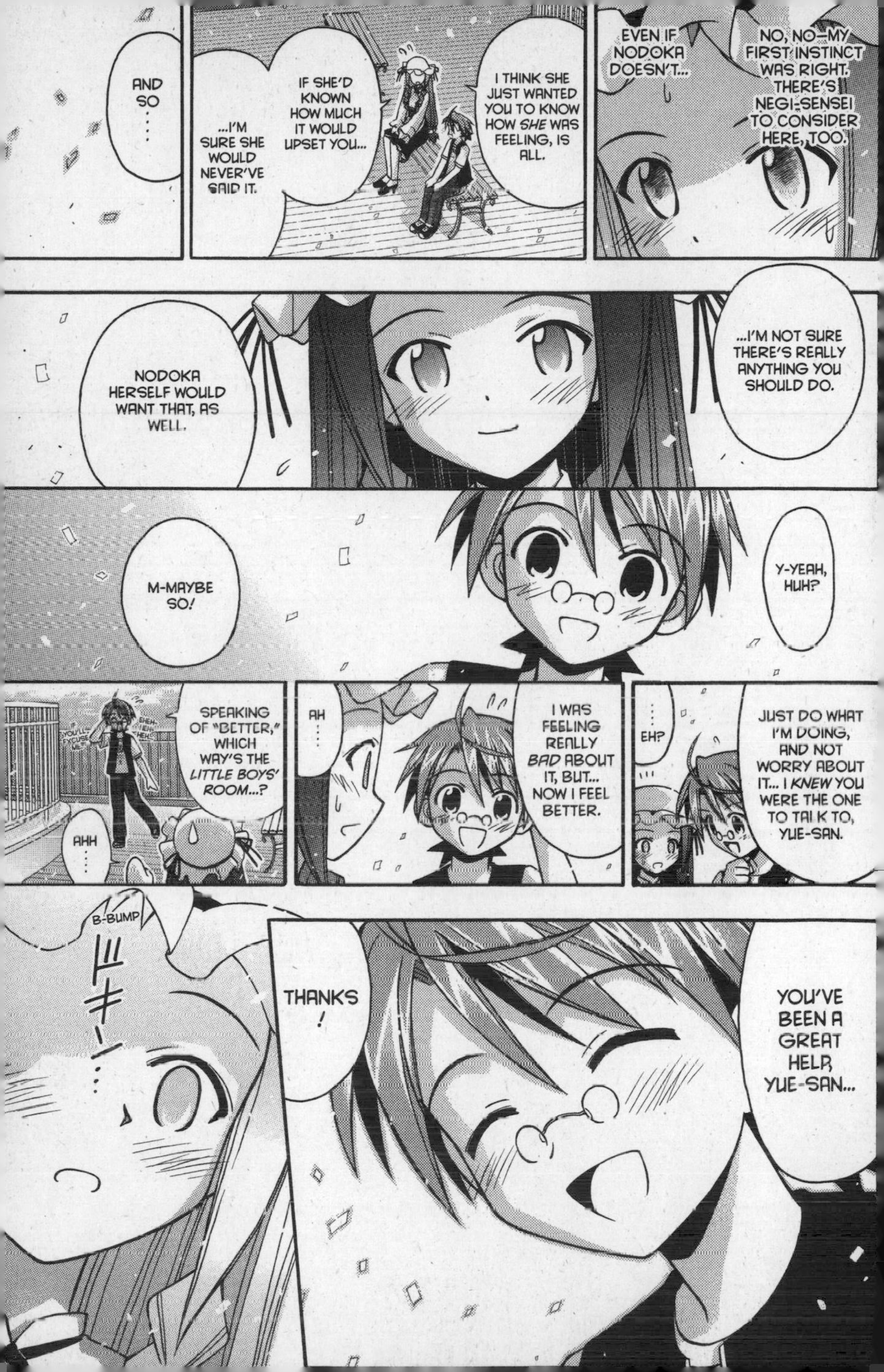
NO, NO—MY FIRST INSTINCT WAS RIGHT. THERE'S NEGI-SENSEI TO CONSIDER HERE, TOO.
EVEN IF NODOKA DOESN'T...
I THINK SHE JUST WANTED YOU TO KNOW HOW *SHE* WAS FEELING, IS ALL.
IF SHE'D KNOWN HOW MUCH IT WOULD UPSET YOU...
...I'M SURE SHE WOULD NEVER'VE SAID IT.
AND SO ......
...I'M NOT SURE THERE'S REALLY ANYTHING YOU SHOULD DO.
NODOKA HERSELF WOULD WANT THAT, AS WELL.
Y-YEAH, HUH?
M-MAYBE SO!
JUST DO WHAT I'M DOING, AND NOT WORRY ABOUT IT... I *KNEW* YOU WERE THE ONE TO TALK TO, YUE-SAN.
...EH?
I WAS FEELING REALLY *BAD* ABOUT IT, BUT... NOW I FEEL BETTER.
AH ......
SPEAKING OF "BETTER," WHICH WAY'S THE *LITTLE BOYS' ROOM*...?
IF YOU'LL EXCUSE ME.
AHH ......
YOU'VE BEEN A GREAT HELP, YUE-SAN...
THANKS!
B-BUMP

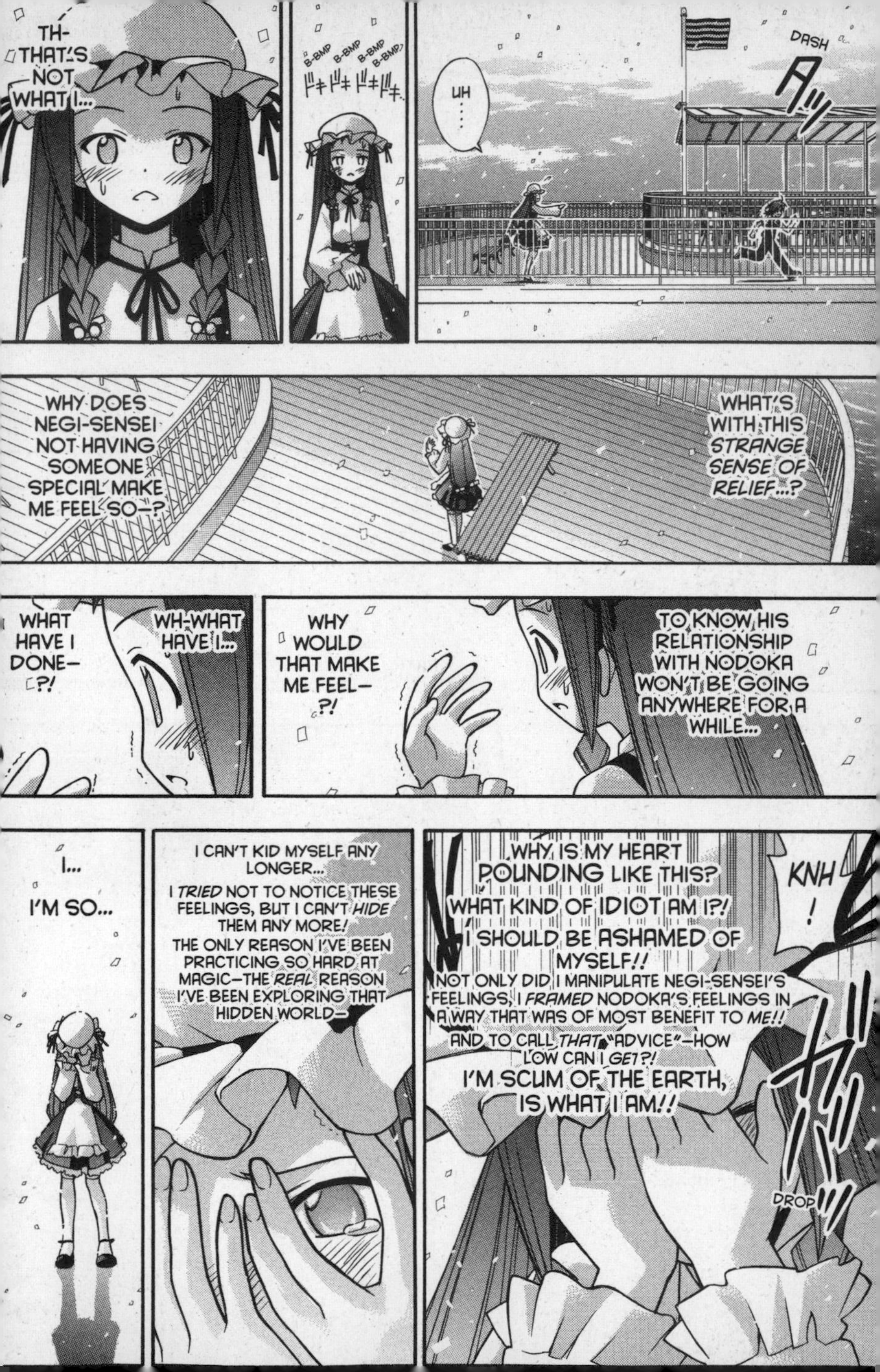
DASH
UH...
B-BMP B-BMP B-BMP B-BMP
ドキドキドキドキ
TH- THAT'S NOT WHAT I...
WHAT'S WITH THIS STRANGE SENSE OF RELIEF...?
WHY DOES NEGI-SENSEI NOT HAVING SOMEONE SPECIAL MAKE ME FEEL SO—?
TO KNOW HIS RELATIONSHIP WITH NODOKA WON'T BE GOING ANYWHERE FOR A WHILE...
WHY WOULD THAT MAKE ME FEEL—?!
WH-WHAT HAVE I...
WHAT HAVE I DONE—?!
KNH!
WHY IS MY HEART POUNDING LIKE THIS? WHAT KIND OF IDIOT AM I?! I SHOULD BE ASHAMED OF MYSELF!!
NOT ONLY DID I MANIPULATE NEGI-SENSEI'S FEELINGS, I *FRAMED* NODOKA'S FEELINGS IN A WAY THAT WAS OF MOST BENEFIT TO *ME*!!
AND TO CALL *THAT* "ADVICE"—HOW LOW CAN I *GET*?!
I'M SCUM OF THE EARTH, IS WHAT I AM!!
DROP!!
I CAN'T KID MYSELF ANY LONGER...
I *TRIED* NOT TO NOTICE THESE FEELINGS, BUT I CAN'T *HIDE* THEM ANY MORE!
THE ONLY REASON I'VE BEEN PRACTICING SO HARD AT MAGIC—THE *REAL* REASON I'VE BEEN EXPLORING THAT HIDDEN WORLD—
I...
I'M SO...

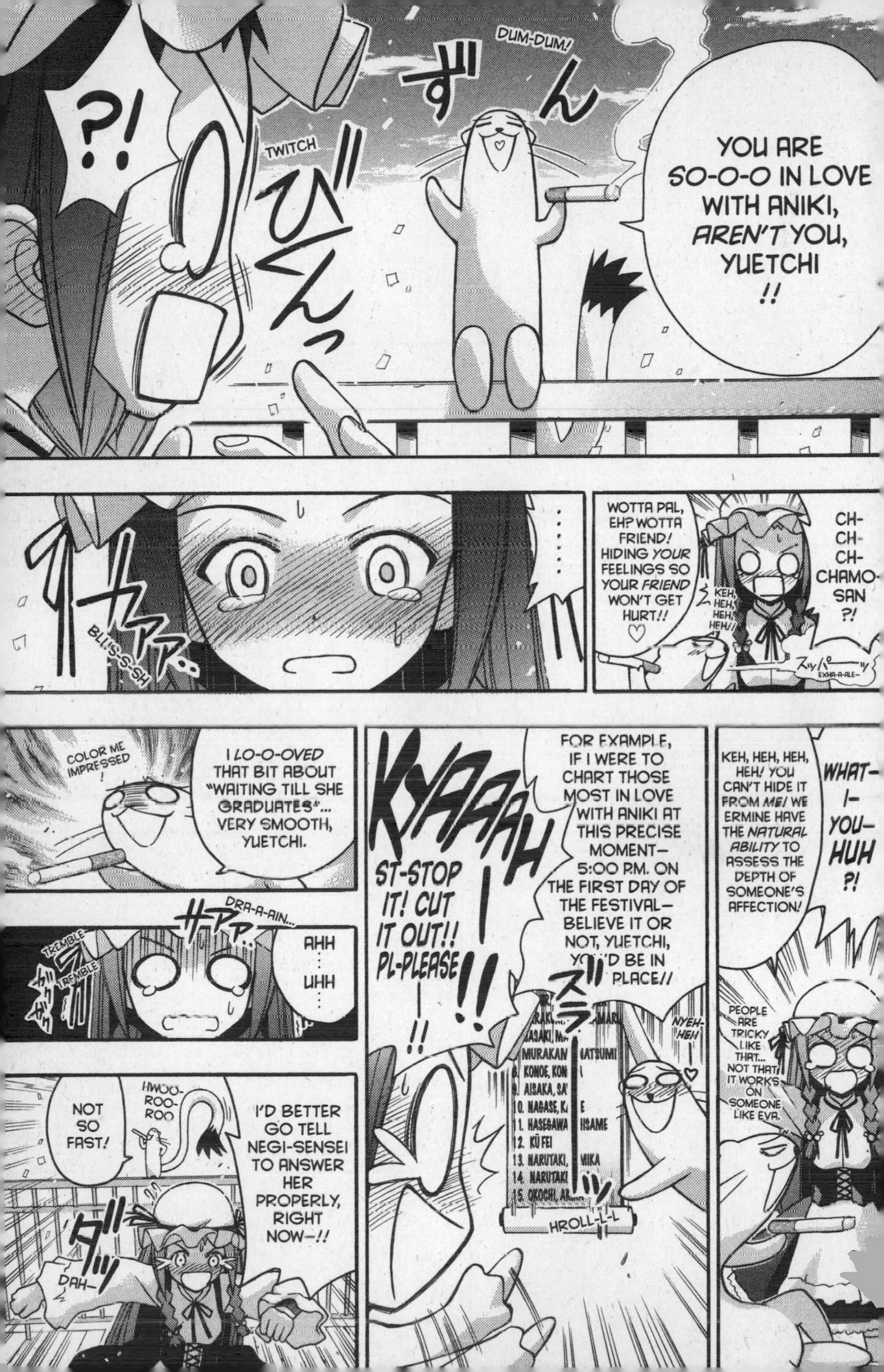
DUM-DUM!
YOU ARE SO-O-O IN LOVE WITH ANIKI, AREN'T YOU, YUETCHI!!
TWITCH
?!
CH-CH-CH-CHAMO-SAN?!
WOTTA PAL, EH? WOTTA FRIEND! HIDING YOUR FEELINGS SO YOUR FRIEND WON'T GET HURT!! ♡
KEH, HEH, HEH, HEH!!
EXHA-A-ALE—
......
WHAT-I-YOU-HUH?!
KEH, HEH, HEH, HEH! YOU CAN'T HIDE IT FROM ME! WE ERMINE HAVE THE NATURAL ABILITY TO ASSESS THE DEPTH OF SOMEONE'S AFFECTION!
PEOPLE ARE TRICKY LIKE THAT... NOT THAT IT WORKS ON SOMEONE LIKE EVA.
FOR EXAMPLE, IF I WERE TO CHART THOSE MOST IN LOVE WITH ANIKI AT THIS PRECISE MOMENT—5:00 P.M. ON THE FIRST DAY OF THE FESTIVAL—BELIEVE IT OR NOT, YUETCHI,
PLACE!!
KYAAAH!!!
ST-STOP IT! CUT IT OUT!! PL-PLEASE—!!
NYEH-HEH!♡
12. KŪ FEI
HROLL-L-L
COLOR ME IMPRESSED!
I LO-O-OVED THAT BIT ABOUT "WAITING TILL SHE GRADUATES"... VERY SMOOTH, YUETCHI.
DRA-A-AIN...
AHH... UHH...
TREMBLE TREMBLE
I'D BETTER GO TELL NEGI-SENSEI TO ANSWER HER PROPERLY, RIGHT NOW—!!
HWOO-ROO-ROO
NOT SO FAST!
DAH—

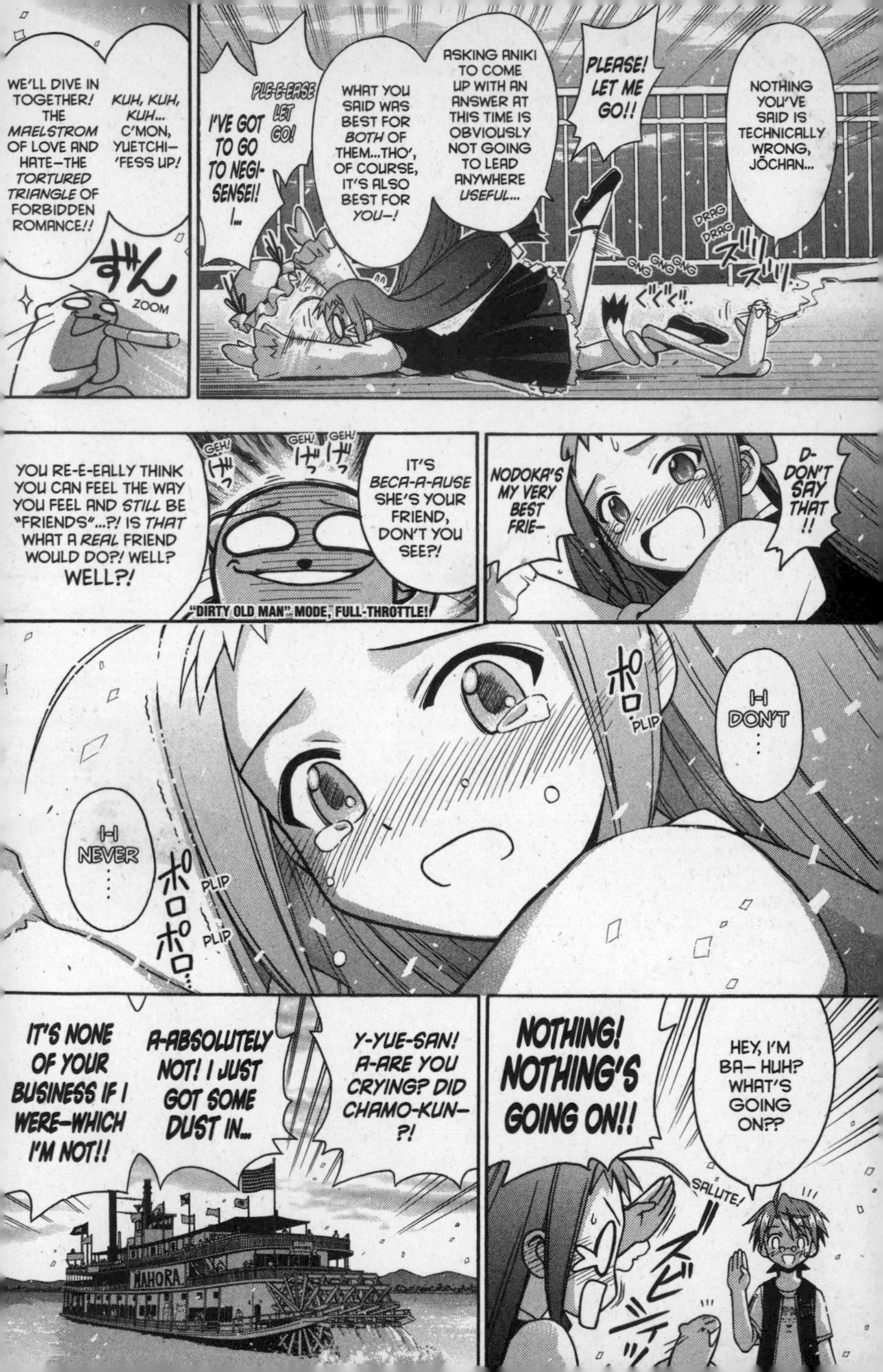
NOTHING YOU'VE SAID IS TECHNICALLY WRONG, JŌCHAN...
DRAG DRAG
PLEASE! LET ME GO!!
ASKING ANIKI TO COME UP WITH AN ANSWER AT THIS TIME IS OBVIOUSLY NOT GOING TO LEAD ANYWHERE USEFUL...
WHAT YOU SAID WAS BEST FOR BOTH OF THEM...THO', OF COURSE, IT'S ALSO BEST FOR YOU—!
PLE-E-EASE LET GO!
I'VE GOT TO GO TO NEGI-SENSEI! I...
GNG GNG GNG
KUH, KUH, KUH... C'MON, YUETCHI—'FESS UP!
WE'LL DIVE IN TOGETHER! THE MAELSTROM OF LOVE AND HATE—THE TORTURED TRIANGLE OF FORBIDDEN ROMANCE!!
ZOOM
D-DON'T SAY THAT!!
NODOKA'S MY VERY BEST FRIE—
IT'S BECA-A-AUSE SHE'S YOUR FRIEND, DON'T YOU SEE?!
GEH! GEH! GEH!
YOU RE-E-EALLY THINK YOU CAN FEEL THE WAY YOU FEEL AND STILL BE "FRIENDS"...?! IS THAT WHAT A REAL FRIEND WOULD DO?! WELL? WELL?!
"DIRTY OLD MAN" MODE, FULL-THROTTLE!
I-I DON'T . . .
PLIP
I-I NEVER . . .
PLIP
PLIP
HEY, I'M BA— HUH? WHAT'S GOING ON??
SALUTE!
NOTHING! NOTHING'S GOING ON!!
Y-YUE-SAN! A-ARE YOU CRYING? DID CHAMO-KUN—?!
A-ABSOLUTELY NOT! I JUST GOT SOME DUST IN...
IT'S NONE OF YOUR BUSINESS IF I WERE—WHICH I'M NOT!!
MAHORA

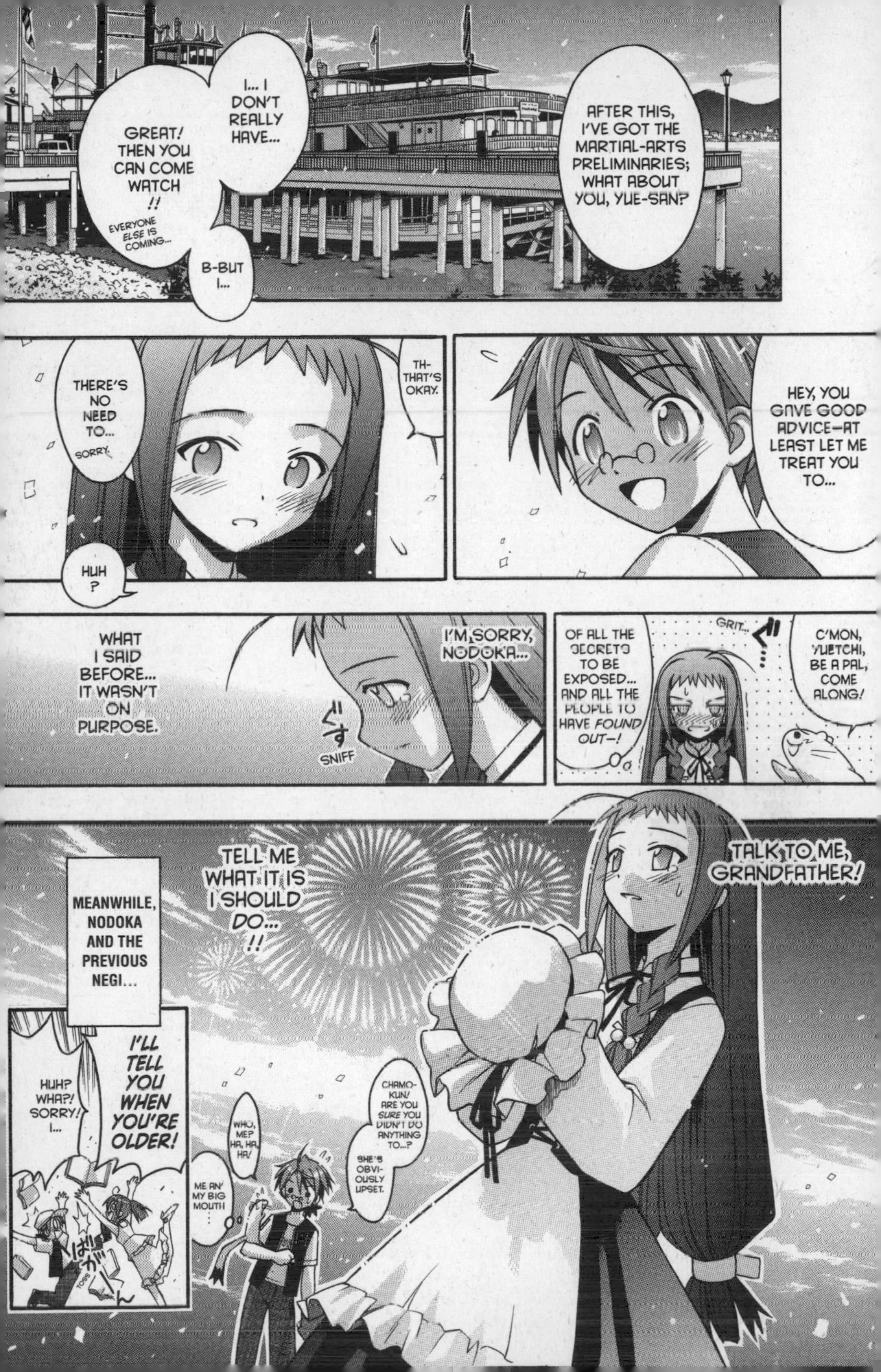
AFTER THIS, I'VE GOT THE MARTIAL-ARTS PRELIMINARIES; WHAT ABOUT YOU, YUE-SAN?
I... I DON'T REALLY HAVE...
GREAT! THEN YOU CAN COME WATCH!!
EVERYONE ELSE IS COMING...
B-BUT I...
HEY, YOU GAVE GOOD ADVICE—AT LEAST LET ME TREAT YOU TO...
TH-THAT'S OKAY.
THERE'S NO NEED TO...
SORRY.
HUH?
C'MON, YUETCHI, BE A PAL, COME ALONG!
GRIT...
OF ALL THE SECRETS TO BE EXPOSED... AND ALL THE PEOPLE TO HAVE FOUND OUT—!
I'M SORRY, NODOKA...
WHAT I SAID BEFORE... IT WASN'T ON PURPOSE.
ぐす
SNIFF
TALK TO ME, GRANDFATHER!
TELL ME WHAT IT IS I SHOULD DO...!!
MEANWHILE, NODOKA AND THE PREVIOUS NEGI...
CHAMO-KUN! ARE YOU SURE YOU DIDN'T DO ANYTHING TO...?
SHE'S OBVIOUSLY UPSET.
WHO, ME? HA, HA, HA!
ME AN' MY BIG MOUTH...
I'LL TELL YOU WHEN YOU'RE OLDER!
HUH? WHA?! SORRY! I...
TOSS

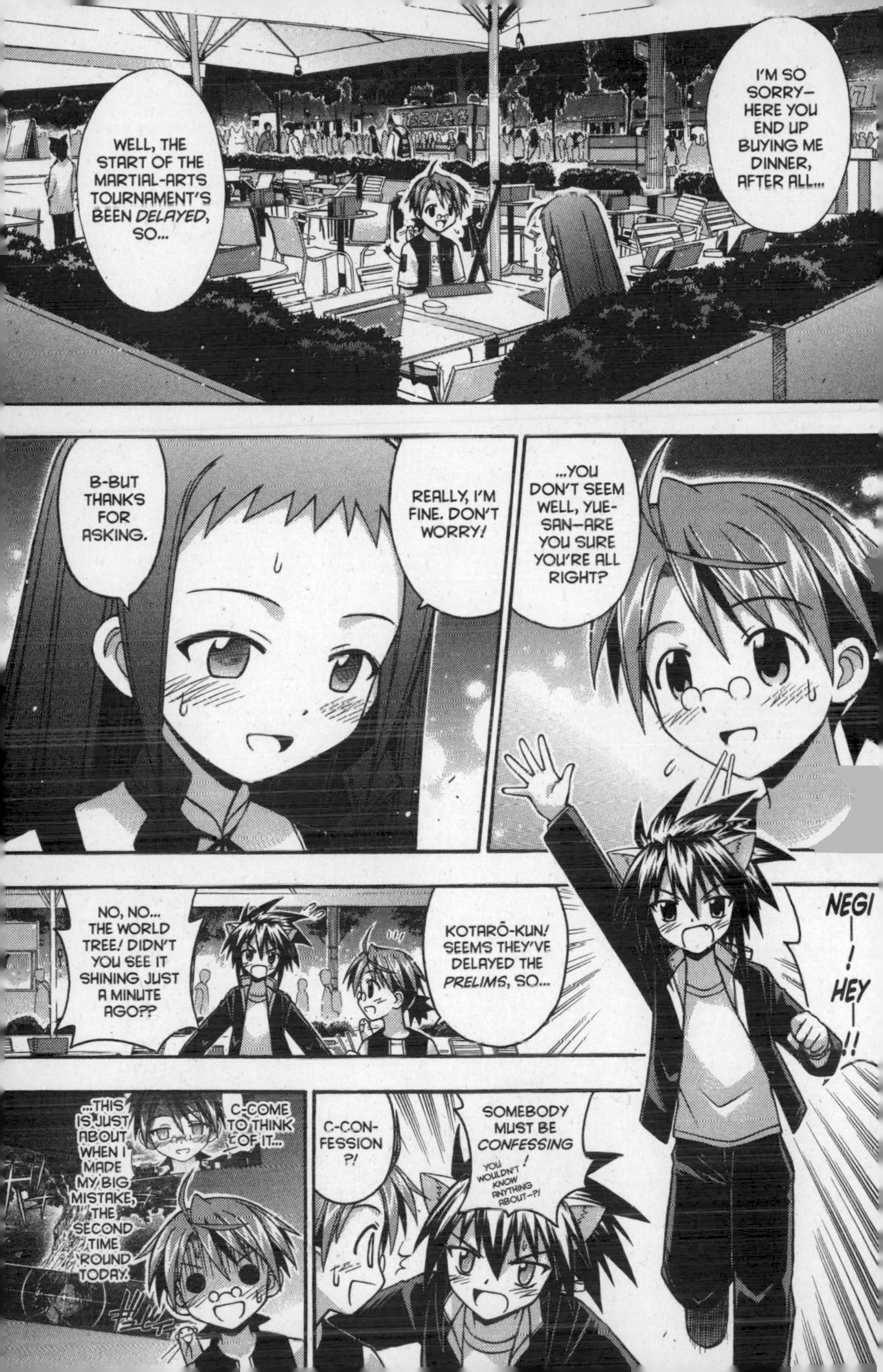
I'M SO SORRY—HERE YOU END UP BUYING ME DINNER, AFTER ALL...
WELL, THE START OF THE MARTIAL-ARTS TOURNAMENT'S BEEN *DELAYED*, SO...
...YOU DON'T SEEM WELL, YUE-SAN—ARE YOU SURE YOU'RE ALL RIGHT?
REALLY, I'M FINE. DON'T WORRY!
B-BUT THANKS FOR ASKING.
NEGI—! HEY—!!
KOTARŌ-KUN! SEEMS THEY'VE DELAYED THE *PRELIMS*, SO...
NO, NO... THE WORLD TREE! DIDN'T YOU SEE IT SHINING JUST A MINUTE AGO??
SOMEBODY MUST BE *CONFESSING*!
YOU WOULDN'T KNOW ANYTHING ABOUT—?!
C-CON-FESSION?!
C-COME TO THINK OF IT...
...THIS IS JUST ABOUT WHEN I MADE MY BIG MISTAKE, THE SECOND TIME ROUND TODAY.

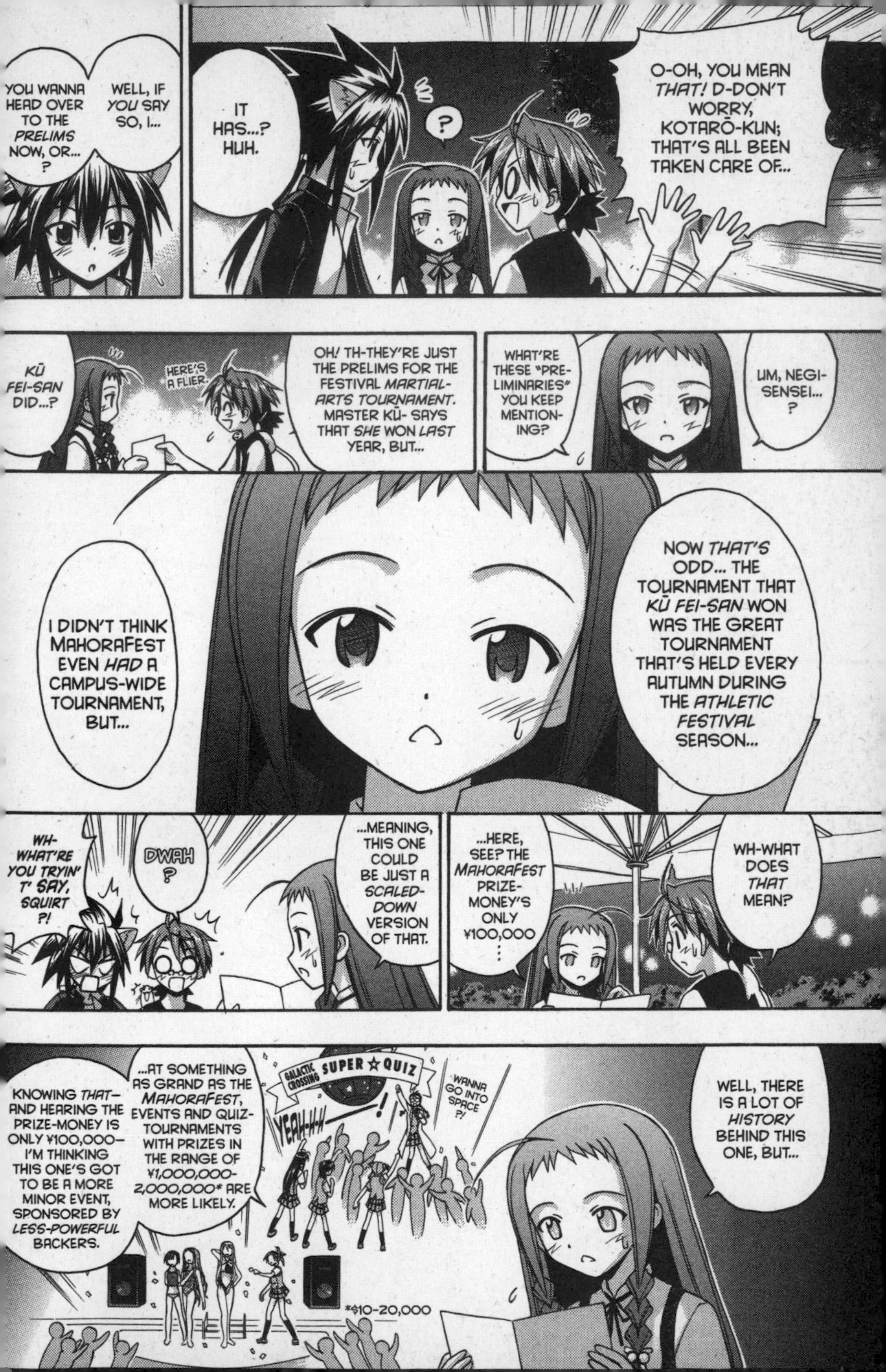

O-OH, YOU MEAN THAT! D-DON'T WORRY, KOTARŌ-KUN; THAT'S ALL BEEN TAKEN CARE OF...
?
IT HAS...? HUH.
WELL, IF YOU SAY SO, I...
YOU WANNA HEAD OVER TO THE PRELIMS NOW, OR...?
UM, NEGI-SENSEI...?
WHAT'RE THESE "PRELIMINARIES" YOU KEEP MENTIONING?
OH! TH-THEY'RE JUST THE PRELIMS FOR THE FESTIVAL MARTIAL-ARTS TOURNAMENT. MASTER KŪ- SAYS THAT SHE WON LAST YEAR, BUT...
HERE'S A FLIER.
KŪ FEI-SAN DID...?
NOW THAT'S ODD... THE TOURNAMENT THAT KŪ FEI-SAN WON WAS THE GREAT TOURNAMENT THAT'S HELD EVERY AUTUMN DURING THE ATHLETIC FESTIVAL SEASON...
I DIDN'T THINK MAHORAFEST EVEN HAD A CAMPUS-WIDE TOURNAMENT, BUT...
WH-WHAT DOES THAT MEAN?
...HERE, SEE? THE MAHORAFEST PRIZE-MONEY'S ONLY ¥100,000...
...MEANING, THIS ONE COULD BE JUST A SCALED-DOWN VERSION OF THAT.
DWAH?
WH-WHAT'RE YOU TRYIN' T' SAY, SQUIRT?!
WELL, THERE IS A LOT OF HISTORY BEHIND THIS ONE, BUT...
GALACTIC CROSSING SUPER ☆ QUIZ
WANNA GO INTO SPACE?!
YEAH-H-H
...AT SOMETHING AS GRAND AS THE MAHORAFEST, EVENTS AND QUIZ-TOURNAMENTS WITH PRIZES IN THE RANGE OF ¥1,000,000-2,000,000* ARE MORE LIKELY.
KNOWING THAT—AND HEARING THE PRIZE-MONEY IS ONLY ¥100,000—I'M THINKING THIS ONE'S GOT TO BE A MORE MINOR EVENT, SPONSORED BY LESS-POWERFUL BACKERS.
*$10-20,000

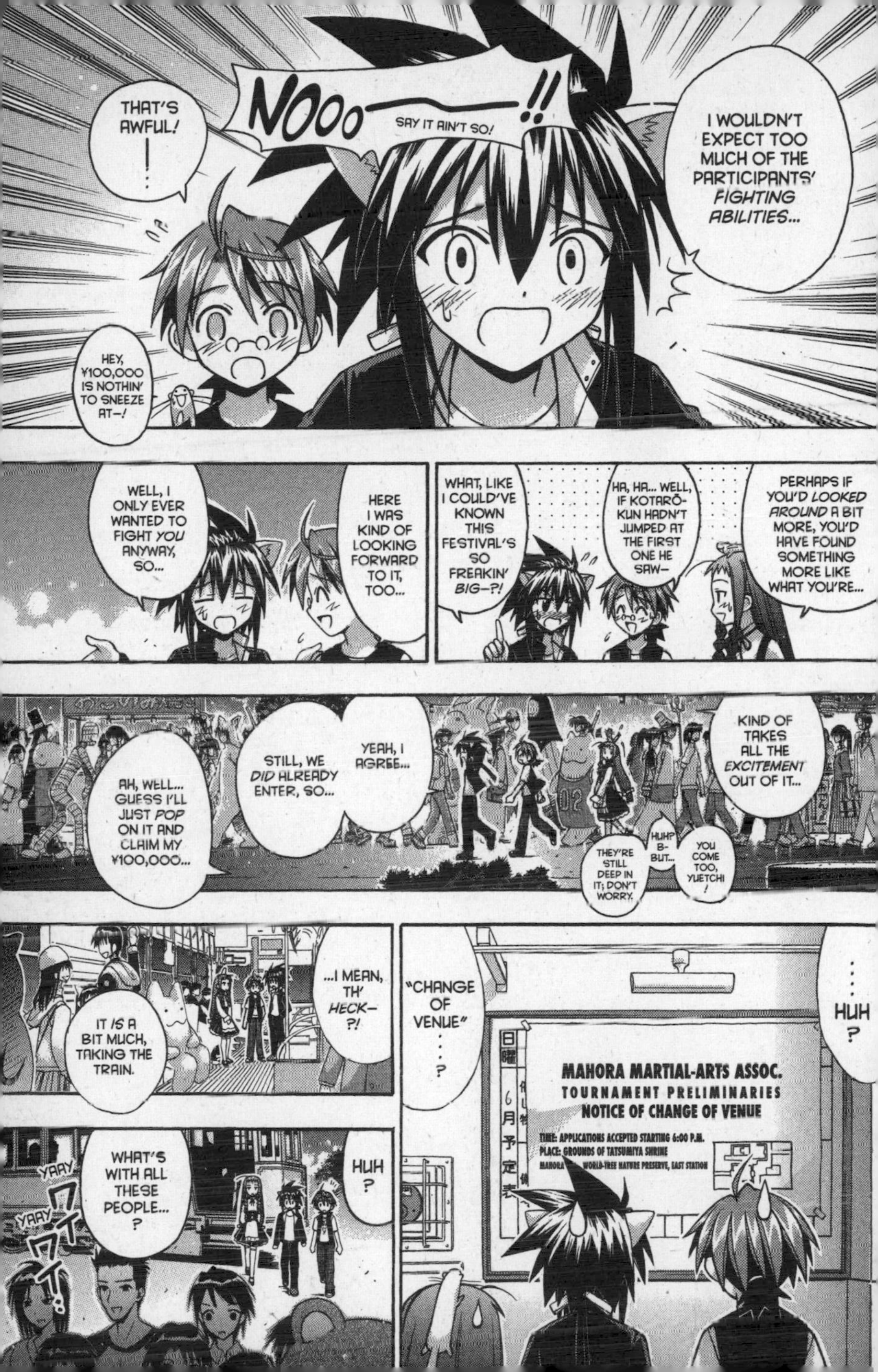

I WOULDN'T EXPECT TOO MUCH OF THE PARTICIPANTS' *FIGHTING ABILITIES*...
NOOO——!!
SAY IT AIN'T SO!
THAT'S AWFUL!
HEY, ¥100,000 IS NOTHIN' TO SNEEZE AT—!
PERHAPS IF YOU'D *LOOKED AROUND* A BIT MORE, YOU'D HAVE FOUND SOMETHING MORE LIKE WHAT YOU'RE...
HA, HA... WELL, IF KOTARŌ-KUN HADN'T JUMPED AT THE FIRST ONE HE SAW—
WHAT, LIKE I COULD'VE KNOWN THIS FESTIVAL'S SO FREAKIN' *BIG*—?!
HERE I WAS KIND OF LOOKING FORWARD TO IT, TOO...
WELL, I ONLY EVER WANTED TO FIGHT *YOU* ANYWAY, SO...
KIND OF TAKES ALL THE *EXCITEMENT* OUT OF IT...
YOU COME TOO, YUETCHI!
HUH? B-BUT...
THEY'RE STILL DEEP IN IT; DON'T WORRY.
YEAH, I AGREE...
STILL, WE *DID* ALREADY ENTER, SO...
AH, WELL... GUESS I'LL JUST *POP* ON IT AND CLAIM MY ¥100,000...
...HUH?
"CHANGE OF VENUE" ...?
日曜
6月予定表
MAHORA MARTIAL-ARTS ASSOC.
TOURNAMENT PRELIMINARIES
NOTICE OF CHANGE OF VENUE
TIME: APPLICATIONS ACCEPTED STARTING 6:00 P.M.
PLACE: GROUNDS OF TATSUMIYA SHRINE
MAHORA WORLD-TREE NATURE PRESERVE, EAST STATION
...I MEAN, TH' *HECK*—?!
IT *IS* A BIT MUCH, TAKING THE TRAIN.
HUH?
WHAT'S WITH ALL THESE PEOPLE...?
YAAY
YAAY
ワイワイ

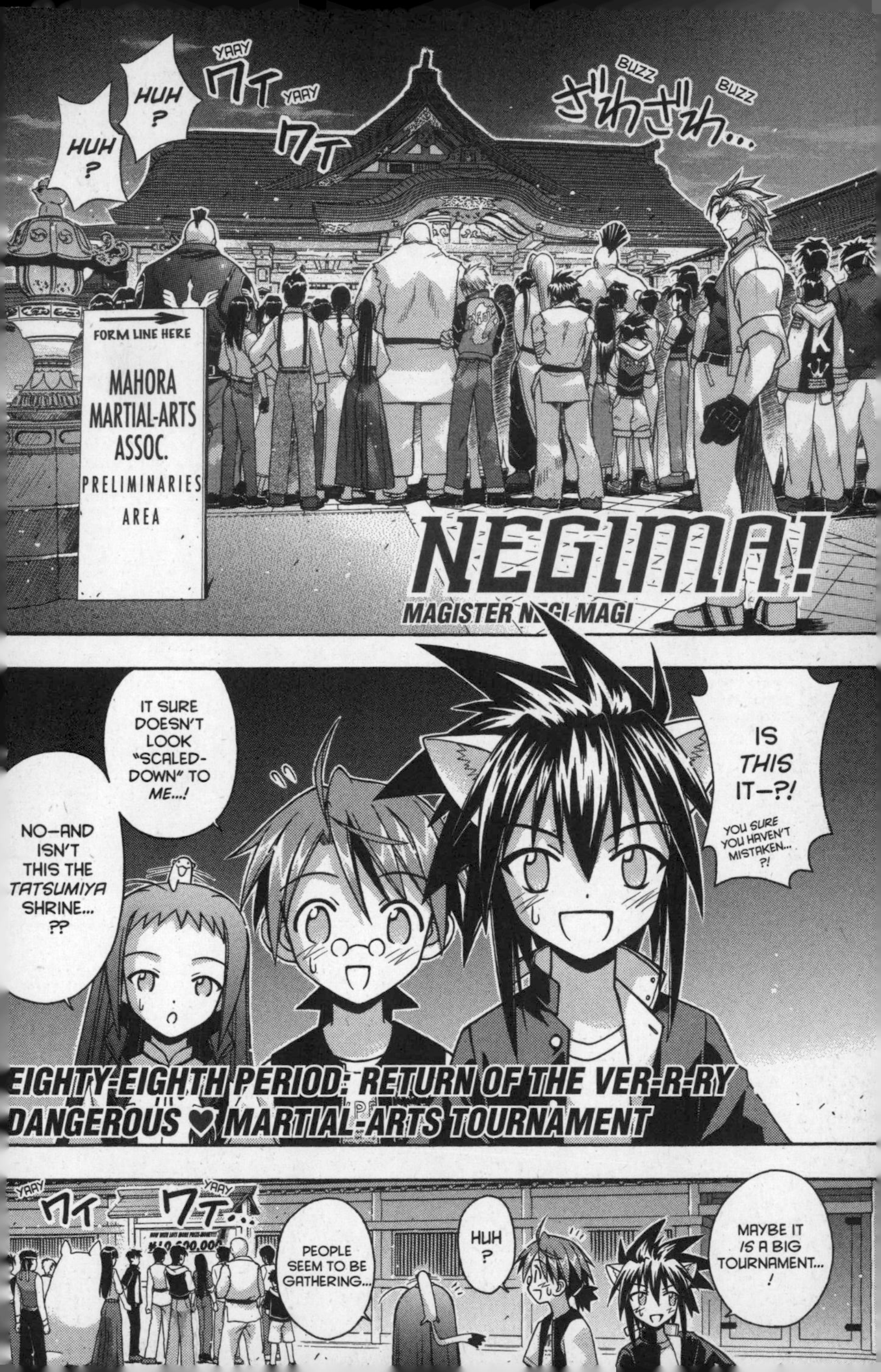
BUZZ
ざわざわ...
BUZZ
YAAY
ワイ
YAAY
ワイ
HUH ?
HUH ?
FORM LINE HERE
MAHORA MARTIAL-ARTS ASSOC.
PRELIMINARIES AREA
NEGIMA!
MAGISTER NEGI MAGI
IS THIS IT—?!
YOU SURE YOU HAVEN'T MISTAKEN...?!
IT SURE DOESN'T LOOK "SCALED-DOWN" TO ME...!
NO—AND ISN'T THIS THE TATSUMIYA SHRINE...??
EIGHTY-EIGHTH PERIOD: RETURN OF THE VER-R-RY DANGEROUS ♥ MARTIAL-ARTS TOURNAMENT
MAYBE IT IS A BIG TOURNAMENT...!
HUH ?
PEOPLE SEEM TO BE GATHERING...
YAAY
ワイ
YAAY
ワイ...

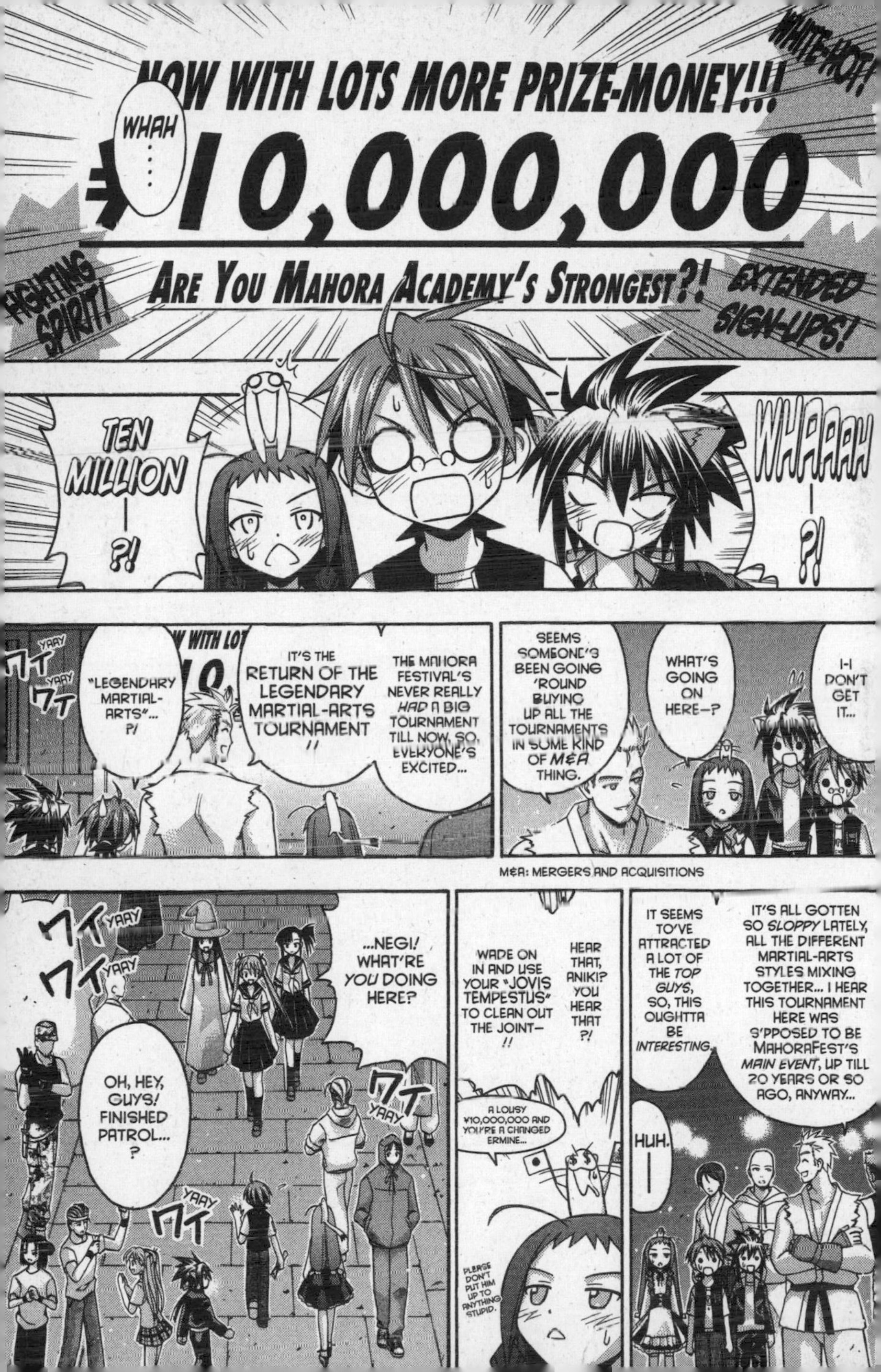
WHITE-HOT!
NOW WITH LOTS MORE PRIZE-MONEY!!!
WHAH ....
¥10,000,000
EXTENDED SIGN-UPS!
ARE YOU MAHORA ACADEMY'S STRONGEST?!
FIGHTING SPIRIT!
WHAAAH —?!
TEN MILLION —?!
I-I DON'T GET IT...
WHAT'S GOING ON HERE—?
SEEMS SOMEONE'S BEEN GOING 'ROUND BUYING UP ALL THE TOURNAMENTS IN SOME KIND OF M&A THING.
THE MAHORA FESTIVAL'S NEVER REALLY HAD A BIG TOURNAMENT TILL NOW, SO, EVERYONE'S EXCITED...
IT'S THE RETURN OF THE LEGENDARY MARTIAL-ARTS TOURNAMENT!!
"LEGENDARY MARTIAL-ARTS"...?!
ワイ YAAY
ワイ YAAY
M&A: MERGERS AND ACQUISITIONS
IT'S ALL GOTTEN SO SLOPPY LATELY, ALL THE DIFFERENT MARTIAL-ARTS STYLES MIXING TOGETHER... I HEAR THIS TOURNAMENT HERE WAS S'PPOSED TO BE MAHORAFEST'S MAIN EVENT, UP TILL 20 YEARS OR SO AGO, ANYWAY...
IT SEEMS TO'VE ATTRACTED A LOT OF THE TOP GUYS, SO, THIS OUGHTTA BE INTERESTING.
HUH. —
HEAR THAT, ANIKI? YOU HEAR THAT?!
WADE ON IN AND USE YOUR "JOVIS TEMPESTUS" TO CLEAN OUT THE JOINT—!!
A LOUSY ¥10,000,000 AND YOU'RE A CHANGED ERMINE...
PLEASE DON'T PUT HIM UP TO ANYTHING STUPID.
...NEGI! WHAT'RE YOU DOING HERE?
ワイ YAAY
ワイ YAAY
ワイ YAAY
ワイ YAAY
OH, HEY, GUYS! FINISHED PATROL...?

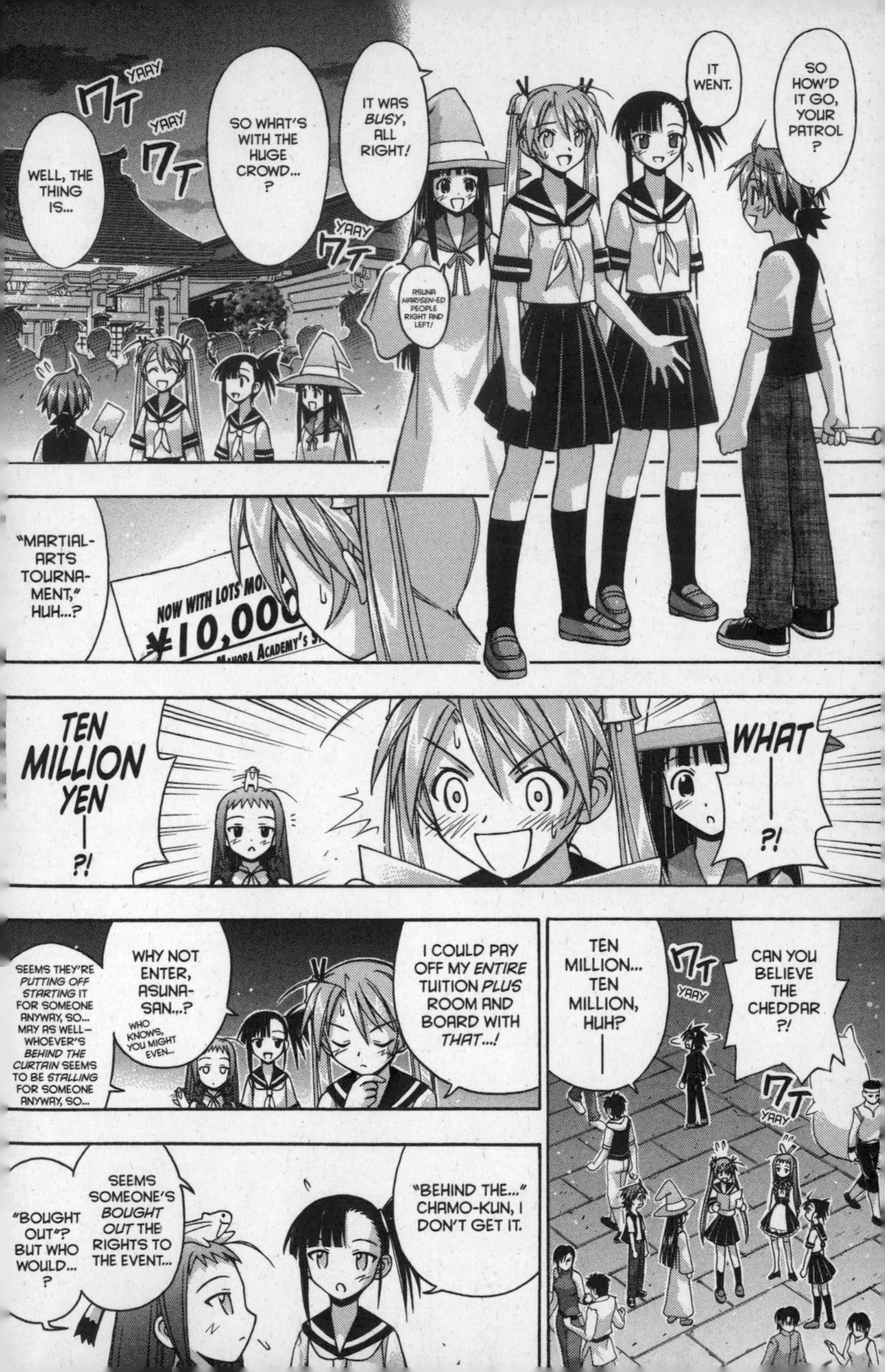
SO HOW'D IT GO, YOUR PATROL ?
IT WENT.
IT WAS *BUSY*, ALL RIGHT!
ASUNA *HARISEN-ED* PEOPLE RIGHT AND LEFT!
YAAY
YAAY
SO WHAT'S WITH THE HUGE CROWD... ?
YAAY
WELL, THE THING IS...
"MARTIAL-ARTS TOURNAMENT," HUH...?
NOW WITH LOTS
¥10,000
MAHORA ACADEMY'S
WHAT—?!
TEN MILLION YEN—?!
CAN YOU BELIEVE THE CHEDDAR ?!
YAAY
TEN MILLION... TEN MILLION, HUH?—
YAAY
I COULD PAY OFF MY *ENTIRE* TUITION *PLUS* ROOM AND BOARD WITH *THAT*...!
WHY NOT ENTER, ASUNA-SAN...?
WHO KNOWS, YOU MIGHT EVEN...
SEEMS THEY'RE *PUTTING OFF STARTING* IT FOR SOMEONE ANYWAY, SO... MAY AS WELL— WHOEVER'S *BEHIND THE CURTAIN* SEEMS TO BE *STALLING* FOR SOMEONE ANYWAY, SO...
"BEHIND THE..." CHAMO-KUN, I DON'T GET IT.
SEEMS SOMEONE'S *BOUGHT OUT* THE RIGHTS TO THE EVENT...
"BOUGHT OUT"? BUT WHO WOULD... ?

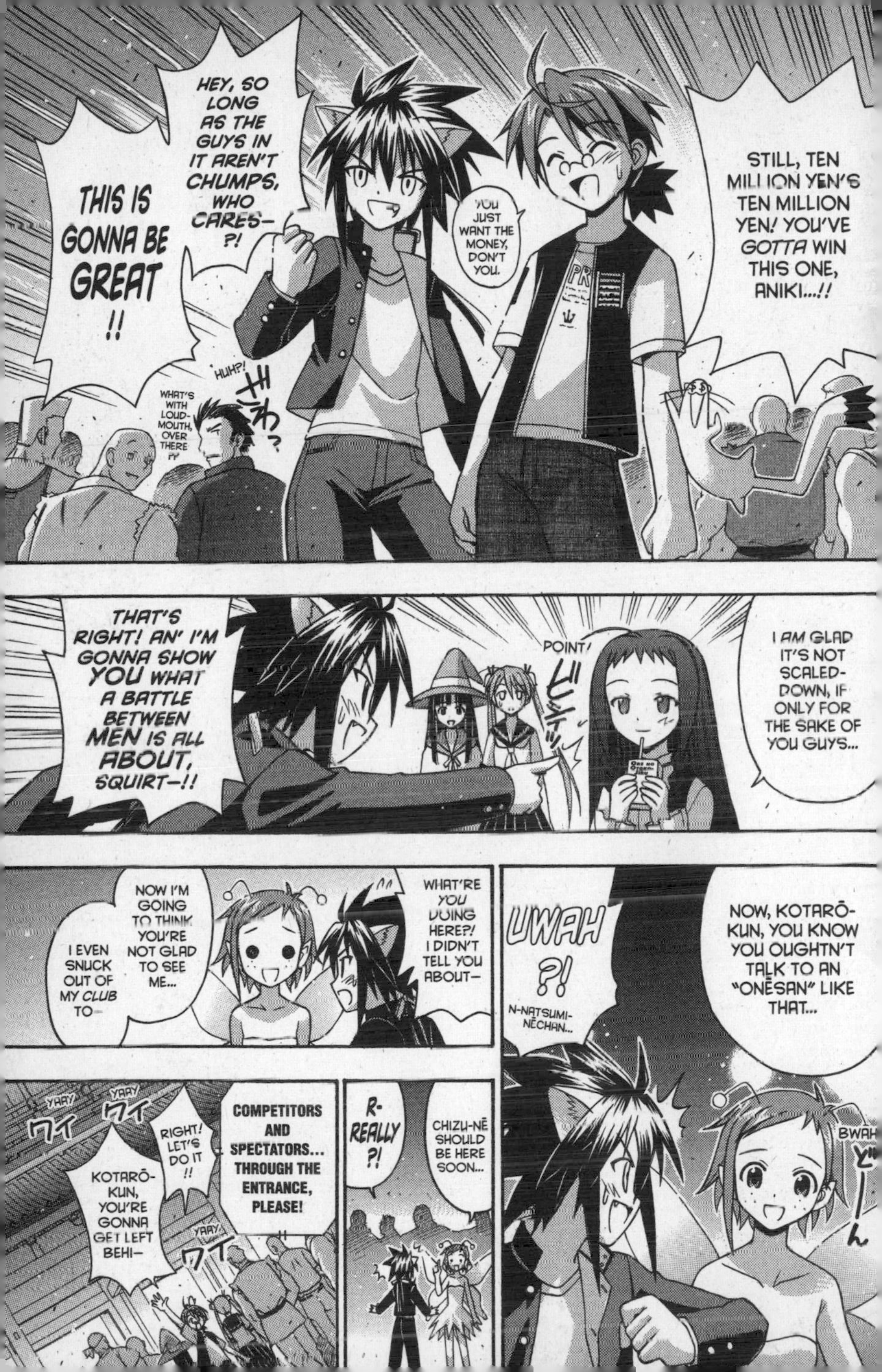
STILL, TEN MILLION YEN'S TEN MILLION YEN! YOU'VE GOTTA WIN THIS ONE, ANIKI...!!
YOU JUST WANT THE MONEY, DON'T YOU.
HEY, SO LONG AS THE GUYS IN IT AREN'T CHUMPS, WHO CARES—?!
THIS IS GONNA BE GREAT!!
HUH?!
WHAT'S WITH LOUD-MOUTH, OVER THERE?!
I AM GLAD IT'S NOT SCALED-DOWN, IF ONLY FOR THE SAKE OF YOU GUYS...
POINT
THAT'S RIGHT! AN' I'M GONNA SHOW YOU WHAT A BATTLE BETWEEN MEN IS ALL ABOUT, SQUIRT—!!
NOW, KOTARŌ-KUN, YOU KNOW YOU OUGHTN'T TALK TO AN "ONĒSAN" LIKE THAT...
UWAH?!
N-NATSUMI-NĒCHAN...
WHAT'RE YOU DOING HERE?! I DIDN'T TELL YOU ABOUT—
NOW I'M GOING TO THINK YOU'RE NOT GLAD TO SEE ME...
I EVEN SNUCK OUT OF MY CLUB TO—
BWAH
CHIZU-NĒ SHOULD BE HERE SOON...
R-REALLY?!
COMPETITORS AND SPECTATORS... THROUGH THE ENTRANCE, PLEASE!
YAAY
YAAY
RIGHT! LET'S DO IT!!
KOTARŌ-KUN, YOU'RE GONNA GET LEFT BEHI—
YAAY

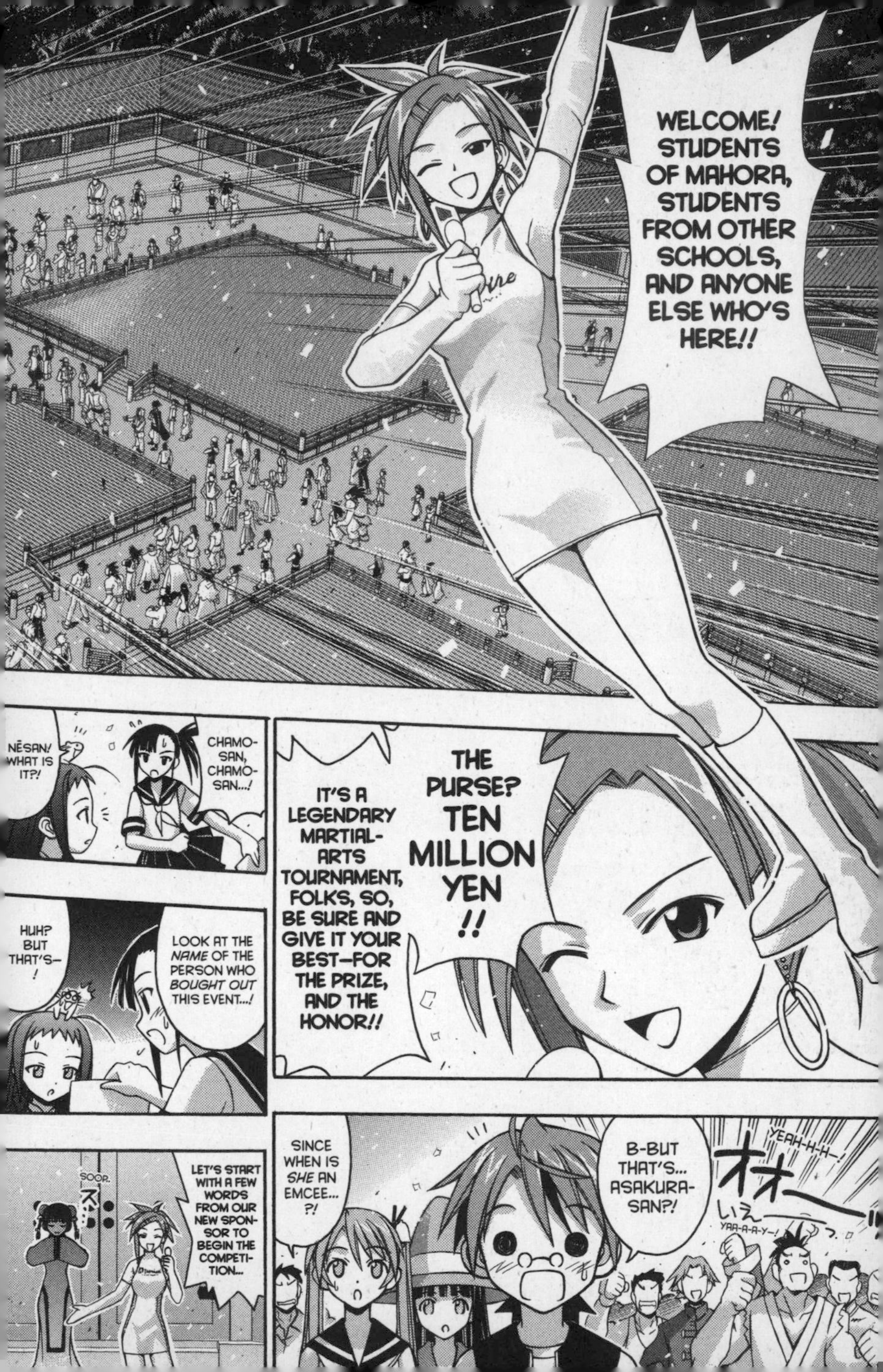
WELCOME! STUDENTS OF MAHORA, STUDENTS FROM OTHER SCHOOLS, AND ANYONE ELSE WHO'S HERE!!
THE PURSE? TEN MILLION YEN!!
IT'S A LEGENDARY MARTIAL-ARTS TOURNAMENT, FOLKS, SO, BE SURE AND GIVE IT YOUR BEST—FOR THE PRIZE, AND THE HONOR!!
CHAMO-SAN, CHAMO-SAN...!
NĒSAN! WHAT IS IT?!
LOOK AT THE *NAME* OF THE PERSON WHO *BOUGHT OUT* THIS EVENT...!
HUH? BUT THAT'S—!
YEAH-H-H-!
オオー
いえー
YAA-A-A-Y-!
B-BUT THAT'S... ASAKURA-SAN?!
SINCE WHEN IS *SHE* AN EMCEE...?!
LET'S START WITH A FEW WORDS FROM OUR NEW SPONSOR TO BEGIN THE COMPETITION...
SOOP.
ス…

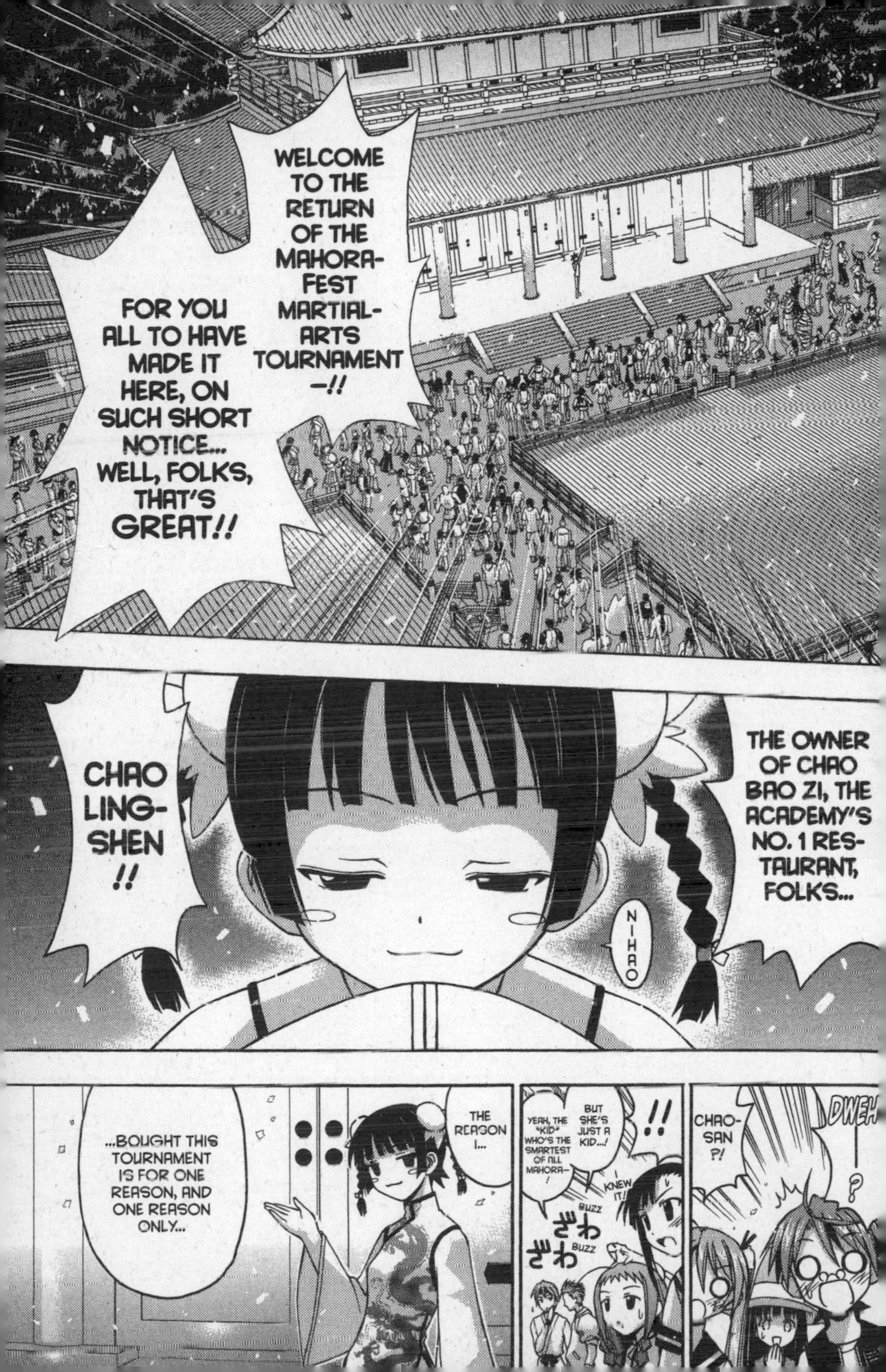
WELCOME TO THE RETURN OF THE MAHORA-FEST MARTIAL-ARTS TOURNAMENT—!!
FOR YOU ALL TO HAVE MADE IT HERE, ON SUCH SHORT NOTICE... WELL, FOLKS, THAT'S GREAT!!
THE OWNER OF CHAO BAO ZI, THE ACADEMY'S NO. 1 RESTAURANT, FOLKS...
NIHAO
CHAO LING-SHEN!!
DWEH
CHAO-SAN?!
?
!!
BUT SHE'S JUST A KID...!
YEAH, THE "KID" WHO'S THE SMARTEST OF ALL MAHORA—!
I KNEW IT!
ざわ BUZZ
ざわ BUZZ
THE REASON I...
...BOUGHT THIS TOURNAMENT IS FOR ONE REASON, AND ONE REASON ONLY...

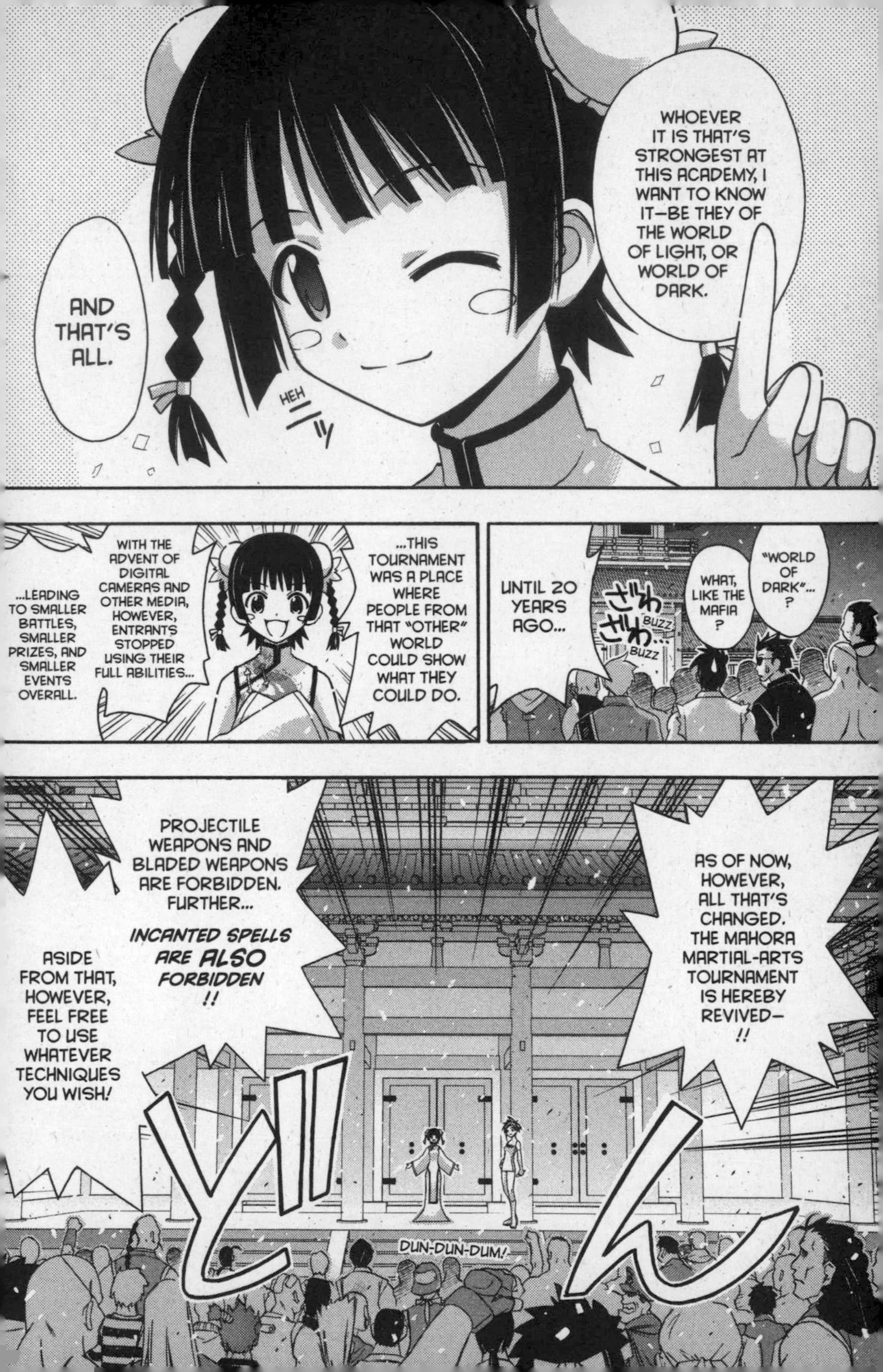
WHOEVER IT IS THAT'S STRONGEST AT THIS ACADEMY, I WANT TO KNOW IT—BE THEY OF THE WORLD OF LIGHT, OR WORLD OF DARK.
HEH
AND THAT'S ALL.
"WORLD OF DARK"...?
WHAT, LIKE THE MAFIA?
BUZZ
BUZZ
UNTIL 20 YEARS AGO...
...THIS TOURNAMENT WAS A PLACE WHERE PEOPLE FROM THAT "OTHER" WORLD COULD SHOW WHAT THEY COULD DO.
WITH THE ADVENT OF DIGITAL CAMERAS AND OTHER MEDIA, HOWEVER, ENTRANTS STOPPED USING THEIR FULL ABILITIES...
...LEADING TO SMALLER BATTLES, SMALLER PRIZES, AND SMALLER EVENTS OVERALL.
AS OF NOW, HOWEVER, ALL THAT'S CHANGED. THE MAHORA MARTIAL-ARTS TOURNAMENT IS HEREBY REVIVED—!!
PROJECTILE WEAPONS AND BLADED WEAPONS ARE FORBIDDEN. FURTHER...
INCANTED SPELLS ARE ALSO FORBIDDEN!!
ASIDE FROM THAT, HOWEVER, FEEL FREE TO USE WHATEVER TECHNIQUES YOU WISH!
DUN-DUN-DUM!

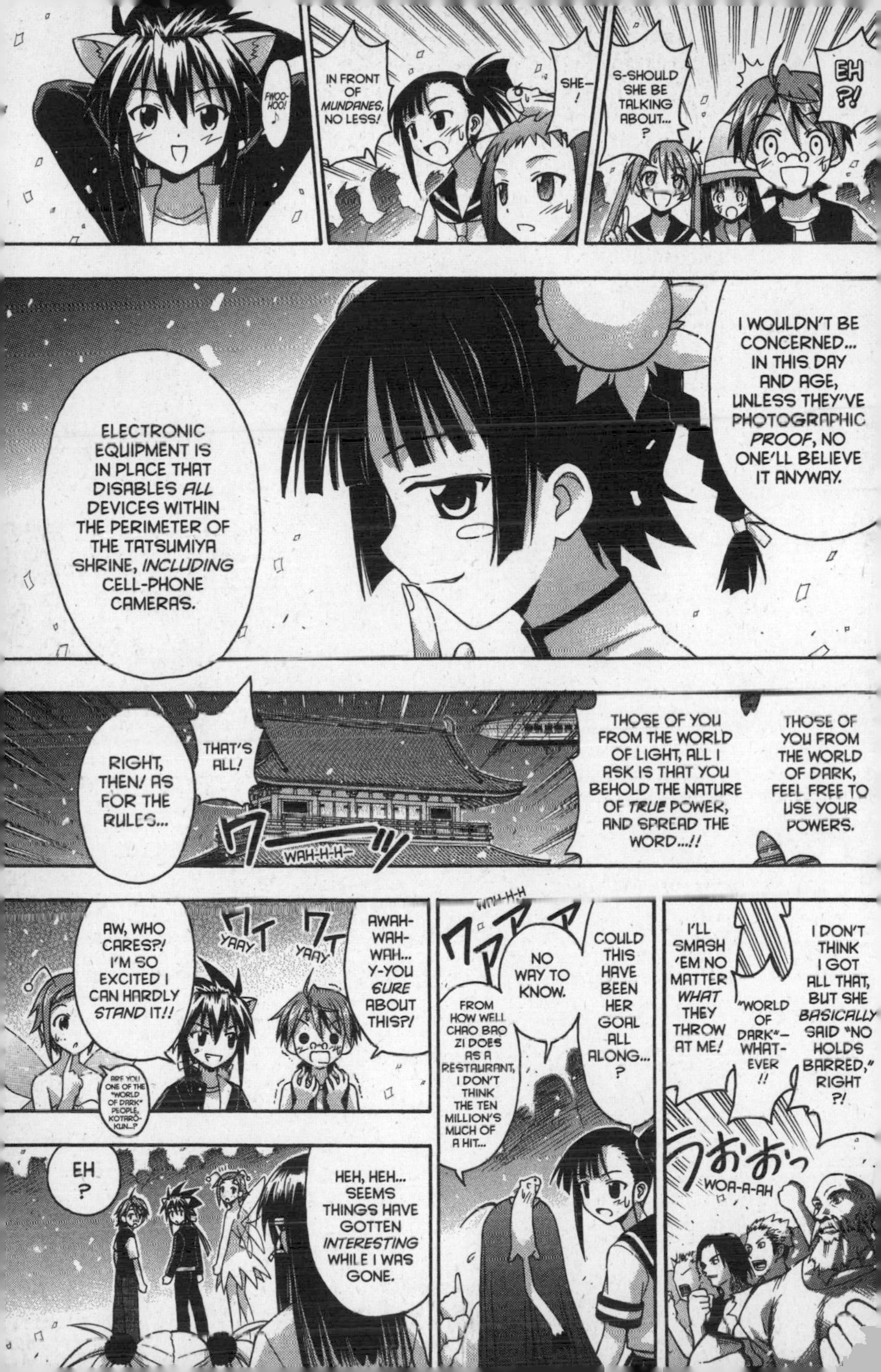
EH ?!
S-SHOULD SHE BE TALKING ABOUT... ?
SHE— !
IN FRONT OF *MUNDANES*, NO LESS!
FWOO-HOO! ♪
I WOULDN'T BE CONCERNED... IN THIS DAY AND AGE, UNLESS THEY'VE PHOTOGRAPHIC *PROOF*, NO ONE'LL BELIEVE IT ANYWAY.
ELECTRONIC EQUIPMENT IS IN PLACE THAT DISABLES *ALL* DEVICES WITHIN THE PERIMETER OF THE TATSUMIYA SHRINE, *INCLUDING* CELL-PHONE CAMERAS.
THOSE OF YOU FROM THE WORLD OF DARK, FEEL FREE TO USE YOUR POWERS.
THOSE OF YOU FROM THE WORLD OF LIGHT, ALL I ASK IS THAT YOU BEHOLD THE NATURE OF *TRUE* POWER, AND SPREAD THE WORD...!!
THAT'S ALL!
RIGHT, THEN! AS FOR THE RULES...
WAH-H-H-
I DON'T THINK I GOT ALL THAT, BUT SHE *BASICALLY* SAID "NO HOLDS BARRED," RIGHT ?!
I'LL SMASH 'EM NO MATTER *WHAT* THEY THROW AT ME!
"WORLD OF DARK"—WHATEVER !!
WOA-A-AH
WAH-H-H
COULD THIS HAVE BEEN HER GOAL ALL ALONG... ?
NO WAY TO KNOW.
FROM HOW WELL CHAO BAO ZI DOES AS A RESTAURANT, I DON'T THINK THE TEN MILLION'S MUCH OF A HIT...
AWAH-WAH-WAH... Y-YOU *SURE* ABOUT THIS?!
YAAY
YAAY
AW, WHO CARES?! I'M SO EXCITED I CAN HARDLY *STAND* IT!!
ARE YOU ONE OF THE "WORLD OF DARK" PEOPLE, KOTARÔ-KUN...?
HEH, HEH... SEEMS THINGS HAVE GOTTEN *INTERESTING* WHILE I WAS GONE.
EH ?

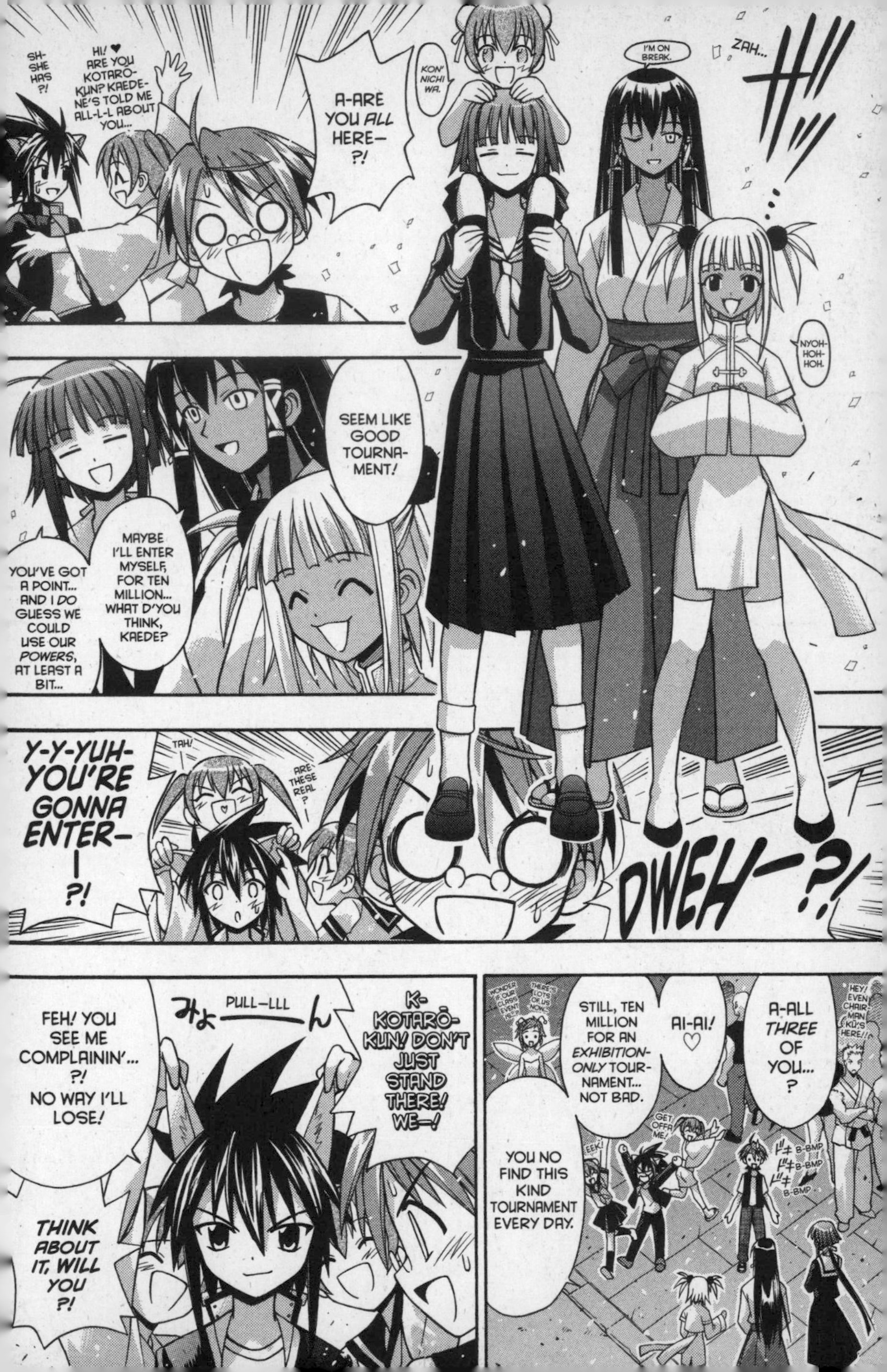
ZAH...
I'M ON BREAK.
KON' NICHI WA.
NYOH-HOH-HOH.
A-ARE YOU ALL HERE—?!
HI! ♥ ARE YOU KOTARŌ-KUN? KAEDE-NE'S TOLD ME ALL-L-L ABOUT YOU...
SH-SHE HAS?!
SEEM LIKE GOOD TOURNAMENT!
MAYBE I'LL ENTER MYSELF, FOR TEN MILLION... WHAT D'YOU THINK, KAEDE?
YOU'VE GOT A POINT... AND I DO GUESS WE COULD USE OUR POWERS, AT LEAST A BIT...
DWEH—?!
ARE THESE REAL?
TAH!
Y-Y-YUH-YOU'RE GONNA ENTER—I?!
HEY! EVEN CHAIRMAN KU'S HERE!!
A-ALL THREE OF YOU...?
AI-AI! ♡
STILL, TEN MILLION FOR AN EXHIBITION-ONLY TOURNAMENT... NOT BAD.
YOU NO FIND THIS KIND TOURNAMENT EVERY DAY.
THERE'S LOTS OF US NOW...
GET OFFA ME!
EEK!
ドキ B-BMP
ドキ B-BMP
K-KOTARŌ-KUN! DON'T JUST STAND THERE! WE—!
みょーーーん PULL—LLL
FEH! YOU SEE ME COMPLAININ'...?! NO WAY I'LL LOSE!
THINK ABOUT IT, WILL YOU?!

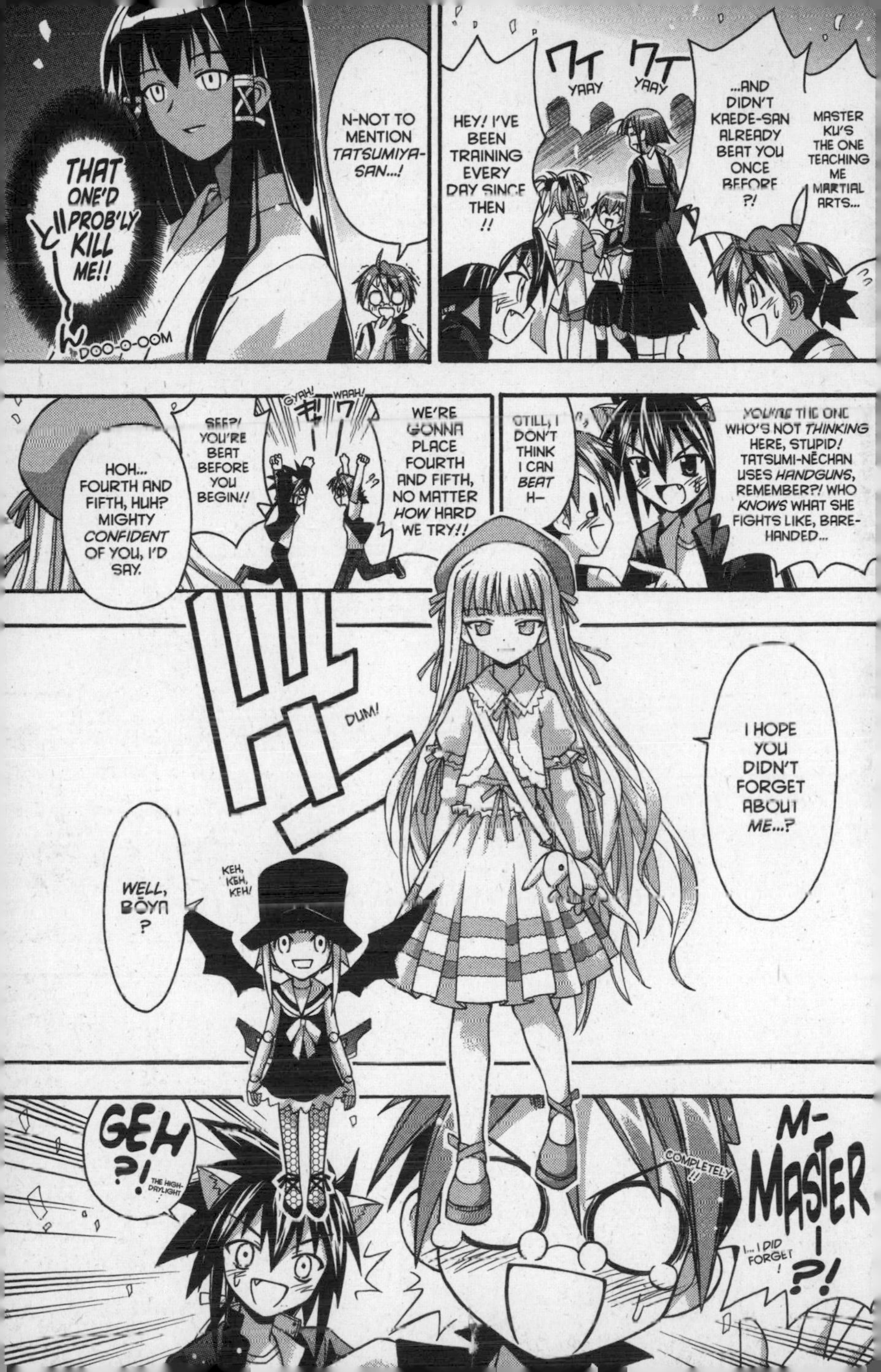
MASTER KU'S THE ONE TEACHING ME MARTIAL ARTS...
...AND DIDN'T KAEDE-SAN ALREADY BEAT YOU ONCE BEFORE?!
ワイ YAAY ワイ YAAY
HEY! I'VE BEEN TRAINING EVERY DAY SINCE THEN!!
N-NOT TO MENTION TATSUMIYA-SAN...!
THAT ONE'D PROB'LY KILL ME!!
DOO-O-OOM
YOU'RE THE ONE WHO'S NOT THINKING HERE, STUPID! TATSUMI-NĒCHAN USES HANDGUNS, REMEMBER?! WHO KNOWS WHAT SHE FIGHTS LIKE, BARE-HANDED...
STILL, I DON'T THINK I CAN BEAT H–
WE'RE GONNA PLACE FOURTH AND FIFTH, NO MATTER HOW HARD WE TRY!!
WAAH!
GYAH!
SEE?! YOU'RE BEAT BEFORE YOU BEGIN!!
HOH... FOURTH AND FIFTH, HUH? MIGHTY CONFIDENT OF YOU, I'D SAY.
I HOPE YOU DIDN'T FORGET ABOUT ME...?
DUM!
KEH, KEH, KEH!
WELL, BŌYA?
M-MASTER!?!
I... I DID FORGET!
COMPLETELY!!
GEH?!
THE HIGH-DAYLIGHT...

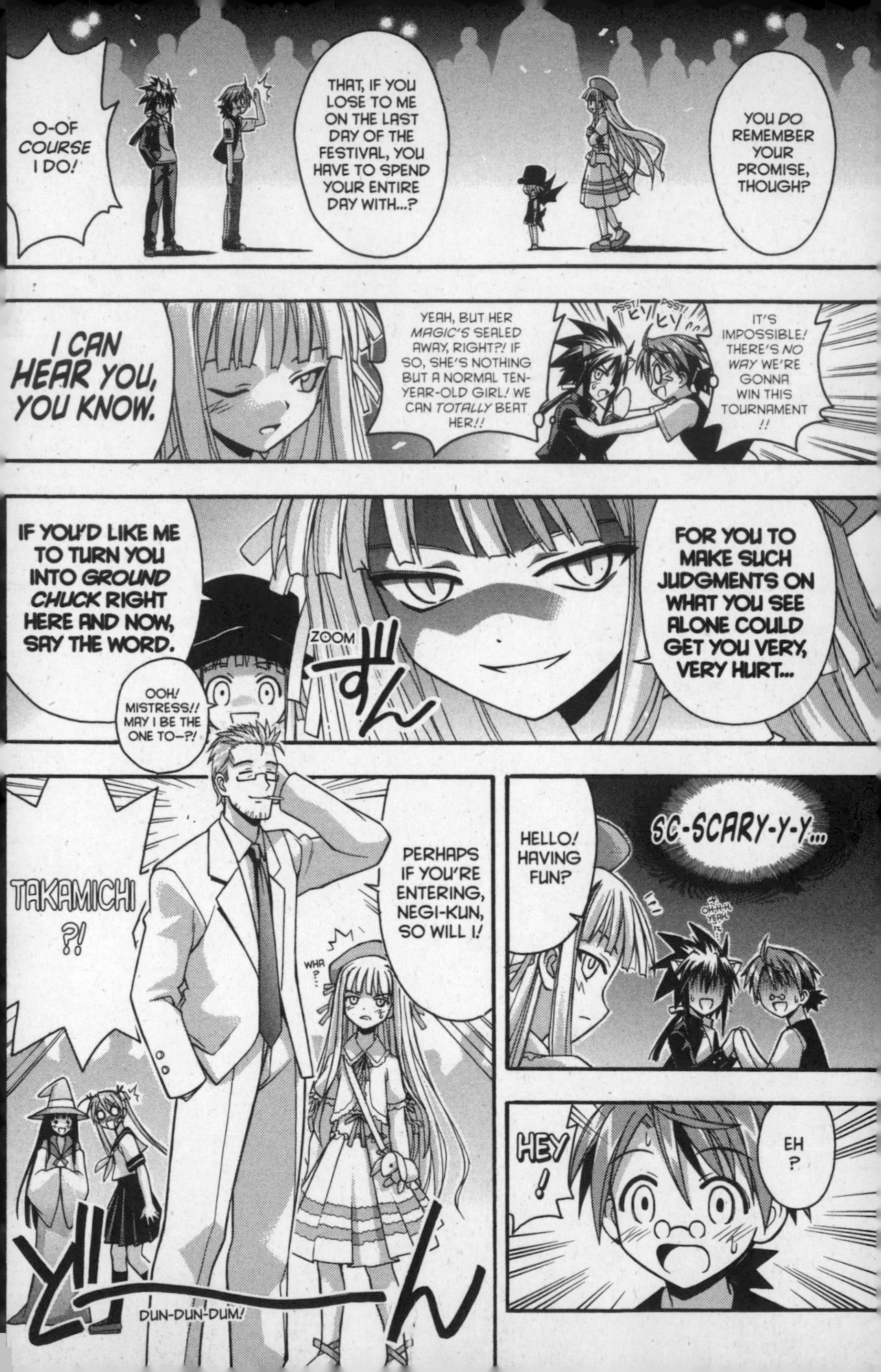
YOU *DO* REMEMBER YOUR PROMISE, THOUGH?
THAT, IF YOU LOSE TO ME ON THE LAST DAY OF THE FESTIVAL, YOU HAVE TO SPEND YOUR ENTIRE DAY WITH...?
O-OF *COURSE* I DO!
IT'S IMPOSSIBLE! THERE'S *NO WAY* WE'RE GONNA WIN THIS TOURNAMENT!!
PSST!
PSST!
YEAH, BUT HER *MAGIC'S* SEALED AWAY, RIGHT?! IF SO, SHE'S NOTHING BUT A NORMAL TEN-YEAR-OLD GIRL! WE CAN *TOTALLY* BEAT HER!!
I CAN HEAR YOU, YOU KNOW.
FOR YOU TO MAKE SUCH JUDGMENTS ON WHAT YOU SEE ALONE COULD GET YOU VERY, VERY HURT...
ZOOM
IF YOU'D LIKE ME TO TURN YOU INTO *GROUND CHUCK* RIGHT HERE AND NOW, SAY THE WORD.
OOH! MISTRESS!! MAY I BE THE ONE TO—?!
SC-SCARY-Y-Y...
HELLO! HAVING FUN?
EH?
HEY!
PERHAPS IF YOU'RE ENTERING, NEGI-KUN, SO WILL I!
WHA?
TAKAMICHI?!
DUN-DUN-DUM!

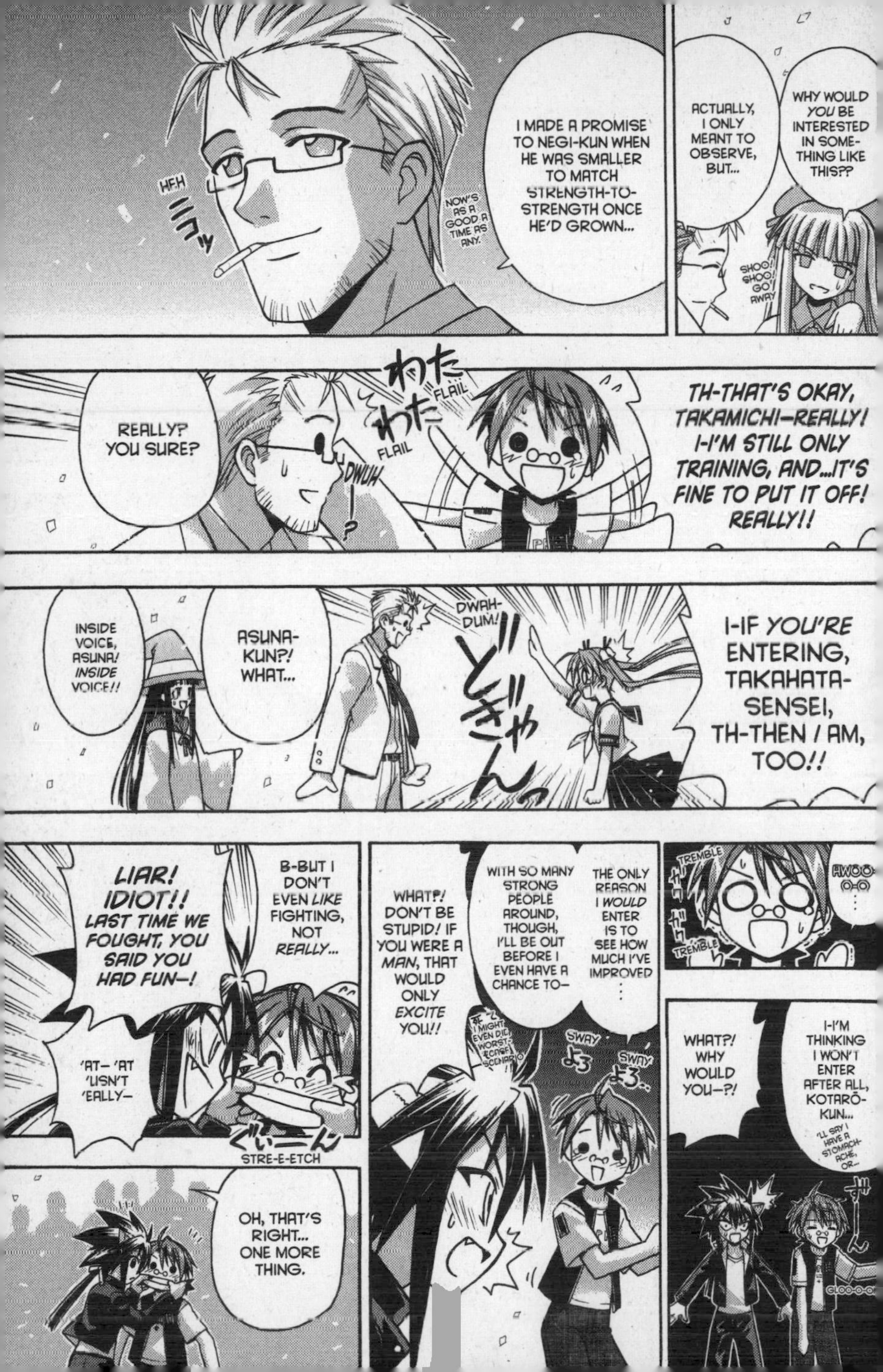
WHY WOULD *YOU* BE INTERESTED IN SOMETHING LIKE THIS??
ACTUALLY, I ONLY MEANT TO OBSERVE, BUT...
SHOO! SHOO! GO! AWAY
I MADE A PROMISE TO NEGI-KUN WHEN HE WAS SMALLER TO MATCH STRENGTH-TO-STRENGTH ONCE HE'D GROWN...
NOW'S AS A GOOD A TIME AS ANY.
HEH
ニコッ
TH-THAT'S OKAY, TAKAMICHI—REALLY! I-I'M STILL ONLY TRAINING, AND...IT'S FINE TO PUT IT OFF! REALLY!!
わた FLAIL
わた FLAIL
DWUH !?
REALLY? YOU SURE?
I-IF *YOU'RE* ENTERING, TAKAHATA-SENSEI, TH-THEN *I* AM, TOO!!
どぎゃーん DWAH-DUM!
ASUNA-KUN?! WHAT...
INSIDE VOICE, ASUNA! *INSIDE VOICE!!*
AWOO (O-O) ...
TREMBLE
TREMBLE
I-I'M THINKING I WON'T ENTER AFTER ALL, KOTARŌ-KUN...
'LL SAY I HAVE A STOMACHACHE, OR...
WHAT?! WHY WOULD YOU-?!
GLOO-O-O
THE ONLY REASON I *WOULD* ENTER IS TO SEE HOW MUCH I'VE IMPROVED...
WITH SO MANY STRONG PEOPLE AROUND, THOUGH, I'LL BE OUT BEFORE I EVEN HAVE A CHANCE TO—
I MIGHT EVEN DIE (WORST-CASE SCENARIO)
よろ SWAY
よろ SWAY
WHAT?! DON'T BE *STUPID!* IF YOU WERE A *MAN*, THAT WOULD ONLY *EXCITE* YOU!!
B-BUT I DON'T EVEN *LIKE* FIGHTING, NOT *REALLY*...
LIAR! IDIOT!! LAST TIME WE FOUGHT, YOU SAID YOU HAD FUN—!
'AT— 'AT 'ISN'T 'EALLY—
ぐいーん STRE-E-ETCH
OH, THAT'S RIGHT... ONE MORE THING.

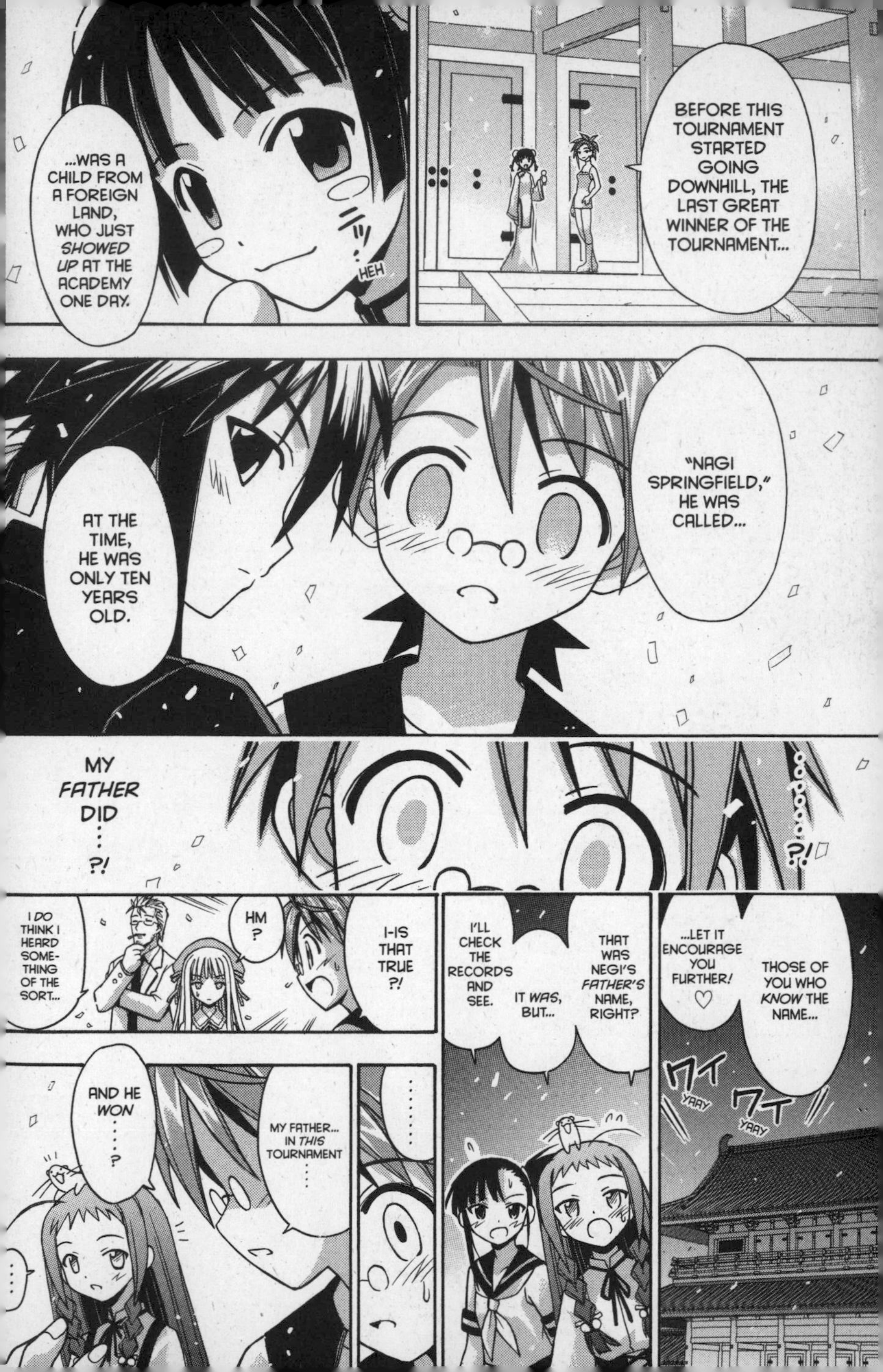
BEFORE THIS TOURNAMENT STARTED GOING DOWNHILL, THE LAST GREAT WINNER OF THE TOURNAMENT...
...WAS A CHILD FROM A FOREIGN LAND, WHO JUST *SHOWED UP* AT THE ACADEMY ONE DAY.
HEH
"NAGI SPRINGFIELD," HE WAS CALLED...
AT THE TIME, HE WAS ONLY TEN YEARS OLD.
?!
MY *FATHER* DID...?!
THOSE OF YOU WHO *KNOW* THE NAME...
...LET IT ENCOURAGE YOU FURTHER! ♡
ワイ
YAAY
ワイ
YAAY
THAT WAS NEGI'S *FATHER'S* NAME, RIGHT?
IT *WAS*, BUT...
I'LL CHECK THE RECORDS AND SEE.
I-IS THAT TRUE?!
HM?
I *DO* THINK I HEARD SOMETHING OF THE SORT...
......
MY FATHER... IN *THIS* TOURNAMENT...
AND HE *WON*.....?
...

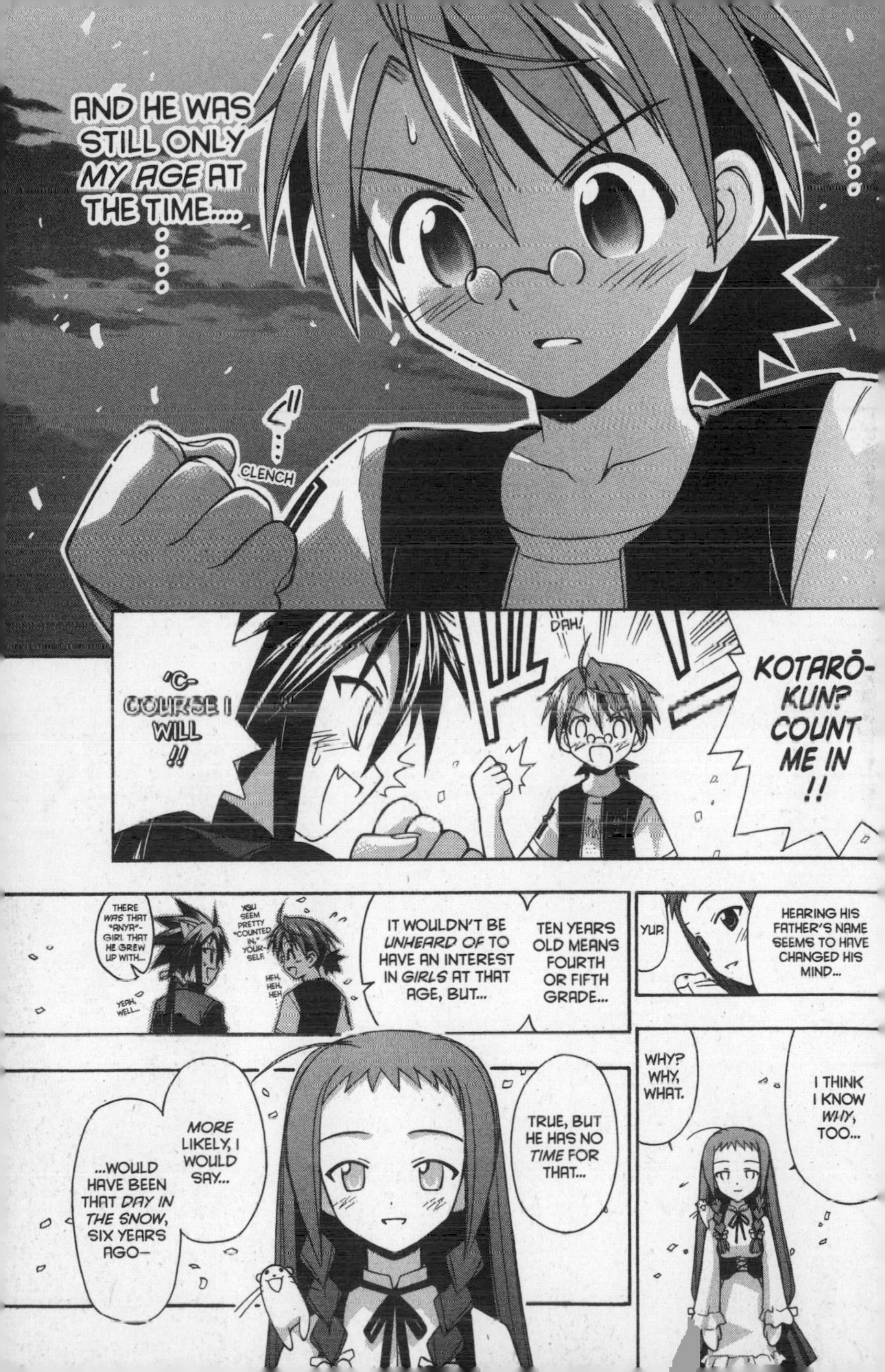

AND HE WAS STILL ONLY MY AGE AT THE TIME....
CLENCH
KOTARŌ-KUN? COUNT ME IN !!
DAH!
'C-COURSE I WILL !!
HEARING HIS FATHER'S NAME SEEMS TO HAVE CHANGED HIS MIND...
YUP.
TEN YEARS OLD MEANS FOURTH OR FIFTH GRADE...
IT WOULDN'T BE UNHEARD OF TO HAVE AN INTEREST IN GIRLS AT THAT AGE, BUT...
YOU SEEM PRETTY "COUNTED IN," YOURSELF.
HEH, HEH, HEH
THERE WAS THAT "ANYA"-GIRL THAT HE GREW UP WITH...
YEAH, WELL...
I THINK I KNOW WHY, TOO...
WHY? WHY, WHAT.
TRUE, BUT HE HAS NO TIME FOR THAT...
MORE LIKELY, I WOULD SAY...
...WOULD HAVE BEEN THAT DAY IN THE SNOW, SIX YEARS AGO—

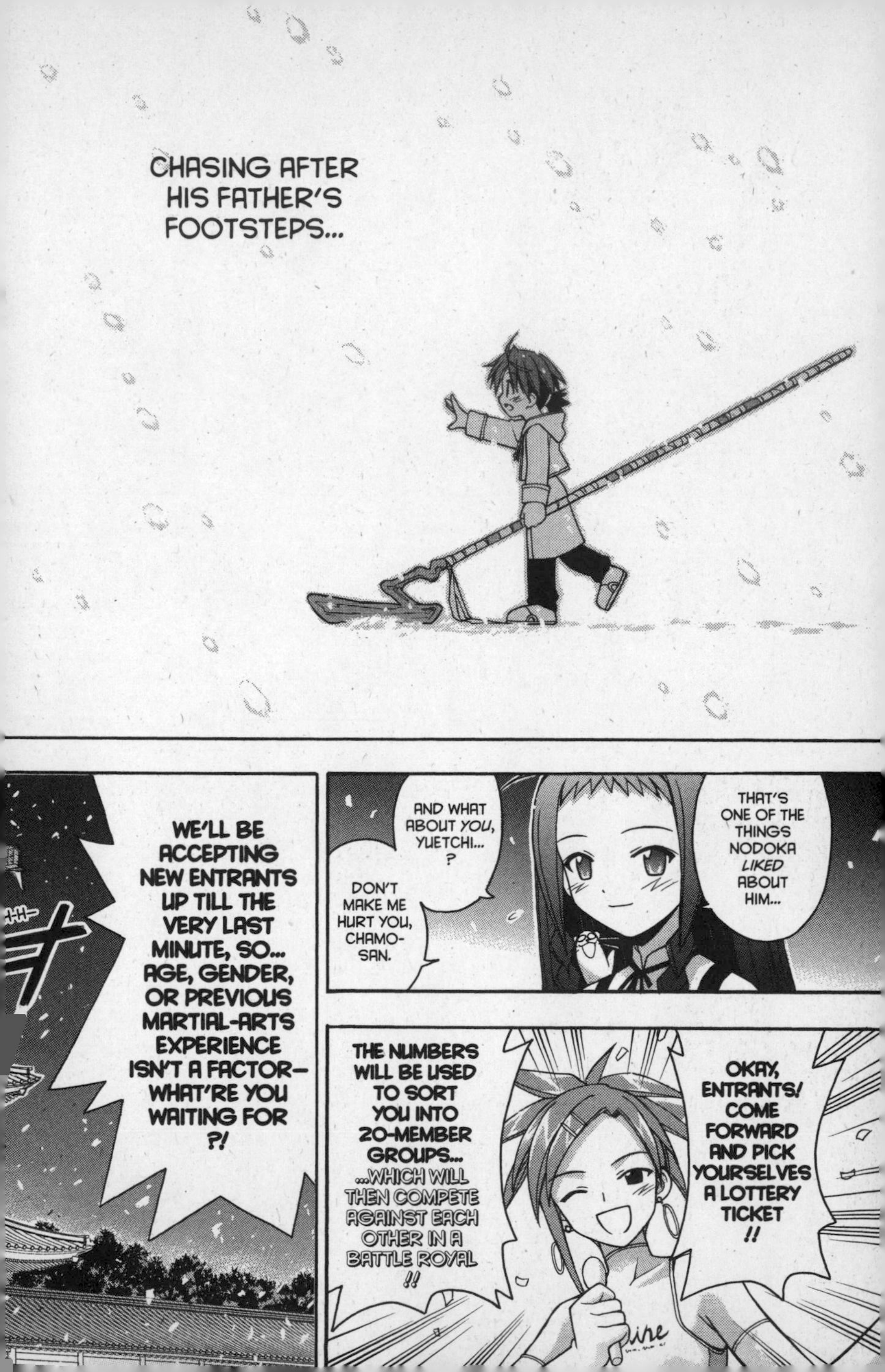
CHASING AFTER HIS FATHER'S FOOTSTEPS...
THAT'S ONE OF THE THINGS NODOKA *LIKED* ABOUT HIM...
AND WHAT ABOUT *YOU*, YUETCHI...?
DON'T MAKE ME HURT YOU, CHAMO-SAN.
OKAY, ENTRANTS! COME FORWARD AND PICK YOURSELVES A LOTTERY TICKET!!
THE NUMBERS WILL BE USED TO SORT YOU INTO 20-MEMBER GROUPS...
...WHICH WILL THEN COMPETE AGAINST EACH OTHER IN A BATTLE ROYAL!!
WE'LL BE ACCEPTING NEW ENTRANTS UP TILL THE VERY LAST MINUTE, SO... AGE, GENDER, OR PREVIOUS MARTIAL-ARTS EXPERIENCE ISN'T A FACTOR—WHAT'RE YOU WAITING FOR?!

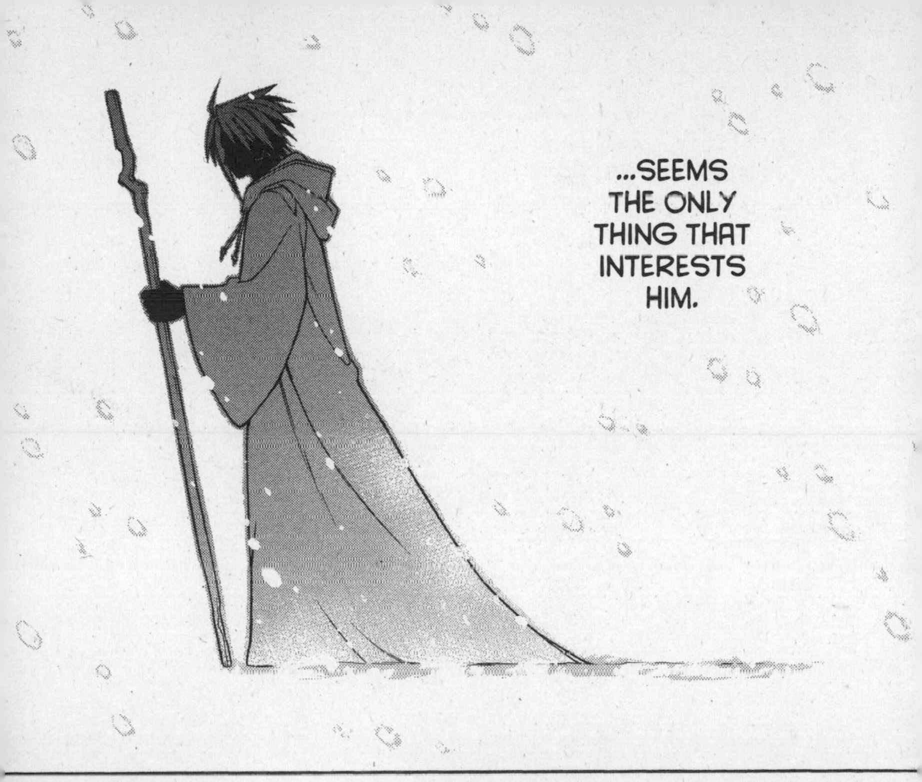
...SEEMS THE ONLY THING THAT INTERESTS HIM.

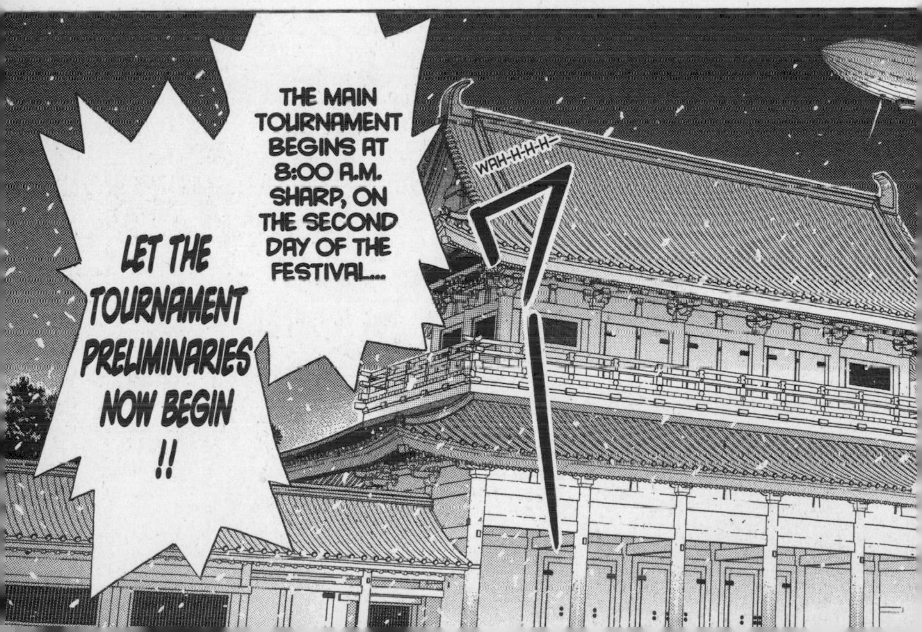
WAH-H-H-H-
THE MAIN TOURNAMENT BEGINS AT 8:00 A.M. SHARP, ON THE SECOND DAY OF THE FESTIVAL...
LET THE TOURNAMENT PRELIMINARIES NOW BEGIN !!

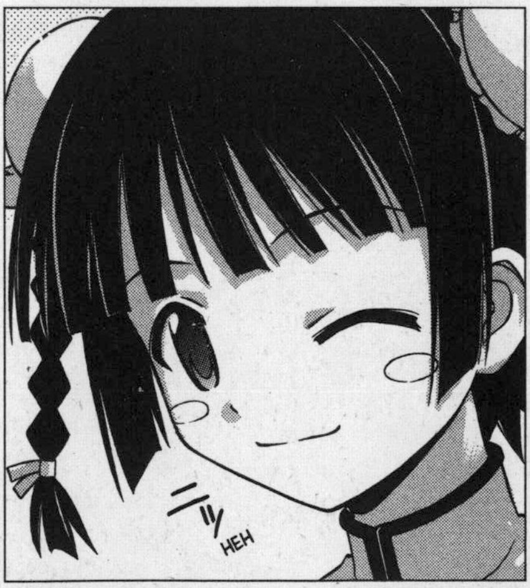
HEH

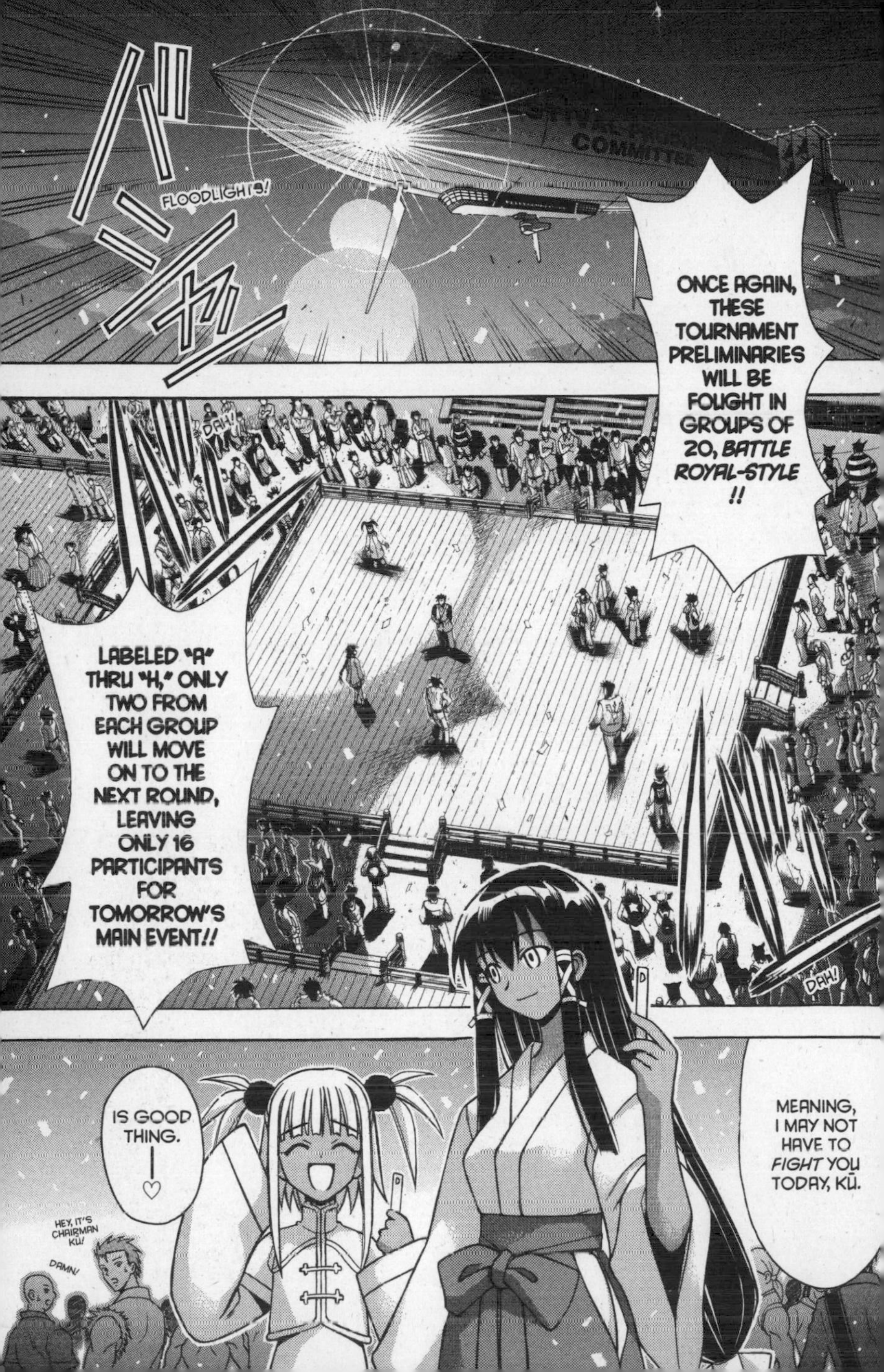
FLOODLIGHTS!
ONCE AGAIN, THESE TOURNAMENT PRELIMINARIES WILL BE FOUGHT IN GROUPS OF 20, *BATTLE ROYAL-STYLE* !!
DAH!
DAH!
LABELED "A" THRU "H," ONLY TWO FROM EACH GROUP WILL MOVE ON TO THE NEXT ROUND, LEAVING ONLY 16 PARTICIPANTS FOR TOMORROW'S MAIN EVENT!!
MEANING, I MAY NOT HAVE TO *FIGHT* YOU TODAY, KŪ.
IS GOOD THING. ♡
HEY, IT'S CHAIRMAN KŪ!
DAMN!

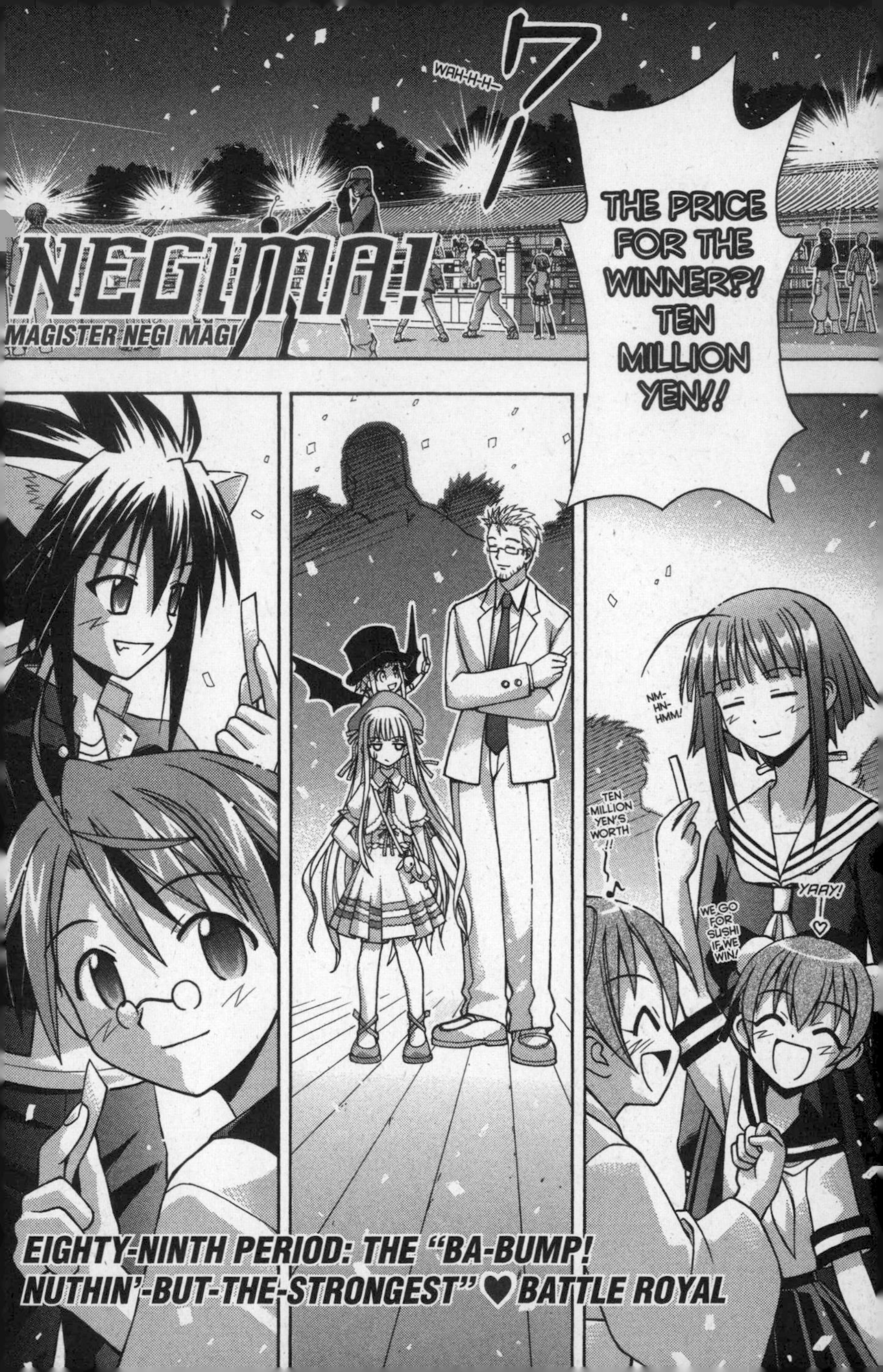
THE PRICE FOR THE WINNER?! TEN MILLION YEN!!
WAH-H-H-H—
NEGIMA!
MAGISTER NEGI MAGI
NM-HN-HMM!
YAAY!
TEN MILLION YEN'S WORTH!!
WE GO FOR SUSHI IF WE WIN!
EIGHTY-NINTH PERIOD: THE "BA-BUMP! NUTHIN'-BUT-THE-STRONGEST" ♥ BATTLE ROYAL

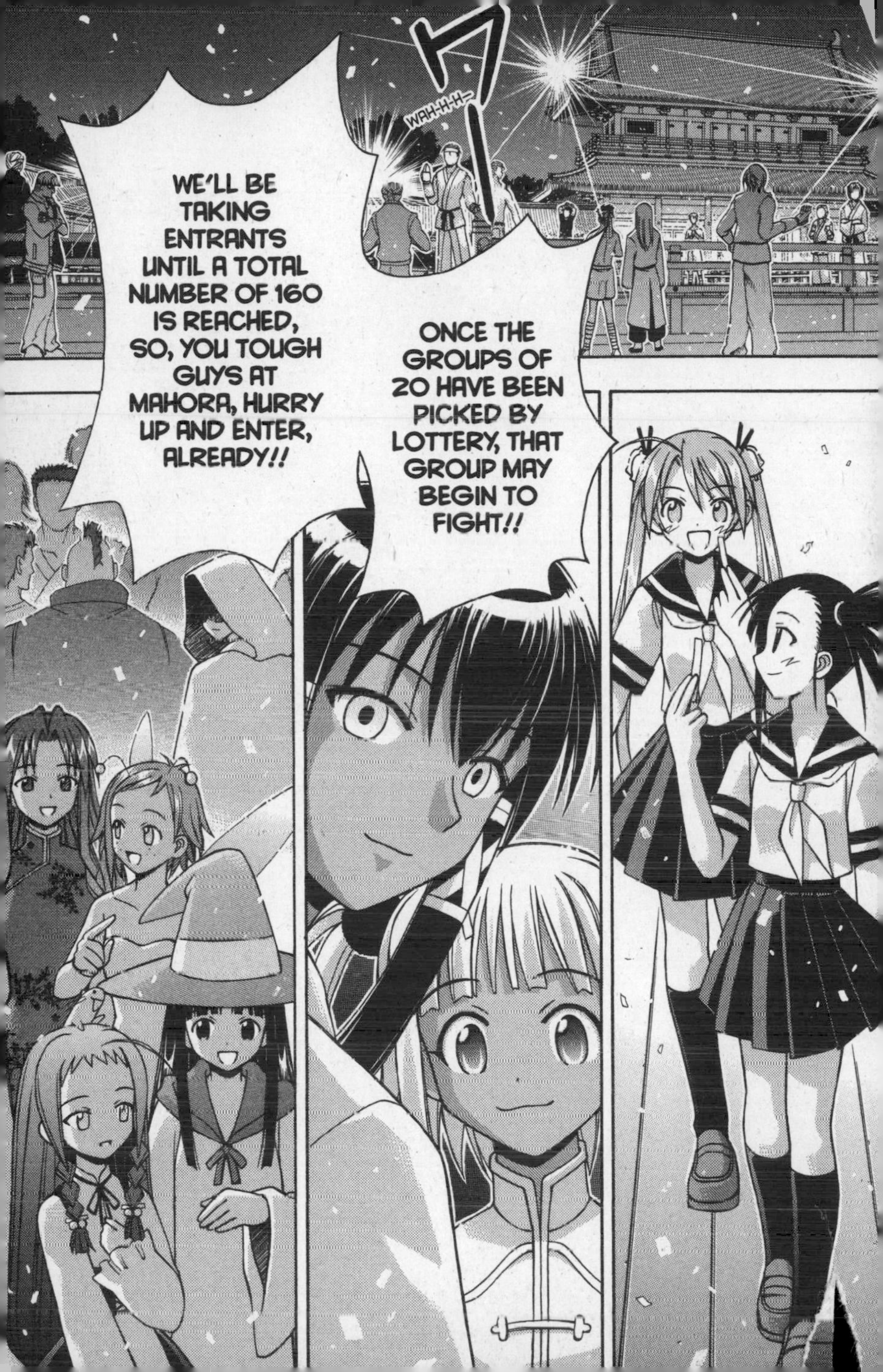
WAH-H-H-
WE'LL BE TAKING ENTRANTS UNTIL A TOTAL NUMBER OF 160 IS REACHED, SO, YOU TOUGH GUYS AT MAHORA, HURRY UP AND ENTER, ALREADY!!
ONCE THE GROUPS OF 20 HAVE BEEN PICKED BY LOTTERY, THAT GROUP MAY BEGIN TO FIGHT!!

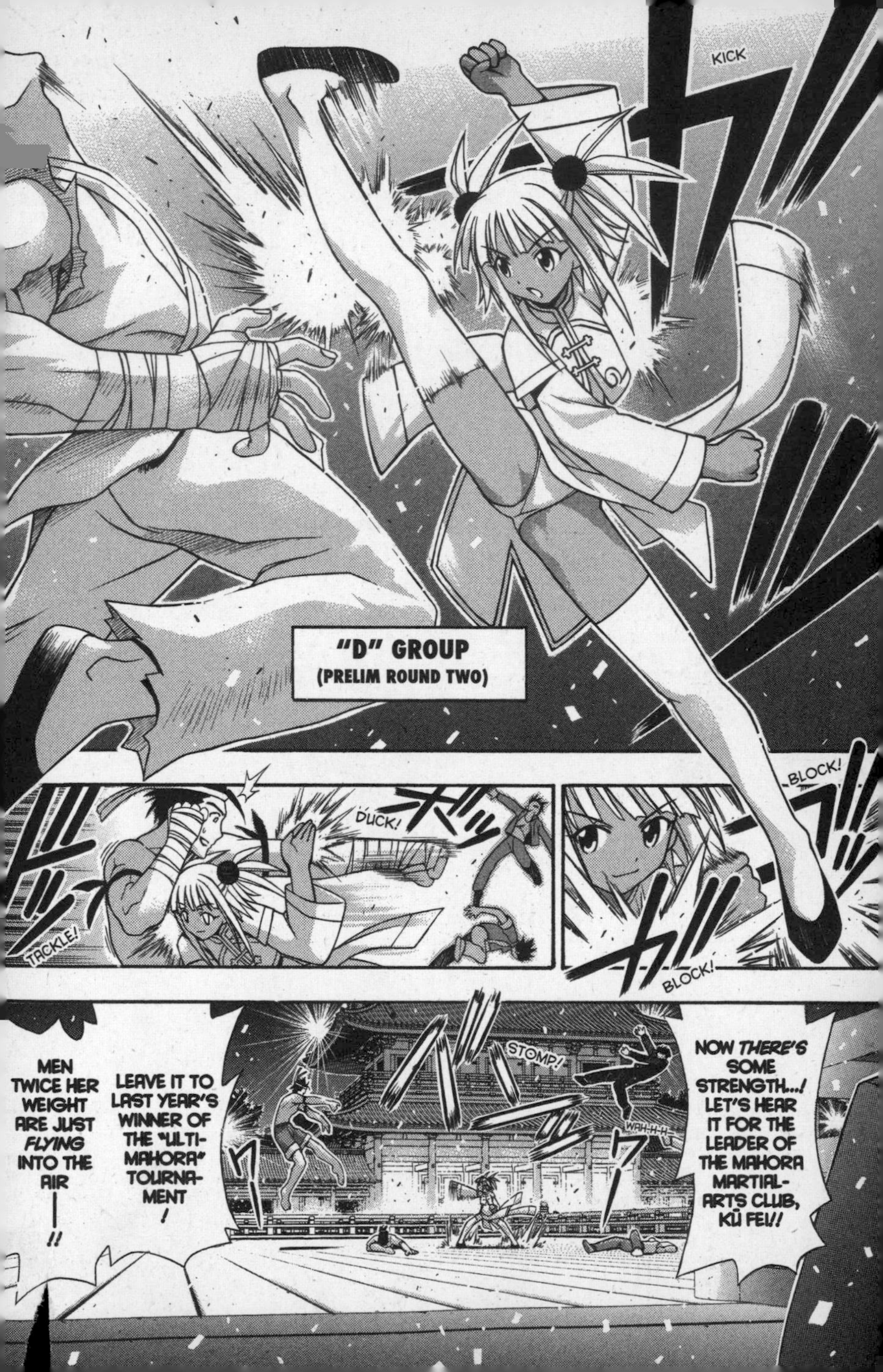
KICK
"D" GROUP
(PRELIM ROUND TWO)
BLOCK!
BLOCK!
DUCK!
TACKLE!
NOW THERE'S SOME STRENGTH...! LET'S HEAR IT FOR THE LEADER OF THE MAHORA MARTIAL-ARTS CLUB, KŪ FEI!!
STOMP!
WAH-H-H
LEAVE IT TO LAST YEAR'S WINNER OF THE "ULTI-MAHORA" TOURNAMENT!
MEN TWICE HER WEIGHT ARE JUST FLYING INTO THE AIR—!!

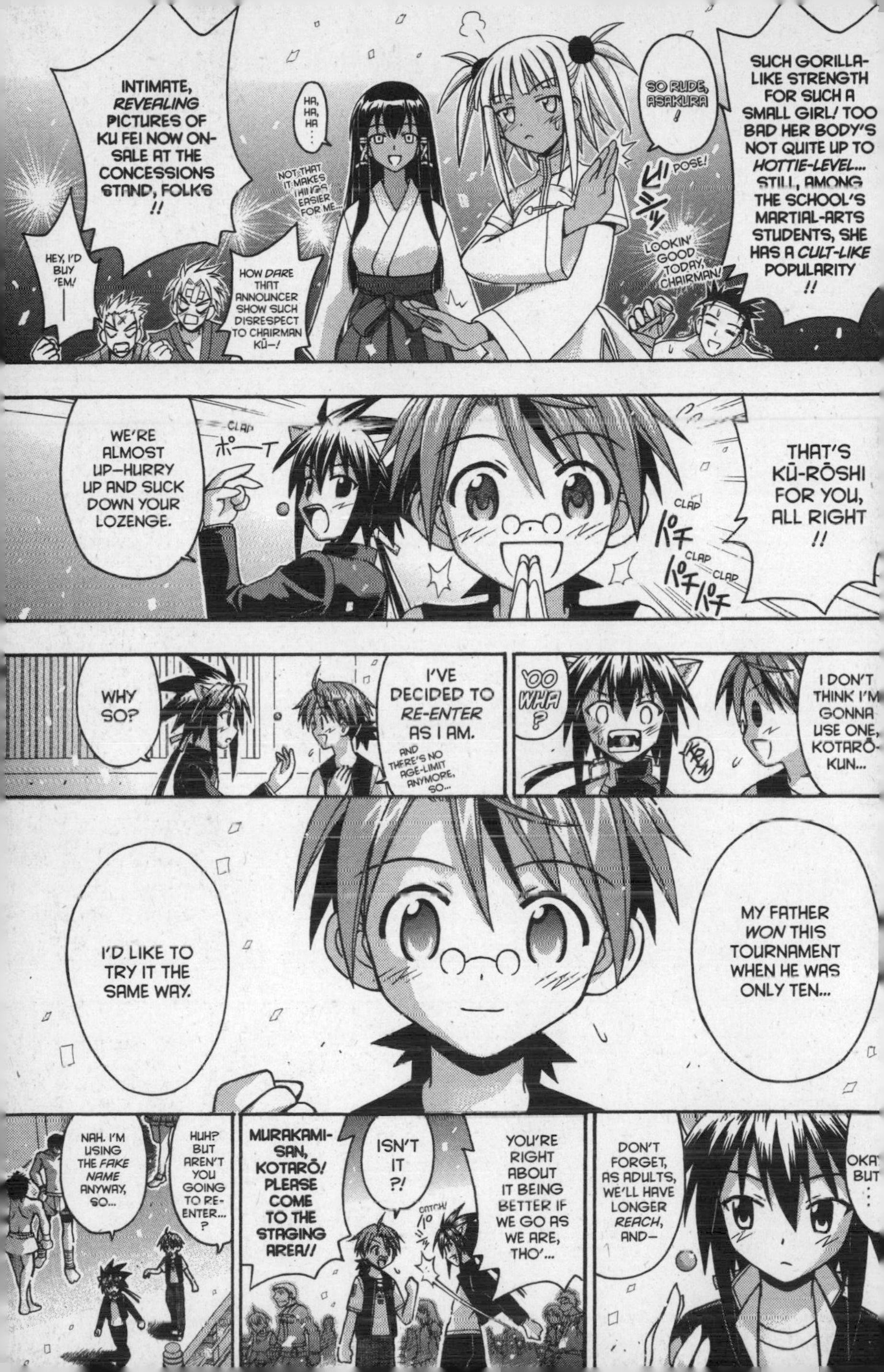
SUCH GORILLA-LIKE STRENGTH FOR SUCH A SMALL GIRL! TOO BAD HER BODY'S NOT QUITE UP TO *HOTTIE-LEVEL*... STILL, AMONG THE SCHOOL'S MARTIAL-ARTS STUDENTS, SHE HAS A *CULT-LIKE* POPULARITY!!
SO RUDE, ASAKURA!
POSE!
LOOKIN' GOOD TODAY, CHAIRMAN!
HA, HA, HA...
NOT THAT IT MAKES THINGS EASIER FOR ME...
INTIMATE, *REVEALING* PICTURES OF KU FEI NOW ON-SALE AT THE CONCESSIONS STAND, FOLKS!!
HOW *DARE* THAT ANNOUNCER SHOW SUCH DISRESPECT TO CHAIRMAN KŪ–!
HEY, I'D BUY 'EM!
THAT'S KŪ-RŌSHI FOR YOU, ALL RIGHT!!
CLAP
CLAP
CLAP
CLAP
WE'RE ALMOST UP—HURRY UP AND SUCK DOWN YOUR LOZENGE.
I DON'T THINK I'M GONNA USE ONE, KOTARŌ-KUN...
YOO WHA?
I'VE DECIDED TO *RE-ENTER* AS I AM.
AND THERE'S NO AGE-LIMIT ANYMORE, SO...
WHY SO?
MY FATHER *WON* THIS TOURNAMENT WHEN HE WAS ONLY TEN...
I'D LIKE TO TRY IT THE SAME WAY.
OKA BUT...
DON'T FORGET, AS ADULTS, WE'LL HAVE LONGER *REACH*, AND—
YOU'RE RIGHT ABOUT IT BEING BETTER IF WE GO AS WE ARE, THO'...
ISN'T IT ?!
CATCH!
MURAKAMI-SAN, KOTARŌ! PLEASE COME TO THE STAGING AREA!!
HUH? BUT AREN'T YOU GOING TO RE-ENTER...?
NAH. I'M USING THE *FAKE NAME* ANYWAY, SO...

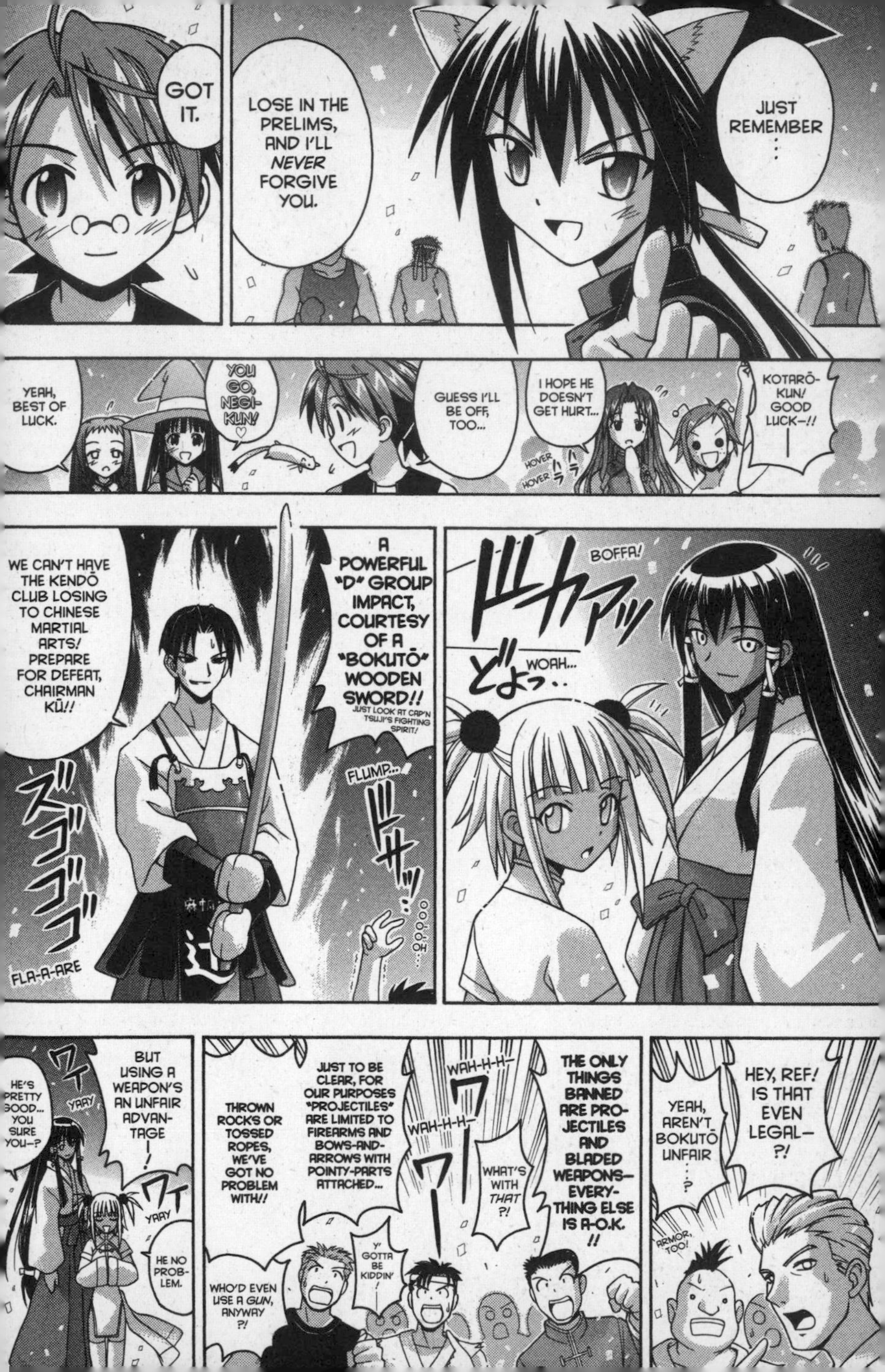
JUST REMEMBER . . .
LOSE IN THE PRELIMS, AND I'LL *NEVER* FORGIVE YOU.
GOT IT.
KOTARŌ-KUN! GOOD LUCK—!!
HOVER HOVER
I HOPE HE DOESN'T GET HURT...
GUESS I'LL BE OFF, TOO...
YOU GO, NEGI-KUN! ♡
YEAH, BEST OF LUCK.
BOFFA!
WOAH...
A POWERFUL "D" GROUP IMPACT, COURTESY OF A "BOKUTŌ" WOODEN SWORD!!
JUST LOOK AT CAP'N TSUJI'S FIGHTING SPIRIT!
WE CAN'T HAVE THE KENDŌ CLUB LOSING TO CHINESE MARTIAL ARTS! PREPARE FOR DEFEAT, CHAIRMAN KŪ!!
FLUMP...
OOOO-OH...
FLA-A-ARE
HEY, REF! IS THAT EVEN LEGAL—?!
YEAH, AREN'T BOKUTŌ UNFAIR . . . ?
ARMOR, TOO!
THE ONLY THINGS BANNED ARE PROJECTILES AND BLADED WEAPONS—EVERYTHING ELSE IS A-O.K.!!
WAH-H-H-
WAH-H-H-
WHAT'S WITH *THAT*?!
JUST TO BE CLEAR, FOR OUR PURPOSES "PROJECTILES" ARE LIMITED TO FIREARMS AND BOWS-AND-ARROWS WITH POINTY-PARTS ATTACHED...
THROWN ROCKS OR TOSSED ROPES, WE'VE GOT NO PROBLEM WITH!!
Y' GOTTA BE KIDDIN'!
WHO'D EVEN USE A *GUN*, ANYWAY?!
BUT USING A WEAPON'S AN UNFAIR ADVANTAGE!
YAAY
HE'S PRETTY GOOD... YOU SURE YOU—?
YAAY
HE NO PROBLEM.

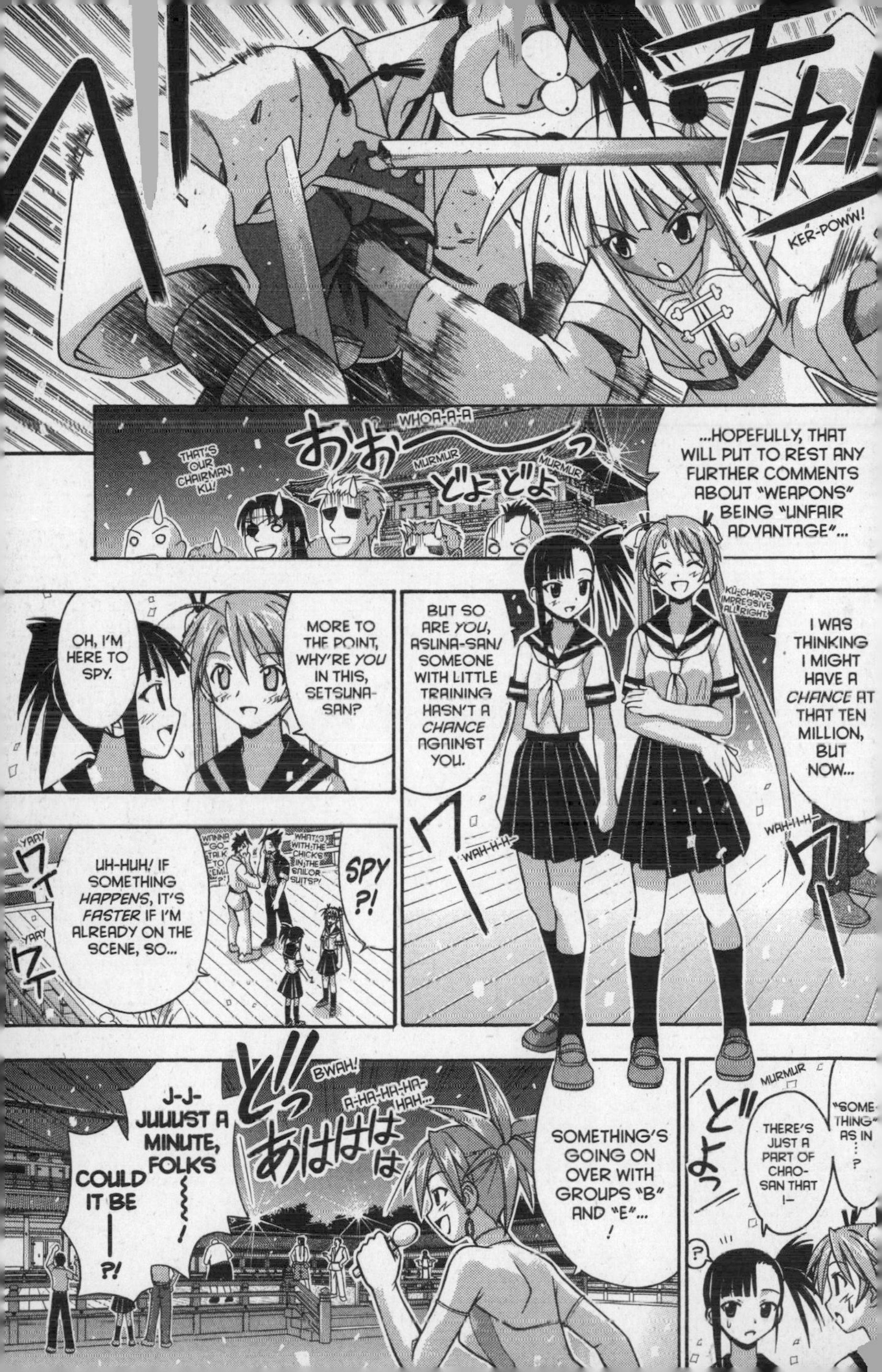
KER-POWW!
...HOPEFULLY, THAT WILL PUT TO REST ANY FURTHER COMMENTS ABOUT "WEAPONS" BEING "UNFAIR ADVANTAGE"...
おおーーっ
WHOA-A-A
どよどよ
MURMUR
MURMUR
THAT'S OUR CHAIRMAN KU!
KU-CHAN'S IMPRESSIVE, ALL RIGHT.
I WAS THINKING I MIGHT HAVE A *CHANCE* AT THAT TEN MILLION, BUT NOW...
BUT SO ARE *YOU*, ASUNA-SAN! SOMEONE WITH LITTLE TRAINING HASN'T A *CHANCE* AGAINST YOU.
ワー
WAH-H-H
ワー
WAH-H-H
MORE TO THE POINT, WHY'RE *YOU* IN THIS, SETSUNA-SAN?
OH, I'M HERE TO SPY.
SPY?!
WHAT'S WITH THE CHICKS IN THE SAILOR SUITS?
WANNA GO TALK TO EMI?
UH-HUH! IF SOMETHING *HAPPENS*, IT'S *FASTER* IF I'M ALREADY ON THE SCENE, SO...
ワイ
YAAY
ワイ
YAAY
"SOMETHING" AS IN...?
THERE'S JUST A PART OF CHAO-SAN THAT I—
どよっ
MURMUR
?
SOMETHING'S GOING ON OVER WITH GROUPS "B" AND "E"...!
どっ
BWAH!
あははは
A-HA-HA-HA-HAH...
J-J-JUUUST A MINUTE, FOLKS~~~!
COULD IT BE—?!

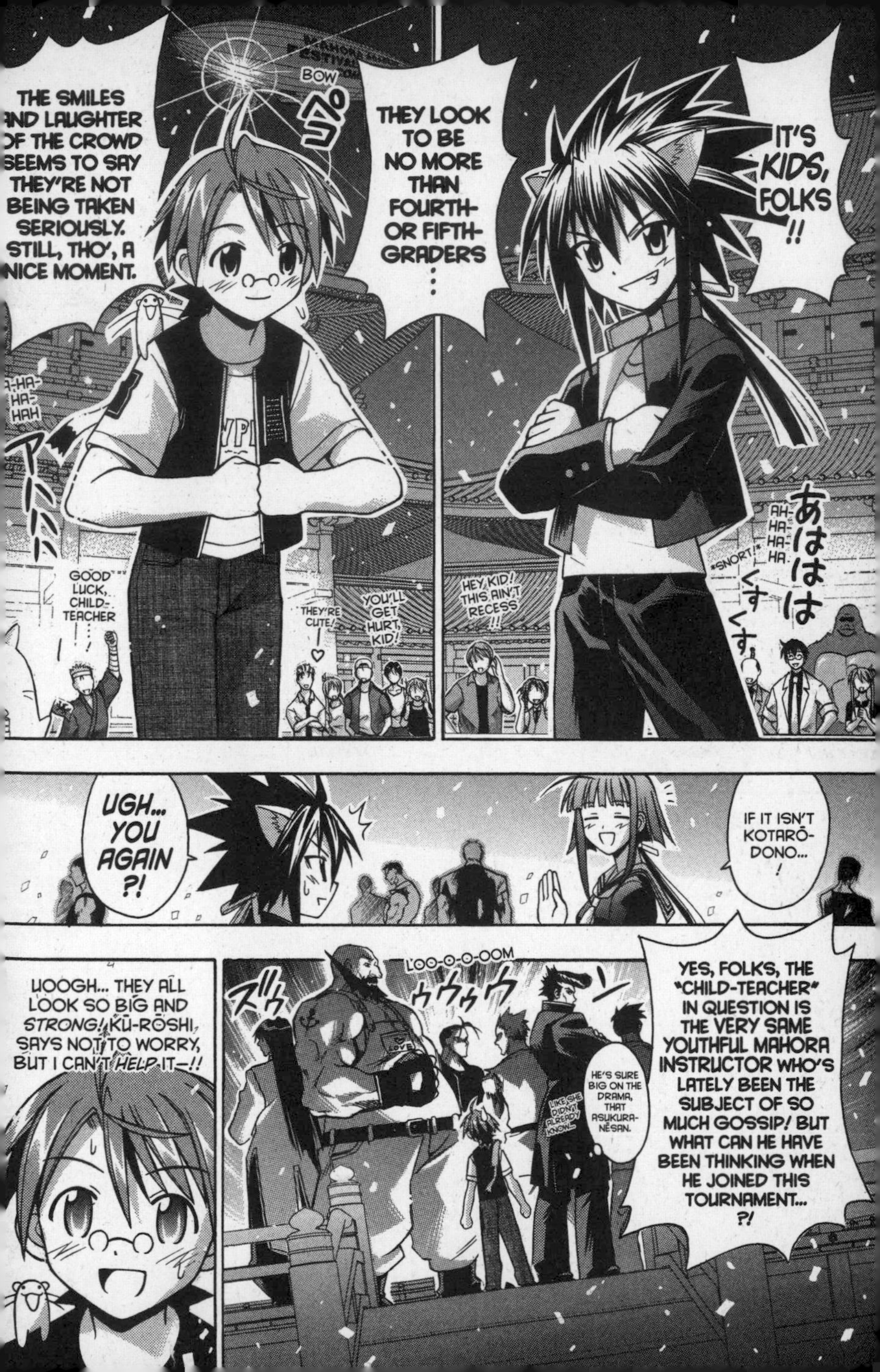

IT'S KIDS, FOLKS!!
THEY LOOK TO BE NO MORE THAN FOURTH- OR FIFTH-GRADERS...
AH-HA-HA-HA
あはは
SNORT
くすくす
HEY KID! THIS AIN'T RECESS!!
BOW
ぺこ
THE SMILES AND LAUGHTER OF THE CROWD SEEMS TO SAY THEY'RE NOT BEING TAKEN SERIOUSLY. STILL, THO', A NICE MOMENT.
YOU'LL GET HURT, KID!
THEY'RE CUTE! ♡
GOOD LUCK, CHILD-TEACHER!!
A-HA-HA-HAH
アハハハ
IF IT ISN'T KOTARŌ-DONO...!
UGH... YOU AGAIN?!
YES, FOLKS, THE "CHILD-TEACHER" IN QUESTION IS THE VERY SAME YOUTHFUL MAHORA INSTRUCTOR WHO'S LATELY BEEN THE SUBJECT OF SO MUCH GOSSIP! BUT WHAT CAN HE HAVE BEEN THINKING WHEN HE JOINED THIS TOURNAMENT...?!
LOO-O-O-OOM
ウウウウ
ズゥ
HE'S SURE BIG ON THE DRAMA, THAT ASUKURA-NĒSAN.
LIKE SHE DIDN'T ALREADY KNOW...
UOOGH... THEY ALL LOOK SO BIG AND STRONG! KŪ-RŌSHI SAYS NOT TO WORRY, BUT I CAN'T HELP IT—!!

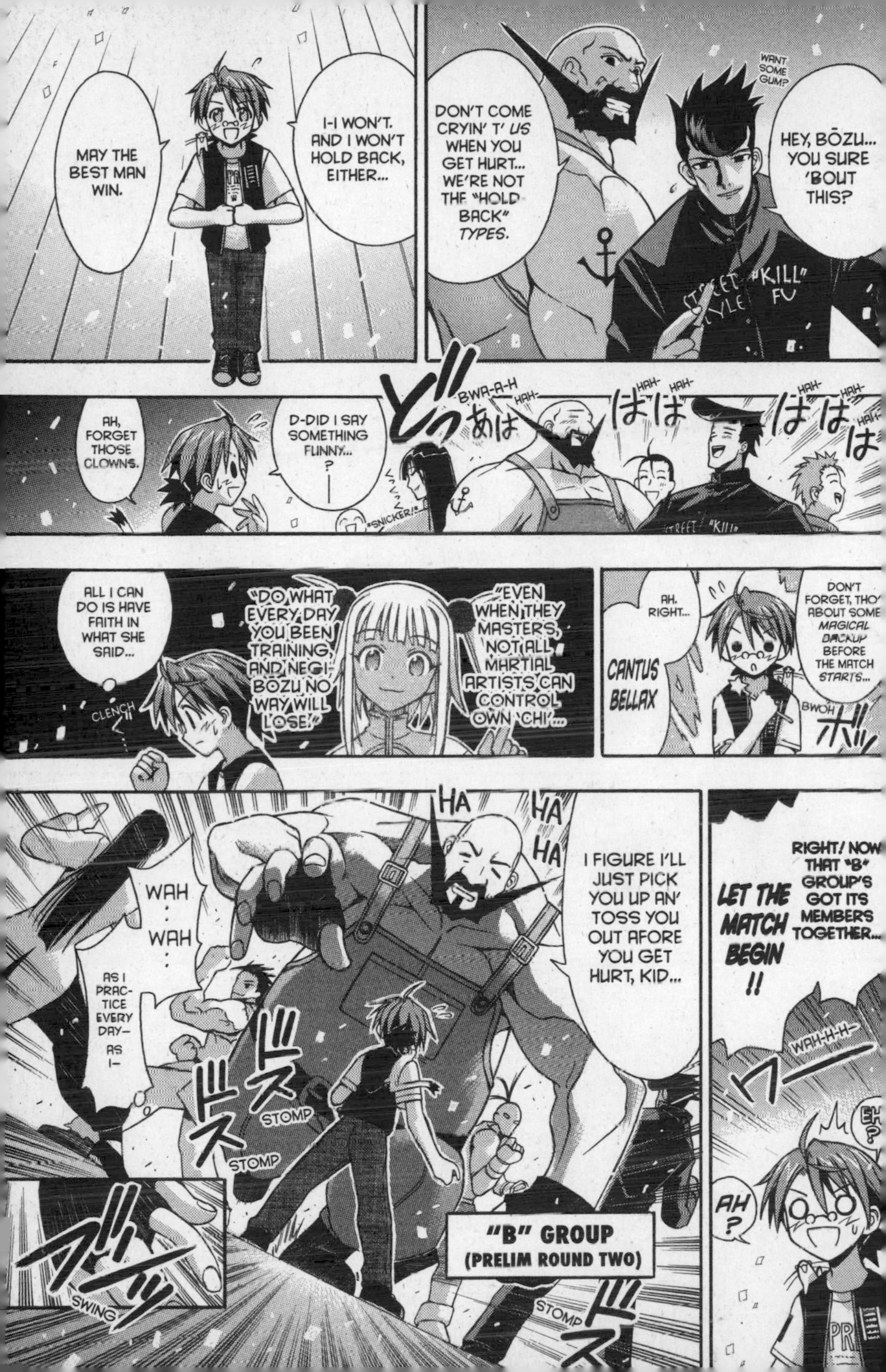
WANT SOME GUM?
HEY, BŌZU... YOU SURE 'BOUT THIS?
DON'T COME CRYIN' T' US WHEN YOU GET HURT... WE'RE NOT THE "HOLD BACK" TYPES.
STREET "KILL" STYLE FU
I-I WON'T. AND I WON'T HOLD BACK, EITHER...
MAY THE BEST MAN WIN.
HAH- HAH-
ははは
HAH- HAH-
ばば
BWA-A-H HAH-
どっあは
D-DID I SAY SOMETHING FUNNY...?
"SNICKER!"
AH, FORGET THOSE CLOWNS.
DON'T FORGET, THO' ABOUT SOME MAGICAL BACKUP BEFORE THE MATCH STARTS...
AH. RIGHT...
CANTUS BELLAX
BWOH
ボッ
"EVEN WHEN THEY MASTERS, NOT ALL MARTIAL ARTISTS CAN CONTROL OWN 'CHI'...
"DO WHAT EVERY DAY YOU BEEN TRAINING, AND NEGI-BŌZU NO WAY WILL LOSE."
ALL I CAN DO IS HAVE FAITH IN WHAT SHE SAID...
CLENCH
RIGHT! NOW THAT "B" GROUP'S GOT ITS MEMBERS TOGETHER...
LET THE MATCH BEGIN!!
WAH-H-H-
ワー
EH?
AH?
HA HA HA
I FIGURE I'LL JUST PICK YOU UP AN' TOSS YOU OUT AFORE YOU GET HURT, KID...
WAH... WAH...
AS I PRACTICE EVERY DAY— AS I—
ドス
STOMP
ドス
STOMP
"B" GROUP (PRELIM ROUND TWO)
ブンッ
SWING
STOMP
ドス

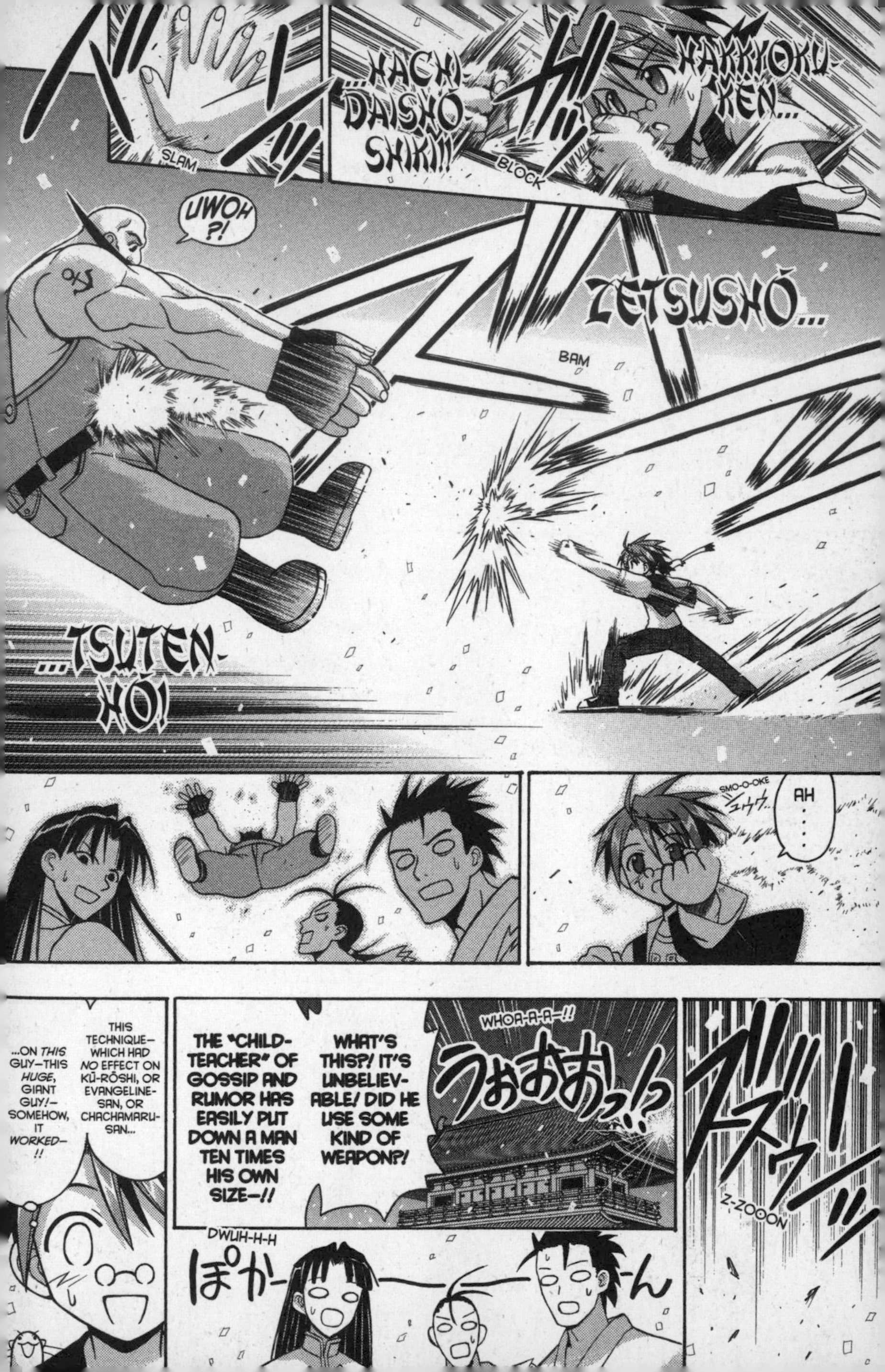
HAKKYOKU-KEN...
HACHI-DAISHŌ SHIKI!!
BLOCK
SLAM
UWOH ?!
ZETSUSHŌ...
BAM
...TSUTEN-HŌ!
SMO-O-OKE
AH ...
Z-ZOOON
WHOA-A-A-!!
うぉおおっ!?
WHAT'S THIS?! IT'S UNBELIEVABLE! DID HE USE SOME KIND OF WEAPON?!
THE "CHILD-TEACHER" OF GOSSIP AND RUMOR HAS EASILY PUT DOWN A MAN TEN TIMES HIS OWN SIZE—!!
THIS TECHNIQUE—WHICH HAD *NO* EFFECT ON KŪ-RŌSHI, OR EVANGELINE-SAN, OR CHACHAMARU-SAN...
...ON *THIS* GUY—THIS *HUGE*, GIANT GUY!—SOMEHOW, IT *WORKED*—!!
DWUH-H-H
ぽかーーーん

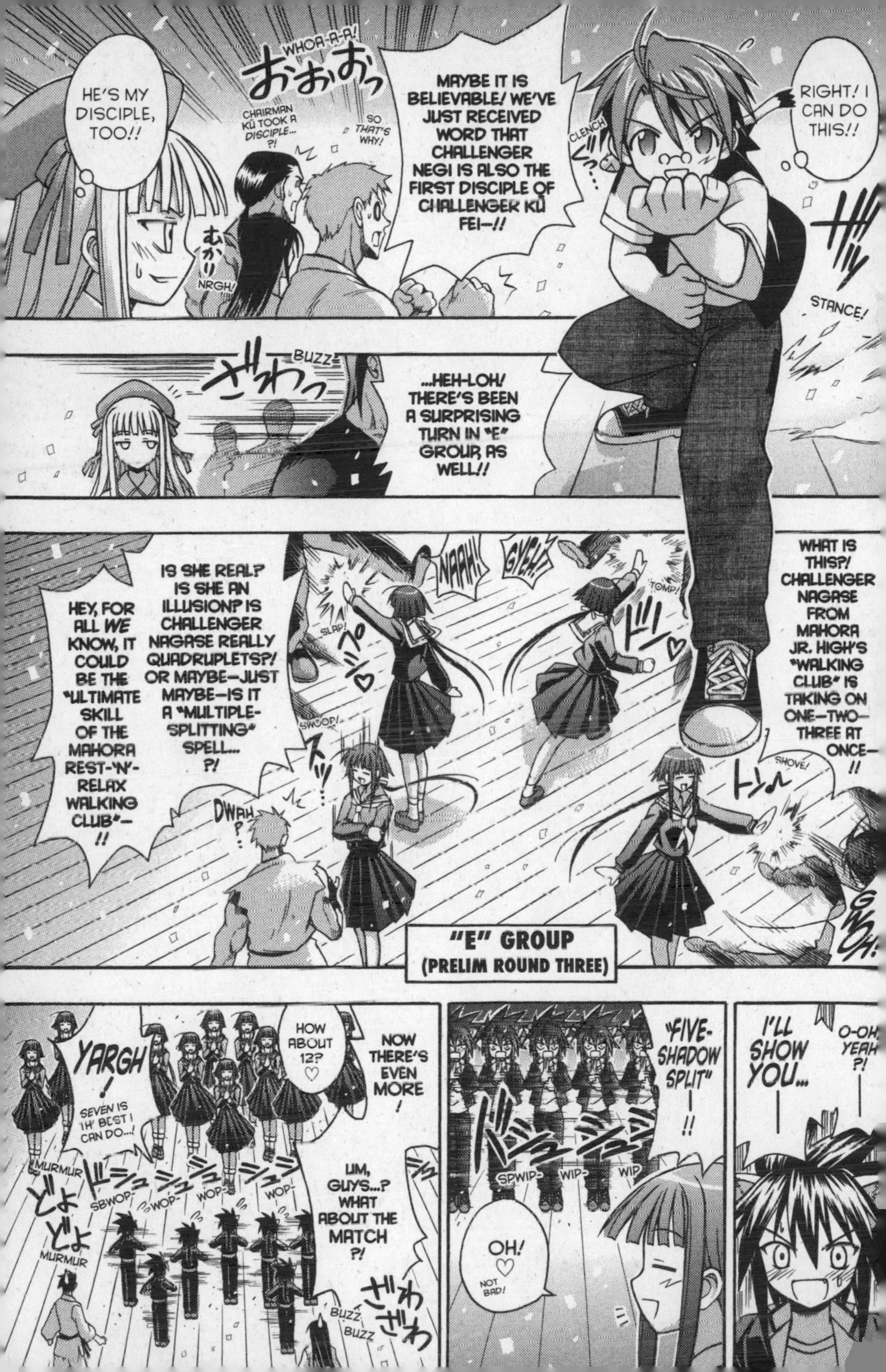
RIGHT! I CAN DO THIS!!
CLENCH
STANCE!
MAYBE IT IS BELIEVABLE! WE'VE JUST RECEIVED WORD THAT CHALLENGER NEGI IS ALSO THE FIRST DISCIPLE OF CHALLENGER KŪ FEI—!!
SO THAT'S WHY!
CHAIRMAN KŪ TOOK A DISCIPLE...?!
WHOA-A-A!
おおおっ
HE'S MY DISCIPLE, TOO!!
むかり
NRGH!
...HEH-LOH! THERE'S BEEN A SURPRISING TURN IN "E" GROUP, AS WELL!!
BUZZ
ざわっ
WHAT IS THIS?! CHALLENGER NAGASE FROM MAHORA JR. HIGH'S "WALKING CLUB" IS TAKING ON ONE—TWO—THREE AT ONCE—!!
GWOH!
SHOVE!
TOMP!
GYEH!
NAAH!
SLAP!
IS SHE REAL? IS SHE AN ILLUSION? IS CHALLENGER NAGASE REALLY QUADRUPLETS?! OR MAYBE—JUST MAYBE—IS IT A "MULTIPLE-SPLITTING" SPELL...?!
HEY, FOR ALL WE KNOW, IT COULD BE THE "ULTIMATE SKILL OF THE MAHORA REST-'N'-RELAX WALKING CLUB"—!!
SWOOP!
DWAH?
"E" GROUP
(PRELIM ROUND THREE)
O-OH, YEAH?!
I'LL SHOW YOU...
"FIVE-SHADOW SPLIT"!!
SPWIP- WIP- WIP
OH! ♡
NOT BAD!
NOW THERE'S EVEN MORE!
HOW ABOUT 12? ♡
YARGH!
SEVEN IS TH' BEST I CAN DO...!
MURMUR
どよどよ
MURMUR
SBWOP- WOP- WOP- WOP-
UM, GUYS...? WHAT ABOUT THE MATCH?!
ざわざわ
BUZZ BUZZ

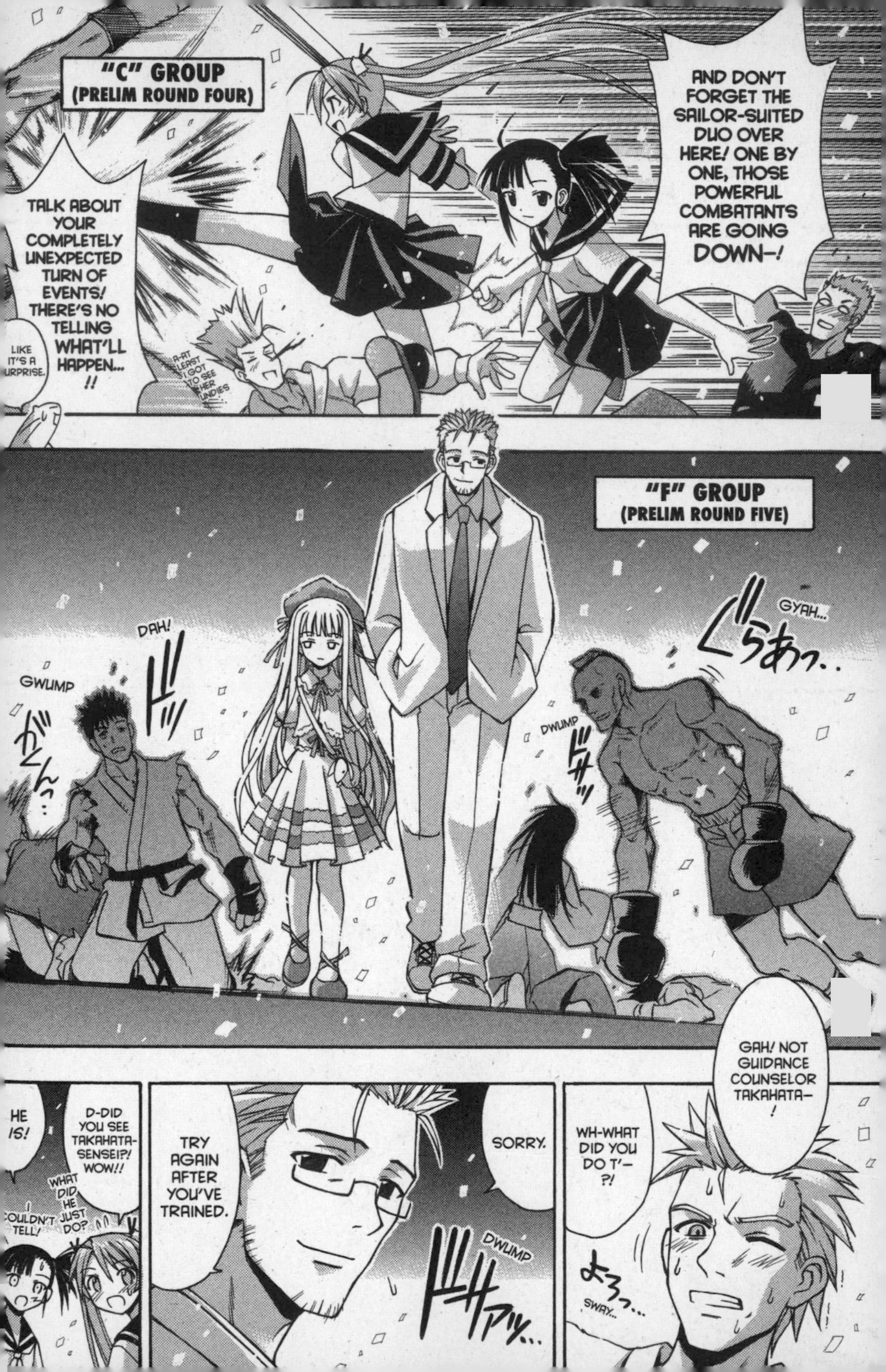
AND DON'T FORGET THE SAILOR-SUITED DUO OVER HERE! ONE BY ONE, THOSE POWERFUL COMBATANTS ARE GOING DOWN–!
"C" GROUP (PRELIM ROUND FOUR)
TALK ABOUT YOUR COMPLETELY UNEXPECTED TURN OF EVENTS! THERE'S NO TELLING WHAT'LL HAPPEN... !!
A-AT LEAST I GOT TO SEE HER UNDIES
LIKE IT'S A URPRISE.
"F" GROUP (PRELIM ROUND FIVE)
ぐらあっ..
GYAH...
ドサッ
DWUMP
ドッ
DAH!
がくんっ..
GWUMP
GAH! NOT GUIDANCE COUNSELOR TAKAHATA–!
WH-WHAT DID YOU DO T'–?!
よろっ...
SWAY...
SORRY.
TRY AGAIN AFTER YOU'VE TRAINED.
ドサァッ...
DWUMP
D-DID YOU SEE TAKAHATA-SENSEI?! WOW!!
HE IS!
WHAT DID HE JUST DO?
I COULDN'T TELL!

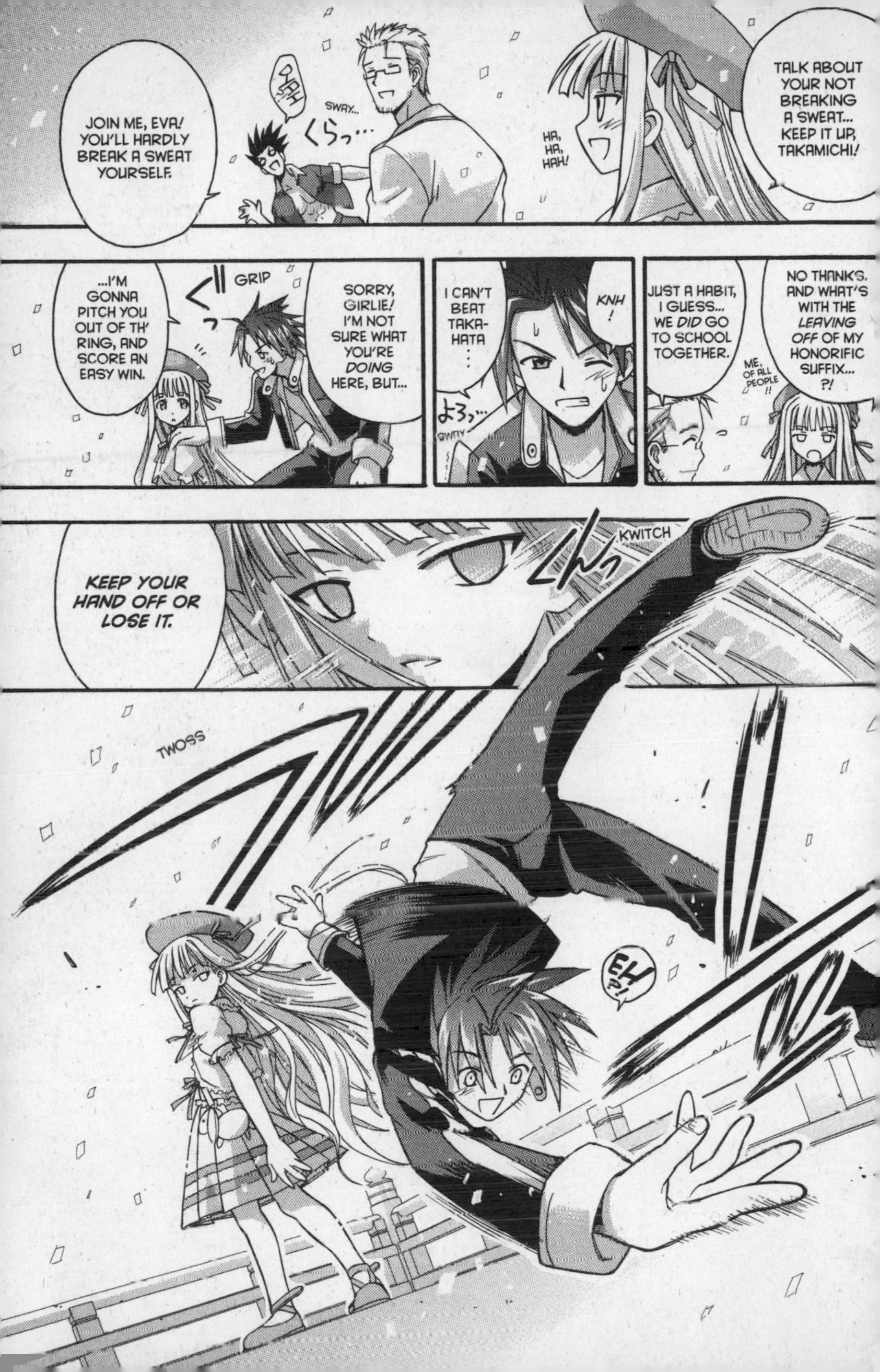
TALK ABOUT YOUR NOT BREAKING A SWEAT... KEEP IT UP, TAKAMICHI!
HA, HA, HAH!
SWAY...
くらっ...
JOIN ME, EVA! YOU'LL HARDLY BREAK A SWEAT YOURSELF.
NO THANKS. AND WHAT'S WITH THE *LEAVING OFF* OF MY HONORIFIC SUFFIX...?!
ME, OF ALL PEOPLE!!
JUST A HABIT, I GUESS... WE *DID* GO TO SCHOOL TOGETHER.
KNH!
I CAN'T BEAT TAKA-HATA...
よろっ...
SWAY
SORRY, GIRLIE! I'M NOT SURE WHAT YOU'RE *DOING* HERE, BUT...
GRIP
...I'M GONNA PITCH YOU OUT OF TH' RING, AND SCORE AN EASY WIN.
KWITCH
KEEP YOUR HAND OFF OR LOSE IT.
EH?!
TWOSS

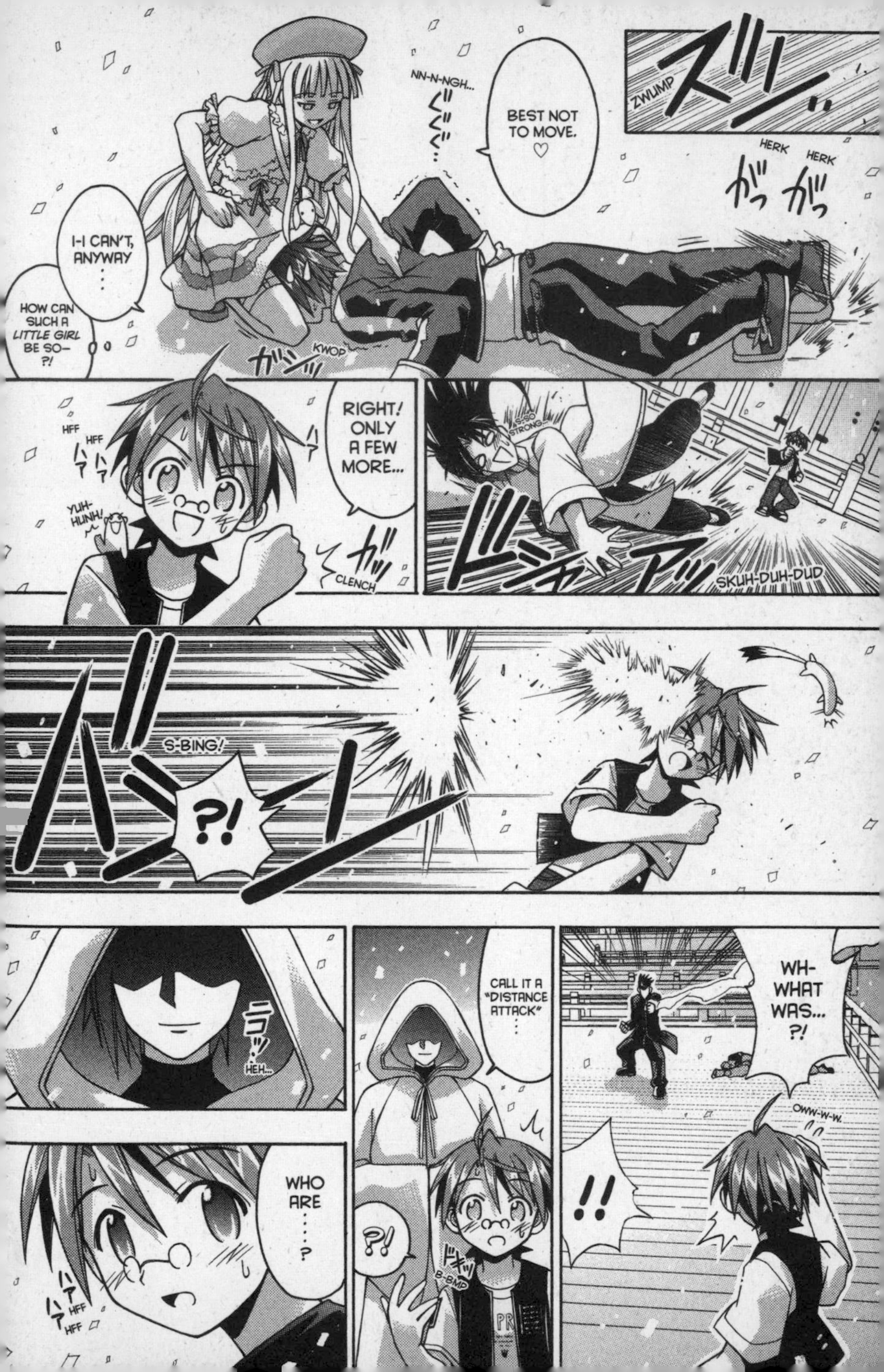
ZWUMP
HERK
HERK
BEST NOT TO MOVE. ♡
NN-N-NGH...
I-I CAN'T, ANYWAY...
HOW CAN SUCH A LITTLE GIRL BE SO—?!
KWOP
S-SO STRONG...
SKUH-DUH-DUD
RIGHT! ONLY A FEW MORE...
HFF
HFF
YUH-HUNH!
CLENCH
S-BING!
?!
WH-WHAT WAS...?!
OWW-W-W.
!!
CALL IT A "DISTANCE ATTACK"...
?!
B-BMP
HEH...
WHO ARE.....?
HFF
HFF

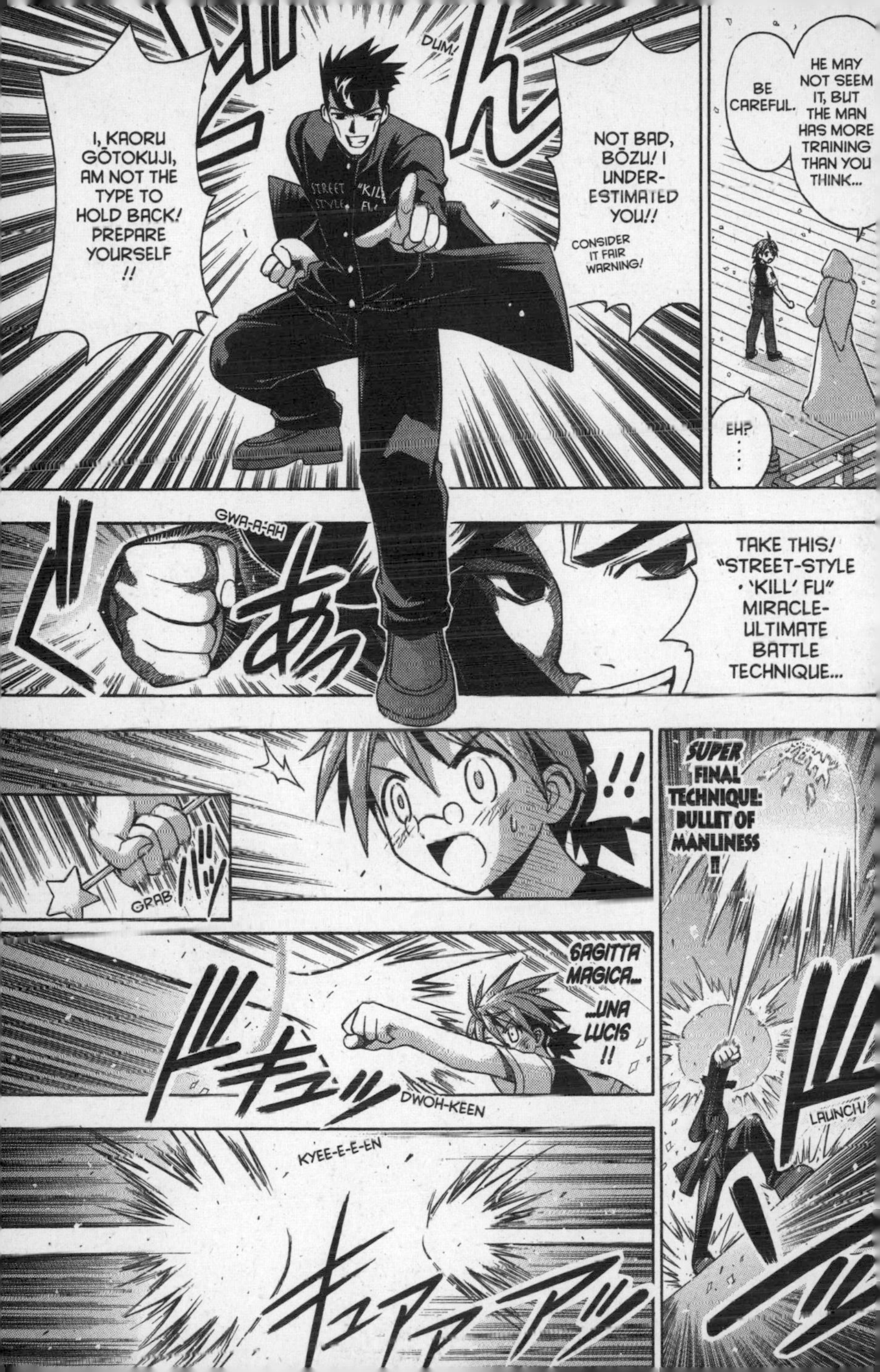
HE MAY NOT SEEM IT, BUT THE MAN HAS MORE TRAINING THAN YOU THINK...
BE CAREFUL.
EH?
.....
DUM!
NOT BAD, BŌZU! I UNDER-ESTIMATED YOU!!
CONSIDER IT FAIR WARNING!
I, KAORU GŌTOKUJI, AM NOT THE TYPE TO HOLD BACK! PREPARE YOURSELF !!
STREET STYLE "KILL" FU
TAKE THIS! "STREET-STYLE · 'KILL' FU" MIRACLE-ULTIMATE BATTLE TECHNIQUE...
GWA-A-AH
SUPER FINAL TECHNIQUE: BULLET OF MANLINESS !!
LAUNCH!
!!
GRAB
SAGITTA MAGICA...
...UNA LUCIS !!
DWOH-KEEN
KYEE-E-E-EN

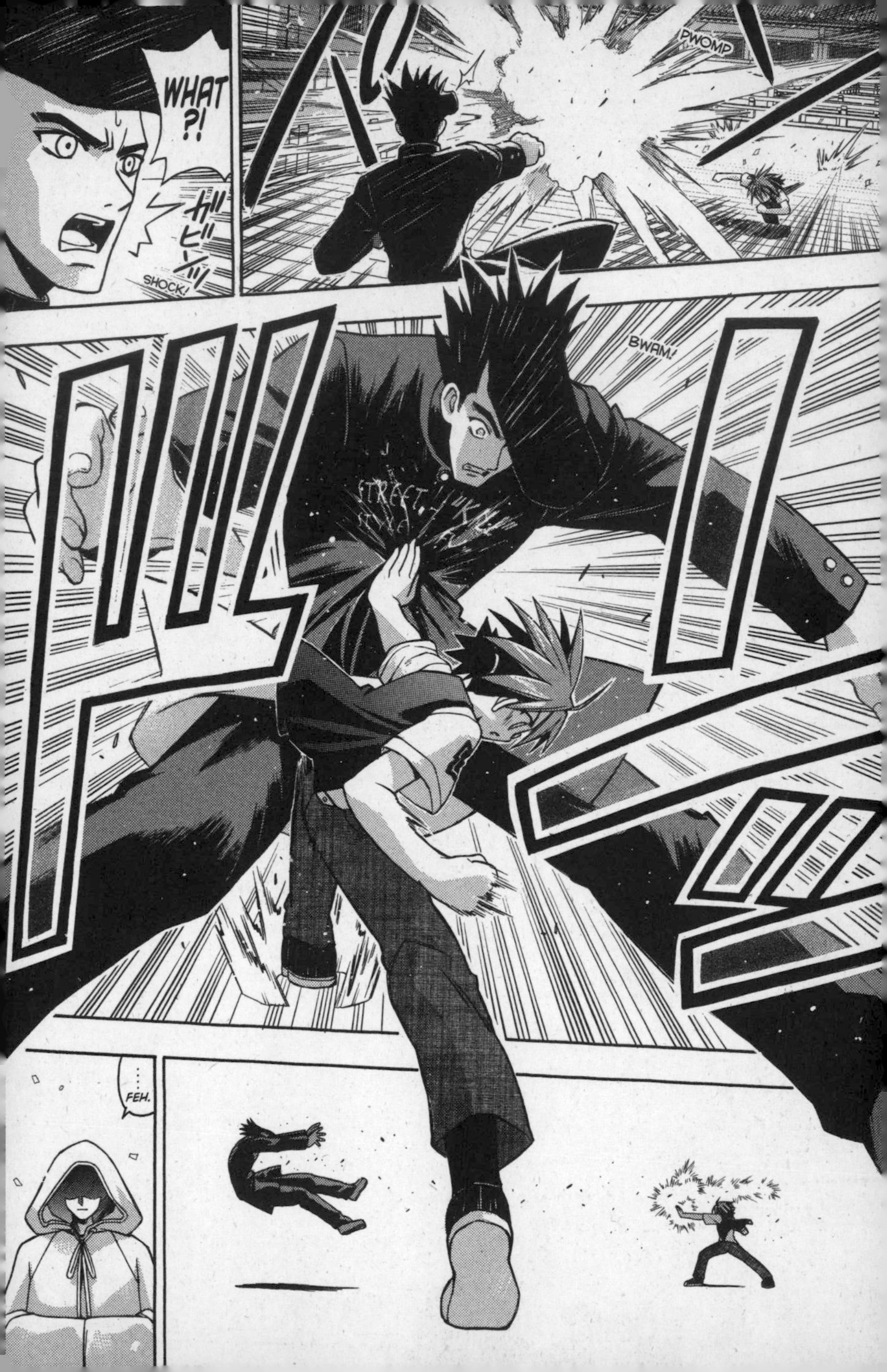
PWOMP
WHAT ?!
ガビーン
SHOCK!
BWAM!
...
FEH.

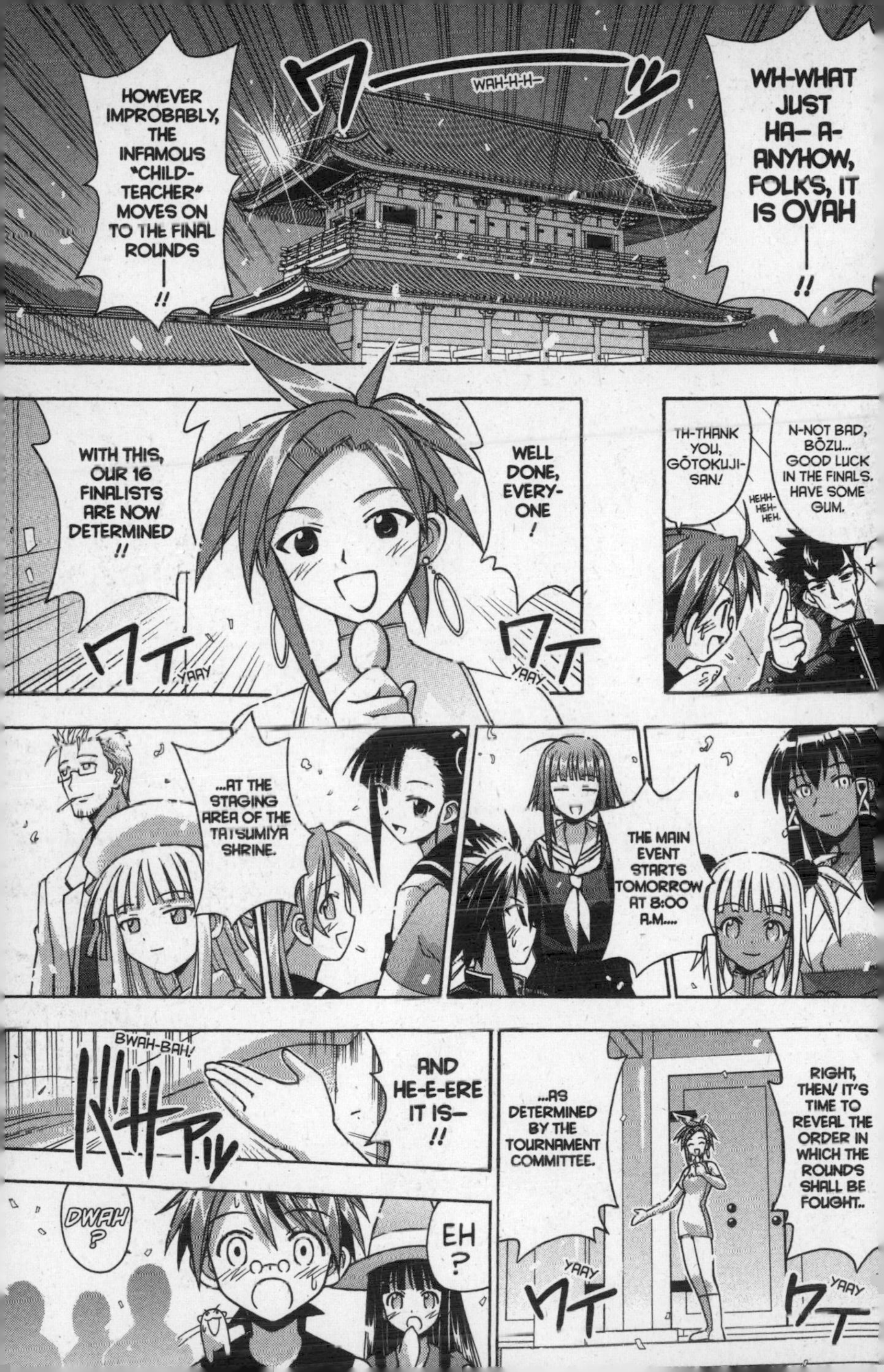
WH-WHAT JUST HA— A- ANYHOW, FOLKS, IT IS OVAH —!!
WAH-H-H—
HOWEVER IMPROBABLY, THE INFAMOUS "CHILD-TEACHER" MOVES ON TO THE FINAL ROUNDS —!!
N-NOT BAD, BŌZU... GOOD LUCK IN THE FINALS. HAVE SOME GUM.
HEHH-HEHH-HEH.
TH-THANK YOU, GŌTOKUJI-SAN!
WELL DONE, EVERY-ONE!
YAAY
WITH THIS, OUR 16 FINALISTS ARE NOW DETERMINED!!
YAAY
THE MAIN EVENT STARTS TOMORROW AT 8:00 A.M....
...AT THE STAGING AREA OF THE TATSUMIYA SHRINE.
RIGHT, THEN! IT'S TIME TO REVEAL THE ORDER IN WHICH THE ROUNDS SHALL BE FOUGHT..
...AS DETERMINED BY THE TOURNAMENT COMMITTEE.
YAAY
YAAY
AND HE-E-ERE IT IS—!!
BWAH-BAH!
EH?
DWAH?

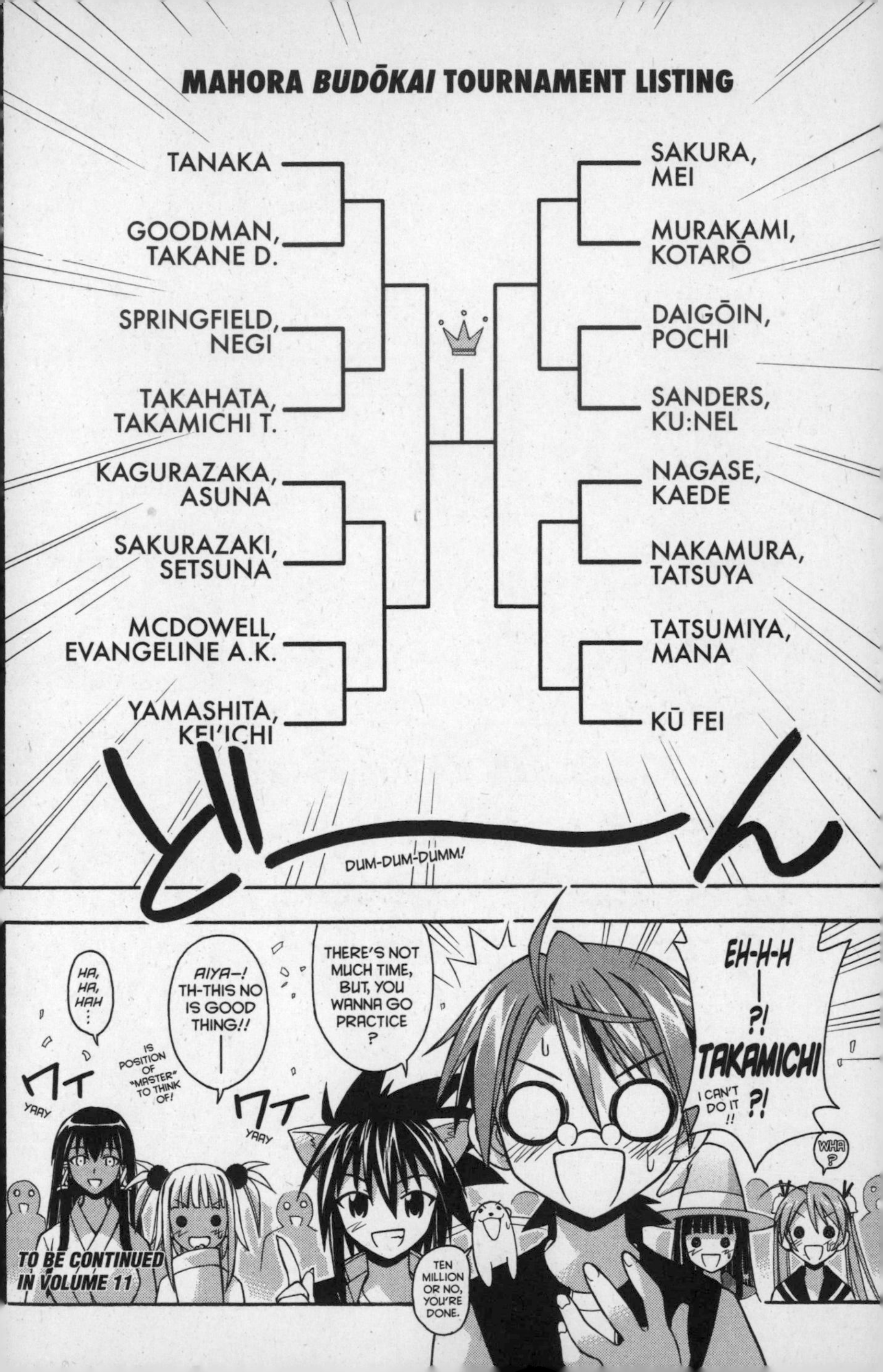
MAHORA BUDŌKAI TOURNAMENT LISTING
TANAKA
GOODMAN, TAKANE D.
SPRINGFIELD, NEGI
TAKAHATA, TAKAMICHI T.
KAGURAZAKA, ASUNA
SAKURAZAKI, SETSUNA
MCDOWELL, EVANGELINE A.K.
YAMASHITA, KEI'ICHI
SAKURA, MEI
MURAKAMI, KOTARŌ
DAIGŌIN, POCHI
SANDERS, KU:NEL
NAGASE, KAEDE
NAKAMURA, TATSUYA
TATSUMIYA, MANA
KŪ FEI
どーん
DUM-DUM-DUMM!
EH-H-H —?! TAKAMICHI ?!
WHA ?
I CAN'T DO IT !!
TEN MILLION OR NO, YOU'RE DONE.
THERE'S NOT MUCH TIME, BUT, YOU WANNA GO PRACTICE ?
ワァ
YAAY
AIYA—! TH-THIS NO IS GOOD THING!!
IS POSITION OF "MASTER" TO THINK OF!
HA, HA, HAH...
ワァ
YAAY
TO BE CONTINUED IN VOLUME 11

— STAFF —

Ken Akamatsu
Takashi Takemoto
Kenichi Nakamura
Masaki Ohyama
Keiichi Yamashita
Chigusa Amagasaki
Takaaki Miyahara

Thanks To

Ran Ayanaga

NEGIMA!
FAN ART CORNER

THANKS, EVERYONE, FOR ALL YOUR LETTERS! (^^)I NOTE THE TREND RECENTLY FOR PEOPLE TO SEND IN PICTURES OF SETSUNA, EVA, AND CHACHAMARU. WE APPRECIATE YOUR WORK—ALWAYS—AND ALSO LOOK FORWARD TO SEEING OTHER CHARACTERS, TOO, SO PLEASE KEEP THAT ART COMING IN!

TEXT: ASSISTANT MAX

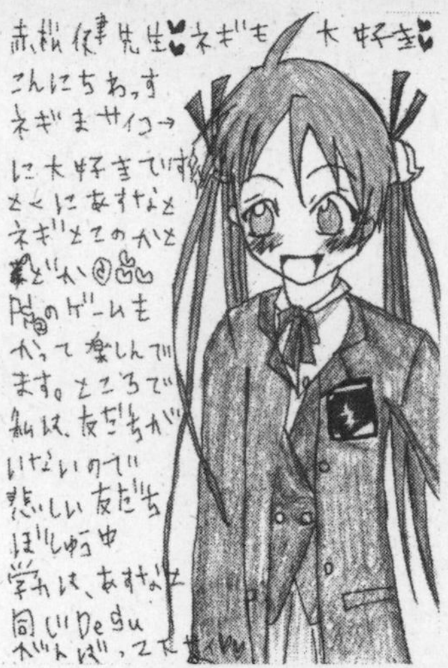
こんにちわっす

▲ IF YOU CAN DRAW ASUNA AS CUTE AS THIS, YOU'RE SURE TO FIND MANY FRIENDS.

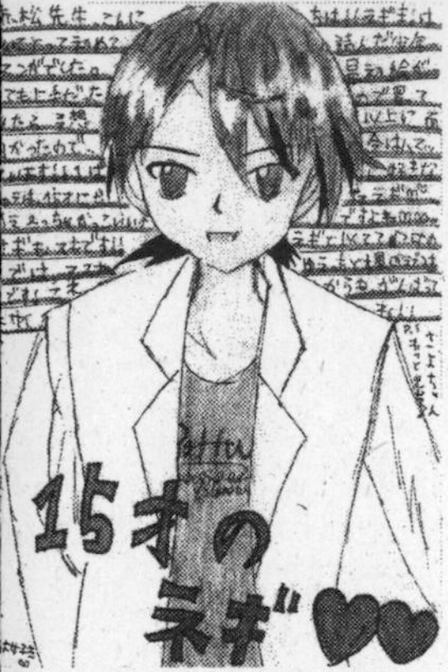
15才の
ネギ♥♥

◀ A VERY DASHING-LOOKING NEGI. MOST AWESOME!

▼ AKIRA PICTURES ARE PRETTY RARE. KEEP SENDING 'EM IN, PLEASE!

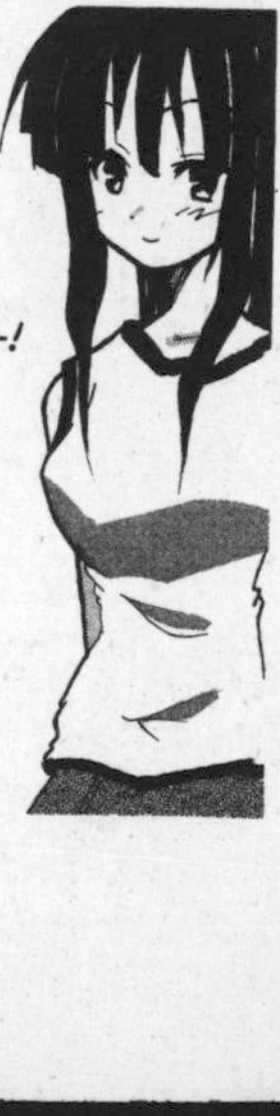

◀ ARIGATŌ—!

SEEMS YOU'VE BECOME QUITE TAKEN BY EVA, HAVEN'T YOU. (HEH.) ▼

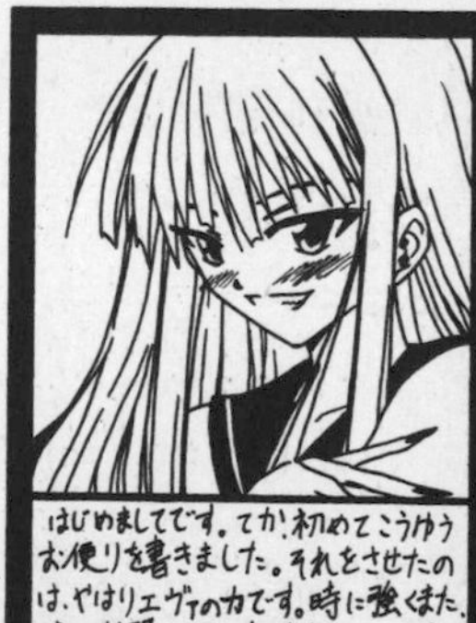
はじめましてです。てか、初めてこうゆうお便りを書きました。それをさせたのは、やはりエヴァの力です。時に強くまた、時にか弱く、そんな所がいいです。
・これからもおうえんするので
ガンバってください。

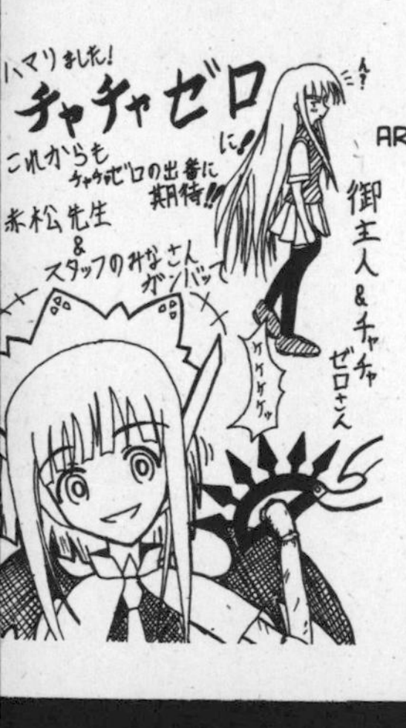
ハマりました!
チャチャゼロ
に!
これからも
チャチャゼロの出番に
期待!!
赤松先生
&
スタッフのみなさん
ガンバッて
御主人
&
チャチャゼロさん
ケケケケッ

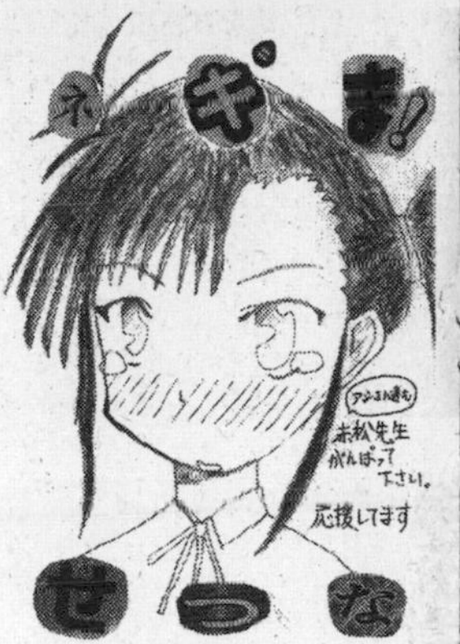
ネギま!
アジさん頑張ろ
赤松先生
がんばって
下さい。
応援してます
せつな

THIS ▶ TEARY-EYED SETSUNA IS SO CUTE.

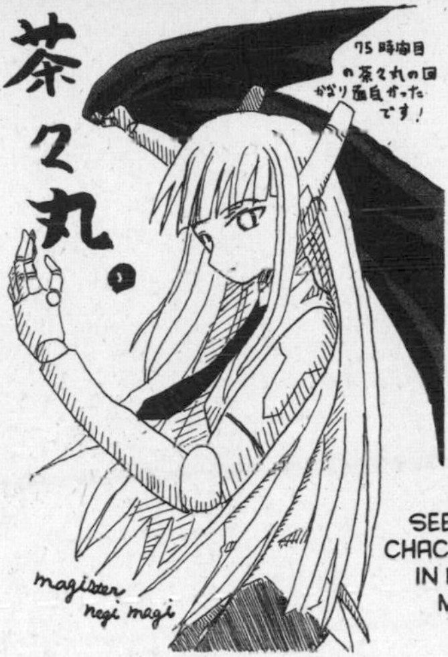
茶々丸
75時間目の茶々丸の回かなり面白かったです!
magister negi magi

◀ SEEMS LIKE CHACHAMARU'S IN BATTLE-MODE!

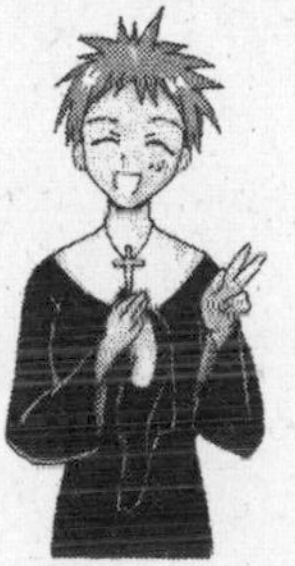

◀ KASUGA LOOKS QUITE HOLY, HERE. (HEH.)

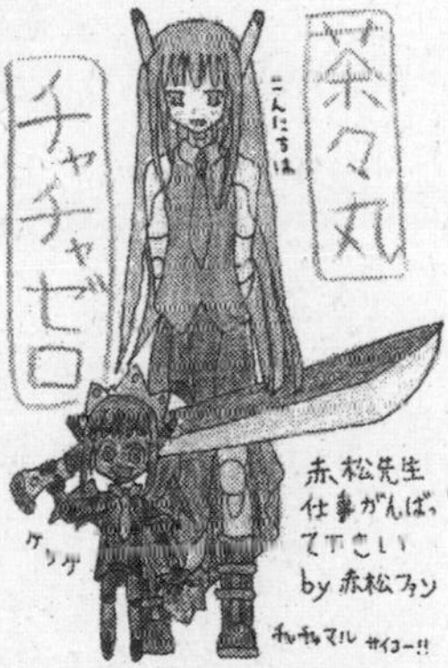
茶々丸
チャチャゼロ
こんにちは
赤松先生
仕事がんばってください
by 赤松ファン
ケケケ
チャチャマル サイコー!!

▶ CHACHAMARU'S A GOOD THING!

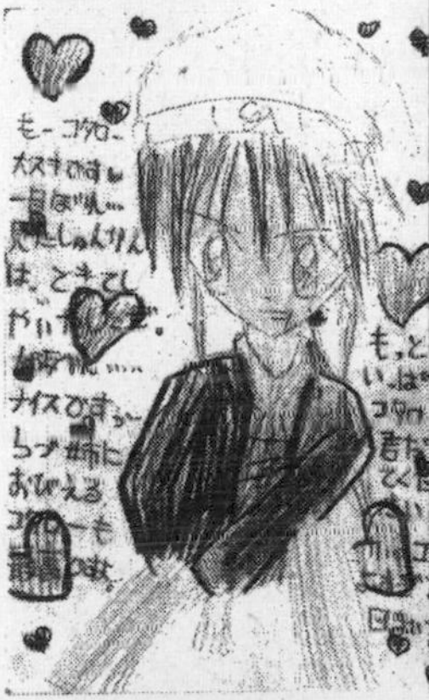

TALK ▶ ABOUT YOUR "KOTARŌ-LOVE"...!

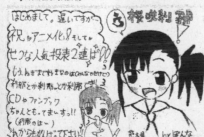

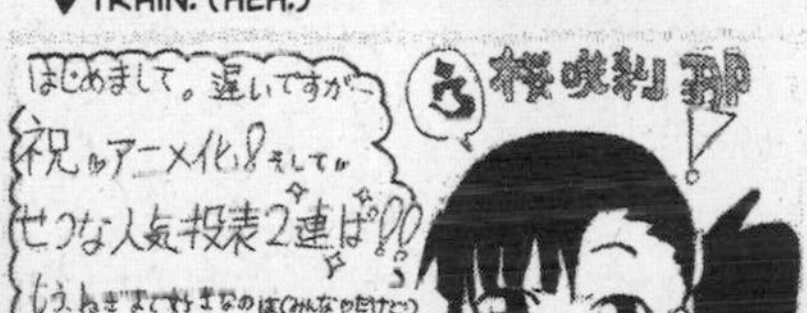
桜咲刹那
はじめまして。遅いですが～
祝♡アニメ化!! そして♡
せつな人気投票2連ぱ!!
CDやファンブック
ちゃんともってまいす。!!
これからもがんばって下さい!!
by ぽんな

THERE'S NO STOPPING THE SETSUNA LOVE-▼TRAIN. (HEH.)

MAHORA ACADEMY

EARLY CONCEPT SKETCHES

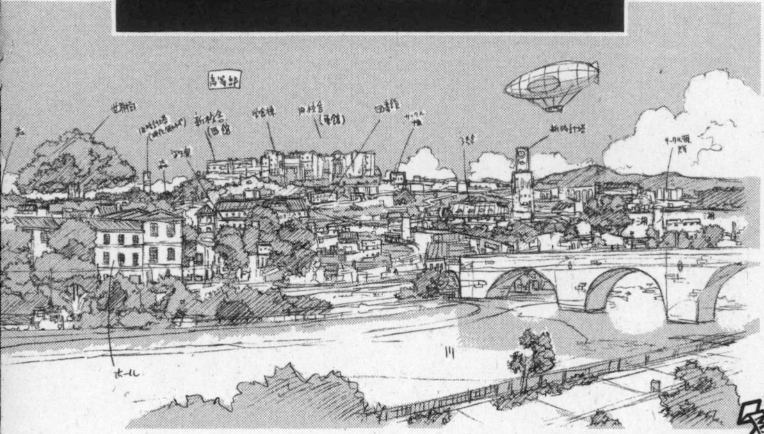

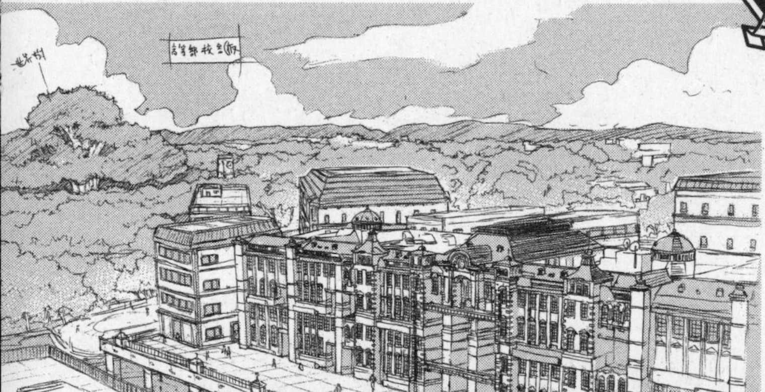

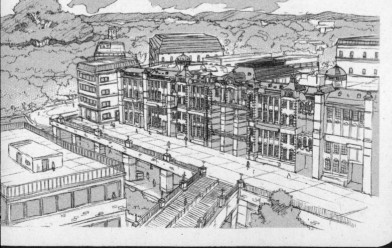

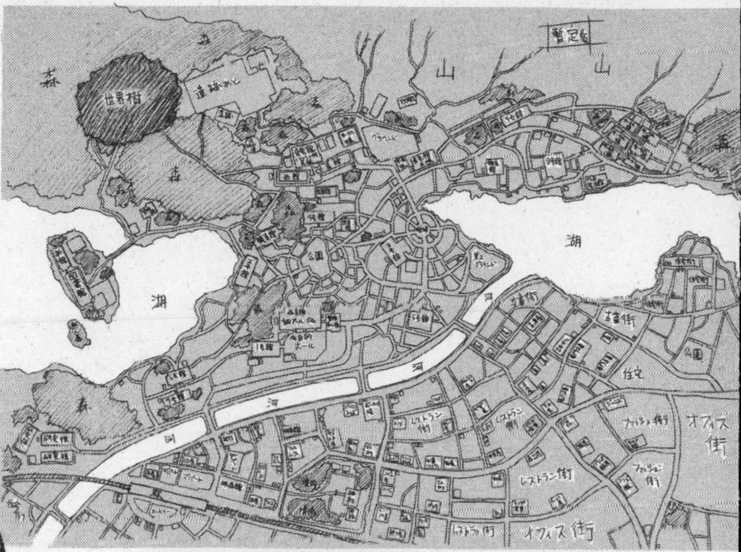
世界樹
森
山
湖
河
オフィス街
レストラン街

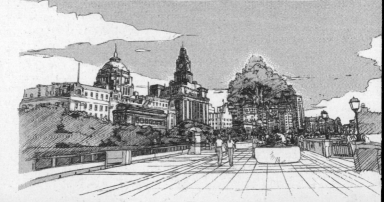

IN THIS VOLUME, WE PRESENT TO YOU THE "IMAGE ILLUSTRATIONS" DRAWN UP BY THE STAFF AND MYSELF DURING A FREE-FOR-ALL, PARTY-TYPE GET TOGETHER HELD BEFORE THE ACTUAL START OF THE SERIES. THIS KIND OF THING'S OFTEN DONE WITH ANIME SERIES, BUT, TAKE IT FROM ME, IT'S PRETTY RARE FOR MANGA.

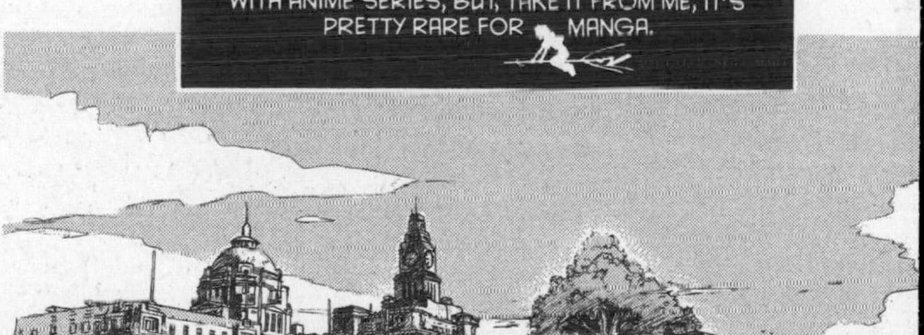

学園中央部 ラフ案

(山)
空中公園
大講堂
アラカシ
テニスコート
野球場
学
世界樹
郵便局
学園中央駅
ゴミ処理場
研究所モノレール
セントラル
校舎?
校舎?
学食食堂工?

上の島は何でもいいです
これは トンガ島とかいうのそのまま

夏場のビーチ
ビーチ
本島
空港島

橋々には
ホテルがたくさんある
中央部は ジャングルあり.

ビーチ
本町
港
ヨットハーバー
ディズニーランド
新都心
しゃー島

学生街
聖蹟を持つ()

公園?
学園都市
学園東寺?
山
海浜公園
学園港
研究部
学園島
霊墓跡

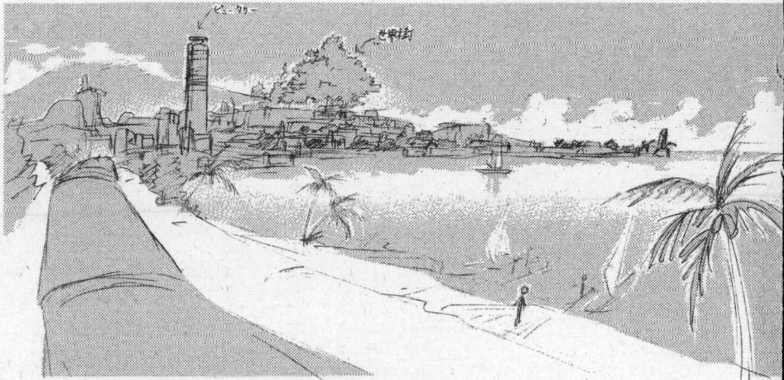

WE'D ALL IMAGINED AN "ISLAND"-TYPE THEME IN THE EARLY STAGES, BUT, BY THE TIME PUBLICATION WAS NEAR, OUR "LAY OF THE LAND" HAD MORPHED INTO A CAMPUS CITY. YOU'LL NOTICE THE WORLD TREE'S PRESENT EVEN NOW; WOULDN'T IT HAVE BEEN FUN TO HAVE HAD A MONORAIL, TOO...? FOR THE SCHOOL COMMUTE, I MEAN.

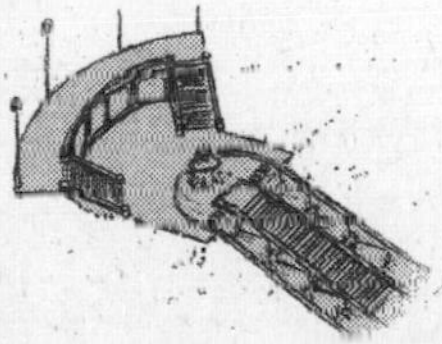

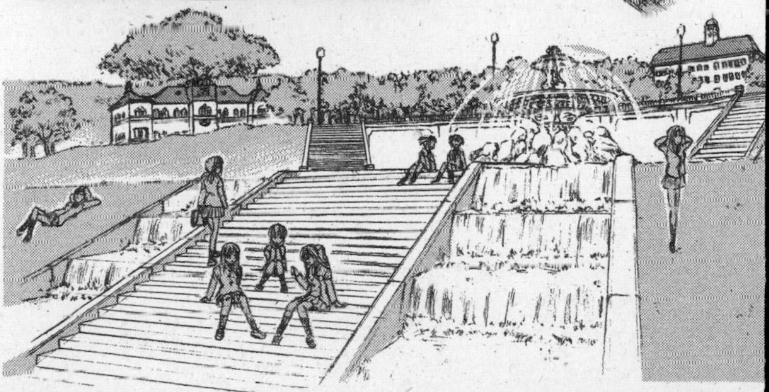

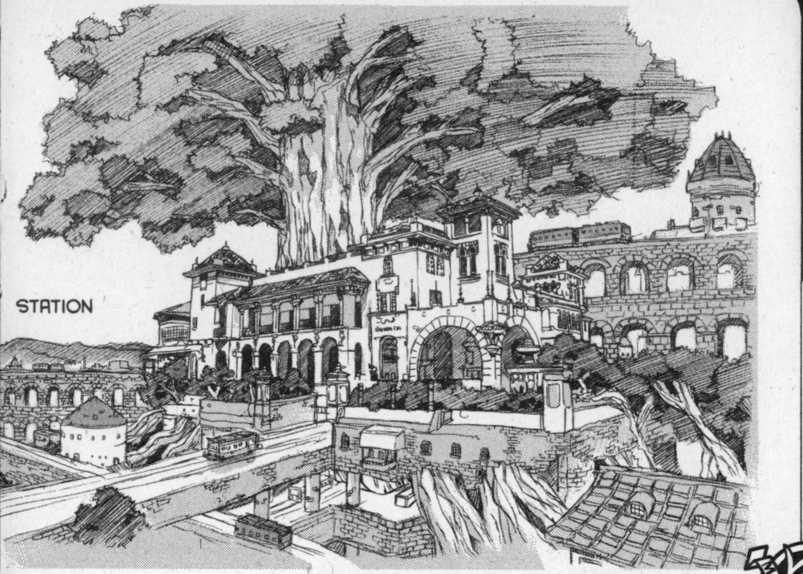
STATION

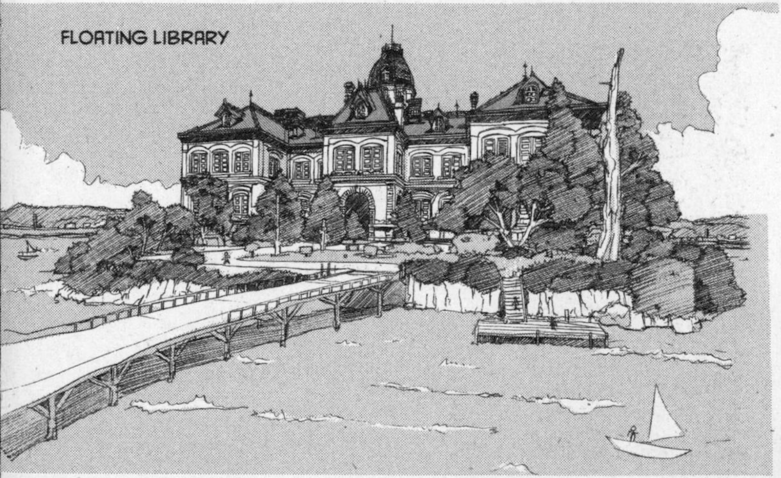
FLOATING LIBRARY

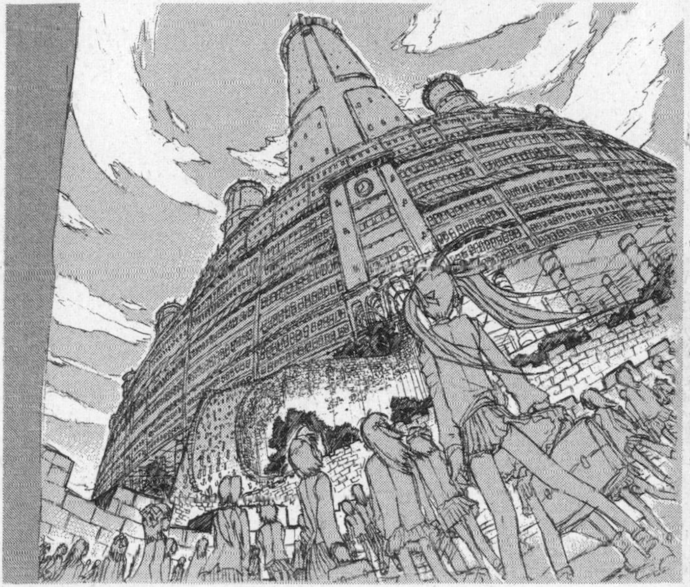

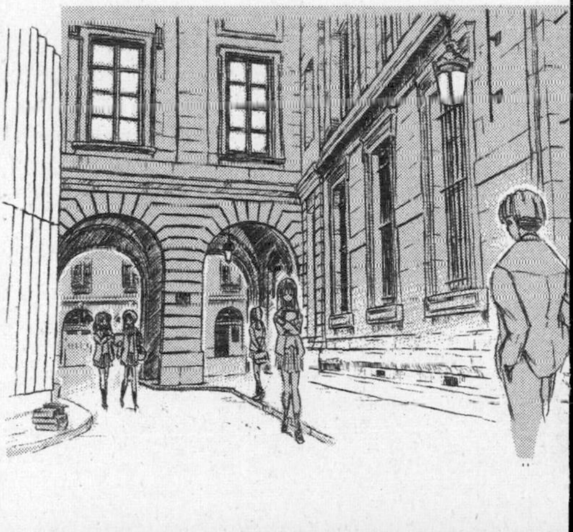

↑

Y-YE GODS, BUT WHAT A HU-U-UGE SCHOOL BUILDING...! (HEH.) CONCEPT DRAWINGS LIKE THESE ARE FUN TO COME UP WITH BUT, ONCE YOU GET DOWN TO THE NITTY-GRITTY OF THE ACTUAL WORK, THEY'RE IMPRACTICAL AND HARD TO KEEP UP. (^^;)

RIGHT, THEN! SEE YOU IN VOLUME 11, OKAY?

赤松

VIII BELLATRIX SAUCIATA

(THE WOUNDED GIRL-WARRIOR)

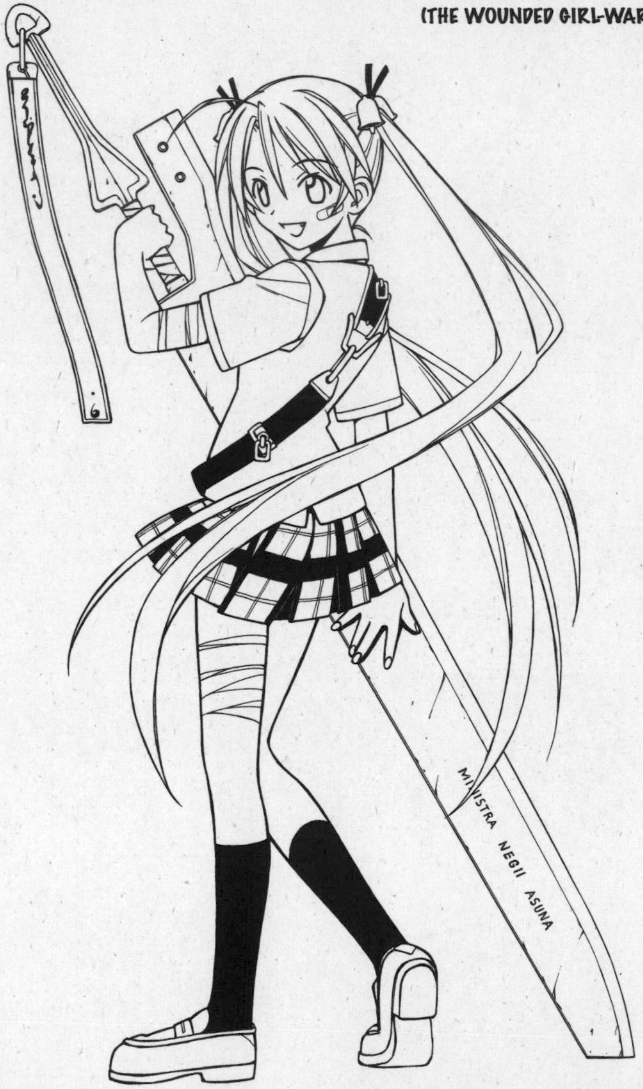
MINISTRA NEGII ASUNA

SOURCE: PACTIO CARD LINE-ART COLLECTION

XIII REGINA MEDICANS

(THE HEALER-PRINCESS)

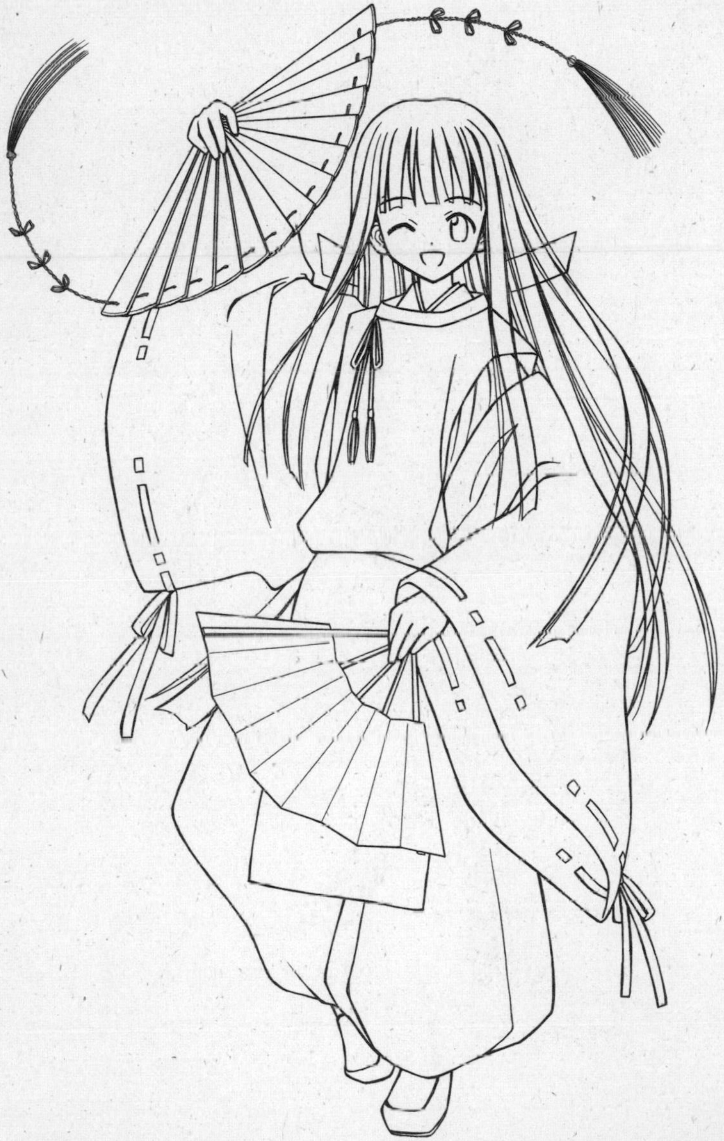

SOURCE: PACTIO CARD LINE-ART COLLECTION

XV GLADIARIA ALATA

(THE WINGED-SWORDSMAN)

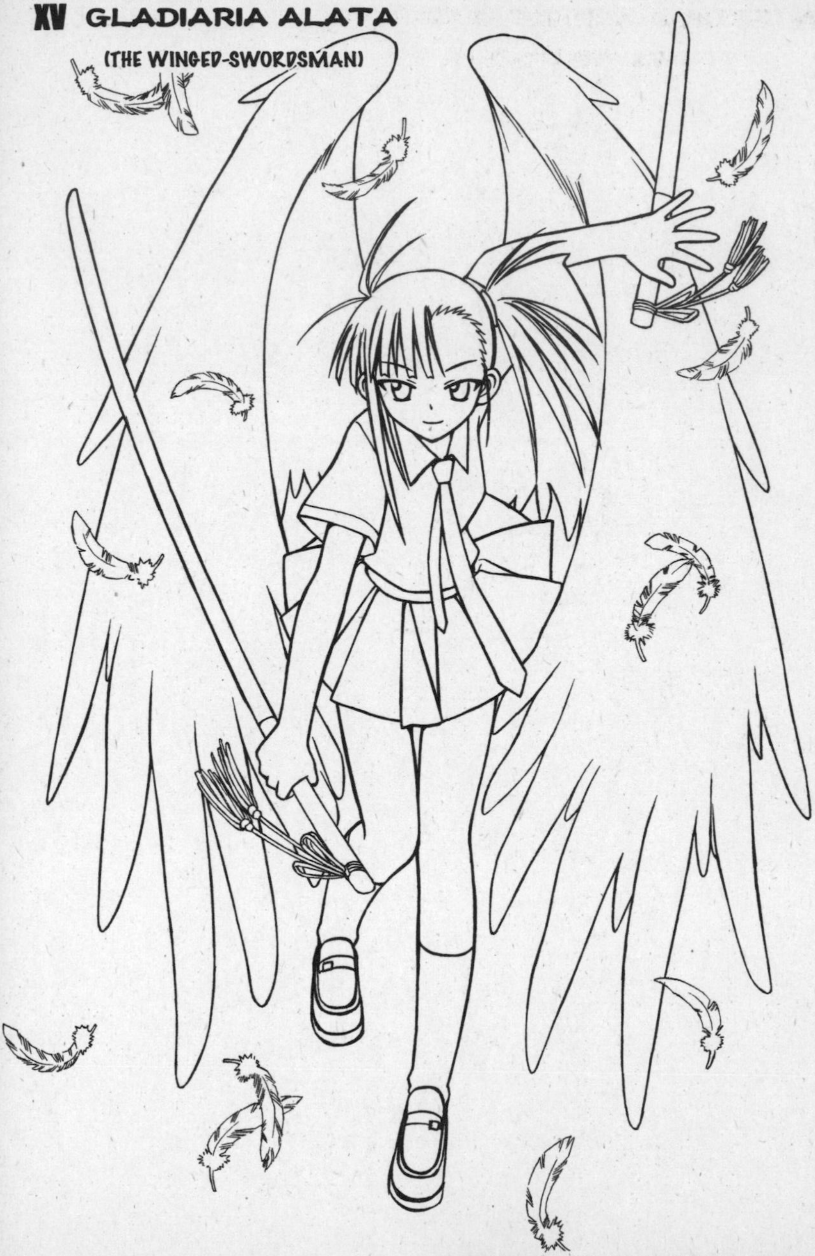

SOURCE: PACTIO CARD LINE-ART COLLECTION

XXVII PUDICA BIBLIOTHECARIA

(THE MODEST LIBRARIAN)

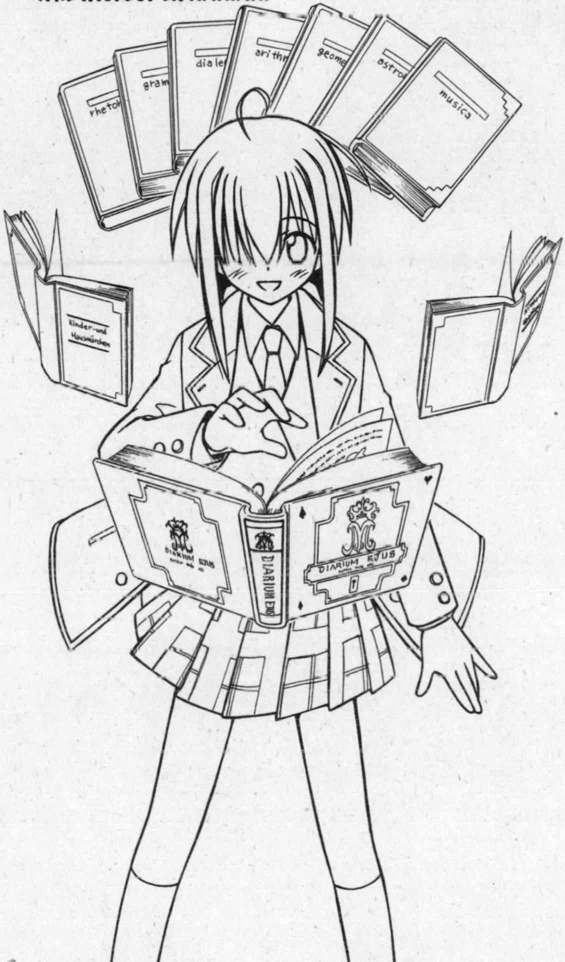
rhetor
gram
diale
arithm
geome
astro
musica
Kinder-und Hausmärchen
DIARIUM EJUS
DIARIUM EJUS
DIARIUM EJUS

SOURCE: PACTIO CARD LINE ART OOLLEOTION

3-D BACKGROUNDS EXPLANATION CORNER

• CAFÉ TERRACE
SCENE NAME: CAFÉ TERRACE   POLYGON COUNT: 367,554

TOP-FLOOR TERRACE USED WHEN NEGI BECAME THE "KISS TERMINATOR," BASED ON THE PIAZZA DELLA SIGNORIA IN FLORENCE.

↓ EXPECT TO SEE THIS TABLE SET USED OVER AND OVER AGAIN FROM THIS POINT FORWARD (HEH).

• WATER PARK
SCENE NAME: WATER PARK   POLYGON COUNT: 556,957

THE FRONT OF THIS STRUCTURE'S BASED ON THE GARDENS OF VILLA GARZONI, IN ITALY. WE ACTUALLY CREATED A REAR VIEW FOR IT, AS WELL, BUT IT SOMEHOW FAILS TO SHOW UP IN THE STORY. (^^;)

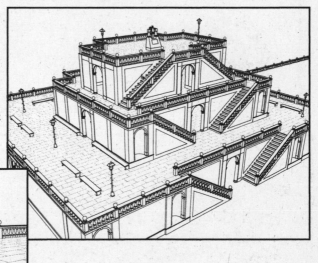

• GATE AT TATSUMIYA SHRINE

SCENE NAME: SHRINE GATE   POLYGON COUNT: 830,952

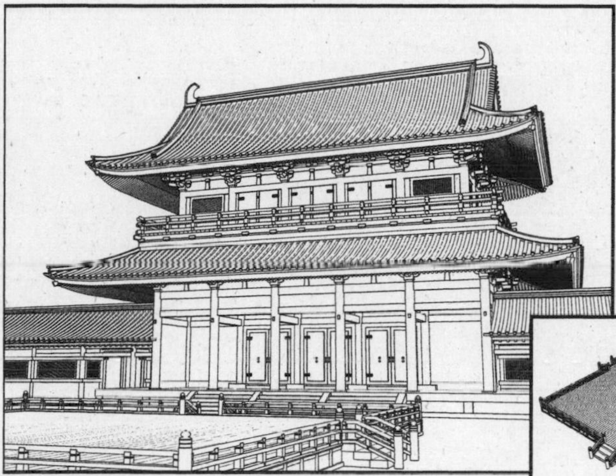

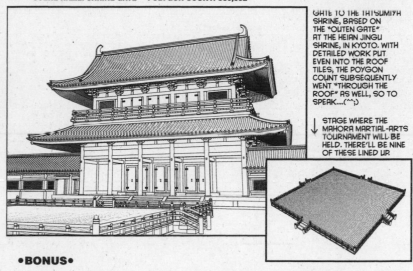

GATE TO THE TATSUMIYA SHRINE, BASED ON THE "OUTEN GATE" AT THE HEIAN JINGU SHRINE, IN KYOTO. WITH DETAILED WORK PUT EVEN INTO THE ROOF TILES, THE POYGON COUNT SUBSEQUENTLY WENT "THROUGH THE ROOF" AS WELL, SO TO SPEAK....(^^;)

↓ STAGE WHERE THE MAHORA MARTIAL-ARTS TOURNAMENT WILL BE HELD. THERE'LL BE NINE OF THESE LINED UP.

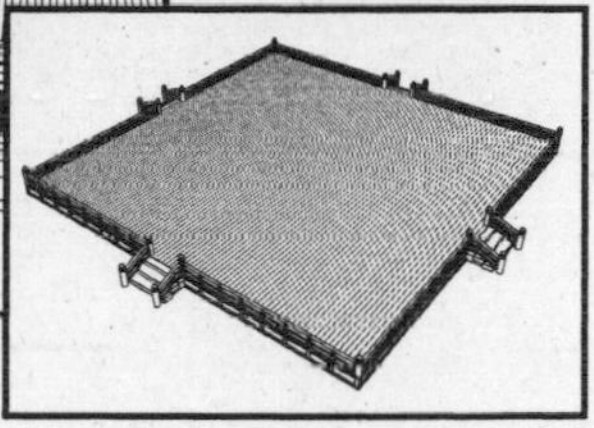

•BONUS•

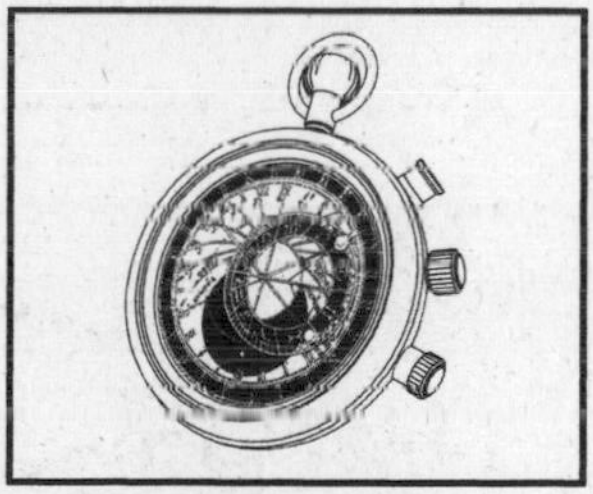

POCKET WATCH-SHAPED TIME MACHINE, "CASSIOPEIA"

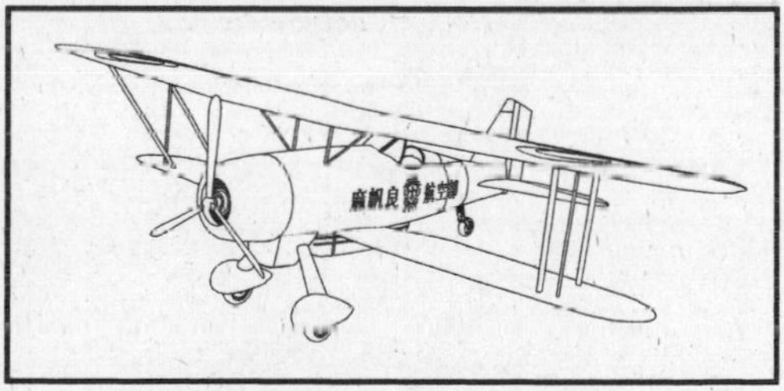

MAHORA AVIATION CLUB ACROBATIC PLANE

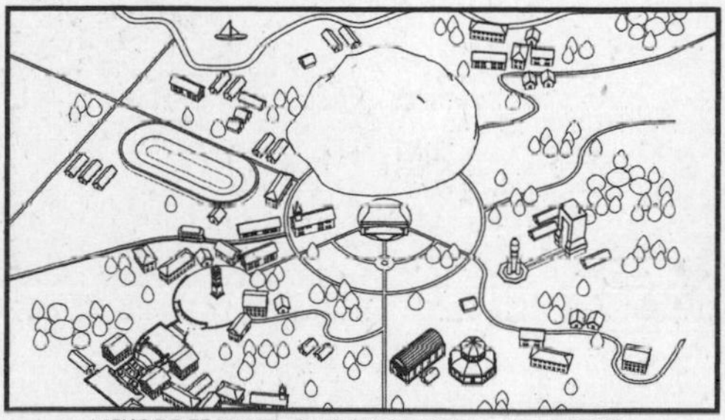

MAHORA FESTIVAL GUIDE MAP, WORLD-TREE AREA

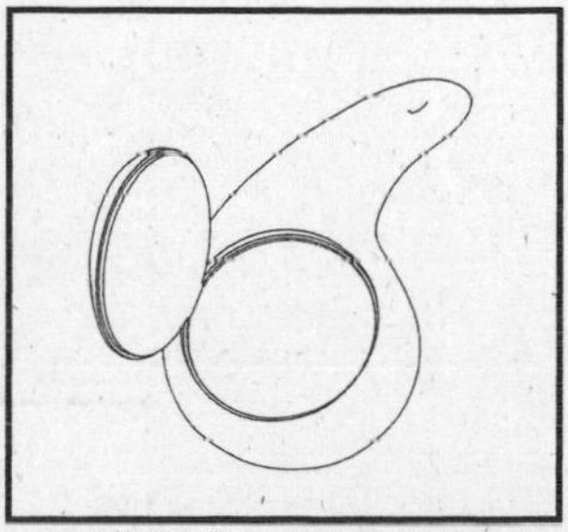

TATSUMIYA JEWEL-SHAPED PENDENT

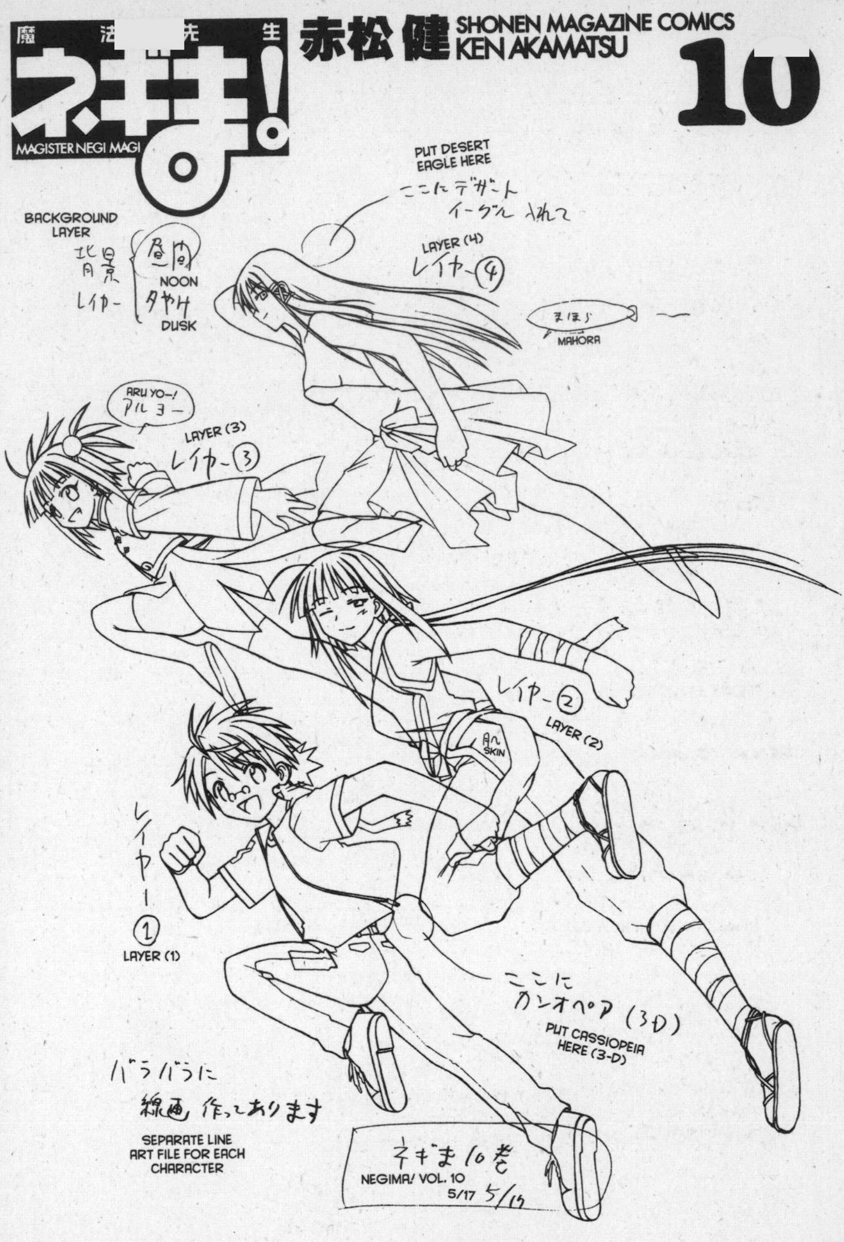
魔法先生
ネギま!
MAGISTER NEGI MAGI
赤松健
SHONEN MAGAZINE COMICS
KEN AKAMATSU
10
PUT DESERT EAGLE HERE
ここにデザートイーグル入れて
BACKGROUND LAYER
背景レイヤー
昼間
NOON
夕やけ
DUSK
LAYER (4)
レイヤー④
まほら
MAHORA
ARU YO—!
アルヨー
LAYER (3)
レイヤー③
レイヤー②
LAYER (2)
肌
SKIN
レイヤー①
LAYER (1)
ここにカシオペア (3D)
PUT CASSIOPEIA HERE (3-D)
バラバラに線画作ってあります
SEPARATE LINE ART FILE FOR EACH CHARACTER
ネギま10巻
NEGIMA! VOL. 10
5/17 5/17

キャラ解説

CHARACTER
PROFILE

④ 綾瀬夕映

④ YUE AYASE

最近 かな〜り人気の ゆえです。

THIS IS YUE, WHO'S RECENTLY CLIMBED THE RANKS IN POPULARITY.

成績は悪いんですけど バカじゃ

ALTHOUGH HER GRADES AREN'T GOOD, SHE'S

ないです。 っていうか 頭いいです。

NO DUMMY. (...SHE IS SMART, YOU KNOW.

〜同感〜！

AWW YEAH〜!

ニーやー一人っているよね〜

お〜 THERE'S LOTS OF PEOPLE LIKE HER, ACTUALLY〜

（うん うん

THERE ARE, THERE ARE!）

声優は 桑谷夏子サンで。 これが

HER VOICE-ACTOR'S NATSUKO KUWATANI, AND THAT

も〜 超ピッタリ！ 本人もそう

IS EVEN GREATER THAN GREAT! IT SHOULD BE—

言ってくれてますし。（笑） 似てるって

THE VOICE-ACTOR HERSELF SAYS SO. (HEH.)

THEY'RE SO ALIKE, THOSE TWO.

アニメの オープニングテーマ

THERE'S THIS BIT IN THE OPENING THEME TO THE TV ANIME

「ハッピー☆マテリアル」で 夕映が

("HAPPY ★ MATERIAL") WHERE YUE SINGS,

ハッピーマテリアル GO！ ゴー とか。

"HAPPI'I MATERIARU GO—!"

（I CAN'T EVEN TELL YOU HOW MUCH

これが

良くて良くて …♥

I LOVE THAT PART: "GO—!" ♥）

今後も マンガ版 アニメ版の

I DO THINK WE CAN COUNT ON YUE TO HOLD UP HER END

両方で 活躍が 期待されますね。

IN BOTH THE MANGA AND ANIME VERSIONS FROM HERE ON IN.

いや〜 良いキャラになった！

...MAN! HAS SHE TURNED OUT TO BE A GREAT CHARACTER, OR WHAT?!

赤松

(AKAMATSU)

About the Creator

Negima! is only Ken Akamatsu's third manga, although he started working in the field in 1994 with *AI Ga Tomaranai* (released in the United States with the title *A.I. Love You*). Like all of Akamatsu's work to date, it was published in Kodansha's *Shonen Magazine*. *AI Ga Tomaranai* ran for five years before concluding in 1999. In 1998, however, Akamatsu began the work that would make him one of the most popular manga artists in Japan: *Love Hina*. *Love Hina* ran for four years, and before its conclusion in 2002, it would cause Akamatsu to be granted the prestigious Manga of the Year award from Kodansha, as well as going on to become one of the best-selling manga in the United States.

Translation Notes

Japanese is a tricky language for most westerners, and translation is often more art than science. For your edification and reading pleasure, here are notes on some of the places where we could have gone in a different direction in our translation of the work, or where a Japanese cultural reference is used.

"*O-Sawari Pub*," page 10

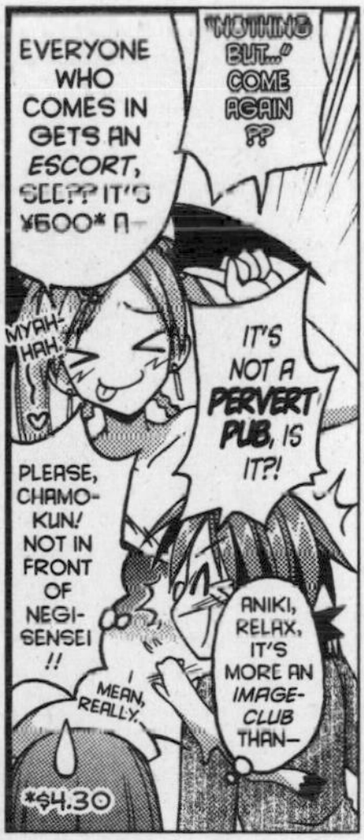
"NOTHING BUT..." COME AGAIN ??
EVERYONE WHO COMES IN GETS AN *ESCORT*, SEE?? IT'S ¥600* A–
MYAH-HAH.
IT'S NOT A **PERVERT PUB**, IS IT?!
PLEASE, CHAMO-KUN! NOT IN FRONT OF NEGI-SENSEI !!
ANIKI, RELAX, IT'S MORE AN *IMAGE-CLUB* THAN–
I MEAN, REALLY.
*$4.30

Similar to the "No-Panty Café" from a previous volume, here's another bit of "colorful" Japanese culture. Sometimes referred to as a "Sexy Pub," the *O-Sawari* or "Feel-Up" Pub operates on the same basic rules of the typical Japanese "cabaret" or upscale bar, where pretty "hostesses" sit and either provide pleasant conversation or a sympathetic ear while pouring drinks for a set fee. But here's where the *O-Sawari* Pub is different: Upon the lowering of the lights and the entering of what some establishments call "downtime," normally "hands-off" hostesses allow patrons a certain amount of kissing and touching. Although the signs in *O-Sawari* Pubs clearly state what a patron may or may not do, it's said that the hostesses ultimately decide what is and isn't allowed...after also taking into account the size of the patron's wallet, of course.

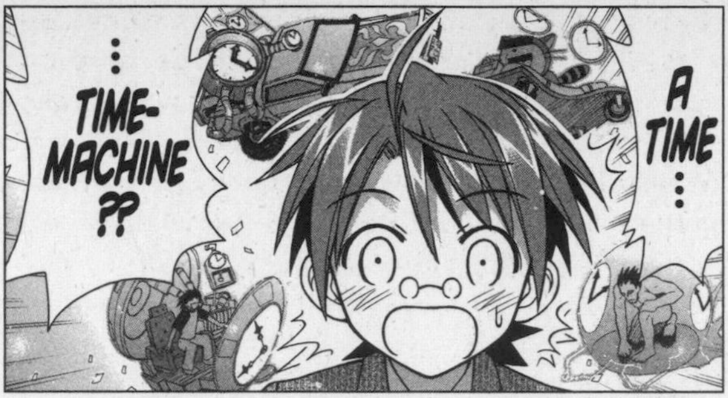
A TIME …
… TIME-MACHINE ??

"*Dwah?* TIME MACHINE?!," page 29

Obvious, perhaps, but for the record (clockwise, left to right): the re-imagined, updated version of the H.G. Wells classic; the converted, stainless-steel car from a certain, mega-blockbuster '80s movie trilogy; a face-obscured "robot cat from the future"; a naked android, making a big impact.

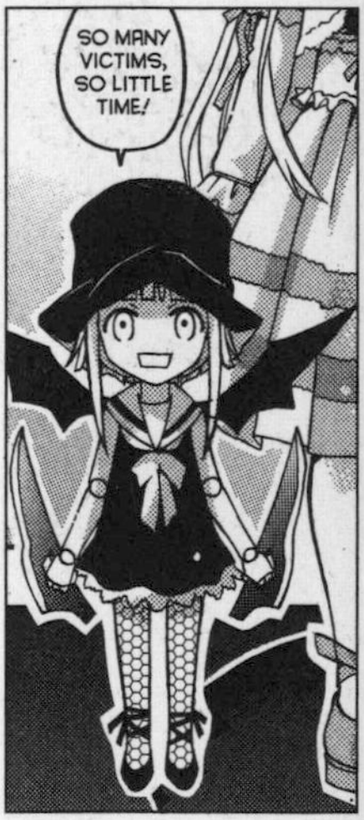
SO MANY VICTIMS, SO LITTLE TIME!

Chachazero, page 31

The reason the normally immobile Chachazero (who is, let's not forget, a puppet) can move on her own power in this segment is only because of the extreme amount of overflow magic in the air during MahoraFest.

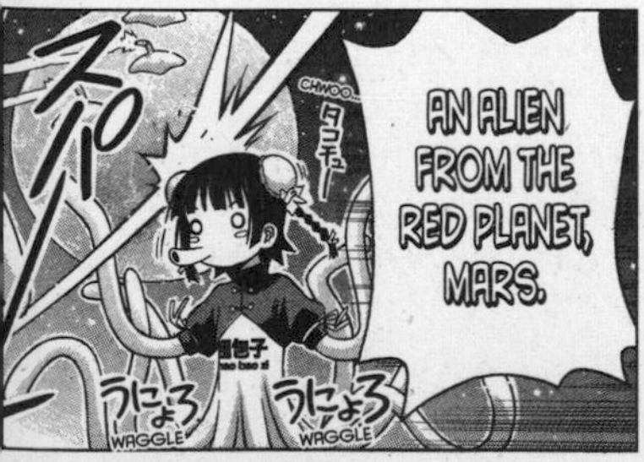
AN ALIEN FROM THE RED PLANET, MARS.
CHWOO...
うにょろ
WAGGLE
うにょろ
WAGGLE

Martians, page 40

Traditionally, Japanese think of Martians as looking like octopi, and here's why. In 1895, astronomer Percival Lowell—one of the best-known Mars observers of the time—speculated that lines visible on the planet's surface must be canals built by intelligent beings. Because of their vast intelligence, their heads would be large, he reasoned, further speculating that the lower gravity of Mars would cause their limbs to be very thin. This thinking is said to have influenced British writer H.G. Wells when he wrote *War of the Worlds* in 1898...and, once *War of the Worlds* was translated into Japanese, it seems that went on to influence generations of Japanese.

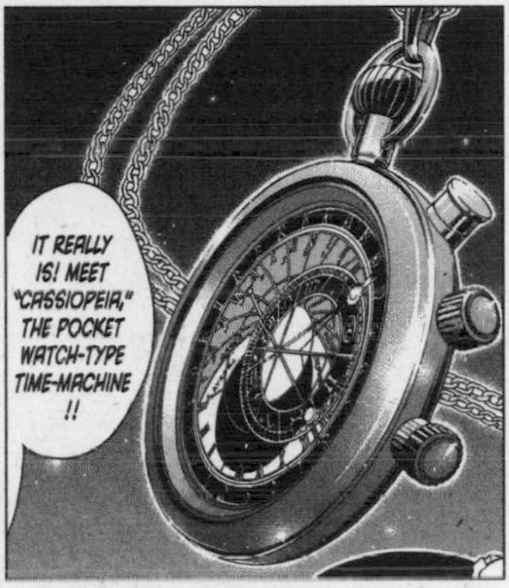
IT REALLY IS! MEET "CASSIOPEIA," THE POCKET WATCH-TYPE TIME-MACHINE !!

Cassiopeia, page 43

The namesake for this pocket watch–shaped time machine is from the novel *Momo* by Michael Ende of *Neverending Story* fame, in which a young orphan girl named Momo has an adventure which spans across time, helped by another mysterious time-traveler with a pet turtle named "Cassiopeia."

Instruction Manual, page 44

Stunningly similar to the manual given to Amuro Rey in the giant-robot *Gundam* saga....

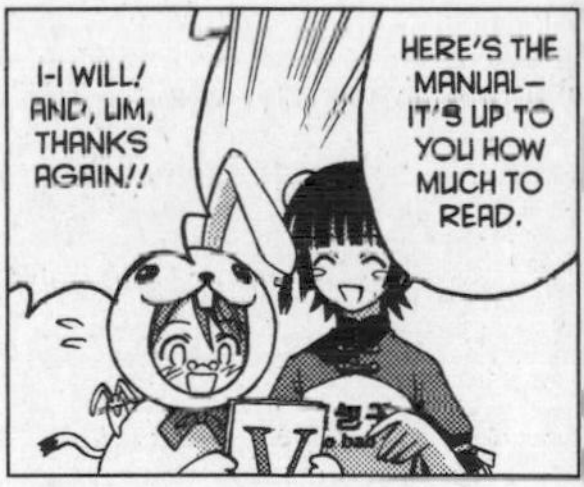
HERE'S THE MANUAL— IT'S UP TO YOU HOW MUCH TO READ.
I-I WILL! AND, UM, THANKS AGAIN!!

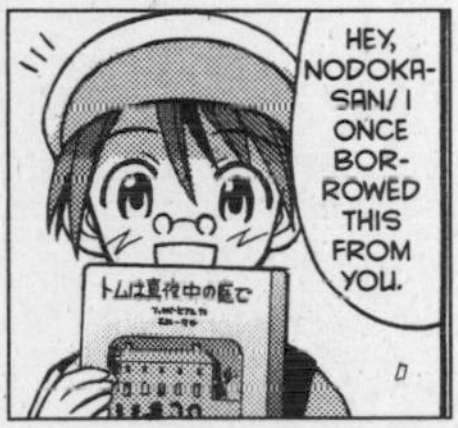
HEY, NODOKA-SAN! I ONCE BOR-ROWED THIS FROM YOU.
トムは真夜中の庭で

Tom's Midnight Garden, page 53

Book borrowed by Negi from Nodoka, in which a magical grandfather clock reveals a secret to ten-year-old Tom and a girl named Hatty almost too amazing to be true.

A Wizard of Earthsea, page 53

THIS ONE'S GOT A MAGE-HERO, TOO...
YEAH, THAT'S A GOOD ONE, TOO...

The volume picked up by Negi in the used-book tent is a Japanese translation of the first book in the "Earthsea" cycle by Ursula K. Le Guin, about the journeys of a young wizard named "Ged." From what we can see in the panel, a literal translation would be "The Battle Against the Shadow," while the name of the series would be "Chronicles of Ged."

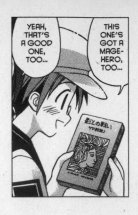

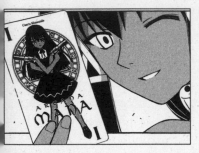

Mana's Pactio Card, page 115

Revealed in this chapter! Because her Magister is unfortunately deceased, Mana is no longer provided with magical support and can no longer call forth her artifact. Because the format of each card differs according to the person invoking the Pactio, the appearance of Mana's card is necessarily different from that, for example, of Asuna's. (Had Chamo invoked the Pactio, Mana's card would have looked like the rest.)

Tournament Schedule, page 174

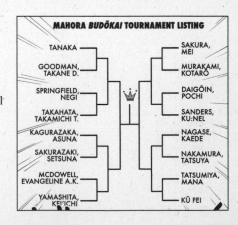

MAHORA BUDŌKAI TOURNAMENT LISTING
TANAKA
GOODMAN, TAKANE D.
SPRINGFIELD, NEGI
TAKAHATA, TAKAMICHI T.
KAGURAZAKA, ASUNA
SAKURAZAKI, SETSUNA
MCDOWELL, EVANGELINE A.K.
YAMASHITA, KEI'ICHI
SAKURA, MEI
MURAKAMI, KOTARŌ
DAIGŌIN, POCHI
SANDERS, KU:NEL
NAGASE, KAEDE
NAKAMURA, TATSUYA
TATSUMIYA, MANA
KŪ FEI

According to Akamatsu's support staff, tournament matches were decided by the roll of a die by Akamatsu himself. The only time he was said to re-roll was when two minor characters ended up in a match together. The staff, it is said, watched these proceedings in utter amazement.

Preview of Volume Eleven

This next volume is available in English now.

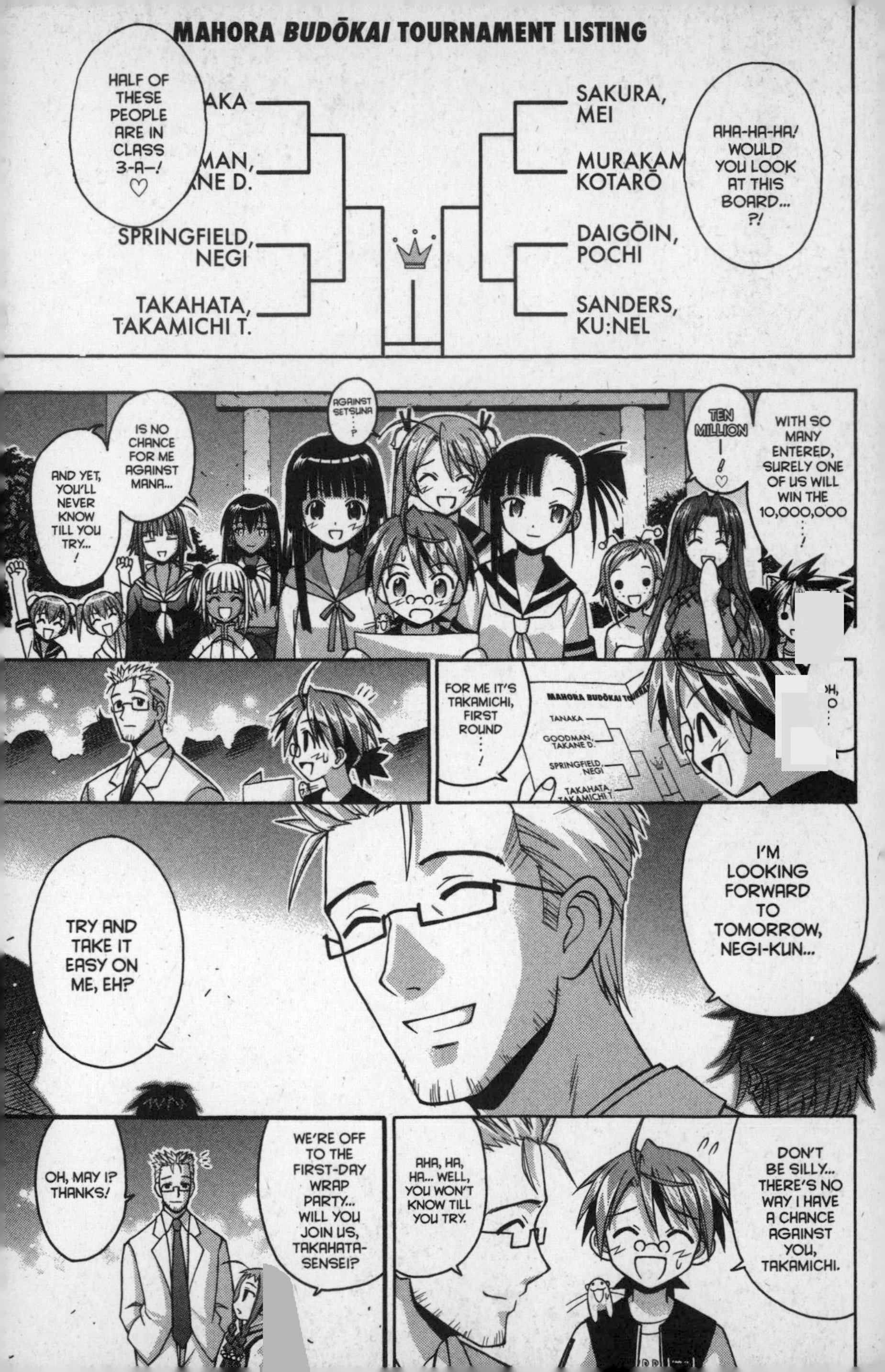
MAHORA BUDŌKAI TOURNAMENT LISTING
AHA-HA-HA! WOULD YOU LOOK AT THIS BOARD...?!
HALF OF THESE PEOPLE ARE IN CLASS 3-A—! ♡
SAKURA, MEI
MURAKAM KOTARŌ
DAIGŌIN, POCHI
SANDERS, KU:NEL
AKA
MAN, NE D.
SPRINGFIELD, NEGI
TAKAHATA, TAKAMICHI T.
WITH SO MANY ENTERED, SURELY ONE OF US WILL WIN THE 10,000,000...!
TEN MILLION—! ♡
AGAINST SETSUNA...?
IS NO CHANCE FOR ME AGAINST MANA...
AND YET, YOU'LL NEVER KNOW TILL YOU TRY...!
MAHORA BUDŌKAI TOURNA
TANAKA
GOODMAN, TAKANE D.
SPRINGFIELD, NEGI
TAKAHATA, TAKAMICHI T.
FOR ME IT'S TAKAMICHI, FIRST ROUND...!
I'M LOOKING FORWARD TO TOMORROW, NEGI-KUN...
TRY AND TAKE IT EASY ON ME, EH?
DON'T BE SILLY... THERE'S NO WAY I HAVE A CHANCE AGAINST YOU, TAKAMICHI.
AHA, HA, HA... WELL, YOU WON'T KNOW TILL YOU TRY.
WE'RE OFF TO THE FIRST-DAY WRAP PARTY... WILL YOU JOIN US, TAKAHATA-SENSEI?
OH, MAY I? THANKS!

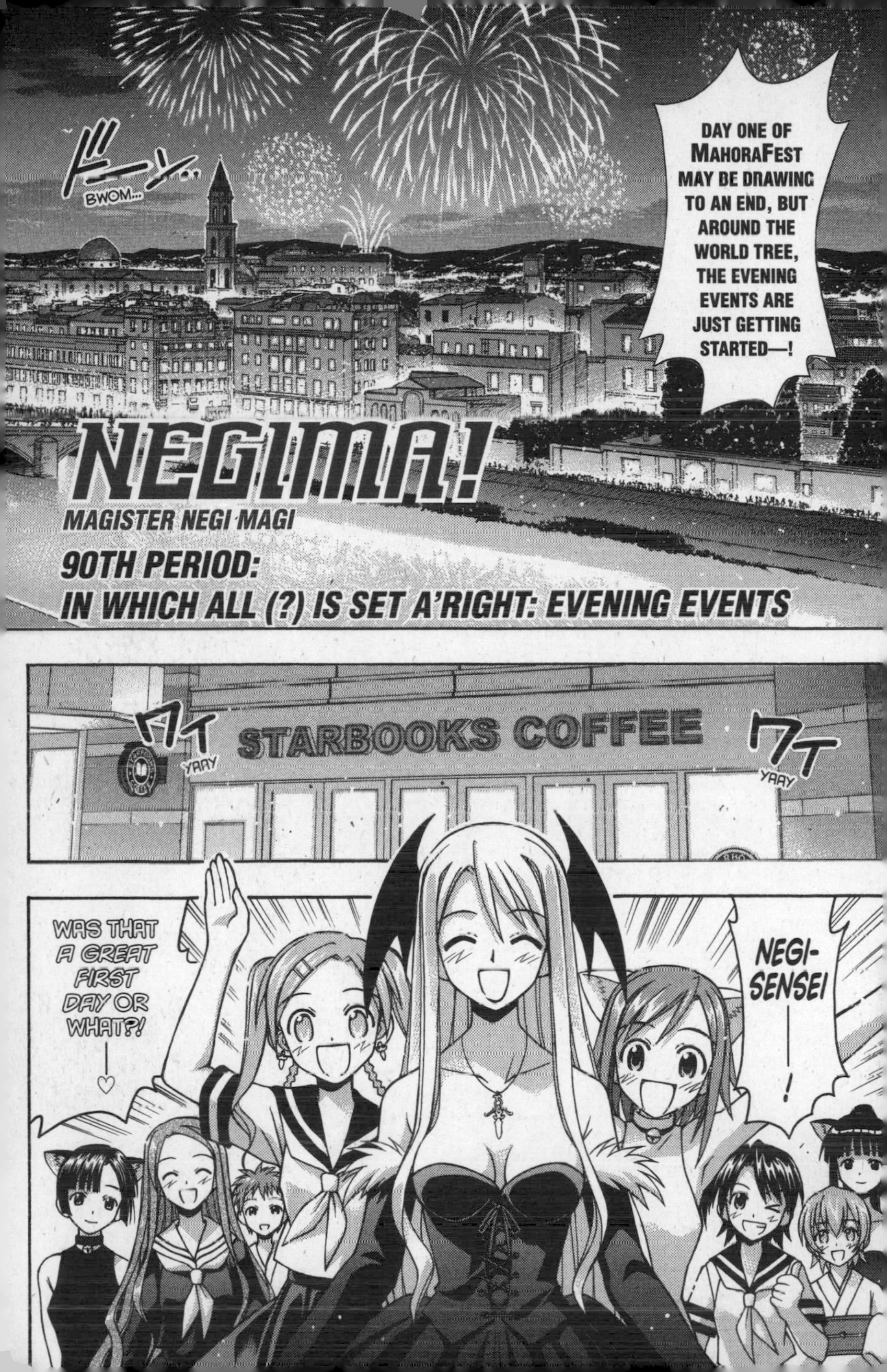
DAY ONE OF MAHORAFEST MAY BE DRAWING TO AN END, BUT AROUND THE WORLD TREE, THE EVENING EVENTS ARE JUST GETTING STARTED—!
BWOM...
NEGIMA!
MAGISTER NEGI MAGI
90TH PERIOD:
IN WHICH ALL (?) IS SET A'RIGHT: EVENING EVENTS
YAAY
STARBOOKS COFFEE
YAAY
NEGI-SENSEI!
WAS THAT A GREAT FIRST DAY OR WHAT?! ♡

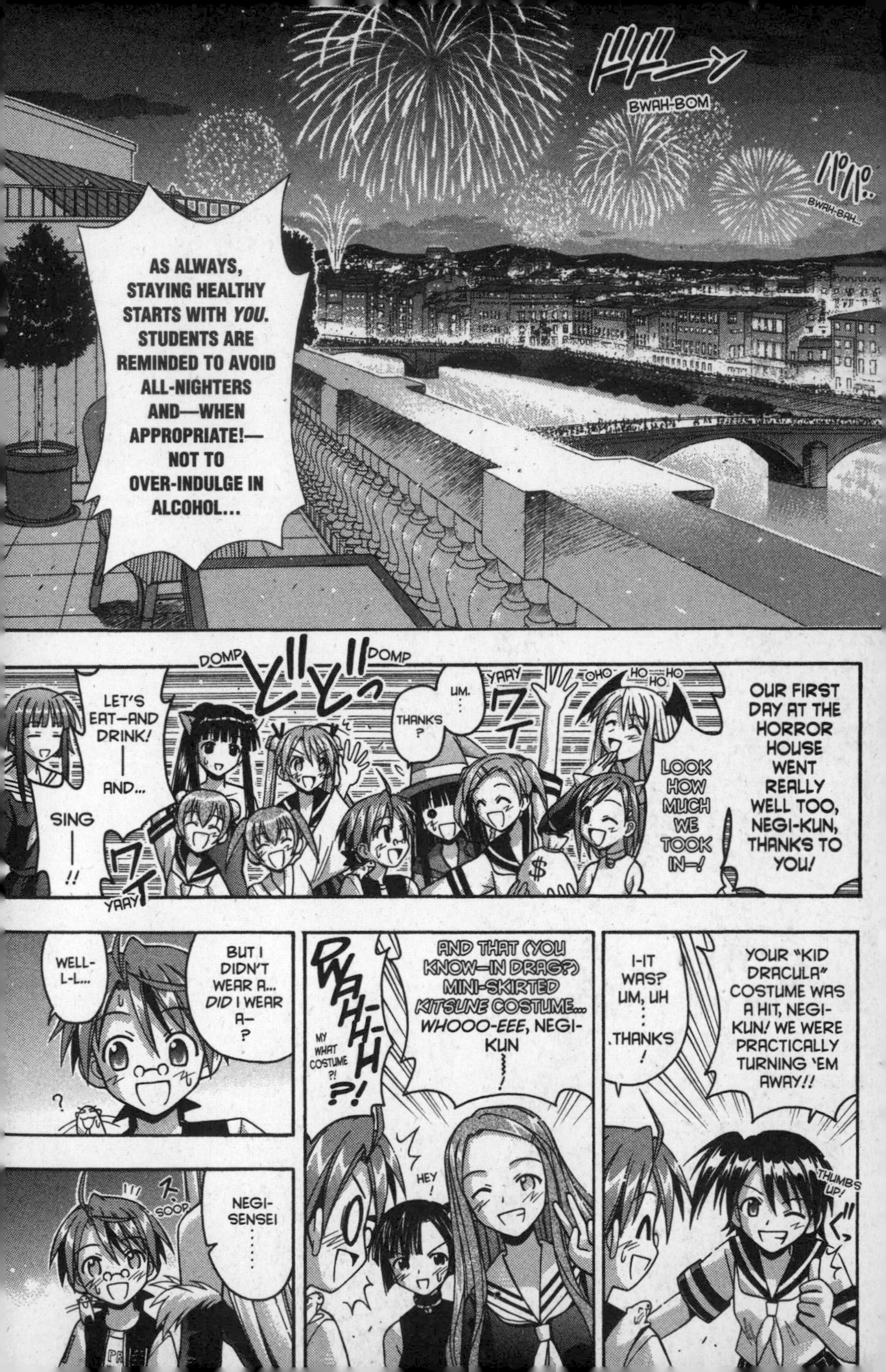
BWAH-BOM
BWAH-BAH...
AS ALWAYS, STAYING HEALTHY STARTS WITH *YOU*. STUDENTS ARE REMINDED TO AVOID ALL-NIGHTERS AND—WHEN APPROPRIATE!—NOT TO OVER-INDULGE IN ALCOHOL...
OUR FIRST DAY AT THE HORROR HOUSE WENT REALLY WELL TOO, NEGI-KUN, THANKS TO YOU!
LOOK HOW MUCH WE TOOK IN—!
OHO HO HO HO
YAAY
UM. ... THANKS?
DOMP
DOMP
LET'S EAT—AND DRINK! — AND...
SING —!!
YAAY
YOUR "KID DRACULA" COSTUME WAS A HIT, NEGI-KUN! WE WERE PRACTICALLY TURNING 'EM AWAY!!
I-IT WAS? UM, UH ... THANKS!
THUMBS UP!
AND THAT (YOU KNOW—IN DRAG?) MINI-SKIRTED *KITSUNE* COSTUME... WHOOO-EEE, NEGI-KUN
BWAHHH?!
MY WHAT COSTUME?!
HEY!
BUT I DIDN'T WEAR A... *DID* I WEAR A—?
WELL-L-L...
NEGI-SENSEI ......
SOOP

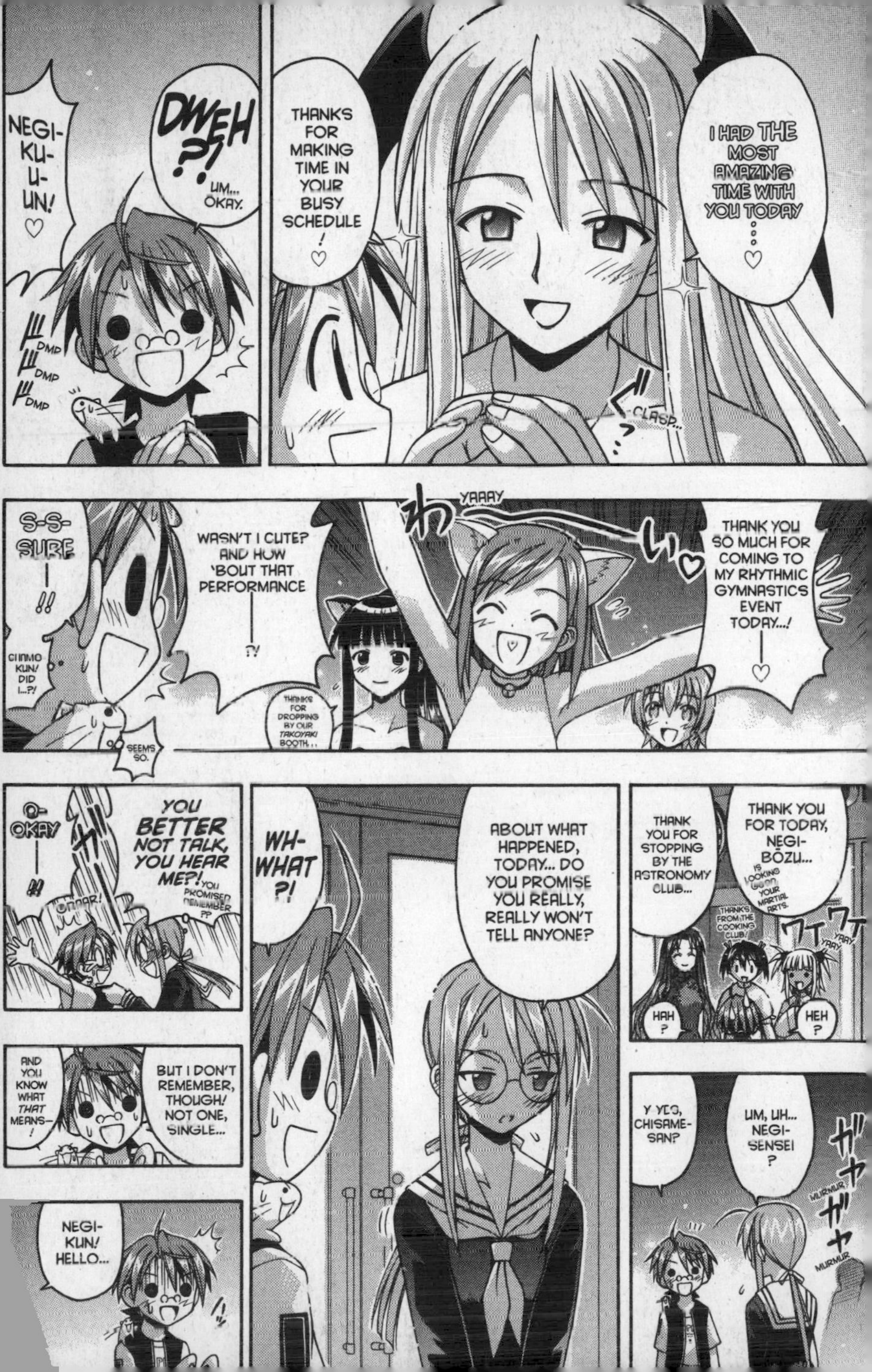
I HAD THE MOST AMAZING TIME WITH YOU TODAY ... ♡
THANKS FOR MAKING TIME IN YOUR BUSY SCHEDULE! ♡
CLASP...
DWEH ?!
UM... OKAY.
NEGI-KU-U-UN! ♡
DMP DMP DMP
THANK YOU SO MUCH FOR COMING TO MY RHYTHMIC GYMNASTICS EVENT TODAY...! ♡
YAAAY
WASN'T I CUTE? AND HOW 'BOUT THAT PERFORMANCE?!
THANKS FOR DROPPING BY OUR TAKOYAKI BOOTH...
S-S-SURE!!
CHAMO-KUN! DID I...?!
SEEMS SO.
THANK YOU FOR TODAY, NEGI-BŌZU...
IS LOOKING GOOD YOUR MARTIAL ARTS.
THANK YOU FOR STOPPING BY THE ASTRONOMY CLUB...
THANKS FROM THE COOKING CLUB!
YAAY
HAH?
HEH?
UM, UH... NEGI-SENSEI?
Y-YES, CHISAME-SAN?
MURMUR
MURMUR
ABOUT WHAT HAPPENED, TODAY... DO YOU PROMISE YOU REALLY, REALLY WON'T TELL ANYONE?
WH-WHAT?!
YOU BETTER NOT TALK, YOU HEAR ME?!
YOU PROMISED, REMEMBER?!
O-OKAY!!
BUT I DON'T REMEMBER, THOUGH! NOT ONE, SINGLE...
AND YOU KNOW WHAT THAT MEANS—!
NEGI-KUN! HELLO...

TOMARE!

[STOP!]

You're going the wrong way!

Manga is a completely different type of reading experience.

To start at the *beginning*, go to the *end*!

That's right! Authentic manga is read the traditional Japanese way—from right to left. Exactly the *opposite* of how American books are read. It's easy to follow: Just go to the other end of the book, and read each page—and each panel—from right side to left side, starting at the top right. Now you're experiencing manga as it was meant to be.